The Original Grands Crus of Burgundy. © by Charles Curtis. All rights reserved. No part of this work may be used or reproduced in any manner whatsoever without written permission except in the case of brief quotations embodied in critical articles or reviews.

Editor: Harriet Bell
Copy editor: Trevor Wisdom
Art direction and design: Madeleine Curtis
Original map design: Madeleine Curtis
Translation copyright © 2014 by Charles Curtis

All rights reserved. No portion of this book may be reproduced—mechanically, electronically, or by any other means, including photocopying—without written permission of the author.

Published by WineAlpha
322 West 57th Street #17H

New York, NY 10019

ISBN 978-0-9906844-0-4

The Original Grand Crus of Burgundy

Charles Curtis MW

WineAlpha

For Carol and Madeleine

• CONTENTS •

Preface   viii
Introduction   x

Part I: Burgundy Wine from the Second to the Twentieth Century

Chapter 1: Origins   15
Chapter 2: André Jullien   26
Chapter 3: Dr. Denis Morelot   36
Chapter 4: Dr. Jules Lavalle   48
Chapter 5: Later Authorities   58

Part II: The Villages from North to South

Chapter 6: The Côte Dijonnaise   66
Chapter 7: Gevrey-Chambertin   85
Chapter 8: Morey   98
Chapter 9: Chambolle   107
Chapter 10: Vougeot   111
Chapter 11: Flagey-Lez-Gilly   122
Chapter 12: Vosne   127
Chapter 13: Nuits and Prémeaux   139
Chapter 14: The Hill of Corton   150
Chapter 15: Savigny-Lez-Beaune   170
Chapter 16: Beaune   176
Chapter 17: Pommard   184
Chapter 18: Volnay and Monthélie   191
Chapter 19: Meursault   200
Chapter 20: Puligny   207
Chapter 21: Chassagne   214
Chapter 22: Santenay   219

Part III: The Legacy

Chapter 23: A Synthesis   223
Appendix I: Glossary (Jullien)   235
Appendix II: Table of Comparative Values (Lavalle)   243
Bibliography   245
Notes   248
Maps   256

• PREFACE •

Jules Lavalle's seminal work *Histoire et Statistique et des Grands Vins de la Côte d'Or*, which appeared in 1855, offers thoughtful insights on Burgundy as well as a historical background on the region that is too often neglected in today's race to find the next "100 point wine." I was surprised that Dr. Lavalle's work had never been translated into English, and for years I dreamt of undertaking this task. One of the things that discouraged me, however, was the very long section at the book's beginning covers grape growing and winemaking in 19th century Burgundy. This material is interesting as history, but it tells us little about today's wines. Grape growing after the phylloxera epidemic is so completely different as to be almost a new endeavor, and new techniques in winemaking have also changed cellar work greatly. However, Lavalle's evaluation of the many vineyards in Burgundy was of enduring importance. This portion of his work has changed little during the past 150 years. The climats of Burgundy date back in their present form 1,000 years, and with luck they will remain essentially the same 1,000 years from now. Once I found time to translate this portion of Lavalle, I posted my translations on my blog winealpha.com.

As I wrote, however, I realized that Lavalle owed a great debt to Dr. Denis Morelot, whose work *Statistique de la Vigne dans le Département de la Côte d'Or* had appeared a generation earlier, and I decided to translate the relevant portions of Dr. Morelot as well. Morelot led me to Andre Jullien and his *Topographie de Tous les Vignobles Connus*, whose first edition was published in 1815, and I translated passages relevant to the Côte d'Or from Jullien's work as well. These three works summarize the essence of pre-modern thought about Burgundy – i.e. what people thought about the terroirs of Burgundy before today's system of Appellations d'Origine Contrôlée (AOC) came into being. These opinions were codified between the beginning of the 18th century and the beginning of the 20th century. Discovering the sources of Jullien, Morelot and Lavalle, I also translated the relevant portions of *Dissertation sur la situation de la Bourgogne, sur les vins qu'elle produit* by Claude Arnoux (1728) and the relevant portions of the *Description Générale et Particulière du Duché de Bourgogne* by Abbé Claude Courtépée and Edme Béguillet (1778). Moving forward in time, I included the classification that appeared in the work credited to Charles Albert d'Arnould Bertall in 1878 entitled *La Vigne, Voyage Autour de Vins de France* and portions of *Les Grands Vins de Bourgogne* by René Danguy and Charles Aubertin (1892) and of *Le Vin de Bourgogne* by Camille Rodier (1920).

The Original Grand Crus of Burgundy brings together the thoughts of these authorities and compares them with today's official AOC system. This system was put into place in the 1930s as a reaction against fraud and deception in the wine trade, and it has been enormously successful. Its foundation was the idea of codifying the rules using the concept of *usages locaux, loyaux et constants*: the "local, honest and traditional" practices of the region. The system, however, departs from these practices in intriguing ways. This book is an appreciation of the thoughts of past generations about the fundamental land units themselves – the *climats*. My hope is that by learning more about these climats that the reader may be drawn to discover new wines and further their appreciation of the unique treasures of this wonderful region.

· INTRODUCTION ·

Burgundy wines are at once mysterious and easily understand. A good Burgundy is a perfectly balanced nectar with a beautiful expression of fruit and a deep complexity that changes from the first sip to the last, with notes of fruit, flowers, spice, and earth that each appear in turn to the careful taster. The best are powerful wines, capable of long aging, and even the least forthcoming among them can have an enchanting perfume and a charming delicacy and finesse.

Yet when those new to Burgundy ask – Where does it come from? Why is it so delicious? –the mysterious side of these wines is encountered. On the one hand, burgundy the beverage with a lower case "b" isn't complicated; it is joyously easy to appreciate. On the other, Burgundy the region with its capital "B" *is* complicated, since it has a documented history of making wine that dates back at least 1,500 years, a distinctive iconography of its winemaking heavens, and a unique viticultural terrain that is anything but self-evident.

The term *grand cru* used in the title of this book is a bit misleading, as it did not exist before the modern era. A *cru* in French is defined by the dictionary *Trésor de la Langue Française* as a "collection of lands considered from the point of view of what is grown there; of a particular cultivation" (*"ensemble de terres considéré du point de vue de ce qui y croît, d'une culture particulière"*). It is a term often used in wine, and the Bureau Interprofessionnel des Vins de Bourgone (BIVB) defines it as a *"terroir* producing wines with specific characteristics." *Terroir* does not mean simply soil, but refers to a specific combination of location, geography, and climate that makes a region or sub-region unique for growing fruits and vegetables or producing cheese or wine. The word *cru* is most often translated into English as "growth", but is commonly used by English speakers to mean "vineyard". However, this usage is not quite accurate, either, since a *cru classé* (classified growth) in Bordeaux is an estate, not a vineyard, and one whose vines are most often located in discontiguous parcels. In Burgundy, if anything, the concept of "cru" is even more complex.

To understand the term cru, begin with the fact that a *lieu-dit* (or *lieudit*; plural *lieux-dits*) is a "named place." This is a general word in French that has a specific meaning in the world of wine, where it refers to the smallest unit of a vineyard, as appellations can be subdivided into lieux-dits. In Burgundy, the particular term *climat* has the same meaning: a vineyard site defined by a specific combination of soil, climate, geology, and topography (exposition, slope, and exposure). Some *crus* may have more than one *climat:* the cru of Échézeaux has eleven climats. Confusingly, one of them is Échézeaux du Dessus. In practice, lieu-dit is used to refer to divisions below the rank of premier cru. Ultimately, each word refers to a wine-growing site, but has a slightly different nuance. For the sake of clarity, French terms (cru, climat, lieu-dit) are used here without translation (or the use of italics).

While the usage of cru in this sense dates to at least the fifteenth century, the specific term "grand cru" in today's usage dates only to the early 20th century. The word "appellation" and its English equivalent give the general sense of "name" with a specific and legal sense of an explicitly defined place producing a product with particular and defined characteristics. French law provides us with a framework for understanding the appellation system. Codified in a process that began in the 1930s and continues today, the AOC system divides Burgundy into 100 appellations that exist within a hierarchy of four levels of quality: regional (51.7% of production), village (36.8%), premier cru (10.1%), and grand cru (1.4%). Regional appellations include a broad swath of vineyards – Bourgogne rouge or Mâcon-Villages, for example – while the village category most often includes just the name of the village, although in some cases a lieu-dit may be added. A premier cru may appear without the mention of a climat, although it is often appended (there are 645 distinct climats classified as premiers crus), and the grand cru usually appears without the name of a climat, although this is not true in Chablis or Corton, and exceptions may be made in other cases, such as in Clos de Vougeot and Échézeaux. In the present volume the names of the villages will be used at they originally appeared, without the vineyard names that have been appended in the 19th century (Gevrey instead of Gevrey Chambertin, Puligny instead of Puligny-Montrachet, et cetera).

With admirable clarity, the AOC system defines and describes how and where each wine must be made as well as all of the particular characteristics that it must possess in order to be worthy of its title. This precise and logical definition of each wine, however, can leave us wondering why the wine it produces is great. To truly understand the wines of Burgundy, it helps to understand not only how they are made today but also their history and context. While the term "grand cru" is itself a modern construct, the concept is not. The title of this book refers to the reputation and character of important vineyards in Burgundy before they were formally defined in the legal sense as grands crus or premiers crus. As the reader will soon discover, the main term used in pre-modern times was *cuvée*. The best wines were called *tête de cuvée*, the second best were known as *première cuvées*, and these were followed in descending levels of interest by *deuxième cuvées*, *troisième cuvées* and *quatrième cuvées*. André Jullien, writing in 1815, has produced a very useful index which I have translated as Appendix I that gives a complete discussion of this and other terms.

The Original Grand Crus of Burgundy is for those who want to discover and learn more about the greatest wines of Burgundy. This is the first time that some of these writings have been translated into English. My goal is not to be encyclopedic; many topics that were once important to these pioneering authors are no longer relevant to the present day, so the works are not translated in their entirety. I have, however, translated everything from them that is relevant to understanding the history of the climats that produce these wines today. If my work gives you a greater appreciation or enjoyment of Burgundy wines, then I have accomplished my aim.

· EPIGRAM ·

Quid non ebrietas dissignat? Operta recludit,
spes iubet esse ratas, ad proelia trudit inertem,
sollicitis animis onus eximit, addocet artis.
Fecundi calices quem non fecere disertum,
contracta quem non in parpertate solutum?

from the Epistles of Horace, book 1 letter 5, Invitation to Dinner

Qui ne sait d'une heureuse ivresse ?
Qui ne sait les heureux effets ?
Elle prodigue la sagesse
Elle révèle les secrets ;
Des Chimères de l'esperence
Elle sait nous faire jouir
C'est dans la coupe du plaisir
Que l'ignorant boit la science
Au lâche elle rend la vaillance
Au fourbe la sincerité
Et dans le sein de l'indigence
Fait trouver la felicité
Gaité, franchise, confiance
Talens, vous êtes ses bienfaits
Eh ! Quel buveur manqua jamais
Ou de courage ou de l'eloquence ?

Oeurves d'Horace traduits par M. Daru

[Used for Topographie de Tous les Vignobles Connus of A. Jullien along with the translation by M. Daru]

What does drunkenness not reveal? It opens that which is closed;
founds hope; pushes the inert into battle;
lifts the burdens of the soul and teaches skill.
To whom has the fecund cup not given eloquence?
Whom, straightened, has not been enriched?

ORIGINS

Bacchus amat colles: Bacchus loves the hills. The principle alluded to by Virgil[1], that grapes grow best on hillside slopes, has been known since classical times. The Romans who spread the culture of the vine in Gaul, and the Christians who replaced them as the Empire fell knew where to plant vines. The wines of the Côte d'Or (the "Golden Slope") in Burgundy are of perpetual fascination to wine lovers. The best of these vineyards date back 1,000 years or more, and wills, bills of sale, and other official documents through time bear testimony to their value, although for the first half of their history from the period of great ecclesiastical plantings around the turn of the first millennia of the common era to the 16th century, the audience for these wines was circumscribed indeed.

Many of the great vineyards of Burgundy were planted (or replanted) at the height of feudalism, during a time of warlords, barbarian invaders, plagues, and crusades. There was little opportunity then to enjoy the finer things of life, and few people who were able to do so. Land ownership was in the hands of feudal warlords or the church, and while the serfs who worked the lands were doubtless acquainted with the wines and the local bourgeoisie had occasion to sample them, few outside the nobility of this region would be truly familiar with these wines. Their renown was spread by dignitaries who visited the area, and slowly these wines were introduced into other markets.

The first wines of Burgundy to be widely known were those of Dijon and Beaune, the largest towns of the time, and those with the most extensive vineyards. Wines produced throughout the region were lumped together under these umbrella names to give them currency in the marketplace and gradually the wines of Nuits also came to prominence. These three proto-appellations stood together in the Middle Ages to represent Burgundy wine. It was not until much later that the villages, such as Gevrey-Chambertin or Volnay, and their respective vineyards became individually recognized.

The first attempt at making a serious inventory of Burgundy and other regions was undertaken by Louis XIV and his finance minister Jean-Baptiste Colbert as part of a new civil code. Colbert is reputed to have said, "The art of taxation consists of plucking the goose in order to obtain a maximum of feathers and a minimum of squawking." Colbert ordered a village-by-village inventory. This enormous undertaking was entrusted to his intendants, or provincial appointees, who each oversaw the administration of a specific region.

Claude Bouchu was the Intendant of Burgundy from 1654 until his death in 1683, during the period when Colbert ordered his inventory. Bouchu's work La

Déclaration des Biens des Communautés (Declaration of the Wealth of the Communities) is a fascinating look at how the French Kingdom functioned under the Ancien Régime, or Old Order, prior to the French Revolution. Bouchu mentioned the reputation of the villages in the Côte d'Or, although without citing individual vineyards. His concern was taxation rather than appreciation.

Claude Arnoux

The earliest known written appreciation of Burgundy wines for their own sake is entitled *Dissertation sur la situation de la Bourgogne, sur les vins qu'elle produit* (Dissertation on the situation of Burgundy, and the wines it produces) by Claude Arnoux, published in 1728. Arnoux, living in London, describes himself as the teacher of the sons of J. Freeman, Esq., and although he writes in French, his work is meant for an English audience and he discusses the suitability of different wines for export to the English market. While he spends a good proportion of his essay relating the mythic and Gallo-Roman origins of the Burgundy, he also commented on the wines:

First Article: Of Vins de Primeur[2]

One calls "Wines of the Year" those that last only a year, or can keep several months into the second year.

The first Vin de Primeur is grown in Volnay, a village situated three miles from Beaune and stretches a mile in breadth and two in length along the slope that is well-exposed to the east; this village as well as Pommard are dependencies of Beaune, whose inhabitants are citizens thereof, which is why I have said above that these two vineyards are subject to the harvest laws of this city's magistrates.

This slope produces the finest, liveliest, and most delicate wine of Burgundy. The bunches and the grapes of the vines of Volnay are very small, and the shoots hardly grow to a height of more than three feet during the entire season; the grapes are so delicate that they cannot suffer the fermentation vat more than twelve to sixteen or eighteen hours, because if one leaves them longer they will take on the taste of the stems to which the grapes are attached.

This vine is a color just a bit darker than partridge-eye; it is lively, heady, and light, almost all spirit; it is finally the most excellent of all Burgundy, which because of its delicacy is not sold and its value is soon dissipated; the wine will keep just from one vintage to another, and it will perish at the hint of hot weather, changing color and beginning to turn; I do not doubt, however, that it would last longer in a cool cellar. The best cuvées issue from a district of vines that are called Champans.

Pommard is the second vineyard of Vin de Primeur, situated between Volnay and Beaune, at a slightly lower elevation than this first and a slightly higher one than the town of Beaune: it produces a wine that has a bit more body than the preceding; it is the color of fire, has much perfume and balm, and it lasts several months longer than Volnay, is easier to sell, and better for the health; if one keeps it more than a year it begins to turn and oxidize and becomes the color of onion skin; the best cuvée is that of La Commaraine; it can last sometimes eighteen months, according to the vintage.

The town of Beaune contains an extensive and considerable vineyard; it covers four hills over the length of four miles from Pommard to Savigny. The first of these hills is called St. Désiré, the second La Montée Rouge, the third Les Grèves, and the fourth La Fontaine des Marconnets. These terroirs produce wines that have the virtues of those of Volnay and Pommard without having their faults. They have a bit more color, many good qualities, and age well, none more than the others, and none more than two years. They are silky, agreeable, and sell more easily than the two preceding wines and much more profitable for the health; the color of these wines is not the same, since it depends on the method of making the wine; one can let it ferment a shorter or longer time according to the delicacy of the climat from which it originates. There are several districts contained in these hills that are of a great reputation: Les Fèves, Aux Cras, Les Grèves, and Clos du Roi are among the most delicious.

Aloxe is the fourth vineyard of Vin de Primeur; it is situated on the slope of a hill three miles from Beaune. This valley is a slope so gentle that one hardly perceives that one is climbing: this little village produces wines of extreme delicacy; they are less lively than the preceding ones, but of a silken and more memorable taste. The color is softer and they sparkle less, but they are beautiful, and since the slope that produces this wine has such a gentle elevation and slope, it does not share the firm acidity of the wines from the tops of the hills; it is tender, with no hard qualities, and consequently able to keep less time; it will begin to turn and take on a sickly quality; it can be shipped abroad but this requires great care.

Pernand is between these vineyards and the large vineyard of Savigny but the character of the wines is so different: these have a more savory character; they have the character of the preceding wines but they are firmer and harder because they are produced from a higher and steeper slope; there are several very delicious cuvées; they are sold abroad, but under the name of Beaune.

Chassagne is a vineyard that is not as considerable in extent as it is in reputation. This is in my opinion perhaps the wine that would be best suited for England, because it can sustain voyages by land and by sea. It is intense, full of fire and smoke, it has a tannic character that renders it more durable than the others; but when one knows to bottle the wine in its season and wait until the tannins resolve, it is one of the greatest wines of the world; if I had an order to fill for the king I would go to Burgundy and choose for him a wine of this climat and be certain of success; this is the only one that one can leave in bottle without fear of having it turn, change color, or become sour; the longer one waits, the more mellow it becomes. I would not advise you to surpass three years, however, and ideally it should be drunk by the end of the second year, although sometimes it can last four years in the proper vintage. It is in the category of Vin de Primeur, although it will last the longest.

Savigny is a large climat between Beaune and Pernand, situated in the hollow between two hills; because the hills that contain the vineyard are open to the rising sun through a valley and close together at the western end, they benefit from the rays of the sun in an oblique fashion rather than directly. This terroir produces excellent, silky wines; they are mellow and have body and delicacy; once they have been bottled, it is necessary to watch them in order not to miss the time when they should be drunk. This wine would also be very good for England; it will last as long or longer than that of Chassagne; it is not as delicate or as lively, but it is more unctuous and very good for the health.

Auxey is in approximately the same situation, in a gap between two hills that open towards Meursault and lead to Saint-Romain, where one can see high mountains crowned with boulders. This vineyard produces wines of the deepest color and a silkier texture than those of Savigny, but they do not have the same reputation; these wines have more body than all of the preceding ones and should be the drink of those lords who would like to avoid shortening their days by drinking these smoky, sparkling wines whose excess can be so dangerous.

Second article: Of Vins de Garde[3]

The wines of Nuits have a great reputation for their ageability and healthful character. Nuits is a very small town nine miles from Beaune along the Route de Dijon; the territory of this village is four to five miles in length; all the lords who prefer healthful drinks to dainty ones order wines from the Côte de Nuits for their table. These wines are harsh at first, bitter and green; it is necessary to wait for them up to five years, but once this green quality has disappeared, they take on a delicious perfume and balm; they have a silky, deep, pure color: Louis XIV drank no other wine.

The Clos de Vougeot is situated a league from Nuits on the way to Dijon, and is owned completely by monks from the famous Cîteaux Abbey that is built between La Saône and this hill. The wine produced is closer to Chassagne than any other; it is excellent, and can be exported to foreign countries.

Chambertin is, in my opinion, the most considerable wine of all Burgundy; it is situated between Dijon and Nuits; it encompasses the qualities of all the other wines yet has none of their faults: this wine you can forget in the cellar and have nothing to fear; I have drunk it six years after the harvest and it was cloudy and troubled when it was poured in our glasses, but it cleared up under our eyes and took on the liveliest and purest color. It is also the most expensive wine of Burgundy. The second to last vintage was sold for forty to forty-two livres[4] per cask, while the wines of Volnay, Pommard and Beaune cost only twenty sterling livres per cask and contained, as noted, four hundred and forty Paris pints.

Third article: Of White Wines

Before speaking of white wines, it is appropriate to note that it is the masculine gender of the grape and it is the male shoot that produces it. It also has two qualities that grapes of color do not have; the first is that if the harvest is late and frost or even colder weather arrives that it can withstand it, while black grapes will wilt and shrivel at the same time. The second is that as soon as the grapes have been cut, they should be thrown in the press without going into the vat and being trod as black grapes are: For if one puts them into the tank they will give a pallid liquid, reddish yellow in color: I want to warn my public.

Meursault is, after Beaune and Nuits, the largest vineyard of Burgundy by its extent; its wines are generally known in Germany, the Netherlands, and throughout France. I do not know if they are in England; the wines that this terroir produces, above all in hot, dry years, are delicious, sparkling, generous, and healthful; they are not expensive, and if they are well-chosen, they will honor England and please those who drink them; when one keeps them more than a year and a half, they oxidize and turn sour.

Puligny is a vineyard bordering Meursault but closer to the plain, which produces very good white wines. They are about the same quality as the wines of Meursault, but their renown is not as widespread and they are almost unknown.

Aloxe, of which we have already spoken in the article on Vins de Primeur, also produces excellent white wine.

Montrachet is a small terroir between Chassagne and Puligny in the plain that is in possession of a vein of earth that renders its terroir unique in its type; it produces a most curious white wine, the most delicious of France; there is no other wine of Côte Rôtie or of Muscat de Frontignan that is its equal; it is produced in very small quantity, and it is sold very dear; to have a small portion it is necessary to have taken it the year before since this wine is always sold before it is produced. But one must be very careful not to be cheated, because vines neighboring this clos sometimes are mistaken for Montrachet: this is why it is necessary to have a trustworthy broker. This wine has such quality that neither Latin nor French can express its sweetness. I have drunk it six or seven times yet I cannot describe its delicacy and excellence.

I have just reported all the renowned vineyards of Haute Bourgogne; those who have passed along the road from Dijon to Lyon along these slopes will render justice to my exactitude, and I pray that those who have not will believe that my relation conforms to the truth.

Courtépée and Béguillet

Description Générale et Particulière du Duché de Bourgogne by Claude Courtépée and Edme Béguillet, a seven-volume work published between 1774 and 1781, remains one of the premier sources for information about Burgundy under the Ancien Régime, and is particularly valued for its geographical insight. Replete with insights on wine as well, it is cited throughout the works of Dr. Morelot and Dr. Lavalle. Courtépée and Béguillet note in the first volume:

As to wine, those of the Dijonnois, and principally le Chambertin, those of La Romanée, of the Clos de Vougeot, Richebourg, and Les Saint-Georges in the district of Nuys, those of Beaune, Pommard & Vollenay, and in white wines, Le Morachet, Le Meursault, those of the Mâconnois, etc., are preferred by gourmets, when they are ready to drink and have what is called bouquet, to all other wines. But one has said, with truth, that this rich nature is as fragile as the vase that contains it, since of seven years there is hardly one which is passable.

The Description Générale provided a document as thorough as the works of l'Intendant Bouchu, but with a lively and fine aesthetic appreciation of all things Burgundian. The work is usually referred to as "Courtépée" after its principal author. L'Abbé Claude Courtépée (1721–1781) was an historian and professor at the College of Dijon, who was ordained as a priest after his law studies. He described himself in his work as a priest and instructor at the College of Dijon. He was also an important contributor to the supplement of Diderot's encyclopedia.

Courtépée was assisted by Edme Béguillet (d. 1786), an agronomist and a lawyer, who worked at the Parlement de Dijon and was an advisor to the King and a notary. A prolific author, his works covered a wide range of topics relative to the production and processing of both grains and vines. He collaborated with Courtépée on the Description Générale et Particulière, where he was referred to as Lawyer, Notary, and Correspondant to the Royal Academies of Science and Belles-Lettres, and an honorary member of the Institut de Bologne and the Academie des Arcades de Rome. Because of his knowledge of agronomy and his interest in oenology, it is likely that the insights into wine production were those of Béguillet and not solely those of Courtépée, although the latter is principally cited as the author of the work.

This wide-ranging work covers every aspect of Burgundy, including its geography, history, politics, and economy. An abbreviated description of the contents of the first volume alone offers an idea of the scope of the authors' work:

> Vol. 1: The abridged history of the Duchy of Burgundy: The first epoch under the Eduens and the Lingons; the second epoch under the Romans (to 410 CE); the third epoch: the first Kingdom of Burgundy (414 – 524 CE); the fourth epoch: the second kingdom of Burgundy under the sons of Clovis (534 – 880 CE); the fifth epoch: Burgundy under the beneficent dukes (880 – 1033 CE); sixth epoch: Burgundy under the first line of royal dukes (1032 – 1361 CE); seventh epoch: Burgundy under the dukes of the second line (1363 – 1477 CE); the latest epoch: Burgundy since its reunion with the crown (1477 – 1674 CE); Dissertation on the former districts of Burgundy, called pagii; A general description of the Duchy of Burgundy: geographical divisions, political divisions, ecclesiastical, civil and military divisions.

Keen insights on Burgundy wines are sprinkled throughout Courtépée et Béguillet, such as this historical mention of the wines of Beaune from the second volume:

> The people of Beaune believe themselves in exclusive possession of the best wines of Burgundy. Except the climats of Chambertin and of Bèze in the area of Dijon; those of Morey, Chambolle, Vosne, where one finds Romanée; those of Vougeot, of Saint-Georges, in the region of Nuits [all] reasonably dispute with them this preference. Keeping to what concerns the people of Beaune, all connoisseurs (following in any case the prices) believe that Volnay is lighter, finer, and purer; Pommard has more body and substance and keeps better in warm countries; Beaune has the most color, is the easiest to drink, and the most purity; Savigny and Chassagne are the most mellow when the vines are young. Several districts of Aloxe, and above all Corton, pretend to equal them, at least in finesse. Pernand is firmer than Aloxe but it doesn't have the bouquet, except for Vergelesses, which is equivalent to the good crus of Savigny. Monthélie is equivalent to Savigny and surpasses Auxey; this last has force and lightness, but it does not have the purity of Savigny, regardless of what is said by M. Gandelot, who has exalted it too far in the opinion of fine gourmets. One compares to Volnay the Santenots of Meursault, whose white wines are excellent and merit their reputation; but Le Montrachet is superior to all white wines of Burgundy and of Europe. One distinguishes again the reds of Morgeot, Le Clavoillon, Les Gravières, Le Clos Tavannes, and the wines of Santenay. Although the climats of Beaune, Pommard, and Volnay, are superior to others, there are nevertheless a certain number of distinguished cuvées from other cuvées, whose possessors are known: they must sustain by their honor and in their own interest the reputation of the wines that they sell.

> Here is the place to give a short essay on the vine in Burgundy and to say a word regarding the reputation of its wines. We have given the general history of the vine and of wines in l'Oenologie[5]; here we will solely treat the principal characteristics that can concern the people of Beaune: all that is concerned with the growth and the best method of making wines will be reserved for a separate dissertation as discussed in the preface.

> Long before Caesar, the inhabitants of Marseille and Gaul Narbonnoise[6] had vines; but there were none in the rest of Gaul. The Belgians forbid wine to enter their country, as they feared that it would sap the courage of the inhabitants, but the Celts were so passionate for this liqueur that they would trade a slave for an amphora of wine. Submitting to the Romans, they applied themselves so to the culture of the vine of Marseille that they neglected their own lands. Domitian, in a poor year for wheat, ordered the pulling up of half of the existing vines and forbid future vine planting in the year of our Lord 92. The excellent Emperor Probus, whose reign was too short for the happiness of humanity, favored all types of agriculture and especially that of the vine, accorded the Gaules the liberty to multiply it in 282. Obstacles removed, the enchanted slopes of the Rhône and the Saône, and those of the country of Eduens[7] were soon covered in vines; these were even found at

Autun, and some believe that to recognize this Vosne gave to its best climat the name of Romanée.

Under Constantine the Great who honored twice the Pays des Éduens[8] with his presence, the vines of the Pagus Arebrignus[9] were already so old that according to Eumenius[10] it was difficult to prune them. From this M. Gandelot thinks that they were of a different genus than those that we cultivate: more likely it is because they were less adept at their cultivation.

In the 6th century, the slopes of Burgundy rejoiced already of a great reputation, which compared its best wines to those of Italy, and which had been exported as far as Gaza in Palestine, which were the delight of good tables throughout the Roman Empire as long ago as the time of Pompey the Great, as we learn from Gregory of Tours when he speaks of our slopes.

> "[Dijon has] Fruitful slopes, filled with vines, that produce a wine which to the noble Falernum and Ascalon [in Gaza] is compared." [Hist. de Fr. liv. 3, ch. 19]

Under Philippe Auguste the wines of Beaune sustained their renown. The poet Guillaume le Breton spoke of them in this manner in the first book of his Philippide:

> "Delighting in its fruitful slopes, wine-loving Beaune, whose reds incite cool heads to war, submitted to the Duke."

The first Dukes of Burgundy had their clos in Chenôve, Vosne, Pommard, Volnay, and presented their wines to the crowned heads of Europe. The city of Reims consumed three hundred casks of wine at the coronation of Philippe of Valois. The majority of it was from Beaune, and cost 56 livres per two casks all expenses included; that of Reims 10 livres, and that of Saint-Pourçain 24 livres.

When the Estates assembled in Paris on the 7th of December 1359, granted to the Dauphin, later Charles V, the tax of one sol per pound of salt, 15 sols for each queue of French wine, and 35 for that of Burgundy. Cluny and Cîteaux furnished the wine to the Papal Court, seated at Avignon, during the 14th century. Jean de Bussières, abbot of Clairvaux, became the abbot of Cîteaux in 1359 and sent thirty casks of the wine of Vougeot to Gregory XI, who thanked him warmly and promised to remember the gift; four years later, he was created Cardinal in 1375.

Petrarch attributed the obstinate refusal of the Cardinals to return to Rome[11]. "In Italy there is no wine of Beaune, and they did not believe themselves able to lead a happy life without this liqueur; they regarded wine as a second element and as nectar of the Gods." This was what he wrote very seriously to Pope Urban V near the end of his days to exhort him to return to Rome in the year 1366[12].

During the deplorable schism that saddened the church for forty years and which only ended with the Council of Constance, the Duke Philippe the Bold was tasked by the Council of the King in 1395 to put an end to it. He made rich presents to Pope Benoit XIII, residing at Avignon, and gave to the Cardinals d'Albane and de

Viviers 20 queues of Beaune wine; but nothing could change their dispositions. Jean sans Peur[13] distributed as much to the Masters of Divinity of the Council of Constance in 1415 in order to spare the doctrine and the memory of Jean Petit, his theologian, a well-earned stigma[14].

Philippe the Bold regaled with his good wine the deputies of Kings Charles and Edward during the peace conferences held in Bruges, and sent some to Paris and to foreign courts. Cities would make a present of it when our Kings would honor them with their presence. The burghers of Bayeux presented to Bertrand du Guesclin, Constable of France in March of 1377 a pipe of the wine of Beaune, a hogshead of oats, and fifty candles. The wine cost 26 livres, the oats 9 livres, and the candles 12 livres. The wine was esteemed as the finest in Europe, and thus this vulgar verse cited by Chausseneuz in the 16th century.

The wine of Beaune above all others reposes

And this other:

Without Volnay there is no perfect joy

Erasmus, in his letters, attributed to the wines of Beaune celebrated excellence and the healing of illnesses of the stomach and colics. He even wanted to move to France, not, as he said, to command armies, but to drink the wine of Beaune.

"*O happy Burgundy* (he wrote in his letter to Laurinus, dated from Bâle in 1522), *who merits to be called the mother of men, since her breast yields such good milk!*"

Roger de Colleryre[15] French poet under Francois 1er, said in 1527:

Picards, Normands, Bretons, & Navarrois,
Love these pink wines of Beaune & Auxerrois
More than all others

Louis XIV allowed the shipment of the wines of Beaune (which he had praised greatly in his council of 1662) on the Moselle and the Meuse. During the convalescence of this monarch after a long illness, his doctor Fagon gave him in 1680 the preference of the wines of Burgundy over those of Champagne: a happy decision which doubled the price of our wines and excited a little war in Parnassus between Charles Coffin, a poet from Champagne, and Bénigne Grenan, a Burgundian poet; and a dispute between Huges de Salins, a doctor in Beaune, and Lepescheur, a doctor in Reims. The first printed in Latin his defense of Burgundian wine in Beaune in 1701 & 1705 (3rd edition). This decision had been approved by the Faculty of Medicine of Paris, where M. Arbinet maintained, in a public thesis in 1665, that the wine of Beaune was the most agreeable and healthful wine; either because of the soil, of the aspect of the sun, or because of the latitude, three degrees more than Reims.

The Cardinal de Bonzy presented to Sobiesky, the king-elect of Poland, wines of Beaune, which were found excellent. Tavernier is said to have drunk some at the court of the king of Persia at the end of the last century. The vines so renowned of the Cape (of Good Hope belonging to the Dutch) were taken from Beaune and the neighboring country. The interesting fact is that this plant has succeeded only on the Cape, and everywhere else it has degenerated. The Grand Dauphin and the Prince de Condé asked M. Brunet, established in Paris, why the wine of the vines that they had procured, were so inferior to those of Beaune? He answered that, "One is not able to transport with the vines the earth and the sun." The Dukes of Berry and of Burgundy, having passed in this last province and tasted the wine, found it so delicious that they renounced the wine of Champagne. The Duke d'Anjou, later Philippe V, king of Spain, accompanied them in 1700, resolved to drink in Madrid only Burgundy wines. The kings of the north drink no other. The Majordomo of the Pope reports each year in his accounting an article on the expense for the wines of Beaune.

The celebrated M. de la Monnoie gave Oudin's Spanish Dictionary to a friend who sent him a dozen bottles of the wine of Beaune; on this gift the poet produced an epigram that finished thus:

> For one thing my tongue, you will learn about the task of
> all thy gifts that I may speak with all tongues

It only remains to describe the ordinance of Philippe the Bold, dated in Dijon in 1395: "Learn, says this prince, that in the slope where the best wine of the kingdom is produced, of which our holy father the Pope, the King of France, and other grand lords have custom to make their provision, one has recently planted the Gamay, a very poor and disloyal vine, which has deceived and defrauded foreign merchants, who our subjects have harmed and impoverished: thus we order that the Gamay vines be cut and utterly removed in a month, under pain to each of a sixty-fold penalty."

A similar ordinance would be necessary as well in these times, where one has multiplied this disloyal plant in the fields where one could grow good wheat.

Philippe the Good, in his judgment rendered in Brussels in 1459 confirming the laws of Beaune, recognized that, "it has long been forbidden to stock wines, other than those produced by the inhabitants, since new Gamay wines could deceive foreign merchants by their sweetness: as the Dukes of Burgundy has always had the reputation to be lords of the finest wines of Christendom, they want to maintain the reputation of the wines of Beaune, Pommard, and Volnay, the inhabitants having hardly any other merchandise."

The vines of Malaga, which several proprietors of houses in the city and the country have planted within their walls to the south, have been brought to Beaune by the Abbot Gandelot. One still sees a vine named the precocious vine, known for the past fifteen years, which ripens a month before the Pinot Noir, etc., etc.

The further comments of Courtépée and Béguillet about the wines of particular villages are incorporated in other chapters of this book. Their work forms a transition from the Middle Ages to early modern times. Their historical work, very thorough for the time in which they wrote, narrates the progression from the chronicles of donations of the Franks in Merovingian and Carolingian times through the land inventories of the Middle Ages under the house of Capet and the Valois kings to the system of taxation developed near the end of the Ancien Régime. These early works and those that follow form a testament to the fact that the wines and vines of Burgundy have been renowned for nearly 1,500 years.

ANDRÉ JULLIEN

Writers from the Ancien Régime convey their general impressions of wines without too many specific details, while authors after the French Revolution revel in the minutiae of the topic. This is due, in part, to the fact that the earliest authors were academics or functionaries, rather than wine professionals. André Jullien, the first writer to come to wide attention who was a member of the wine trade, was the exception. His influence was profound, and he is the precursor of all modern wine writing.

Antoine André Jullien was born on November 10, 1766 in the Burgundy village of Châlons-sur-Saône. He became a wholesale wine trader in Paris at the age of thirty, and came to wider notice with his practical inventions to aid the clarification of wines in cask. He is the author of the modestly titled *Topographie de Tous les Vignobles Connus* (Topography of All Known Vineyards). Jullien traveled the world to gather information on the origin, type, and quality of the world's wines, and described in detail their commerce, packaging, and shipment. The first edition of 1815 was followed by revisions in 1816, 1822, and 1832. The work was translated into English as The Topography of all the Known Vineyards; Containing a Description of the Kind and Quality of Their Products, and a Classification and published in London by G. and W.B. Whittaker in 1824. Jullien was awarded the Prix de Statistiques by the Academy of Sciences of the Institut de France in 1832 for this work. He also wrote Manuel du Sommelier, a practical work on the care and maturation of wines, published in 1822. As Jullien notes in his preface to Topographie:

> We possess several good works on the culture of the vine and on the best procedures to follow for the production of wine but none to my knowledge that treats the distinguishing characteristics of different climats, and even less the nuances of quality that one notes in the product of crus very near to each other, and which, being placed at the same latitude, should seem to give perfectly similar results. I have tasked myself to fill this gap and unite in my work all of the details likely to interest a vineyard owner or someone interested in the quality of their cellar. I indicate first the geographic position of the vineyards, with as much exactitude as possible, and that of the crus whose wines enjoy some reputation; passing next to their produce, I speak of the type, number, and distinguishing qualities, of the rank that they must occupy according to me; the wines of each cru among those of the same type; finally, I give the name and capacity of the casks and measures in usage, the places where the commerce and the shipping of wines takes place, and the means of transport most commonly utilized.

Jullien's work is vast and far exceeds the scope of Burgundy wines. His system, however, remains valid and of interest today, and his section on the wines of the Côte d'Or is worthy of inclusion in full. In fact, Jullien exceeds this brief slightly, since as a native of Chalon-sur-Saône he groups together the wines of his home district with its more illustrious neighbors in the Côte d'Or, a division that is included in this book. Jullien compares all the wines of the Côte d'Or on an equal footing and offers his impressions by arranging the vineyards in what he sees as their order of quality, discerning each with five classes of red wine and five classes of white wines:[16]

> **Département[17] of the Côte d'Or, including the district of Chalon-sur-Saône in the département of the Saône-et-Loire, and divided in five districts: Dijon, Beaune, Châtillon-sur-Seine, Semur[18], and Châlons-sur-Saône.**

> This département owes its name to the chain of little mountains that extends from Dijon, through Nuits, Beaune, Chalon-sur-Saône to Mâcon, which is called the Côte d'Or because of the richness of its products. It is above all between Dijon and Chalon, in the districts of Beaune and Dijon, that one harvests the celebrated wines known under the name of fine wines of Haute-Bourgogne, who, if they have any rivals, are not surpassed by them. The wines of the premiers crus, when they come from a good year, reunite in just proportion all of the qualities that make perfect wines. They have no need of admixture or of any preparation to attain the highest degree of perfection. These actions, known in certain countries as treatments to aid quality, always debase the wines of the Côte d'Or. They have a bouquet all their own which develops after three or four years. It alters them to introduce any aromatic substances or other wines, regardless of their quality. It is not even beneficial to mix them together, for the reunion of two wines of the first quality would result in a loss of their bouquet, and can only produce an inferior wine of the second or even third class.

> The red wines of the Côte d'Or join to a beautiful color a quantity of perfume and a delicious taste; they are full-bodied, fine, delicate, and generous all at once, without being too florid. Drunk in moderation, they will give good tone to the stomach and facilitate digestion. The white wines possess the same qualities; they are mellow [i.e. rich in fruit without being sweet], and their color takes on an amber tint as they age. Those from the premiers crus dispute the honors of the dessert with the best sweet wines available.

> One counts 24,000 ha of vines in the département of the Côte d'Or, and 9,200 in the district of Chalon-sur-Saône, or 33,200 ha, whose production, in an average year, is 779,000 hl of wine; the local inhabitants consume 315,000, and the surplus is delivered to commerce for exportation, either within France or without.

> The vines which are most often cultivated are the Pinot Noir, which is grown almost everywhere that fine wine is made; Giboudot[19], the Melon Noir[20] and the Gamay; the white grapes are Chardonnay, which gives the best wines, Melon Blanc[21], Narbonne or Chasselas, and Gamay, this last vine, in white as in red, gives only inferior wine.

> The vineyards are considered as being spread over three slopes: the Côte de

Nuits, which includes all of the vineyards in the region of Nuits and some of those from Dijon; the Côte de Beaune, which includes all of those from the district of Beaune, with the exception of those from Nuits; and, finally, the Côte Châlonnaise, which includes all of those vineyards in the district of Chalon-sur-Saône.

RED WINES

First Class

The crus that form this first class, with the exception of Chambertin, are all from the district of Nuits, three leagues northeast of Beaune; one orders them as follows:

Romanée-Conti, in the territory of Vosne, three-quarters of a league from Nuits and four and a quarter leagues from Dijon; this celebrated vineyard produces a wine remarkable for its beautiful color, spirited aroma, delicacy, finesse, and delicious taste. It is difficult to procure the authentic article, because the vineyard that produces it occupies only two hectares[22], from which one harvests but 12 to 15 casks in an average year.

Chambertin, situated in the territory of Gevrey, two and a half leagues from Dijon, occupies 25 ha and produces each year 130 to 150 casks of excellent wine, joins a beautiful color to a vigorous and mellow character, finesse, perfect taste and a suave bouquet.

Richebourg, in the territory of Vosne, which differs from Romanée-Conti only in that it more deeply colored and less fine and delicate. It is above all distinguished by great vigor and bouquet.

Clos Vougeot, at the extremity of the territory of Flagey and four leagues from Dijon gives wines that are similar to the preceding [Romanée-Conti, Chambertin, and Richbourg] except they are more generous[23]. The products of different parts of the Clos produce wines of varying quality; the upper parts give a wine that is very fine and delicate; the lower parts, particularly the portions along the main road, give inferior wine.

Romanée-Saint-Vivant, in the territory of Vosne. This vineyard is so named because it belonged to an abbey of the same name. It furnishes wines of the same type as Romanée-Conti but inferior in quality. The vineyard which produces it being larger: this difference comes from the nature of the terrain and the way in which it is cultivated.

La Tâche, in the territory of Vosne. The wines of this slope are more or less similar to the preceding, perhaps even superior, and have a great potential for aging.

Les Saints-Georges[24], in the territory of Nuits; the wine of the clos of this name bears a great resemblance to that of Chambertin, to which it is nevertheless inferior; it has more color, taste, body, and even mellow character than the crus of Vosne which I have just cited, but these are preferred for their finesse and delicacy.

Independent of the wines of which I have just spoken, there are in several less celebrated districts privileged slopes whose wines approach the quality of those I cite. These are the Clos de Prémeaux[25], a half-league from Nuits, Musigny, in the territory of Chambolle, Clos de Tart, Bonnes-Mares, Clos de la Roche and Veroilles in Morey [sic}, Clos Morgeots, Maltroie, and Clos-St.-Jean in Chassagne, and finally Perrière in Fixin, in the district of Gevrey.

These vines are not very extensive, and are not well-known outside of Burgundy, and the wines that they produce are always less expensive than those of the crus with greater reputation, even though they are of similar quality.

Of these wines that compose the first class, those that can be shipped by sea include Chambertin, Saint-George, and Perrière, when they come from a year when the temperature was favorable to the vine.

Second Class

Corton in the territory of Aloxe in the district of Beaune; the wine of this cru is of the same type as that of Saint-George, it is a little mellower, but less agreeable; it is a deeply colored wine, structured, and vigorous that can be kept a long time and supports perfectly well being shipped by sea. It acquires much vigor and bouquet as it ages.

Vosne, at three quarters of a league from Nuits. The wines of this vineyard are generally the finest and the most delicate of the Côte de Nuits. After the premières cuvées of Romanée-Conti, Richebourg, and La Tâche, are those called **Echézeaux** and **La Grande Rue**. They follow immediately and are little different in quality than the wines of La Tâche and Romanée-Saint-Vivant. The other vines, known under the name of premières cuvées, follow closely the two that I have just named.

Nuits, at three leagues north east of Beaune. After the wines of the Clos Saint-George, of which I have already spoken, all of the premières cuvées of Nuits are of approximately equal merit, and appear in the market under the name of wine of Nuits, premier quality. They are more deeply colored, mellower, more generous, and will keep longer than those of Volnay, Pommard, and Beaune, but these last are more precocious and agreeable with more purity of flavor; they can be drunk from the second year after their harvest, while those of Nuits drink well three and even four years after. Finally, these last travel better, both by sea and by land.

Prémeaux, near Nuits, of which I have already cited the Clos among the wines of the first class, has several other crus that take their place with those of the premières cuvées of Nuits; the best vines are the ones next to the Clos.

Volnay, two leagues south of Beaune, produces the lightest, finest, and most agreeable wines of the Côte de Beaune. They have above all a charming bouquet. The most distinguished crus of this territory are Caillerets, Champans, and Chapelle.

Pommard, a half-league southwest of Beaune. The quality of the wines of this territory differ little from the preceding; they have only more color and more body; consequently they have less finesse and are less agreeable at an early age. The cuvées called Rugiens and Épeneaux are superior to the others.

Beaune. The territory of this town is the largest and furnishes the greatest quantities of wine, in first quality as in second; they differ little from those of Volnay and Pommard; there are even several cuvées that are equal to the best from these vineyards. The wines of Beaune have the well-earned reputation of having purest of all Burgundy. The most highly esteemed crus are those of Les Grèves, Les Fèves, Clos des Mouches, Clos du Roi, and Les Cras. This town produces also many wines of the second and third cuvée, which take their places among the third, fourth, and fifth classes.

Chambolle, at three-quarters of a league from Nuits. This vineyard is nicknamed "The Volnay of the Côte de Nuits". Its wines, although very agreeable and fine, have a bit more body and generosity than those of Volnay and much more length, but their taste is less pure. That of the vineyard called Musigny that I have cited with the wines of the first class, is the equal of La Tâche, Saint-George, and Corton; the other premières cuvées differ little from the best of Beaune.

Morey, a half-league from Gevrey, on the Côte de Nuits. The wines of this village are not very inferior to the largest part of those of Nuits; those called the Clos de Tart, Bonnes-Mares, Clos de la Roche, and Véroilles, which I have cited with those of the first class, furnish wine of the same type as that of Chambertin, Saint-George, and Corton, although inferior, not having quite the body or generosity, and aging less well.

Savigny-sous-Beaune, one harvests in this very extensive vineyard a great quantity of wine, of which the major part belongs only to the third or fourth class. There are privileged slopes whose products are little inferior to the premières cuvées of Beaune, such as La Dominode, Les Vergelesses, Les Marconnets, and Les Jarrons.

Meursault, at one and three-quarters leagues from Beaune, harvests in the vineyards called Santenots and Petures[26], wines that are no different from those of Caillerets, the premier cru of Volnay, except that they have more body and will age for a longer time. Those of the vineyard called Les Cras[27] have all of the agreeable finesse of the best wines of Volnay. The others can only be cited in the fourth class.

Third Class

Gevrey, at two leagues from Dijon. This vineyard is situated in the Côte de Nuits. The most highly esteemed crus after Chambertin are Saint-Jacques, Chapelle, Véroilles[1] and Mazy. All of the wines that they produce have body, a beautiful color, bouquet, and are capable of long aging; they are of the type of Nuits, and approach them in quality.

Chassagne, in the district of Nolay, three leagues from Beaune, furnishes agreeable and fine wines, which are more generous and more solid than those of the Côte

---

1 This is not the same vineyard that I spoke of in the section on Morey.

de Beaune, but their taste is less pure and they are not as sought after. Several privileged crus produce wines little inferior to the first class, such as Morgeots, particularly the clos of this name, Maltroie and the Clos St.-Jean, of which the products are well superior to all of the other wines of this village.

Aloxe, at one league from Beaune, gives wines that are full-bodied, fine, and generous and have notable bouquet. One distinguishes as the best the vineyards named Le Charlemagne and Bressandes; they are little inferior to the wine of Corton, of which I have already spoken.

Savigny-sous-Beaune, already mentioned, furnishes wines that can appear here. The best cuvées are of the type and quality of the second wines from Beaune. Here is also made much ordinary wine of the first quality, light and agreeable, which in general does not cellar well.

Blagny, a rural district in the territory of Puligny, at two and a half leagues southwest of Beaune, gives fine wines of good quality.

Santenay, district of Nolay, at three and three-quarters leagues from Beaune. This vineyard, which is part of the Côte de Beaune, gives good tasting wines that age well. The cuvées called Gravières and Clos de Tavanne, close the list of fine wines, and are on a par with the second wines of Beaune, Pommard, and Volnay; all of the others give only ordinary wine of first quality.

Chenôve, at one league from Dijon. The crus that can figure in this class are the Clos du Roi and Le Chapitre. They give wines of deep color, good taste, very solid, which acquire while aging much quality and an agreeable bouquet. They are equal to the second cuvées of Nuits. The other parts of this vineyard produce ordinary wines of first and second quality.

The wines called second-cuvée harvested Vosne, Nuits, Volnay, Pommard, Beaune, Chambolle, and Morey must still figure in this class as "semi-fine" wines; the same vineyards furnish also ordinary wines of the first and second quality, of which the best are often shipped as fine wines, in countries where the first wines are not appreciated at their just value.

Fourth Class

Mercurey, in the district of Touches, at three leagues from Châlons-sur-Saône. One includes here under the name wines of Mercurey not only those of this vineyard, but also those of Touches, Estroy, and Bourgneuf; they distinguish themselves among the wines of the Côte Chalonnaise, by the pleasant quality of their taste, their lightness, and their perfume. They have the greatest purity of fruit of this entire district, and age very well. The best are the most esteemed of the category ordinary wines of the first quality. They should not be bottled until they have aged in cask for two or three years, according to the temperature of the year that has produced them.

All the wines of the Côte Chalonnaise, even those of Mercurey, have little mellowness but a dry taste that characterizes them and distinguishes them from those of the Côte de Beaune, under whose name they are nevertheless often sold in the market.

Givry, the largest town of the district, at two leagues from Chalon-sur-Saône has some privileged crus that furnish wines superior to the premières cuvées of Mercurey, such as Boichevaux, Clos Salomon, Le Cellier, La Baraude, and Vignes-Rouges. The wines they produce are very full bodied and generous, with good taste; when they come from a year where the temperature was favorable to the vine and they have aged properly in cask, then they have finesse and bouquet and approach the fine wines of the third class. The other crus of this district furnish some ordinary wine of first quality and much more of the second and third. They have in general more body but less finesse than the wines of Mercurey, and must be kept longer in cask.

The territory of **Dijon** encloses esteemed vineyards. One sets in the first rank those of Marcs d'Or, whose wines are full-bodied, mellow, and of a very good flavor; they figure with honor among the ordinary wines of first quality. The cru called Ponneaux gives wines that resemble those of Marcs d'Or, but they are of inferior quality.

Monthélie, in the district of Meursault, on the Côte de Beaune. This vineyard has several slopes that furnish wines of the type and quality of the fine wines of the second class of Volnay. One finds here among the others many good ordinary wines of first and second quality.

Meursault. The wines of this village, called passe-tout-grains[2], are solid, full-bodied, and good for reinforcing weak wines. This property, more than the pleasantness of their taste, has placed them among the most esteemed wines of this class. However, when they have aged three or four years in cask and several months in bottle they are very good as ordinary wine, some of the first quality, and some of the second.

Fixin, **Fixey**, and **Brochon**, in the district of Gevrey and the region of Dijon, produce very good ordinary wine, of which the majority is more of the first class than of the second. They have a beautiful color and are more agreeable and pure than the wines of the Côte Chalonnaise, but are not as long-lived. The vineyard called [28]Perrière, in the territory of Fixin, gives fine wines, full-bodied and very solid, that I have already cited following those wines of the first class.

Saint-Martin, in the district of Touches, near Chalon-sur-Saône. The wines of this village are full-bodied and age well; however, they are generally less good than they were twenty years ago, since the owners have substituted common vines for fine ones which were in a majority; the vineyard called Chassières belongs to the ordinary wines of the first quality; others are only of the second quality.

Rully, at three leagues from Chalon-sur-Saône, furnishes from its best vines ordinary wine of the first category.

---

2 One calls passe-tout-grains the wines in Pinot Noir and Gamay, mixed in diverse proportion; they are, in general, considered as ordinary wines of the second quality. Common wines come from Gamay alone, or from vines planted in poor expositions.

Monbogre, a dependency of Saint-Desert, at two and a half leagues from Chalon-sur-Saône, harvests wines of deep color, which although at first very closed, gain greatly by aging and become agreeable. They have, along with the wines of Meursault, the grace of fortifying weak wines which has earned them the name of "doctors" of the Côte Chalonnaise; it is in this capacity that I add them to this class.

Fifth Class

The wines that compose this class are, 1st, the second, third, and fourth cuvées of vineyards composing the first four classes; 2nd the crus whose exposition, the nature of the terrain, and the type of vine give only ordinary wine, inferior to those I have cited. If one compares them to French vineyards producing only ordinary wine, one could divide them into even more categories, of which the first would be ordinary wines of the second class, the others those of the third class, and common wines.

Montagny, **Chenôve**, **Buxy**, **Saint-Vallerin**, and **Saules**, known under the name of the Côte de Buxy, at three and a quarter leagues southwest of Chalon-sur-Saône, producing many ordinary wines of the second and third category, which have a good and agreeable taste; they are precocious wines, and appear at first more agreeable than those of Givry and Saint-Martin, but they do not improve as much with aging.

Jambles, in the district of Givry; **Saint-Jean-de-Vaux** and **Saint-Marc**, in that of Touches, which furnish a great quantity of deeply colored, full bodied, common wine that age well; they do a considerable business in Switzerland and Alsace-Lorraine. Their fault is to lack generosity, and to be hard and somewhat coarse; several other districts give similar wines.

The vineyards in the district of Châtillon-sur-Seine in the département of the Côte d'Or produce only common wines; those of the district of Semur have several slopes that furnish wines for local consumption of the second and third quality, among which one cites Flavigny as having body, a fair amount of generosity, and good flavor; they are, above all, very solid, and gain in quality as they age, and when they voyage. Many other vineyards from the same district furnish common wines which can be distilled to make fairly good eaux-de-vie, but these do not leave the region.

WHITE WINES

First Class

Puligny, in the district of Nolay, two and a half leagues southwest of Beaune. It is in this village that Montrachet is located, celebrated for the excellent white wines it produces. Although they are produced in the same vineyard from the same type of vine, there are several quality divisions, depending on the exposition of the vines. They are known under the names of Montrachet Aîné [the elder], Chevalier

Montrachet, and Bâtard Montrachet. The first, superior to the other two, is harvested in the part exposed to the east and to the south. It unites all of the qualities of a perfect wine; it has body, much generosity, and finesse; it has a very agreeable hazelnut taste which is all its own, and above all a vigor and bouquet whose power and suavity distinguish it from the other white wines of the Côte d'Or. Chevalier Montrachet shares all of the qualities of its elder, but does not possess them to the same degree. Bâtard Montrachet follows Chevalier very closely, and sometimes shares the praises of the connoisseur.

Second Class

Meursault, already cited for its red wines, furnishes many highly esteemed white wines, which, leaving the country, often take the name of Montrachet, which they resemble a bit but do not share all the qualities. The slope called Les Perrières is particularly renowned for the excellence of its wines, which sustain a comparison with Bâtard Montrachet: they have much finesse, delicacy, and perfume. The vineyards named Combottes[29], Les Gouttes d'Or, Les Genevrières, and Les Charmes, furnish wines of the same type, and for their merit should be classed after Perrières in the order that I have followed in naming them.

Third Class

The vineyard called **Les Rougeots** and several others in the territory also give wines that are called première cuvée, and differ from them by only slight nuances; they are full bodied, fine, generous, and endowed with a pretty bouquet.

The rural district of **Blagny**, in the territory of Puligny, furnishes fine white wines that sell for the same price as those of the première cuvée from Meursault.

NOTE: The white wines of Haute-Bourgogne are good in general to bottle at the end of a year or eighteen months; there is little need to leave them two years in cask. The majority of them take on an amber tint while aging that does not alter their quality or their transparence; that of Les Gouttes d'Or in Meursault owes its name to the brilliance of its golden color.

Although carefully bottled and perfectly limpid, all of these wines are subject to maladies, during the course of which they appear to have lost their quality, but it is sufficient to let them rest for several months for them to regain their transparence, their good taste and their bouquet; these maladies are only the work of nature, through which they complete their fermentation, purify themselves, and attain their highest degree of quality; the longer they age, the less they are subject to this.

Fourth Class

The second cuvées of Meursault, of which we distinguish **La Barre**, give wines that have a part of the qualities of those of the première cuvée; they are less fine and less delicate, but very agreeable as ordinary wines of the first class; they alone can figure here.

Fifth Class

The troisième cuvées of Meursault occupy the top rank of this class and give good ordinary wines of the second class.

The **Côte de Buxy**, at three and a quarter leagues from Chalon-sur-Saône, furnishes light and sparkling wines with a pleasant and agreeable taste; they retain their sweetness for a long time, and if one bottles them in the month of March following the harvest, they will sparkle like champagne. This property is common to almost all of the white wines of Burgundy, but one rarely makes the attempt with wines of the first quality. In addition, the sparkle causes many bottles to break, and dissipates at the end of several months, whereas that of champagne will be retained for several years.

Bouzeron, a district of Chagny, at three and a half leagues from Châlons, makes wines that are less light-bodied than those of the Côte de Buxy, but they have a distinguished taste that places them near the troisième cuvées of Meursault.

Givry, already cited, harvests in the part of its vineyards called Champ Poureau a white wine of the type of those of Buxy, but less light and less generous: one drinks it with pleasure when it comes from a year when the temperature has been favorable to the vine. Several other crus produce wines that are for the most part consumed in the countryside cabarets of the district, or mixed with red wines that are too deeply colored.

The principal commerce in the wines of Haute Bourgogne is done in the Dijon, Gevrey, Nuits, and Beaune in the département of the Côte d'Or, and in Chagny, Chalon-sur-Saône, and Givry in the département of Saône et Loire.

The casks in use are called demi-queues, which contain 30 veltes or 228 litres; the wine is sold by the queue, which contains two demi-queues; one also employs, above all for fine wines, quarter queues, called feuillettes, which contain 15 veltes or 114 litres.

Shipping: the wines of the Côte d'Or are normally shipped by ground, above all those of the first quality. Those of the Côte Chalonnaise ship by the same method or by the canal of Chalon, the Loire, and the canals of Briare and of Loing, as far as the Seine, or finally, overland as far as Auxerre, and from there by the Seine to Paris and Rouen. The choice of these diverse means is determined by the price of transport and the greater or lesser urgency of timely delivery.

DR. DENIS MORELOT

Dr. Denis Morelot, a physician and surgeon from Beaune, was the first to attempt a complete analysis of all of the Côte d'Or wines in his 1831 book, La Vigne et le Vin en Côte d'Or. Dr. Morelot was a member of the Academy of Arts, Sciences and Letters of Dijon, the Antiquities Commission of the Côte d'Or, and several other learned societies. He owned a vineyard with a large domaine based in Volnay.

Morelot's approach was thorough, rational, and scientific, and he believed that all aspects of wine and of the vine could be understood through practical experimentation. He begins with a chapter entitled "Of the nature of the soil of the good vineyards and their products, which we will examine village by village" and offers his thoughts on the concept of terroir, to clarify his judgments of the various crus.

> The base of our hills is a limestone that varies in its characteristics according to the different currents that have formed it. The intimate knowledge of this rock is, in my opinion, one of the most useful points in the study of our soil. It is believed that the quantity of more or less pure of calcium carbonate that constitutes the mass of our mountains gives singular influence to the formation of the topsoil, which can only confirm the opinion of the celebrated Sir Humphry Davy[30], that the soils appear to owe their origin to the decomposition of rocks.
>
> This manner of envisaging the nature of the soil in terms of the substances that compose their base to explain the differences in its products appears to me completely new.
>
> All agronomists are agreed that rocks decompose and are reduced to a more or less cohesive dust; that this dust combines with other substances and becomes mixed with a greater or lesser quantity of organic matter, and that this mixture constitutes, properly speaking, the topsoil, whose quality varies according to the good proportion of its constituents. I believe, however, that no one has applied local knowledge of the base of these hills to agricultural theory; nor have they remarked that the identity of such or such a product or the differences of these same products was the result of the decomposition of the bedrock analogous in the first instance and different in the second.
>
> Some have made an objection to this theory that, rather than destroying the theory, validates it. They believe that vines planted in a granite soil such as Hermitages near Tain, or composed of round quartz pebbles such as at Châteauneuf du Pape such as La Nerthe or La Gaude, etc., or formed of schist as at La Malgue near Toulon, give excellent wines. I am far from denying this truth; but each of these wines has a particular quality, a taste absolutely different from the other; none of them have any relationship to those of Burgundy in terms of flavor. It is thus the soil that imprints

the wines and accounts for the differences between them.

I am further convinced that the exposition, the dryness of the soil, the age of the vines and their variety powerfully influence the quality of the wine; but if it is better in a certain part of the same slope, that which is inferior in quality always shares a certain similarity of constituents.

The truth of this assertion will soon be demonstrated by the details that I will reveal. The description that I will give of each of the slopes that compose the vineyard of our département will serve as proof. I will show the slope of each small hill, the nature of the limestone of each group; and I will prove that the products of the same slope being of equal perfection will share the same composition of soil, organic matter and exposition

After this introduction, Morelot launches into his analysis of the vineyards of each village, moving from south to north. Once he reaches Dijon, he continues to examine "the nature of the soil of the inferior vineyards and their products," a topic of little interest to us. He offers a chemical analysis of the soil, a chapter on the debate regarding the time of the first planting of vines in Burgundy, and chapters on vines, vine varieties, and their diseases, vine growing, and wine making. Fascinating topics, but of more interest to the historian than to the wine lover. Starting in 1875, Burgundy vines were largely oblitreated by the ravages of the phylloxera root louse. To save the vines, they were grafted to American rootstock starting in 1888, and thus the vines of Morelot's day are fundamentally different from those found at the end of the 19th century, as is the method of their cultivation. Viticulture and oenology have also progressed to the point where the techniques described by Morelot have less application on today's wines than they once did. Morelot's ninth chapter, however, is still applicable today as he describes what makes certain Burgundy wines great:

> The quality of wines of the first distinction in the Département of the Côte d'Or varies infinitely: in the first place by the nature of the soil. I think that I have sufficiently showed the influence of the earth on the productions of the vine that I need not speak of it here.
>
> Secondly by exposition. The best exposition that one can choose is to be inclined east-southeast; such is the situation of Montrachet, of Santenots, of Champans, of Corton, of Les Saints-Georges, of La Tâche, of La Romanée, of the Clos de Vougeot, of Musigny, and of Chambertin. There are certainly a heap of climats that enjoy a beautiful exposition and yet give only mediocre products; one must attribute this poor quality of grape to a type of soil that is not well suited, that is cold and humid, and does not contain the principals of which I have spoken.
>
> Thirdly by the quality of the vine. The vine is of great importance. I have discussed the vines that are the most widely planted and those which the good winegrower must adopt and use to propagate his vineyard. He must above all keep guard against certain vines that surely could change the quality of his wine.

Fourthly by atmospheric influences as one is convinced by the table in Chapter VIII. Early years are always the most advantageous to the quality of the wines, but it is in precisely these years that one produces the least; it is rare in our region that there are not some April frosts and if the vine has developed already, all is lost, or at least a great part. One must not believe that heat alone with suffice to make good wine, it must be tempered by light rains from time to time. When the sky is constantly dry, the berry hardens, develops poorly, and often dries, and gives thus only a wine of mediocre quality.

Fifthly by the grape growing technique. It is incredible how the work done in the vineyard affects the nature of the wine. Some greedy proprietors cover their supposedly weak vineyards in manure: the next year there is an extraordinary vigor, and they propagate by layering more vines than they should, and the vine gives them a great quantity of grapes, but these juicy grapes contain above all else water and vegetable proteins, and the wine that is produced is subject to a host of maladies and will not keep. I am far from censuring those who bend all of their efforts to cultivate properly the vine, but excessive yields are far from proper cultivation. The quantities are over abundant, and of an artificial and deceptive quality. Those for whom the production of wine is their sole occupation should take close note of this: they will experience fewer disagreements and less loss on their part should they avoid this practice.

In the sixth place, by winemaking technique. I will not return to this topic; what I have said above seems to me sufficient to make known the way in which the manner of producing the wine influences its quality.

Finally, by a multitude of circumstances that can improve or destroy the quality of the wine. For example, we have seen hope of a good harvest destroyed in a few days at harvest time; thus in 1756, in 1801, in 1826, abundant rain lasting several days before the harvest swelled the grapes and given them a taste that was not rot and not mold, but strongly disagreeable, and which the wines retain after aging. In 1826, the villages that harvested before the rains, for example in the Côte de Nuits, had good quality wines with a pure fruit aroma. One can only attribute this detestable flavor to the heavy rains that fell before the harvest, since those that were harvested before it had no off aromas.

I will not continue further on the causes of the variety of qualities of wine, what I have said seems to me sufficient, but I will occupy myself now with the constituent elements, or more appropriately, the intrinsic elements of the wines that have all of the qualities that one desires.

As we know, our choicest wines come from the Pinot Noir vine growing in the best soils and with the most favorable exposition. In propitious years, when the fermentation proceeds perfectly, they should have first a beautiful velvety color; secondly body, that is to say a degree of firmness; thirdly an aroma or a bouquet that is appropriate for our wines; fourthly, generosity; finally a charming flavor that one calls finesse in our district.

First, the velvety red color is the result of the solution of the principal colorant that is attached to the inside of the skin of the grape through the means of fermentation. This principal is never more abundant than in hot and slightly humid years; it is in these circumstances that one has the best color. However, it is in these years when the wines have the best color without having any other distinguished quality.

I have long believed that the principal colorant in grapes was a resinous matter that dissolved best when there was much alcohol in the wine; and this beautiful color, soon after fermentation, acquired a lively character: I soon discovered, however, that this was an error by performing the experiments that I will describe. M. Bailly, pharmacist in Beaune, is very well versed in chemistry and assisted me greatly in this work.

We skinned very ripe black grapes and macerated these skins for several hours in warm alcohol and it was not colored, proof that it was not this substance that aided the development of the color, and that the coloring matter was not a resin but a gummy substance. We introduced a certain quantity of grape skins into very concentrated diethyl ether without attaining any type of coloration. We placed some in acetic acid and a few moments later the liquid had taken on a fairly strong pink tint. This same phenomenon takes place in tartaric acid; the liquid appeared to us perhaps a bit redder. We macerated some skins in distilled water which, a few moments later, was colored a beautiful blue color. Sulfuric acid, introduced in small quantity, caused this blue color to turn slowly red and bit by bit it developed an orange shade. Several drops of potassium produced a very noticeable effect: the liquid became deep blue and even when diluted in a larger quantity of water retained its blue color. We have then concluded from these experiments that the coloring matter in grapes is a gummy substance of a class of its own that turns red in grape acids, blue in alkali solutions, and which we will give the name of uvine[31].

In cold and rainy years, when the grape is only half ripe, there is little uvine, and the little that is there is further diluted by the tartaric acid that is still very abundant in unripe grapes; it is to this that one can attribute the lack of coloration in these wines. I have performed an experiment on this subject. In 1829, ordinary wine was unripe and contained much acid: at the moment of racking the tank, I mixed into the tank containing a certain quantity of this wine four to five ounces of pure potassium for each tonneau, stirred briskly, and proceeded to rack the wines; my wine took on a color double that which it had possessed, and the potassium tartrate that formed removed from the wine a large part of its acidity. The maturation continued without difficulty, and at the end of a year the wine was excellent.

In certain years where the wine is of poor quality, it is possible to obtain, however, a wine of fairly good color; this circumstance is due to the solution of a large quantity of the principal colorant in the juice of the grape and a saturation of tartaric acid to the degree possible; the uvine, remaining in free solution, thus gives its color to the wine.

In hot years, one obtains in general a very deep color; there is much more uvine because there is more maturity and less tartaric acid, two circumstances that favor deep color. However, it should be noted that even in those years most apt to plant growth and to vines, one does not always obtain deep color, a fact that depends on the atmosphere; if the weather has been constantly dry, the skin of the grape hardens and the uvine dries out; but if the weather has been hot and tempered from time to time with soft rain, the skin softened by this watering charges the juice with the greatest amount of colorant and the wine, in favorable years, unites good quality and beautiful color . It has now become a legend in our country that the wine will be good when it takes on color in the first month of its fermentation. This phenomenon takes place because a portion of the tartaric acid, suspended in the wine and causing the color to appear very lively, crystalizes and falls out of solution to the bottom of the tank and the color, absent the effect of this acid, takes on its natural color. The wine, in this case, does not necessarily take on a higher quality, but it loses acidity, a fact which can already be considered an improvement.

Secondly, it is said that a wine has body or that it is mellow when, while drinking, it seems to have a light hardness; it is necessary that this hardness be contained within appropriate limits; if there is not enough, the wine is dull, or to use the expression of the district, it is matte; if on the contrary there is too much body, it is not agreeable to drink and it is necessary to wait a long time for it to become potable.

The wines of the Côte de Nuits are often of the latter case; they are hard for the first two years and their qualities seem to be enveloped; little by little the covering dissipates and they demonstrate much body and perfect flavor. I do not suggest by specifying the Côte de Nuits here that this is only the case with the wines from this region. All of the good crus of the Côte de Beaune have the same characteristic in good years, but these are more often ready to drink at an earlier age.

This hardness in the wine seems to derive from a high charge of alcohol that dissolves some of the tannin contained in the skin of the grape, and several finings are sufficient to make the wine lose this hardness; one can also reduce the tannic charge by macerating a piece of iron in the young wine, which will develop a deep black color that indicated the formation of iron gallate.

Thirdly, the aroma or bouquet is a quality particular to the wines of our slopes. When these wines arrive at the moment to be drunk, they have noticeable bouquet on the nose and on the palate which I have always compared to a slight vanilla odor.

I have often wondered at the cause of this aroma, which does not belong to any great degree to our wines, and how to submit it to analysis. It is a principal so subtle and fleeting that it is impossible to gather enough of it together to test it. This bouquet does depend on the properties as the colorant, for one finds it in old wines that have lost all of their color; it does not belong to the alcohol, as it still exists in wines weakened by age; and when the wine becomes bitter it does not disappear entirely. I am thus led to believe that the bouquet, so flattering to the taste, is no other than an essential oil that is found in such small quantities that it is impossible to extract it.

The late M. Bosc attributes this aroma almost entirely to the choice of vine, which is to say to Pinot Noir, specially endowed with this property. It is possible that this genus of vine is more disposed than another to furnish it, but I am tempted to believe that the sun contributes even more than the vine; and in effect, we remark that certain vineyards furnish it in either greater quantity or more penetrating fashion. Volnay is privileged in this regard; La Romanée and Les Saints-Georges are distinguished above all by an exquisite bouquet that they begin to develop in their second year.

Our good coopers, accustomed to tasting each year the wine of each climat, are able to distinguish the taste of the wines of each vintage. It is the bouquet inherent to each that makes them recognizable; such is the level of their expertise that it is rare that the coopers are fooled. How could they avoid developing this faculty when one thinks that in the years when the wine is reputed to be of good quality that they taste in the space of merely a few days up to two thousand casks of wine? Although often their tongues and palates are overheated by an almost continual tasting of very lively new wines, yet they do not miss the slightest fault of a cask of wine, be it a hint of mustiness or a slight earthy character.

This is knowledge acquired as I have said by practice; but it is the bouquet that resembles an unwithered flower that is their surest guide; when one finds it no longer, the wine has been somehow damaged and is no longer what it should be.

Fourth, the generosity of our wines is recognized only by the palate of our gourmets. No experiments have been done on this important topic; it is necessary to undertake a long suite of experiments that will embrace in a broad manner all that one might say on the subject. It would be useful to examine wine coming from the same climat and the same vine in the same exposition and appreciate the differences that result from the mixture of grapes from different districts; to take note of the specific must weights and the fashion in which they undergo fermentation, and to do these experiments over the course of several years.

These experiments will lead to results that could have a high importance for our country. In waiting for these experiments to be done, I will give succinctly that which I have learned working with M. Pautet of different wines that I have subjected to distillation.

Analysis

Of wines of 1822, performed 2 January 1824

Village	Quality of wine	Alcohol obtained	Degree of alcohol
Pommard	Pinot Noir, 1st quality	18/100	22
Pommard	Passe-tout-grain, 3rd quality	16/100	22
Morteuil	Gamay, inferior quality	11/100	22

The alcohol coming from the first wine had a very suave odor and a pleasant taste;

one would say that it shared the agreeable nature of the wine from which it had come. Count Chaptal, in speaking of the aroma, says that with the exception of the first liquid that comes from the still and conserves a bit of the particular odor of the wine, the eau de vie that comes next has only its most essential characteristics.[3] However, in this particular case, the aroma was conserved until the end of the distillation.

The alcohol coming from the second type of wine was somewhat less fine and less delicate, but it had an agreeable taste; whereas that which had been made from inferior wine had no perfume, and I would say furthermore that it was a very common eau de vie.

The degree of generosity of wine is more considerable in those of a superior quality than it is in those of an inferior quality; however, the musts of these wines present little difference in the measure of their sugars. It is, however, the diverse principals that constitute the grape that differ essentially according to the vine and the soil that has produced it.

All grapes contain an element that resembles animal protein, sugar, vegetable albumin, malic acid, tartaric acid, and water. It is in the just proportion of each of these parts that the quality of the wine is found. If sugar predominates, the wine is sweet and syrupy; such are the wines of the south; if on the contrary, vegetable albumin is in excess, it is acid; such are the majority of wines made from Gamay in cool and rainy years. The protein is the fermentable element: it exists in almost all fruits. One must not confuse it with the sugar: one finds them almost always together, and may under the right conditions change their nature. Sugar leads to fermentation, and its alteration produces alcohol, while vegetable albumin produces acidity.

It is proposed to remedy the inconvenient surfeit of vegetable albumin by the addition of sugar or honey. Several owners have tried to correct their wines in this manner, in the years that have given little natural sugar. They have followed fairly exactly the precepts given on this subject by the knowledgeable Chaptal. They have made better wine, it has aged better, and has a very good flavor; but this wine, thus prepared, if I am not mistaken, is no longer the true wine of Burgundy. Stronger, more generous, more deeply colored, it has lost its bouquet and is closer to southern wines.[4]

This method, in my opinion, is only admissible for the wines of our slopes in rainy and humid years, when the must is overburdened with a considerable amount of water and fermentation completes with great difficulty and the wine has no merit.[5] In this instance nothing can be done and nothing prevents us from adding to the must the sugar that it lacks, and thus, correcting the excess of mucous, and producing a wine of good taste. The ancients employed an analogous procedure in boiling the must to evaporate overabundant water and thus concentrating the sugars and obtaining results similar to the addition of sugar.

In hot years, when the sugars dominate the damp elements, it is a great error to believe that sugars can still be added; any addition, in my opinion, is a loss, as the wines have already all of the requisite qualities. This addition is simply useless as in

---

3 *The Art of Making Wine,* Chaptal

4 This element is named glaïadine or gliadine, by Taddey, from the greek word glia, or gluten

5 I speak here only of the wines of the first quality as the reputation of Burgundy rests solely on these wines

the southern latitudes, for example, where the sugars are in excess, one is obliged in certain years to add yeast in order to make the fermentation more active; or one is forced to keep the wines a great number of years before the fermentation is completely finished.

The following fact supports what I have just told you. M. Julia-Fontenelle, chemistry professor, distilled in Narbonne in 1804 wines of Rivesaltes, Peyretortes, Staget, and Bauquets, which were two years of age. These wines, the best of the Roussillon, furnished him at the distillation with 24% alcohol at 22°, but yet seventeen years later, these same wines distilled gave him the same quantities at 23°.

It is incontestable that the addition of sugar to wines gives them a greater level of alcohol; but it is necessary to recognize that this addition in hot and propitious years does not add to the quality; to the contrary, it retards the moment when the wines will be fit to drink, a fact that is always unfavorable for the proprietor and the merchant. Furthermore I would say that through exaggerated additions of sugar one does not obtain the desired effect, since it is absolutely necessary to add a certain dose of tartaric acid to the must to obtain a good fermentation as the experiments of the Marquis de Bullion have showed. If one saturates the must with sugar, the fermentation will be suspended and even impeached for a greater or lesser time.

Let us content ourselves, therefore, when the year is favorable with the advantages that have been given us, without recourse to often imaginary improvements, and let us reserve for the years which are cold, damp and late the resources that chemistry has created for us. If in these circumstances we do not have true Burgundy wine, we can have wine of good flavor, and one can admit it to the best tables as grand ordinaire or the wine for a roast.

I have completed several experiments to measure the alcohol that wines of superior quality from different crus can contain. It is almost the same in all, or the difference is so small that it is not measurable. From this I have concluded that the quality and superiority of the wines of such or such climat was the result of inherent qualities of the wine that come from the vine, the soil, and its exposition, and not either a greater or lesser quantity of alcohol. One can thus conclude that the wines refuse all analysis, and that it is only through taste alone that one can appreciate their quality, their value, and their merit.

This has thus convinced me, and I can give it as a positive fact, that the distillation of the wines of our country shall never become a useful branch of commerce. However little may be the value of our vines, one will always profit by selling them as wine rather than by converting them to eau-de-vie. Our ordinary wines in a common year will never render more than nine percent eau-de-vie at 20°, and regardless of the low price obtained, one will realize at least double than if they were converted into alcohol.

Fifthly, the finesse is another particularity of our wines: one recognizes an agreeable sensation when drinking a cuvée of choice; it seems that this quality depends on a sort of delicacy of the molecules that constitute the wine. This property seems so inherent to them that it serves to distinguish them, since they are generally known under the name the fine wines of Burgundy.

I have said that it is because our wine has delicate molecules; in effect, our superfine wines contain less potassium bitratrate, more generosity, a red color that is more brilliant and distinct from the color of Gamay, which is more violet-hued. Although this property is in itself appreciable to the sight, the real difference is in the flavor; it is the palate that will best recognize all of the differences and that will decide in the final analysis the greater or lesser degree of finesse in our wines.

The wines that reunite in high degree all of the properties that I have just enumerated come from vines known in our country as têtes de cuvées. These include Chambertin and the Clos de Bèze in Gevrey; in Morey, the Clos de Tart; in Chambolle, Musigny, and Les Amoureuses; in Vougeot, the magnificent clos of the same name; in Vosne, the Romanées, Richebourg, and La Tâche; in Nuits, Le Saint-George; in Aloxe, Le Corton; in Savigny, La Bataillère; in Beaune, Les Fèves and Les Grèves; in Pommard, Les Épeneaux and Le Clos de Cîteaux; in Volnay, Les Champans and Les Caillerets; in Meursault, Le Santenots; in Chassagne, Le Morgeot. [Emphasis added]

Immediately after these têtes de cuvées come the wines that are called in our country the premières cuvées; these approach the preceding, but some of their qualities are lacking; it is hardly appreciable, but tasters know how to distinguish them. These nuances are the result of the union in the same tank of grapes from different climats, which, although they come from climats with a good exposition, are not of a homogeneous nature as those are that one harvests in the same district. In a favorable year, the premières cuvées replace the têtes de cuvées and even the most knowledgeable gourmets will not be able to distinguish them.

It is to this cause that one must attribute the nuances that one observes in the wines of the Côte de Nuits and the Côte de Beaune. In the first, the climats generally belong to one owner; they make one cuvée with the grapes from one parcel, identical in character and in quality. In the Côte de Beaune, ownership is incredibly fragmented; it is impossible that the grapes are everywhere of the same nature; the amalgamation of all of these products is well accomplished in the tank, but it lacks this exquisite quality that distinguishes so eminently the wines that come from the same cru, with a beautiful exposition, having the proper soil, planted with a choice vine. If the wines of the distinguished districts of Volnay, Pommard, Beaune, etc., were made solely with grapes coming from these parcels, I am convinced that they were be more appreciated than those of the Côte de Nuits; I offer as proof the wine of Corton and that of Santenots. I do not think that there is better in our country.

After these cuvées come those that are "good"[32]. The wines of *bonnes cuvées* approach the preceding, but they have less finesse, sometimes less body, and often they are distinguished by a deeper color. The grapes that provide the wines of this quality come from vines that grow in a less favorable terrain and are less well-exposed; they can never equal the premières cuvées nor replace them. It is this type of wine that has been too greatly expanded in the past thirty years; it is unfortunately too abundant, and more than once it has besmirched our superfine wines. If these qualities are examined superficially they may seem similar to the premières cuvées, but they have nor the merit nor the value of those.

One gives the name of *cuvées rondes* [round] to wines that come from vines planted on the highest part of the slope or completely at the bottom, almost in the plain. These are from Pinot Nor, but often from compacted soil with lots of clay, mixed with only a bit of the marl that one finds in the upper portions; it is a thin, rocky, poor soil and offers only the least possible amount of earth necessary for planting. In addition, one sees that neither the soil nor the exposition can contribute to the quality of these wines, which have, nonetheless, color and body, but lack finesse and, above all, bouquet. They can make distinguished but ordinary wines; thus are those of Fixin, Fixey, Marsannay, etc.

After the wines of which I have just spoken, one places those which are called in the term of the countryside passe-tout-grains, which are furnished by half Pinot Noir and half Gamay. Several villages have the reputation of furnishing such wines of a superior quality, such as Puligny, Meursault, Chorey, Comblanchien, Fixin, Fixey, and Marsannay, etc.

The passe-tout-grains makes, in propitious years, an excellent ordinary wine, above all, if care has been taken in its fermentation. It presents a beautiful, velvety, and brilliant red color, lots of body, generosity, and a particular bouquet that is not without charm, yet lacking finesse. This type of wine still has one great advantage: it is less susceptible to the diseases of the vine, and will keep a long time without deteriorating; often, in fact, one has recourse to wines of this type to prop up wines of the first quality that have been weakened or are tending towards bitterness or sourness.

The villages that form what is called the arrière-côte[33] because they occupy a range of hills behind the good slopes; these villages, I tell you, furnish in abundance wines of quality equal to those I have just described; but they are good only in very hot years; their exposition on more elevated summits demands more intense heat for the grapes to reach perfect maturity. One distinguishes among the wines of the arrière-côte those of St.-Romain, Meloisey, Nantoux, Arcenant. One can also classify in this category Plombières, Talant, Fontaine, etc.

The last wine is pure Gamay. This is what one harvests on the slopes of the Auxois and on the plain, in clay with little admixture of chalk. The grapes of this vine, as I have already said, ripens sufficiently only in precocious and very hot years; it is also only in these years that Gamay has color and body; but it never has much generosity, since the wine of Gamay of 1822, the best year for Burgundy wine in human memory, gave only 11% alcohol by volume. There are villages where the Gamay is better than others: this relates to the soil, exposition, and even the means of cultivation. One may cite, among these communes, Corcelles-les-Arts,

Bligny-sous-Beaune, Couchey, Perrigny-lez-Dijon; however superior, this Gamay still lacks finesse and bouquet.

White wines offer less variety than reds; one can hardly count but three: to wit, Montrachet, Meursault, and the ordinary wines.

Le Montrachet has such a great superiority over all white wines that we can name it alone as tête de cuvée. In good years its lightness, perfume, finesse, extreme delicacy; generosity without dryness, and sweet flavor without heaviness, make of it one of the best wines that one can drink; One must make every effort to maintain it without color, and for that one must always top up the cask; with this precaution one prevents the absorption of oxygen, which, being incorporated in the wine causes the wine to turn yellow and lose a part of its bouquet and its lightness.

As the district that produces this delicious wine is very small and only furnishes a small quantity, it is always expensive; and despite its elevated price, it is rare that its sale provides an adequate return for its producers given the expenses they incur.

Chevalier-Montrachet, Bâtard-Montrachet, Meursault, and Blagny are all fairly similar in their taste and in their qualities. Less fine than the Vrai Montrachet, they are nevertheless very agreeable in flavor, and very generous. It is also recognized that they will make you drunk easily. One must also place in this class the white wines of Fixin that are harvested in the Clos du Chapitre. There are still several climats, in the territory of Dijon, that one cannot place completely in this same line, but approach it. The white wines of all of these vineyards are normally sold in the market at the same prices as red wines of the first quality from these localities.

The common white wines are always more or less acid; without body or pleasantness, they come from marl or clay soils that stamp them with their character and mediocre quality. In good years they retain for several months a bit of their original sugar that has not fermented to dryness and which gives them a slightly sweet taste. This flavor causes the wines to be avidly sought after. But whether they have it or not, these wines drink well young and are mostly consumed in the first year after their production.

One could, if one desired it, conserve for a longer time this sweet flavor by making what is known in certain countries a *vin muet*. This is normally done with sulfur, that is, by burning several sulfur candles in the casks at the moment when one racks the must from the press. All fermentation is thus suspended and the wine keeps all of its sweetness. At the end of several days one can fine it, and one is assured of drinking sweet wine, very clear and limpid. There is another very easy method of arresting all alcoholic fermentation, which is to introduce into the casks a pound or two of mustard seed very lightly bruised. By this means, the wine will also keep its sweet taste and it is not altered at all by the addition of these seeds. I will observe only that the white wine cannot have begun its fermentation in the slightest degree.

Vin muet is not bad, above all when it has been fined, and the substances that trouble it have been removed; to the contrary, it is very agreeable to drink, and it resembles the white wines of the Midi.

Some have even counseled the addition of plaster[34] to the casks to arrest fermentation. As I do not know the result of this experiment, I merely note the proposed technique. I am persuaded that one could have recourse to this method without danger, since it must cause a chemical decomposition of this salt whose base is a blend of tartaric and malic acids and releases sulfuric acid in a free state leading to the suspension of all fermentation.

To sum up all that has been said of the mutage of wine, one can infer that the most certain means of obtaining it is to release into the tank a determined quantity of sulfur dioxide, and that the best way to arrive at this is to burn sulfur candles in the casks when they are one quarter full and then to agitate the liquid in order to impregnate it with the sulfur, to recommence this activity when what has filled the cask half full, and finally to do it a third time when it is three quarters full. At each sulfuring, one must be very careful not to drop the burned sulfur candle into the wine because this will give it an unpleasant taste.

I will speak further on about the usefulness of mutage to cure several maladies of wine. That which I have said here is sufficient to teach proprietors of vineyards with white grapes how to procure an agreeable beverage, above all in poor years, when the white wine resembles verjus more than wine.

DR. JULES LAVALLE

Dr. Jules Lavalle published *Histoire et statistique de la vigne et des grands vins de la Cote-d'Or* [*History and Statistics of the Vine and of the Great Wines of the Côte d'Or*], the major work on 19th century Burgundy wines in Dijon in 1855. In the same year, the Bordeaux negociant trade published its classification of the wines of the Gironde. Both works classify the wines produced in each region, but the Bordeaux classification is the work of a committee of wine professionals, while Dr. Lavalle's is that of a passionate amateur. Another differene is that the Bordeaux classification is based strictly on the price attained by each wine in the marketplace. Dr. Lavalle makes use of commercial factors in his evaluation of different wines, but this is only one element in his analysis. Most striking, however, is the fact that the Bordeaux classification has changed very little since 1855 and is still is in use, whereas Dr. Lavalle's work is often overlooked and the present Burgundy system resembles his schema only approximately.

Dr. Lavalle based his work on that of his predecessor Dr. Morelot, but they differ in several ways. Dr. Lavalle's work goes into great depth regarding the individual crus of each village and provides an in depth analyses of the wines' qualities. Dr. Lavalle's work served as the basis for the 1860 classification of the vineyards of Burgundy by the Beaune Agriculture Committee (Comité d'Agriculture de Beaune, or CAB), of which he was a member. This is the most complete and well-documented classification prior to modern times. Although flawed in some regards, the CAB classification gives a more nuanced view of the wines of Burgundy than exists today. It has come down (almost!) to the modern day in the reproduction in the Atlas de la France Viticole by Louis Larmat, a series published in the years just after the Second World War. It was in fact this map that hangs in my study that prompted my investigation of the present topic. The differences between this map and maps of the present-day appellations fascinated me, and I began to investigate the origins of this previous classification. I was delighted to discover the work of Dr. Lavalle but surprised that few of my contemporaries shared my enthusiasm and shocked that there is no translation of Dr. Lavalle's work into English.

As with Morelot and Jullien, significant portions of Lavalle are of more interest to the historian than to the wine lover. The first section, *Historique*, describes wine production under the Romans and in the following centuries; winegrowers and their salaries; the methods of grape growing, harvest, and vinification in these antique times; animals and insects that attack the vine; ancient laws and ordinances relative to the vine; taxes on wine; barrels and barrel makers; tasters, gourmets, and courtiers; the commerce in wine; the price of wine in different epoques; and several Burgundian proverbs relative to the wine and other matters.

Lavalle tells us that he is a "medical doctor and doctor of the natural sciences, a professor of natural medical history at the medical school of Dijon, director of the botanical garden of the same city, member of the Geographical Society of France, secretary of the Horticultural Society of the Côte d'Or, a member of the Central Agricultural Committee of the Côte d'Or, and of several learned societies." Pointedly, not a vineyard owner or a trader in wine, yet certainly someone well positioned to understand the intricacies of grape growing in Burgundy. It is evident from the text that he is also a great lover and connoisseur of the wines of his native region.

Lavalle notes that he has worked with the assistance of Joseph Garnier, "archivist of the city of Dijon, correspondent of the Ministry of Public Instruction for Historical Work, member of the Commission of Antiquities of the Côte d'Or, and secretary adjunct of the Academy of Art, Science and Literature of Dijon," and M. Delarue, pharmacist of Dijon, member of the Academy of Art, Science and Literature of Dijon, secretary of the Council of Health and Well-Being of the Côte d'Or, editor of the Acts of the Congress of Winegrowers of 1845...and of a great number of proprietors and winegrowers." In his preface, he writes:

> Everyone, in France and abroad, speaking about the wines of the Côte d'Or; each of us knows the most popular names; it is at once the glory and the riches of our region and our whole country; and yet, there is no complete history of these great wine regions. Wine lovers and merchants ask in vain where one might find the most indispensable information: Burgundy has not been able to offer them until the present more than a few general facts and vague descriptions, and did not even possess a complete inventory of the sites most worthy of appreciation, and 100 climats worthy of being inscribed in letters of gold upon its shield have remained as forgotten and unknown several kilometers outside of their territory as if they had been planted with vulgar shrubs.
>
> It is this void that I have tried to fill. I hope to make this book worthy of the country in whose history it must be an important page, and no sacrifice or work has been avoided in arriving at this end. Would that I have not strayed too far from this goal.
>
> The base of any conscientious study must be a topographical map executed on a scale sufficiently large to allow the reader to find without pain the smallest climats, and sufficiently exact to serve the most serious research. Nor have I neglected anything to give this part of my work a sufficient development and exactitude. All of the division of climats have been scrupulously plotted and drawn according to today's cadastral survey. Wherever able, I have indicated the height above sea level, and the contours of the land have been studied with care sufficient to show not only diverse undulations of the soil, but so that one might conclude its relation to any other point, as each contour line indicated a slope of ten meters.
>
> It is not without interest, certainly for the foreigner, to be able to study the exact design, obtained most often through photography, of these rich slopes, these fecund

hills, whose culture seems not to have changed in fourteen centuries, that Gregory of Tours admired as we do today, and where we find planted the same vines and cultivated in the same manner the fields that Charlemagne possessed. The map itself can reveal a thousand of the most important details of exposition of these climats: a book was thus a useful complement. The sketches of all maps were done under my supervision by M. Gentet, whose talent as a precise draftsman is most remarkable, and I have confided to M. Tirpenne, distinguished lithographer of Paris, the care of executing in stone these charming scenes that accompany this work.

As to the text, it could only be completed with the assistance of all of the men who, either from the theoretical or practical point of view, have studied the multiple questions that have been the object of this book. Thus my first concern has been to assure the active and precious collaboration of all those who, either proprietors or winegrowers, had made a serious study of the vine. My first duty must be here to gratefully acknowledge their assistance. If this work is to be of any interest, if I have treated the most delicate questions of appreciation and resolved them without raising too many protests, I owe it above all to the patient research of several, to the extreme kindness with which they have met my requests, and, above all, the absolute integrity of each with regard to the information of which I had need.

I will make here mention of the name of M. Garnier, who offered an important part of what in this book is interesting and new, and that of M. Delarue, who never ceased to aid me in my research. I offer to M. Vernette-Lamothe my lively thanks for eagerness and kindness in letting me draw upon his numerous publications. I will seize the occasion to render public homage to the truth that I am beholden to the numerous documents of Dr. Morelot, from whom I have borrowed several interesting pages, to M. Clerc, and MM.

Marion, banker of Dijon; Genret-Perrotte, proprietor of Gevrey; Marion, proprietor of Fixey; Vienne, ex-archivist of Gevrey; Groffier, proprietor and winegrower of Morey; Lapertot, proprietor of Dijon; Changenet, proprietor and winegrower of Chenôve; Michel, teacher of Gevrey; Liegeard, proprietor of Brochon; Chanut, medical doctor of Dijon; Duret, medical doctor of the town of Nuits; Marey (Félix), proprietor of Nuits; Viénot, mayor of Premeaux; de Laloyère, proprietor of Savigny; Roux, director of the Clos Vougeot; Marillier, notary of Beaune; Rougeot, proprietor of Beaune; Michaud (Edouard), proprietor of Beaune; Marey, proprietor of Pommard; Jobard, proprietor of Pommard; Goulier, proprietor of Meursault; Paquelin, proprietor of Chassagne; Abord-Belin, proprietor of Santenay.

Lavalle continues with the main part of the work, which he entitles "*History of the vine and wines of the Côte d'Or.*" The first portion of this is subtitled "*The present time*", with a further subtitle of "*Preliminary considerations*," under which he notes:

The region of the Côte d'Or possesses today approximately 26,500 hectares [ha] consecrated to the growth of the vine. The different vineyards of this region, dispersed over almost all of the points of its territory, are divided into two groups: the first, planted in Gamay in every type of soil and exposition, give only ordinary wine, often even the most mediocre, and serve only for local consumption; the second, planted with the vines called *noiriens* or *pinots*, are all found on the slope that, from Dijon to Santenay, divides the chain of mountains designated by the name of the Côte d'Or.

The vines planted in Gamay cover more than 23,000 ha, which one meets under the name of *plant de Mâlain, plant d'Arcenant, plant de Bévy*, etc., etc. It is remarkable that no pink or grey varieties are grown. The yield can often extend to 50 and even 60 hectolitres per hectare (hl/ha)

The vineyards composed of Pinots occupy barely 2,500 ha, of which the average yield can be evaluated at most at 18 hl/ha, giving 45,000 hl for the average annual production of the Côte d'Or in fine wine.

The history of these last vineyards offers only a general interest; the wines produced by them are avowed everywhere as wines of the Côte d'Or, and merit the high reputation from which they benefit. It thus happens that the story of our fine wines finds itself limited to a small number of localities all situated in roughly equivalent and contiguous condition.

This book, specially destined to the vineyards whose production has carried so far the name of Burgundy and the Côte d'Or, will thus contain only the story of those slopes planted in Pinots. I will refer you for all of the details relative to the culture of Gamay, to the work published by Dr. Morelot in 1831 under the title of *Statistique de la vigne dans le département de la Côte d'Or.*

In truth, the situation could not be more different today, at least with respect to the grape blend. According to the CIVB, there are 27,966 hectares of vines under production in Burgundy as a whole, which seems superficially similar to Lavalle's figure. Today's figure from the CIVB, however, includes all of modern Burgundy -- Chablis and the surrounding region, the Grand Auxerrois (Tonnerrois, Vézelien, Jovinien, and le Châtillonnais, for a total of 5, 982 ha); the Côte d'Or, including both the Côte de Nuits and Hautes Côtes de Nuits (approximately 2,614 ha), and the Côte de Beaune and Hautes Côtes de Beaune (approximately 4,752 ha); the Côte Chalonnaise and the Couchois (approximately 2,124 ha); and the Mâconnais, 5,813 ha.

The current iteration of the BIVB does not include Beaujolais as one of the regions of Burgundy. Beaujolais has always been related, but kept separate and certainly not seen as equal. Historically attached to the Duchy of Burgundy, part of Beaujolais is included in the administrative region of Burgundy, which includes the Côte-d'Or and the Saône-et-Loire as well as the Yonne and the Nièvre.

Part of Beaujolais lies in the department of the Rhône-Alpes and straddles Burgundy and the Rhone. For wine lovers, however, the chief difference is the dominance of the Gamay grape in Beaujolais wines, irrevocably separating it in the eyes of wine lovers from the rest of Burgundy.

Like nearly every other commentator of the *Ancien Régime*, Lavalle rails against the Gamay grape, because it is generally seen as inferior since it was outlawed by Philippe le Hardi in 1395. Today this view has triumphed. While it is allowed throughout Burgundy as an auxillary grape variety, its plantings are quite limited: only 8% of the surface area, as compared to 49% for Chardonnay, 35% for Pinot Noir, 6% for Aligoté, 1% for Sauvignon, and 1% for all other varieties. Interestingly, although the war of the noble varieties has been won, the composition and extent of the vineyards in the Côte d'Or has changed dramatically. We note 7,366 ha planted today in the Côte d'Or (Hautes Côtes included), demonstrating a threefold expansion of plantings of noble varieties since the 19th century. However, Lavalle's figure of 26,500 ha under vine in the Côte d'Or demonstrates that the *total* area under vine was more than 3.5 times larger than it is today.

Note that Lavalle wrote his work before the phylloxera epidemic, when vines were not grafted, but planted on their own roots and propagated through *provinage*, or layering. (In the provinage system, a trench is dug and canes are laid down in the earth and buried over, causing the cane to throw down roots from which future canes will spring. This planting method is no longer used because of the susceptibility of vines grown in this way to the deadly effects of the phylloxera root louse). Planting a vineyard in this way, the density of plantation was nearly three times higher on average. However, the yield was three times lower, demonstrating that pre-phylloxera wines had a very different character indeed.

Maximum yields today are a matter of legislation. Each appellation has a base yield, which is modified each year by government decree (*plafond limite de classement*, or PLC), and which cannot be higher than the maximum limit, called the *rendement butoir*, as fixed by the AC legislation. For example, the base yield for Bourgogne blanc is 68 hl/ha, and for Bourgogne rouge, 60 hl/ha. The rendement butoir is 75 hl/ha and 69 hl/ha for white and red, respectively, and in 2011 the PLC was 70 hl/ha and 62 hl/ha, respectively. This is more than 10% more than the maximum yields described by Lavalle, because the techniques of viticulture have become more sophisticated and the vines themselves were grafted and changed as a result of the phylloxera infestation. Quality-minded growers produce what they feel is an ideal quantity for a given vine on an individual basis, rather than a maximum amount.

If anything, however, the differences between the 18 hl/ha cited by Lavalle and today's legal limits are even more startling. For a grand cru such as

Chambertin, the *rendement de base* is 42 hl/ha while the rendement butoir is 49 hl/ha. Particularly in the grands crus, however, yields are kept low by the top estates, and are often only 50% to 75% of the rendement de base, or even less, depending on vintage conditions. It is for the reasons outlined above that Lavalle's discussions of wine-making and grape growing have little bearing on wine production today.

Lavalle returns to the history of his beloved region before analyzing the vineyards:

Of the wines of the Côte d'Or and their antique renown

If there is a subject that is in all countries the cause of frequent discussions, certainly it is that which gives the title of this chapter. Wherever one may be, one is listened to attentively while speaking of Burgundy wines in general, and particularly of the wines of the Côte d'Or. The names of Romanée, of Vougeot, of Saint-Georges, of Chambertin, or Corton, of Montrachet, of Richebourg, etc., have long ago made their flight 'round the world, and I don't know if there is a corner of land anywhere in our old Europe where these names are not celebrated.

One does not fall into exaggerated patriotic sentiment by proclaiming the immense, incontestable superiority of our wines. It is only to repeat after a thousand others to affirm that they are at the first rank and perhaps several of them have no rivals. Exquisite finesse of bouquet, a savor at the same time warm and delicate, prolonging several instants and leaving after the taste a fresh and fragrant breath; vermillion color, perfectly limpid; of a beneficent action on the organs of digestion; such are the high qualities that make the wines of the Côte d'Or the first wines of the world, qualities that exist in almost all of the most renowned wines, and suffice often to assure their brilliant reputation.

I do not want to deprecate the other good French wines nor be unjust in their regard; but it seems impossible not to recognize that almost all of these wines are far from possessing a bouquet as developed as ours, or lack this warmth that is an essential condition of a perfect wine.

A large number of people that know our good Burgundy wines only by name and by several bottles that commerce has furnished them think it sage to repeat the charge that they are too rich in alcohol. By way of response I would that stocks of our wines issued from a trusty source be established in all of the great cities and delivered to consumers only when they are ready to be drunk. This would be the best advocacy to make in their favor; it would assure them the triumph with every distinguished wine lover.

Precisely because of their perfection, the wines of Burgundy demand, it is true, to be cared for as intelligently as these splendid flowers that one cultivates with the greatest care over several years before seeing their petals open magnificently, full of dash and perfume; it demands a knowledgeable steward to lead them with patience and art to the moment where they are most worthy to be offered to the man of taste.

If you impute a crime to the wine of Burgundy, this demand of effort and the fact that they reveal their treasures only to he who is worthy, you then address the same reproach to all that is beautiful and to all that is delicate and perfect.

Without doubt, our great wines demand to be cared for carefully; but they demand neither more nor less than many others, such as the first growths of Bordeaux, for example; and the contrary opinion can only find credence because a great number of people, above all in foreign lands, have received as wines of Burgundy adulterated or processed wines, as unworthy of the name that one accords them as of the price that they command. Buy your Burgundy wines from trustworthy persons and you will soon agree with this opinion; then keep your wines neither too long nor yet not long enough; seize the moment when they present themselves in all their perfection, and, at the least, if you can but once appreciate one of our great wines in all its splendor, you will be numbered among its enthusiastic admirers.

Wine, to merit the vote of the gourmet, must be of a pure color and not too deep. No cloud, no matter how slight, must alter its transparence, and, if spread in a thin layer on a white metallic surface or dispersed in small droplets, must be comparable only to the purest ruby. The most experienced taste must find nothing, neither during nor after tasting, of this acerbity that is the character of the wines that have not acquired by age the precious qualities of which I have just spoken. The alcohol held within must be appreciable only by the light and moist warmth that develops in all parts of the palate. The taste and the aroma must be struck at the same time and by the flavor and the aroma that are loosed, and the perception must be so equal in all the organs of taste and smell, that it would be impossible to say which creates the more agreeable impression.

To recognize all of these qualities, the Burgundian wine lover emeritus begins by receiving in a silver cup with semi-spherical hollows in its base a small quantity of wine that he will taste, and thus appreciates the color and transparence of the wine even in dim light or lamp light; then he begins slowly with one or two mouthfuls in such a manner that all the parts of the palate are put in contact with the wine, which he then spits out. It is rare that one or two tastes are insufficient for him to pronounce with certainty his opinion. But if he wants to appreciate the wine in all its finesse, to analyze the bouquet in all its details, to take joy in all its treasures, then the gourmet takes a large glass which he will envelop with both hands so that he communicates a certain heat; then, pouring in the bottom of the glass a small quantity of wine, he agitates the precious liquid, raises it to the level of the eye so as to enjoy the reflections of the light as they play across its vermillion waves, and tastes it after having thus, by an agitation of several instants, developed all of the perfumes that it contains.

It is truly regrettable that some have taken the detestable habit of drinking Burgundy wines in the little glasses called *verres à bons vins*. Let us leave these shells for wines without aroma that can be good for the mouth but have nothing to offer for the smell, and let us come back to the good habits of our ancestors. Would that large glasses circulated again on our tables so that the inimitable perfume of our wines might develop on its vast surface. If Burgundy would but do this, it would do as much for the reputation of its wines as one might do in twenty years. I have always considered the usage of these narrow and deep glasses a trap to ensnare us that we have walked right into unawares. It seems to me that Burgundy wine thus offered in a narrow glass resembles a rose presented in the bottom of a box.

Also let the guest not forget too long the wine in his glass and he will not lose in the air the first fruits of its precious perfume. When the bottle was opened; when, after several hours at a mild temperature, it allows to escape the waves of its divine bouquet, the true wine lover will not lose a minute, and, recalling our joyous refrain, will love to repeat in chorus:

> Never leave in your hand
> Your glass nor empty nor full

If, in order to be praised, the wines of the Côte d'Or had need that one recall all of the glorious deeds of their past, it would be a brilliant and very ancient history. From the 4th century, the epoch when Eumenius wrote that our wines were the object of admiration for foreigners; from Gregory of Tours, who, two centuries later, compared them to Falernian and how many other praises!

The first Dukes of Burgundy had their walled vineyards at Chenôve, at Vosne, at Pommard, at Volnay, and presented their wines to all the crowned heads. Cîteaux furnished the Papal court, seated in Avignon during the 14th century. Jean de Bussières, who from abbot at Clairvaux became the abbot at Cîteaux, in 1359 sent thirty barrels of Vougeot wine to Gregory XI, who thanked him extravagantly and promised to remember his present; in effect, four years later, he was made cardinal.

Petrarch attributed in 1366 the obstinacy of the college of cardinals not to return to Rome to the wines of Burgundy. It is a fact that in Italy there is no wine of Beaune and [the cardinals] do not believe that they can lead a happy life without this liquid; that they see this wine as a second "nectar of the gods".

Our archives are full of testaments of the shipment of wines made by the Dukes of Burgundy or by the cities of Dijon and Beaune to kings, popes, and other grand dignitaries, etc. The bourgeois of Bayeux presented to Bertrand du Guesclin, Constable of France, a pipe of Beaune wine in March 1377. It was the first wine of Europe.

Erasmus, in his letters, attributed to the wines of Beaune celebrated excellence and the healing of illnesses of the stomach and colics. He even wanted to move to France, not, as he said, to command armies, but to drink the wine of Beaune. "*O happy Burgundy* (he wrote in his letter to Laurinus, dated from Bâle in 1522), *who merits to be called the mother of men, since her breast yields such good milk!*"

Louis XIV permitted the transport of the wines of Beaune on the Moselle and the

Meuse, which he had greatly praised in the judgment of his council in 1662. During the convalescence of this monarch after a long illness, Dr. Fagon gave in 1680, preference to Burgundy wines over those of Champagne; happy decision, which doubled the price of our wines and excited a "war of the muses" between Charles Coffin, a poet from champagne, and Bénigne Grenan, Burgundian poet, and a dispute between Hugues de Salins, doctor in Beaune, and Lepescheur, doctor in Reims, in 1704 and 1705. This decision had already been approved by the faculty of medicine in Paris, where M. Arbinet submitted a public thesis in 1665 that "the wine of Beaune is of all wine the most agreeable and salubrious."

The cardinal of Bonzy presented to Sobieski, elected king of Poland, wines from Beaune that he found excellent. Tavernier is said to have drunk some at the court of the king of Persia near the end of the 17th century. Everyone knows that Napoleon put our great wines in the best possible light.

The Cape is proud to have borrowed vines from the Côte d'Or, and on these two continents one serves with respect in the midst of the most exquisite dishes, a bottle of our great wines.

Should I recall all the couplets made throughout the centuries in honor of Burgundy wines, couplets written in all languages and that all know how to sing? Should I speak the prodigious praises of our wines by the most eminent men of taste or the most celebrated oenologists? I have already given on this subject the opinion of Count Odart; here now is what Baron Cussy wrote several years ago:

> "The last cellarmaster of the Cîteaux Abbey was Dom Gobelet. This illustrious gourmet, forced, with tears in his eyes to quit the precious cellars dedicated to his leisure, did not want to leave without carrying off a sample of the sacred fire. He conserved it so well without sparing it that some remained in 1813 when this estimable hermit passed from this life to the next in Dijon, his native country.

> "In 1803, Mr. A***, war commissioner, was invited while passing through Dijon with a number of his friends to dine at the home of Dom Gobelet. After dinner, watered with numerous libations of this nectar, Mr. A***, thanking and congratulating the honorable amphytrion, proposed to exchange for a purse of 50 Louis of 24 francs.

> "This proposition was welcomed with a cold disdain, and brought this response: *"Sir, every time you pass through Dijon, do me the honor of coming to dine with me: we will drink as much of this wine as you like; but, I shall never sell you a bottle..."*

On the subject of the wine of La Romanée, harvested by the princes of Conti, M. de Cussy added: "The prince made a gift to those who he honored with these bounties. He gave, in 1782, to Monseigneur de Juigné, archbishop of Paris.

It is by this munificence that we were happy to make the acquaintance of this precious wine, which was at once velvet and satin in the bottle." For Montrachet he couldn't have too many praises:

"O Montrachet! Dear Montrachet, divine Montrachet!!! The first, the most fine of white wines produced in our rich France! You who has remained pure and without tarnish in the hands of your honorable owner, the Marquis de La Guiche!" Whatcan we add to such praise?

LATER AUTHORITIES

Dr. Lavalle had a tremendous influence on the Burgundy wine authorities that came after him. Most of them agreed with or adopted his judgments with relatively little change in terms of composition. However, there was a movement away from the more nuanced views of earlier authors to a system that forces all climats into a tripartite division of première, deuxième, and troisième cuvées, without distinguishing têtes de cuvées above this level.

Camille Rodier notes in his 1920 work *Le Vin de Bourgogne* that "*...the difference that exists between these têtes de cuvées and premières cuvées not always being very distinct, the Commission did not believe it necessary to adopt this sub-division, susceptible too often to produce regrettable errors.*" It must be this sensibility that informed the modern system, which also includes three divisions. Amateurs with a broad tasting experience of Burgundy wines may well regret this streamlining of the classification - for example, the wines of Bordeaux are classified into a five-fold division. Although it is impossible to compare the wines of the two regions, yet one can only admire the additional flexibility of a five-tiered system over one with only three classes of vineyard.

René Danguy and Charles Aubertin

Les Grands Vins de Bourgogne was written by René Danguy and Charles Aubertin in 1892 (referred to throughout by their French associative name Danguy et Aubertin). This was an interesting moment in the history of Burgundy wine because it was was the first major work to be written after the phylloxera epidemic. Accordingly, it reflects a viticultural reality closer to that of our own day. On the other hand, as *Les Grands Vins de Bourgogne* was published just thirty-seven years after Lavalle's work, and it is in some ways closer to this than it is to the modern day.

René Danguy was a professor at the Beaune School of Viticulture, while Charles Aubertin was an officer of the Academie Française, a correspondent of the Minister of Public Instruction, and a justice of the peace. The authors adopted the classifications of Dr. Lavalle and of the Comité d'Agriculture de Beaune without change. Their avowed purpose was to update the work of Dr. Lavalle without changing its essence. As they note, "Without ever having the thought of surpassing Doctors Morelot and Lavalle, whose esteemed works have been out of print and nearly unfindable for many years, we believe that a publication of the same nature, based upon the current state of vineyard ownership in the Côte d'Or would be welcome..."

Danguy and Aubertin did find it necessary to update some portions of the previous classifications. They used a convention that appears as "C. Loc" in their classification. They explain that C. Loc. refers to local tradition. They comment in their "Important Note" just prior to the first usage (for the village of Santenay, since they, like Morelot, move south to north) that, "In the above classifications [Lavalle and the Comité d'Agriculture de Beaune] certain climats have been omitted and others have been constituted after the appearance of these works; to make our classification, we have had recourse to the information that we have been given by tradition, which has the status of authority in the villages of the Côte d'Or. We designate this local classification as C. Loc. and decline in this place any personal responsibility." In some cases, however, Danguy et Aubertin include the C. Loc. opinion when it seems to disagree with that of Dr. Lavalle.

In his preface to the reissue of the work in 1978, Pierre Poupon notes that the publishers of the original work accepted advertising from certain wine producers who wanted to be noted. This may strike some readers as an odd, although the practice is not unknown in wine writing in France, even today. One may find, however, that this method produces a result that strives to present every village and every climat in its best possible light. Although the reader will discover some very useful information in Danguy et Aubertin, it is sometimes necessary to read between the lines to arrive at a just opinion of the wines presented.

Since much of the content of *Les Grands Vins de* Bourgogne was taken from Morelot and Lavalle, only the author's comments à propos the vineyards of the Côte d'Or are translated and quoted in this book.

The Generalists

In their book, Danguy et Aubertin included an 1878 classification that was featured in a work signed Bertall and entitled *La Vigne: Voyage Autour des Vins de France - Etude physiologique, anecdotique, historique, humoristique, et même scientifique*. (*The Vine: a Voyage Around the Wines of France - a physiological, anecdotal, historic, humorous, and even scientific study*) Bertall was the pen name of Charles-Albert Arnoux (1820 - 1882), who was a popular Second Empire illustrator. As the title suggests, the amount of space devoted to the wines of Burgundy is relatively modest. Bertall, however, does include without further comment a *Classification of the Principal Wines of the Côte d'Or*, "according to the opinion of the most authoritative experts".

Bertall's classification is substantially similar to Lavalle's, with some notable changes. Bertall elevates the wines of Richebourg and La Tâche to the highest category *"hors ligne"* [outstanding], and adds Pommard Arvelets and Rugiens as têtes de cuvées n° 2, although Lavalle refused to distinguish any above the rest. In addition, the classification used by Bertall removes the following climats from the list of têtes de cuvées: Clos-Saint-Jacques, Mazy, and Varoilles, in Gevrey; Clos-Saint-Jean and Clos Pitois, in Chassagne; Corvées, Didiers, and Forêts, in Prémeaux ; Les Fèves and Les Grèves, in Beaune.

Bertall's exact list appears without being credited in a book written by G. M Guillon entitled *Étude Générale de la Vigne* (General Study of the Vine). Guillon is described as the director of the viticultural station in Cognac. Like Bertall, his is a wide-ranging work. Guillon covers all the vineyards of the world (including Asia, Africa, and South, Central and North America) in 166 pages, and then spends 259 additional pages to cover all of viticulture and terroir. The work was published in Paris by Masson et Cie in 1905. Both Bertall and Guillon rank the vineyards of the Côte d'Or as follows:

RED WINES

Hors Ligne

Romanée-Conti
Chambertin
Clos Vougeot
Richebourg
La Tâche

Tête de Cuvée n° 1

Musigny
Romanée-Saint-Vivant
Les Saints-Georges
Le Corton
Bonnes-Mares
Clos de Tart

Tête de Cuvée n° 2

Pommard Arvelets and Rugiens
Vosne Beaumonts
Nuits Aux Boudots, Les Cailles, Aux Cras, Aux Murgers, Les Porrets-Saint-Georges, Les Pruliers, Aux Thorey and Les Vaucrains
Volnay Les Caillerets and Champans
Puligny Clavoillon
Chassagne Clos Morgeot
Santenay Clos Tavannes and Noyer Bart
Corton (a part of it)
Échézeaux
Beaune Fèves and Grèves

Fixin Clos de la Perrière
Volnay Santenot

WHITE WINES

Hors Ligne
Montrachet

Première Cuvée
Chevalier-Montrachet
Bâtard-Montrachet
Meursault Charmes, Combettes, Genevrières, and Goutte d'Or
Corton Charlemagne

Camille Rodier

Le Vin de Bourgogne (La Côte d'Or) (The Wine of Burgundy: the Côte d'Or) was written by Camille Rodier in 1920 and published by L. Damidot in Dijon. Rodier (1890 – 1963) was the grandson of Albert-Sebastien Rodier, the founder of the Maison Henri de Bahèzre in Nuits, which he led with his brother Albert. Rodier was also the head of the Syndicate d'Initiative de Nuits-Saint-Georges. He went on to publish a book on Clos du Vougeot in 1931, and in 1932 to found the Confrerie des Chevaliers du Tastevin. Each year there is a meeting or *chapitre* of the Confrerie just prior to the sale of the Hospices de Beaune wines. These two events, along with La Paulée de Meursault form the *Trois Glorieuses* – three glorious days that celebrate Burgundian wine.

Rodier begins his preface with a quote from Dr. Lavalle, and his work owes much to Lavalle. He also incorporates elements from the works of Dr. Morelot as well as those of Danguy et Aubertin. Adopting nearly the same formulation as these last authors, he notes that without hoping to improve on their work, he wishes to bring them up to date. He updated the lists of proprietors and introduced changes to Dr. Lavalle's classification. The first part of the book starts with a review of the history of the Burgundy region and an overview of its grape growing and winemaking techniques, before classifying the great wines of Burgundy in the second part as follows:

> The wines of Burgundy are highly varied, being produced from diverse grape varieties and in diverse regions: the Haute-Bourgogne with the Côte d'Or, Basse-Bourgogne with the Yonne; the Côtes Chalonnaise and Mâconnaise in the Saône-et-Loire, and Beaujolais with the Rhône above Lyon.
>
> The wines of Haute-Bourgogne produce the great wines of Burgundy, those that have gained for this privileged region the beautiful name of the Côte d'Or, are the

only ones that interest us here. This work, especially dedicated to the vineyards that have carried the renown of Burgundy and of the Côte d'Or so far, is thus concerned only with the story of "*La Côte*" and the vineyards that produce fine wines.

For a long time, growers, merchants and consumers have established two great divisions of La Côte: the Côte de Beaune and that of Nuits. These two produce highly characteristic wines, each of which excel in their type, and no one is able to compare.

A very ancient work, *Le Grand Dictionnaire Anglais* of Miller says of this subject, "one distinguishes in the Côte d'Or two varieties of wine produced from the same plant: the Vins de Primeur and the Vins de Garde. The Côte de Beaune, which produces Vins de Primeur, extends in the Côte d'Or over the villages of Santenay, Chassagne-Montrachet, Puligny-Montrachet, Meursault, Auxey-le-Grand, Monthélie, Volnay, Pommard, Beaune, Savigny-les-Beaune, Pernand, Aloxe-Corton, and Ladoix-Serrigny. The wines of the Côte de Beaune possess a great finesse, much bouquet, and are sweeter, readier to drink at an earlier age, but in general less long lived than those of the Côte de Nuits.

The Vins de Garde produced by the Côte de Nuits are harvested throughout the villages of Corgoloin, Comblanchien, Prissey, Premeaux Nuits-Saint-Georges, Vosne-Romanée, Flagey-Echézeaux, Vougeot, Chambolle-Musigny, Gevrey-Chambertin, Brochon, Fixin, and Fixey.

As with the wines of the Côte de Beaune, those of the Côte de Nuits are also very fine, but they acquire their qualities less quickly than the preceding. Miller continues to say that, "The vins de garde are at first harsh and bitter, but that this will pass and that they become perfumed and delicious. The wines of the Côte de Nuits are effectively wines for aging, very robust, that gain much bouquet and mellowness as they age. These are distinguished crus that constitute very certainly the most beautiful emblems of Burgundy.

"We will now pass in review each of the villages of the Côte, and for this statistic, we will follow the order established by Dr. Lavalle, beginning in the Côte de Nuits and ending in the Côte de Beaune."

After this preamble, Rodier includes a review of the geographic and geologic background of the Côte d'Or, and notes of viticulture and oenology; these duplicate the works of earlier authors, so they are omitted here. Here are his thoughts on classification:

> We testify here so that it be firmly established that we have not set out to do a new classification, but that the work that we present to the reader is the result of two classifications of different authority. To wit:
>
> 1. That established by Dr. Lavalle in his 1855 work on the Great Wines of the Côte d'Or

2. That given in 1860 by the Comité d'Agriculture of the Arrondissement of Beaune and of Viticulture of the Côte d'Or in the Statistical Map of the Vineyards producing the Great Wines of Burgundy.

The map of the climats that accompanies this work has been laid out through the efforts of a Commission chosen by the Comité d'Agriculture de Beaune and presents all of the desired guarantees of sincerity and exactitude.

The classification includes three classes or categories noted in the map by tints or distinct colors: it has been done separately for each village, *without prejudice to the comparative merit of their products.*

The first class (premières cuvées) includes the vines that reunite to a great degree all of the conditions for which one could wish to produce a choice wine, above all the triple virtue of bouquet, of finesse, and of longevity: it includes in a single division all of what one would normally call Têtes de Cuvées and Premières Cuvées: the difference that exists between these Têtes de Cuvées and Premières Cuvées not always being very distinct, the Commission did not believe it necessary to adopt this sub-division, susceptible too often to produce regrettable errors.

The deuxième classe (deuxièmes cuvées) includes vines placed in conditions a bit less favorable according to the nature of their exposition, their grade, or to their greater or lesser altitude.

It sometimes happens, above all in the years when the favorable temperature diminishes or more properly modifies the importance of these diverse conditions of inferiority, that the produce of the vines of the deuxièmes cuvées approaches that of the vines of the premières.

One includes in the troisième classe (troisièmes cuvées) the vines that produce wines that, while still worthy to be classified among fine wines, are found at the boundary of the good climats and lack something either of finesse or of longevity.

We have not judged it appropriate to include in this classification the vines producing Gamay or *vin ordinaire*. We wanted to restrain our work to that fairly compact part of the Côte whose merit has carried so far the reputation of the Burgundian soil and name.

One must not conclude from the divisions that we give further on, which are those of the Comité d'Agriculture de Beaune, that the wines harvested exclusively in the privileged climats are necessarily preferable to those produced in other climats: many circumstances, difficult to enumerate, and notably the care taken during the vinification, can modify the quality. It is even the case at times that the mixture of grapes harvested in vines placed in premières and deuxièmes cuvées will produce a superior wine. Likewise, wine coming from several parcels in the same climat, reunited in the same barrel will present by the fact of this homogeneity, a particular cachet that a great number of consumers will seek out.

This accordingly prepares the case for winemaking cooperatives, where certain owners of parcels from the same climate can combine their grapes and thus obtain a better result than if they had each produced their own cuvée.

Buyers thus must not act solely on the indications provided in our work: they must act according to their tastings assisted when necessary by supplementary information regarding the past performance of the same vines.

We insist on the observation made above that this classification offers no point of comparison between different climats in diverse villages.

Everyone will understand why we have not sought to make this comparison: the tastes are so different and the qualities esteemed in one are so often mutually exclusive to those favored in another that we cannot assume the responsibility of appreciations so difficult and subject to dispute.

As to the designation of the names of the owners, we have encountered a great deal of difficulty. Everyone knows that the ownership of La Côte is highly fragmented: it is dispersed among a great number of owners, and it happens that a very small number of people make cuvées of a single climat. On the other hand, a great number obtain wines, often of great value, by blending together the harvest of diverse points of the [same] territory, or even in neighboring villages, as we have noted above.

The result of these facts is that in spite of our attention and all of our good will, it has often been impossible to note some proprietors who have extensive holdings but who do not have any parcel of sufficient size in any one climat and that the classification by climat gives only an approximate relative value of each.

We would also add that we have consulted the best sources possible on this subject. This work is as exact as possible, but we do not know if there could have been changes made before the time of its appearance.

To all those who understand the interest of this enterprise and who have given us through their encouragement the most precious assistance; Mayors, Negociants, Owners, and Growers, we address here the most lively thanks.

Particularly to MM:

Savot, President of the Confederation of Burgundy Winegrowing Associations
Marquis d'Angerville, President of the Agricultural Committee of the district of Beaune and of winegrowing of the Côte d'Or
Alexis Chanson, President of the Chamber of Commerce of the Wines of Beaune, Owner and Negociant of Beaune
Etienne Amiot, Proprietor and Grower in Morey
Prosper Bavard, Proprietor in Puligny-Montrachet
Edouard Belorgey, Proprietor in Morey
J. Boudier, Proprietor in Corgoloin
Bernard Bourée, Negociant in Gevrey-Chambertin

Brenot, Proprietor in Santenay
Breuillot, Wine Broker in Beaune
Dusserre, Wine Broker in Beaune
Paul Gauthiot, Mayer of Couchey
Gilles, Proprietor and Mayor of Comblanchien
Henri Gouroux, Proprietor and Mayor of Flagey-Echezeaux
Fernand Grivelet-Modot, Proprietor in Chambolle-Musigny
Jules Gros-Renaudot, Proprietor in Vosne-Romanée
Jeantot, Mayor of Vougeot
Albert Joliet, Curator of the Muiseum of Dijon
Jouard, Mayor of Chassagne-Montrachet
H. Laligant, President of the Vintners Cooperative of Brochon
René Lamblin, Proprietor in Fixin
Mallard-Gaulin, Mayor of Ladoix-Serrigny
Pavelot, Proprietor and Mayor of Pernand
Petiot, Wine Broker in Savigny-les-Beaune
Jean Poisot, Proprietor and Negociant in Premeaux
Gabriel Poupon, Proprietor in Meursault
Rieusset, Wine Broker in Pommard
Thomas Bassot, Proprietor and Negociant in Gevrey-Chambertin
Armand Veau, Proprietor and Mayor of Auxey-le-Grand
Charles Viénot, Proprietor and Negociant in Premeaux.

Vineyard Ownership

Since the original works of Lavalle, Morelot, and Jullien form the basis of all that followed them regarding the wines of Burgundy, this book focuses on them with some comments by Arnoux and Courtépée for their historical interest and relative brevity. If I omit many worthy comments from the works of both Danguy et Aubertin and Rodier it is in the interest of concision, as their works are based upon the earlier authors. Where comments by these earlier authors are incomplete, however, I will translate from the latter two works to fill in the gaps. For example, Lavalle left out Pernand; I include the thoughts of these later authors on this village. I also endeavor to note where Danguy et Aubertin and Rodier deviate or appear to deviate from their predecessors. Finally, I note the changes in vineyard ownership documented by all of these authors, since they are of interest to the serious student of Burgundy wine and allow readers to trace the evolution of principal climats. I add the names of the proprietors who appear in Danguy et Aubertin and Rodier for all of the vineyards that are presently considered to be grands crus, as well as for those vineyards that were considered in former times to be têtes de cuvees, to add this historical perspective.

VI THE CÔTE DIJONNAISE

The name *Côte Dijonnaise* was once used to indicate the wines produced between Dijon and Gevrey and I modestly propose reviving the term here. For while wine production almost died out in what is effectively the suburbs of a medium-sized town, there are now there are signs that it may be coming back. In general, however, these wines from the northernmost reaches of the Côte de Nuits are seldom seen today, but in pre-phylloxera times they were renowned. AC regulations still make provisions for wines produced within the city of Dijon, notably with the memorable name Bourgogne Montrecul[35].

The Côte Dijonnaise was included in the works of Jullien, Morelot, and Lavalle, all of whom singled out the vineyard called Marcs-d'Or in Dijon. As Anthony Hanson points out in *Burgundy*, Marcs-d'Or was located in the village of Larrey, which no longer exists and is now part of Dijon. Lavalle also mentions Violettes and Montrecul. Modern AOC regulations make provision for only two regional appellations to be produced in Dijon: the wine can either be labeled Bourgogne (red, white, or pink), or Bourgogne Montrecul (or Montre-Cul, or En Montre-Cul) as appropriate. The legislation makes no particular mention of the use of Pinot Blanc here, as is noted by Lavalle. For the most part, these wines have slipped into vinous history. Wine production here was eclipsed long ago by the twin influences of the phylloxera crisis and the encroachment of the city of Dijon.

Chenôve lies immediately to the south of Dijon, and as with this larger city, the only AOC that is today located completely in Chenôve has been demoted to regional status: Bourgogne Le Chapître, corresponding to the lieu-dit mentioned by three of our authors. This appellation's history can be traced back to its ownership by the Dukes of Burgundy at least as far as the 13th century, although Courtépée notes that lands at Chenôve were given by Amalgaire to the Abbey of Bèze in 612 AD. His comment on Chenôve in full:

> [Chenôve has] Three lords; the Cathedral Chapter of Autun for the belltower and the high street, the Benedictines of St. Bénigne for the low street, and the king for the Clos. It was the clos of our Dukes with a very beautiful wine press and a large barrel room. The press was constructed in 1238 by Alix de Vergy, widow of Eudes III, who assigned from her pressroom in Chenôve a hogshead of wine to the monks of Saint Bénigne, instead of the 5 sols that the Jacobins owed: she left the press to her son Hugues IV. The clos was willed by Eudes IV to Jean, Duke of Normandy, the eldest son of the King in 1348. The Intendant of the clos was called Cloutier or Clousier.

Le Chapître today is 5 ha 4 a 61 ca. Just to the south of Le Chapître lies the Clos du Roy (24 ha 34 a 66 ca), today producing red wine classed as AC Marsannay. The other lieux-dits in Chenôve that still produce wine are currently classified as Marsannay Rosé, and include Clos de l'Etoile and Clos Monniaux (also known as Le Village), and the Bas du Clos.

Couchey, like Chenôve, is today a dependency of Marsanny whose vineyards are very ancient, as documented by Courtépée when he notes that, "The Chronicle of Bèze mentions vines in Couchey, given by Amalgaire in 630 and called Cochoiacum." They go on to document the equally venerable origins of Marsannay:

> The vineyards of [Marsannay] produce fairly good wines: from 658 vines have grown here (see Spicil. Book 1, p. 499). Aubert gave in 882 to the Priory of St. Etienne seven parcels of vines in Marsannay in the district of Oscheret.

By the time of Dr. Lavalle, the vineyard of Marsannay was in serious decline, but today the village has moved in the opposite direction of the rest of the Côte Dijionnaise and is now flourishing. The BIVB makes note of thirty producers of Marsannay, and explains that the appellation began to grow again in the 1930s. From the middle 1930s the wines were sold simply as generic Bourgogne; in 1961 they acquired the right to append "Marsannay" (for red and white) and "Rosé de Marsannay" to their labels. In 1987 the wines received the recognition of full AC status.

The current appellation of Marsannay (or at least its plantable area), along with its dependencies in Couchey and Chenôve, covers 302 ha 31 a 48 ca, while Lavalle states that there were no more than 10 or 12 ha of Pinots in Chenôve. He mentions none in Marsannay or Couchey, noting that nearly all of Chenôve is planted to Gamay. As elsewhere, the overall area under vine has shrunk, but the grape blend has improved. The vines today are all either Pinot Noir or Blanc or Chardonnay (with Pinot Gris listed as an accessory grape). Today the production of AC Marsannay is roughly 70% red wine and 15% each white wine and rosé, and follows the same nomenclature as Chenôve.

What follows are translations of both Morelot's and Lavalle's opinions of these wines, leading with Morelot. And while Lavalle begins his dissertation with the wines of Dijon, following a north to south orientation, Morelot begins in Santenay and works from south to north. For the sake of clarity, I will take Morelot as I find him, re-ordering the paragraphs to combine the comments of each author into one section. Dr. Morelot:

> Leaving the village of Gevrey, just a short distance from the houses, one enters Brochon, drawn out from the plain to the summit of a hill which it occupies entirely; the village is built on the lower part, in a very picturesque position[6].

---

6 This village is very old, it is named in the titles Brisco. It was given to the Abbey of Saint-Étienne, who was in 801, according to Betto, the Bishop of Langres.

The rock that forms the base of this slope is a type of limestone of a deep red color, which had led some to falsely believe that it was a type of porphyry. It is very hard, and decomposes only with great difficulty; thus the terrain of Brochon does not offer the lightness of the other soils on our slopes; one also does not find in this village a very considerable mass of distinguished climats. There is one exception, named "Crai-Billon or Cré-Billon[7]" furnishing a wine that when it is mature and originates in a good year, is the equal of the good wines of our region. All of the other climats give a wine in general well above the common level but which however cannot be considered as a wine of the first class.

As one leaves the territory of Brochon, one is upon that of Fixin; it forms, along with those that it borders a long band that starts at the top of an isolated hill and descends towards the plain. The village of Fixin is constructed in the middle of this band, at about mid-slope. Its position is very agreeable, and the view is very wide.

The rock that forms the base of this hill is, as at Brochon, a type of limestone, extremely hard, which can even be polished. Its grain is even more fine than that which I spoke of above: one calls this as well porphyry because at first glance it can be taken it as such. In a memoir of 1769, it was proposed as a replacement for the marble of Burgundy and that of the entire kingdom.

In spite of the quality of this stone, it appears that it is less susceptible than that of other slopes to combine with soil, as the vineyard of Fixin furnishes few distinguished districts. There are only two that enjoy a high reputation: La Perrière and Le Chapitre. The first of these is a clos, belonging to a wealthy proprietor, who for many years has not propagated his vines so that the vines are now rare and become daily more so; in this way each of them, so isolated, is stressed and the grapes ripen in a more perfect manner. One part of this clos is planted in Pinot Blanc, and the wine that comes from it is excellent when mature. The quantity harvested is very low and its entry into the marketplace is but a memory.

Le Chapitre is worth a bit less than La Perrière, however the wine of this climat is classed among the good cuvées. All the rest of the slope of Fixin produces only wines just above the ordinary; and as for those of Brochon, they cannot be counted among the first class.

The territory contiguous to Fixin is that of Fixey, which offers the same forms as the first: an absolutely isolated slope with the vineyard starting in the middle and extending in a long band almost to the plain; finally, the village is built at mid-slope in about the same line as that of Fixin. The bedrock is similar to the two others; it is still fake porphyry that is its base. The earth is even less favorable to Pinot Noir. One hardly finds this vine variety, except mixed with Gamay, which gives only passe-tout-grain of a good quality, fairly agreeable, light in body and in color.

The village of Couchey, which borders that of Fixey, depends also from the summit of an isolated hill, but offers a more considerable extent than those of which we have just spoken. The vineyard starts only at the very foot of the slope; all of the upper part is barren, and little grows in these rocky, infertile slopes. The village of

---

7 This is the Clos from whom Prosper Jolyot, tragic poet who is the honor of our départment, had taken his surname of Crébillon.

Couchey occupies a level place at the foot of the slope[8], and the rest of the territory extends over the plain. The lower parts of Couchey were planted to vines but a few years ago; it is nothing more than a crest or bar of sand that formerly grew only rye. It is probably that the first years compensated the owners for their investment. But it is to be feared that these vines will not last long, at least without constantly renewing the soil to sustain the former plantings.

The wines of Couchey are pass-tout-grains, light good ordinary wine; they are of approximately the same value as those of Fixey. At least, the lands are taxable at the same rate; and if one compares directly the products they are more or less the same; however, those of Fixey are worth a bit more.

The slope of Couchey is separated from that of Marsannay by a deep and narrow little valley, which defines perfectly the small hills at the foot of which are found these two villages: that of Marsannay is much broader of the two of which we have spoken; instead of lying parallel to this last, it takes its direction in a valley that turns toward the north, and its exposition is north-north-east. Vines exist only on this slope on the lower third; the other two-thirds are covered by a wood that joins to other larger ones and covers the *arrière-côte*[36].

The bedrock is still the same limestone that one finds in Fixin, Fixey, etc., and the earth offers the same composition as at Couchey: the same soil structure and principals. I would here remark, however, that the territory of Marsannay offers several fairly distinguished climats; but I would also remark that they are not found at the foot or on the slopes of the hill that I have just referred to, but on another isolated hill which I will have occasion to speak of soon. The territory of Marsannay is very widespread, and occupies not only the slope that touches that of Couchey, but also a portion of the hills of Chenôve.

This hill is but a league across, leaving Marsannay to finish at Larray, above Dijon. It offers a very agreeable aspect, and the exposition is magnificent. It is turned towards the east-south-east, and is two-thirds covered with rich vineyards in which the superb village of Chenôve is built in an amphitheater.[9]

The bedrock of this slope is a limestone entirely different from that which we have just examined. The stone is of a very fine grain, and is perfect for lithography, which is beginning to be widely used. Half of the village of Marsannay, placed on the side and at the foot of a slope whose bedrock is little disposed to combine with other types of soil, gives only ordinary wine; the other half, placed on the other slope, whose bedrock has greater affinity for other types of soil, offers several climats that furnish excellent wines, deeply colored, generous, with purity of fruit and the ability to age for the long term. Less fine, less agreeable than those of the slopes of Beaune or Nuits, they are not without merit, even next to these.

That which I say here regarding the wines from the part of Marsannay found on the slope of Chenôve can apply equally to the vines of this village, which in general are very good, and of about the same quality when they are harvested on the slopes of this hill. I have tasted wines of nearly fifteen years that still had a fire, a vinosity

---

8 Couchey is very old. According to the Chronicle of Bèze, Duke Amalgaire gave vines in this village (named Cochoineum) to this abbey in 630. One may still see the ruins of an ancient castle, with its tower and its deep moats. In 1253, the inhabitants obtained their independence and named a mayor and two aldermen. The village today has seven hundred inhabitants.

9 According to M. Legouz, this village is one of the most ancient of the entire Côte d'Or and must have been inhabited in the times of the Romans; he thinks that even Titus Veter had a house here in the first century. [Saint] Gontran [the 6th century Frankish king] gave lands to Sant-Benigne [cathedral, in Dijon] in 584. Amalgaire gave vines to the abbey of Bèze in 612, and Saint-Léger gave Chenôve in 660 to the cathedral of Autun.

worthy of being appreciated in the marketplace. They did not have the finesse or delicacy that one finds in the most privileged parts of our Côte d'Or, yet in spite of this they were of a very pleasant smell and taste.

The most distinguished climat of Chenôve is the Clos du Roi. But, as I have observed, all of the vines that are on this slope furnish good wine; those that grow on the lower parts give only ordinary wine, but are not without merit; for it is in this sandy and dry terrain that they are found and this type of soil, in general not favorable for quantity, is fairly favorable for quality.

Leaving the territory of Chenôve, one enters into that of Dijon. Here one finds the vineyard of Marcs-d'Or, whose wine has much in common with that of Chenôve, however it has little of the same finesse. In spite of these qualities, I cannot classify it among the têtes de cuvées. I have tasted wine coming from the best parts of this climat, and from a good year, and I found that, as with the wines of the good climats of Marsannay and Chenôve, those of Marcs-d'Or can only qualify as a wine to serve with the roast; it is well above the *grand ordinaires*, but it lacks something to be classed among the superior wines. There are still several choice districts in the territory of Dijon that approach the Marcs-d'Or, but as they are not as good, I will say nothing of them."

For Lavalle, working in the opposite direction (from north to south), the quality vineyards begin in earnest in Fixey and Fixin, which are today both included in the appellation Fixin. Lavalle follows Courtépée, who comments upon the reputation of the local wines, noting "[Fixin or Fissin has] its entire slope in vines, which give wine above the common level." Lavalle's formal classification is first introduced here, although it isn't enumerated completely until he arrives in Gevrey Chambertin. For the sake of clarity, I give an overview here, as it is different from the one we use today. And while it is tempting to equate his classifications to elements of today's system, they are not equivalent at all. Tête de cuvée is Dr. Lavalle's top classification, and the sense as the top wine of a particular region is plain enough.

What's more, while it is tempting as well to equate this to the grands crus of today, his list is different in that it is more exclusive (in that the total number of sites receiving this distinction is smaller than the grands crus of today), and, too, differently composed. Also, Lavalle's is slightly more nuanced, with further subdivisions and distinctions of these categories when traveling down the Côte. Significant here is his designation of *cru hors ligne*, also plain enough – an extraordinary site – and the term *vin extra* is similarly intuitive.

Following this top level of distinction are a variety of others, including première cuvée ("first blend"), which is much more limited than today's premiers crus, but Lavalle adds deuxième cuvée, troisième cuvée, some of which have no equivalent in the system of Appellation d'Origine Controllée. Today's system offers 645 premiers crus, all of which are technically of the same rank. One appealing factor of Dr. Lavalle's work is the additional nuance that he provides. The best way to understand Lavalle's terms is to define them contextually without insisting on a verbatim translation. Lavalle's classification system changes slightly as it is adapted to different communes throughout the Côte d'Or, with each explained in turn.

Fixin presents the first of Lavalle's têtes de cuvées, the Clos de la Perrière. This site is classified as Fixin Premier Cru in the modern AOC system, and includes the original clos of 4 ha 90 a 31 ca along with a small amount of En Suchot (17 a 42 ca) just underneath the wood at the top of the hill. This lieu-dit is not mentioned in Lavalle and does not appear on the 1869 map from the Comité d'Agriculture de Beaune. Clos de la Perrière is also extended slightly into Brochon, with 1 ha 62 a 33 ca of the lieu-dit Queue de Hareng enjoying the same appellation.

Although Lavalle goes to some length to establish Fixin's pedigree, it did not make the grade as a grand cru during the formulation of the appellation system. Lavalle goes on to enumerate a number of famous climats within Fixin: in addition to the Clos de la Perrière, there are seven première cuvées, thirteen deuxième cuvees, and eleven troisième cuvées.

Modern authorities are much less interested in Fixin and its environs. The hamlet of Fixey (located between Fixin and Marsannay), treated separately by Lavalle, has today been absorbed by Fixin, which features five premiers crus in total, including three Clos (not all of which retain their walls). In addition to the Clos de la Perrière, there is Clos Napoléon, which today includes the original Clos as well as 7 a 65 ca of Le Village and 1 ha 75 a 47 ca of Aux Cheusots, spelled Echéseaux by Lavalle. Clos du Chapitre, mentioned by Morelot and Lavalle, is still premier cru, as is Arvelets.

Arvelets has 3 ha 35 a 71 ca and Hervelets has 3 ha 82 a 63 ca in modern AOC legislation, while allowing both (along with 49 a 40 ca of Meix-Bas) to be marketed as either Arvelets or Hervelets. In Lavalle's day the spelling was Hervelets which shares the same etymology as Arvelets. Hervelets did not exist at this time, so we refer to the portion in the former Fixey as Arvelets and that found in Fixin proper as Hervelets.

A further curiosity of the modern iteration is the inclusion of Les Meix Bas as a premier cru, which figures eighth in the estimation of Dr. Lavalle. It is at the foot of the Clos Napoléon, just at the edge of the village. Clos Napoléon is downslope from La Perrière, and Meix Bas further still, with a northern exposition.

Overall, Lavalle cites 100 ha in Fixey and 134 in Fixin, whereas the total today for AC Fixin (which includes the two as well as a small bit of Brochon) is 115 ha, with 4% of the area producing white wine.

Lavalle explains the character of the Côte Dijonnaise:

COMMUNE DE DIJON

Hardly a century ago, one could still find in the territory of this commune wines of great value, appreciated at the same time locally and abroad. Today, there remain but a few hectares cultivated in quality vines, and the small quantity of the harvest has distanced the buyers of this market. It is very remarkable that the culture of Pinot, very developed in the 14th, 15th, and 16th century in the vicinity of Dijon, has continually declined since this time, and everything indicated that soon these last good wines will have disappeared from their vineyard. In the previous century, Courtépée pointed out the wines of Crais de Pouilly, Poussots, Roses, and Perrières as the lightest and most delicate wines. He considered the wines of Les Violettes and Les Marcs-d'Or as excellent from the third and fourth harvest, and as capable of being shipped abroad.

Gamay has invaded all of these climats. Few if any Pinot vines remain in Perrières and Crais de Pouilly. In Poussots and Roses there haven't been any for some time; Les Marcs-d'Or, Les Violettes, and Montrecul are nearly alone a witness to their former reputation.

M. Morelot considers the wine of Marcs-d'Or as well above the grands ordinaires[37], but nevertheless cannot be classed among the têtes de cuvées[38].

These wines present a great fire and vinosity. They age very well, and are ready to drink only after a certain number of years, often six or eight. It is only by aging them that they acquire their finesse and bouquet.

These are truly remarkable wines. If we add to these qualities that the wines travel well, one will understand how regrettable it is that this vineyard has been neglected.

One can say as much of the wines produced by old Pinot vines in the climates of Les Violettes, Echaillons, and Champs-Perdrix, and it is probably because to this necessity of long aging that one can attribute the general removal of the fine vines of this vineyard.

The climat of Montrecul produces very renowned white wines from Pinot Blanc. Many people believe these wines to be the equal of the good wines of Meursault. There remain only a few hectares (ha).

The principal proprietors of fine vines in these climats are:

Les Marcs-d'Or: MM. de Courtivron, 4 ha; de Vesvrotte, 1 ha 67 ares (a); de Loisy, 2 ha 50 a; id., 60 a; de Boissieux, 1 ha; Larché, 25 a.

Les Violettes: MM. The Duleu heirs, 50 a; de Palaiseau, 15 a; Bizouard, 50 a.

En Montrecul: MM. Cousturier (Valère), 1 ha; Chagenet-Gallois (Jacques), in

Chenôve, 15 a; Bizouard, 1 ha 65 a; Michelot, 13 a; de Montillet, 1 ha 40 a; the Bartet heirs, 40 a.

Ez Echaillons: M. Mathieu, 25 a; Mme Widow Boudier, 1 ha.

En Champ-de-Perdrix: MM. Thiébaut-Meulien, 50 a; Bruet, 60 a.

Fontaine-d'Ouche: MM. Bruet, 33 a; Berger, 50 a; Colardot, 1 ha.

Ez Gremeaux: the Faivre heirs, 40 a.

Ez Valandons: M. Lesénécal, 66 a; Widow Raviot, 85 a.

Les Grands-Monts-de-Vignes: MM. Jacob, 33 a; Lesénécal, 50 a; id., 33 a; Colnet, 66 a; Guillé, 40 a.

Ez Roussotes: the Bartet heris, 22 a.

En Pisse-Vin: M. Billette, 33 a.

En Saint-Jacques: the Bartet heirs, 40 a.

Ez Sausses: Mme. Raviot, 13 a.

En Pavet: M. Colnet, 40 a.

COMMUNE DE CHENÔVE

As at Dijon, Chenôve has little by little lost its great vineyards. Gamay, to which this commune was ceded long ago, has climbed little by little onto the slopes, and the Clos-du-Roi itself is today its domain. One will hardly fine 10 or 12 ha of fine vines in the climats called *Clos-du-Roi, Chenevary, Seloncourt, Chapitre, Bas-du-Chapitre,* and *Valandons.*

The vast climat of *Clos-du-Roi*, after having belonged to the Dukes of Burgundy, passed to the kings of France, and was engaged and definitively sold during the Revolution. The walls that surrounded it have almost disappeared, although the superb grape press constructed in 1238 by Alix de Vergy, widow of Eudes III, who left it to her son Hugues IV and is still in use today, still remains. This magnificent press, or more correctly two magnificent presses, because it is two placed side-by-side, are arranged in the center of an immense hall that also contains the vats. They are in a perfect state of conservation and merit to be carefully respected.

During the time that *Clos-du-Roi* belonged to the crown, the wines harvested there enjoyed a very high reputation. One also made, as I indicated on page 30 [in the chapter on vinification], highly esteemed vin cuit[39]. It was the same with the wines of the Cathedral Chapter[40]. This name recalls the considerable property possessed in this commune by the Canons of Autun.

In the previous century, the vineyards of Chenôve still enjoyed a great renown. Coutépée considered the wines produced there as *comparable to those of Nuits, when they had been aged five or six years.*

Today, the good wines of Chenôve still merit one of the most honorable places among the most excellent wines with roast meat. They have body and color, they age well, and with age often acquire the most sought-after qualities.

If one wanted to classify the wines harvested at Chenôve, one could adopt the following order:

Chevary: Proprietor: M. de Palaiseau, 1 ha 71 a.

En Seloncourt, Chapitre, Clos-du-Roi: Proprietors : MM. Masson-Naigeon, 1 ha 54 a; Lesénécal, 1ha 2 a; *Grillet*, 4 ha, 28 a; Changenet, 20 a.

Au Piquon (Bas-du-Chapitre): Proprietor: M. Jolibois, 1 ha 70 a.

Pinot Noir, mixed with hardly one part in twenty of Pinot Blanc is the only plant cultivated in the vines of this commune giving fine wines. The planting of these vines goes back at least eight or ten centuries. If one wants to obtain quality, it is necessary to avoid any compost but grape marc and to only renew the vines by using a shoot from the same plant.

These considerations are completely applicable to the vines situated in the territory of Dijon, except those which give white wines, where the Pinot Blanc exists alone.

In these two communes, the renowned climats are placed at the middle of the slope, whose top is completely bare. In the last several years, plantations of pine trees have been made by the city of Dijon or by M. Berlier on the fallow places above *Montrecul, Les Violettes,* and *Le Chapitre*.

COMMUNE OF MARSANNAY-LA-COTE

Another territory where the climats devoted to Pinot Noir have diminished from day to day and have disappeared almost completely. Fifty years ago, one would have still found a considerable number of quality vines and some wines worthy of notice, but since this time the invading march of Gamay has hardly ceased making progress.

The last few Pinots were pulled up from *Les Argillières* about twenty years ago, and from *Les Recilles* eight or ten years ago. Today there are still a few climats where one finds a certain number of Pinot vines, but nowhere do they cover enough space to make a special cuvee.

I am assured, however, that several proprietors, notably M. Poupier, have just replanted several hectares of Pinot in the climat *Les Portes*. This climat appears to have been planted long ago in vines. It was given in 1189 to the monks of Epoisses by Hugues III, the founder of their abbey.

The climats where formerly the best vines were found were Les Favières, Les Crais, Diénay, Les Argillières, Etale, Les Recilles, Dessus-des-Longeroies, Guidon, Fer-Meulin. It is still these climats that produce the best Gamay wines.

More than 310 ha are consecrated to this culture and give esteemed vins ordinaires.

COMMUNE OF COUCHEY

The vineyard of this commune, today planted entirely in Gamay, is more than 220 ha and gives good vin ordinaire.

As with the preceding communes, Couchey possessed for many years vines producing fine wine in the part situated above the road that goes from Couchey to Fixey.

The *Chronique de Bèze* mentions the vines of Couchey given by Duke Amalgaire in 630.

COMMUNE DE FIXEY

This commune contains around 100 ha, which yield annually an average of 200 hectolitres (hl) of fine wine and 2,700 hl of common wine, as follows:

Première Cuvée

Les Arvelets, 3 ha 33 a 15 centiares (ca), of which 2 ha 69 a 55 ca belong to MM. Lamblin and Magnin-Philippon, and the Widow Drevon. They are planted in Pinot Noir mixed with one part in twenty of Pinot Blanc; they give a wine that is firm, colored, heady, and ages well; it is fine and gains in bouquet as it ages. It resembles the St.-Jacques in Gevrey. The part in Pinot in this climat can yield annually an average of 15 hl/ha, which is to say in all about 40 hl.

This climat has been cultivated in vines for a great number of centuries, and one can without error place its planting in the 8th or 9th century.

The part planted in Gamay, consisting of 63 a 60 ca, belongs to several growers, and can produce on average 24 hl/ha, or 15 hl in total.

La Mazière, 2 ha 21 a 45 ca, of which 84 a 35 ca belong to M. Marion and are planted in Pinot Noir mixed with one fortieth part of white; these give a fine wine, colored, heady, agreeable, and a bit earlier drinking than Les Arvelets, which can yield on average 20 hl/ha, or 16 hl in total.

The part planted in Gamay, containing 1 ha 37 a 10 ca belongs to several growers and can yield on average 30 hl/ha, or 40 hl in all.

We observe that one diminishes by one part in forty the quantity as we shall do with all of the yields for Gamay that follow, although on a different basis, to take into account the part not producing due to the necessity of pulling up the vines after 25, 30, or 40 years as this type of vine ceases to produce and it is necessary to renew it. This explanation will not be repeated, although this reduction will have been taken in all of the following articles on Gamay that you will read.

The annual production of this first class is 56 hl.

<u>Rodier</u> demotes La Mazière to a deuxième cuvée.

Deuxième Cuvée

Le Rosier, 1 ha 21 a 5 ca of which 49 a 95 ca are planted in Pinot Noir mixed with one twentieth part of Pinot Blanc, and give a fine and delicate grand ordinaire; the can yield on average 20 hl/ha, for ten in all [of Pinot Noir].

1 ha 12 a 10 ca are planted in Gamay and can yield 31 hl/ha.

Champennebau, 88 a 80 ca, of which 41 a 95 ca are planted in Pinot Noir mixed with one fortieth part of Pinot Blanc; they give a wine equal to the preceding, and can yield 15 hl on average per hectare, or 6 in all.

46 a 85 ca are planted in Gamay and yield 37 hl/ha, or 17 in all.

Les Clos, 1 ha 44 a 20 ca, of which 64 a 60 ca are planted in Pinot Noir and yield 20 hl/ha, or 13 in all.

79 a 60 ca are planted in Gamay and yield 30 hl/ha, or 23 in all.

Le Clos, 87 a 50 ca, which belongs to MM. Lamblin and Violle, is planted in Pinot Noir with one twentieth part of Pinot Blanc, and can yield on average 17 hl/ha, or 15 in all.

Les Foussottes, 2 ha 68 a 40 ca, of which 1 ha 26 a 5 ca are planted in Pinot Noir with one thirtieth part of Pinot Blanc, and can yield on average 20 hl/ha, 25 in all.

1 ha 42 a 35 ca are planted in Gamay and can yield 31 hl/ha, for 43 in all.

Les Mogottes, 1ha 47 a 20 ca, of which 41 a 20 ca are planted in Pinot Noir mixed with one twentieth part of white, and can yield 7 hl.

1 ha 6 a planted in Gamay, yielding 37 hl/ha on average, or 38 in all.

Champ-Perdrix, 1 ha 50 a 55 ca, of which 20 a 85 ca are planted in Pinot Noir with one twentieth in white, yielding 15 hl/ha, or 3 in all.

1 ha 20 a 70 ca in Gamay, yielding 24 hl/ha, for 30 in all.

The average annual production of this second class is 79 hl.

Troisième Cuvée

Meix-Tournant, 1 ha 80 a 5 ca, belonging almost entirely a M. Boudrot, which includes the clos terminating with his house – 1 ha 72 a 70 ca are planted in Pinot Noir with a mixture of one thirtieth of white; it gives a light, colored, wine, agreeable for the ordinary wine of good tables, and yields on average 14 hl/ha, for 20 in all.

7 a 35 ca are planted in Gamay and can yield 3 hl.

Les Echalais, 2 ha 75 a 55 ca, of which 84 a planted in Pinot Noir with one thirtieth in white, yielding 15 hl/ha, for 12 in all.

1 ha 90 a 85 ca in Gamay, yielding 24 hl/ha, for 44 in all.

Tabellion, 38 a 15 ca, of which 10 a 60 ca planted in Pinot Noir with one twentieth of white, yielding 21 hl/ha, for two in all

1 ha 20 a 65 ca in Gamay, yielding 54 hl/ha, for 63 in all.

Les Herbues, 4 ha 1 a 15 ca, of which 34 a planted in Pinot Noir with one fortieth in white, yielding 24 hl/ha, for 8 in all.

3 ha 67 a 15 ca in Gamay, yielding 50 hl/ha, for 179 in all.

Clémofert, 95 a 35 ca, of which 19 a 35 ca planted in Pinot Noir with one fifteenth of white, yielding 15 hl/ha, for 3 in all.

76 a in Gamay, yielding 24 hl/ha, for 18 in all.

Crais-de-Chêne, 5 ha 97 a 40 ca, of which 11 a planted in Pinot Noir with one thirtieth in white, yielding 15 hl/ha, for two in all.

5 ha 86 a 40 ca in Gamay, yielding 24 hl/ha, for 136 in all..

Les Petits-Crais, 1 ha 54 a 75 ca, of which 20 a 35 ca planted in Pinot Noir with a thirtieth part in white, yielding 14 hl/ha, for 3 in all.

1 ha 34 a 40 ca in Gamay, yielding 24 hl/ha, for 30 in all.

La Place, 1 ha 3 a 5 ca, of which 5 a 15 ca planted in Pinot Noir with a twentieth part in white, yielding 15 hl/ha, for 23 in all.

Le Pothey, 1 ca 82 a 20 ca, of which 6 a 55 ca planted in Pinot Noir with a twentieth part in white, yielding 24 hl/ha, for two in all.

1 ha 75 a 65 ca in Gamay, yielding 24 hl/ha, for 75 in all. [sic]

Le Champ des Arrêts, 3 ha 46 a 15 ca, of which 4 a 45 ca planted in Pinot Noir with one twentieth in white, yielding 14 hl/ha, for one hl in all.

3 ha 41 a 60 ca in Gamay, yielding 24 hl/ha for 79 in all

Average annual production of this third class, 57 hl.

The total size of the vineyard is 100 ha 18 a 65 ca, producing 192 hl of fine wine and 2,693 hl of Gamay.

Observations: If one did not want to describe these climats in such minute detail and instead group several together in order to make parcels enclosed by their natural limits such as roads, one could define these parcels thusly:

1st The Arvelets by themselves, that merit a special mention, situated at the top of the villages, against the scrub between Fixin and Fixey, which share this climat;

2nd The Entre-Deux-Velles and Village;

3rd The Clos-Philippon, all the way up to the house;

4th The Mazière and Clémofert, at the edge of the village, against the Clos Marion in Fixin;

5th Jally, Ollivier, and Combe-Lavau, at the top of the village;

6th Floussottes, Comb-Blanche, and Chenaillot, against the scrub between Fixey and Couchey;

7th Rosier, Les Clos, Campennebaut, Mogottes, Tabellion, Champ-Perdrix, between the Chemin de Flavignerot and that that leads above Couchey;

8th Herbues, Poirier-Rougeot, Germets, Pothey, between the two roads that lead to Couchey;

9th *Crais-de-Chêne, Champ-des-Arrêts*, between the rue de Chêne and the village of Couchey;

10th Echalais, Petit-Crais, Brûlées, Treuils, Ravry, between the rue de Chêne and the Chemin des Ravry;

11th Cocarde, Poirier-Gaillard, La Place, between the preceding road and the Rue Tonnat;

12th La Mouille, Les Longues-Pièces, Les Carrottes, between the Chemin de la Maladière and the road.

Nota: We have not deducted from these climats several plantings of mulberry bushes that are there from what we considered as vines, since soon, probably, they will be devoted to this culture. Only the Clos Darras, around 1 ha, planted today in mulberries had its vines pulled up.

As to the culture of Gamay, growing today and threatening everywhere to replace Pinot, we offer the same observation as in the note on Fixin.

COMMUNE DE FIXIN

This vineyard contains approximately 134 ha, with yield annually an average of 450 hl of fine wine and 3,550 hl of common wine, as follows:

Tête de Cuvée

La Perrière – The property known under the name of Clos de la Perrière is composed of 5 ha in a single parcel, of which 3 ha 70 a are planted to vines, and the balance to a courtyard, gardens, buildings, and outbuildings.

This property belonged in former times to the Abbey of Cîteaux. On May 30th, 1622, it was sold by the gentlemen of Cîteaux to M. Boullier, from Dijon. It was acquired next by M. de Frazans. On March 8th 1741 it was sold to M. Loppin, a lawyer at the Parliament of Dijon. It stayed in the Loppin family (who had become first Count and then the Marquis de Montmort) until January 18th, 1853, when it was sold to M. Denis Serrigny, professor at the law school of Dijon.

The buildings include an old castle constructed in two different periods. The most recent part was built in 1102, the date of the construction of the older part is unknown.

Virtue surrounded the house of the abbots of Cîteaux in Fixin, which served, it is said, as a hospital for their sick monks because of the healthy air that circulates there.

There exist in the gardens some old oaks which are as thick as three meters in circumference, and walnut trees as old as the house. All of these trees produce the most picturesque scene, with some situated at the summit and some at the base of a quarry that provided the stones for the construction of the house (from whence its name) and the church of Fixin.

The house offers the most magnificent vista: below the village of Fixin, and all of the villages of the Côtge to the right and to the left as far as Dijon and beyond, and for perspective, the Jura and the Alpes.

100 meters behind the property one finds the Clos of M. Noisot in which is placed the statue of Napoléon, elevated at the expense of these generous citizens and one of the masterpieces of our great artist M. Rude.

The wines of the Clos de la Perrière have been classed for many years among the finest of Burgundy. The characteristics that distinguish them are that they are deeply colored, generous, and that they have the virtue of keeping longer than any of the great wines of Gevrey-Chambertin, and a bouquet that typifies the charm of the wines of Burgundy and places them at the head of the entire world.

The Marquis de Montmort traditionally sold his wines at the same price as Chambertin.

This climat, planted with Pinot Noir with a mixture of one twentieth part of Pinot Blanc, produces on average each year 14 hl/ha, all together 39 hl.

The annual production of têtes de cuvées, 39 hl.

> Danguy et Aubertin note that Clos de la Perrière is a monopole of the Joliet family, a fact confirmed by Camille Rodier. It will be remembered that M. Rodier remarks at the outset of his *Statistique* that he has grouped together the Têtes de Cuvées and the Premières Cuvées in the first category, owing to the difficulty in distinguishing them. The careful reader, however, will note that within his list of Premières Cuvées that he lists certain climats in all capital letters within this category, and others are not. It is reasonable to assume that these merit special attention in his opinion but that his discretion forbids him from elaborating further. In Fixin, he distinguishes La Perrière and Le Chapitre both with capital letters, a small departure from Lavalle, below.

Première Cuvée (climats by order of merit)

Le Chapitre, containing 4 ha 77 a 10 ca and belonging to M. Lamblin, produces a wine which approaches that of La Perrière, from which it is separated only by a small wall; one must say of this wine that it is equally firm, generous, colored, and long-lived; produced by Pinot Noir mixed with one fortieth part of Pinot Blanc, it yields annually an average of 15 hl/ha, 71 altogether.

Les Arvelets, 3 ha 60 a 95 ca, the greatest portion belonging to the widow Drevon, to MM. Lamblin and Magnin-Philippon, is planted in Pinot Noir mixed with one twentieth part Pinot Blanc, and gives a fine wine equal to the preceding one; it yields on average 15 hl/ha, together over the 3 ha 35 a 15 ca planted in this manner, 50 hl.

The small part in Gamay, consisting of 25 a 80 ca which belongs to small growers, can annually yield an average of 6 hl.

Le Tremble, 85 a 60 ca, belonging to M. Marion and which is enclosed by walls, is planted to Pinot Noir mixed with one twentieth of Pinot Blanc; it produces a wine that is distinguished particularly by its finesse; it is less firm than the preceding wines and sooner ready to drink; it is well-colored, generous, and has bouquet; it can yield on average 20 hl/ha, 17 altogether.

Echéseaux and **Clos-Napoléon**, 1 ha 83 a 70 ca, belonging in large part to M. Noisot. 1 ha 40 a are planted in Pinot Noir mixed with one fortieth part of Pinot Blanc; it gives a firm wine, well-colored, and generous; when the vines are more mature it will cede nothing to the Chapitre and the Arvelets, between which it is placed; it can yield an annual average of 20 hl/ha, 28 altogether.

43 a 70 ca are planted in Gamay and belong to several owners; it can yield an average of 24 hl/ha of common wine, and given the necessity of grubbing up this vine after approximately 40 years to renew it, it diminishes by one fortieth the yield. The method will be followed although on a different basis, in for all the articles on Gamay that you will read, without having to repeat the explanation; here, the yield is 10 hl.

The average annual production of premières cuvées is 166 hl.

Deuxième Cuvée

Part of the Clos of M. Marion, 1 ha 90 a 40 ca below the Tremble, which lies above it and is first rate; This part as well is planted in Pinot Noir mixed with one twentieth part of Pinot Blanc and gives a grand ordinaire, fine, agreeable, having a pleasant bouquet, and can yield on average 20 hl/ha, 38 altogether.

Part of the Clos of M. Villette, 73 a planted in Pinot Noir mixed with Pinot Blanc, joining the preceding vineyard and giving an equal wine yielding the same quantity per hectare, that is to say 14 hl.

Les Ormeaux, 1 ha 35 a 80 ca, with belongs almost entirely to M. Noisot, which part is connected and part is to be incessantly replanted [sic] in Pinot Noir, could yield (with age) a wine equal to the preceding ones in the same quantities, that is to say for the 1 ha 30 a 20 ca which belong to M. Noisot, 26 hl, and for the 5 a 60 can in Gamay belonging to someone else, 2 hl.

La Croix-Blanche, 98 a 80 ca, of which 32 a 50 ca belong to M. Noisot, are planted in Pinot Blanc and give an agreeable wine, yielding 20 hl/ha, 6 altogether.

Le Crais, 1 ha 76 a, of which 1 ha 45 a 70 ca belong to M. Boudrot-Pitolet, are planted in Pinot Noir mixed with one hundredth part of Pinot Blanc; with a bit more age it will give a wine equal to the preceding ones, and will yield an average of 20 hl/ha, 29 altogether.

Closmée, 4 ha 21 a 10 ca, of which 1 ha 2 a 84 ca belong to M. Lamblin and are planted in Pinot Noir mixed with one fortieth part of white; with age it will give a wine equal to the preceding ones in the same quantity, which is to say an average of 20 hl/ha.

3 ha 18 a 26 ca, belonging to several owners are planted to Gamay and yield 108 hl.

The average annual production of this second class is 133 hl.

Troisième Cuvée

Les Entre-Deux-Velles, 5 ha 6 a 51 ca, of which 3 ha 95 a 5 ca form the greatest part of the Clos of M. Lamblin, are planted in Pinot Noir with an admixture of one sixtieth part of Pinot Blanc, and give what is called a good and agreeable "ordinaire bourgeois", and can yield on average 20 hl/ha, 97 altogether. 1 ha 11 a 46 ca, belonging to the same owner and to others are planted in Gamay; these can yield on average 40 hl/ha, or 44 altogether.

In this class one must recognize that were all of the parts planted in noble vines, the production of this class would rise by 120 hl on average each year. In total, 134 ha 36 a to produce 458 hl of fine wine and 3,553 hl of Gamay.

Observations: —If one did not want to describe these climats in such minute detail and instead group several together in order to make parcels enclosed by their natural limits such as roads, one could define these parcels thusly:

1st *La Perrière*, which merits special mention, situated at the top of the village, against the mountain scrub between Fixin and Brochon;

2nd *Le Chapitre*, which, immediately underneath La Perrière, also merits, with the next climat, special mention;

3rd *Les Arvelets*, which must be placed in the same rank as Le Chapitre and which also produces great wines;

4th *Le Tremble*, which comprises, with the first article of the deuxième cuvee, the Clos-Marion and its habitable house;

5th *Les Echéseaux* and *Clos-Napoléon*, with the first article of the deuxième cuvée against Le Chapitre to the north in the same zone;

6th *Le Clos Villette, Les Ormeaux, Le Crais, Clomée* and *La Croix-Blanche* taken together;

7th *Les Entre-Deux-Velles*, forming the Clos de M. Lamblin, with its habitable house;

8th The *Boudières* and *Combe-Roi, Meix-Bas, Charmotte* and *l'Arrêt-Chaud*, together, at the mouth of the valley;

9th *Le Village* and *Les Prés*, this last climat in the middle of the village

10th *Les Herbues*, situated below *Le Chapitre*, between the villages of Fixin and Brochon

11th *Les Petits-Crais*, the *Vignes-aux-Grands, Portefeuille, Sergentière*, the *Vionne, Vignois, Coton, Bouteillottes, Fondement, Chantion, Champ-des-Charmes, Chechelin*, and *Les Tellières*, above the Chemin de la Maladière, between the village of Brochon and the high street and below the Maladière with the same boundaries;

12th *Doret* and the *Prielles* together;

13th *Cochon, Poirier-Bâtard, Sarrottes, Rond-les-Os, Clos Sainte-Eloi*, and *Mossière*, below the Maladière and between the high street and the Chemin de la Mossière and the village of Fixey;

14th *Champs de Vogé, Gibassier*, the *Chenevières-Hautes* and *Basses*, above the Chemin de la Maladière, between the Chemin de la Mossière and the village of Fixey;

15th The *Cheminot*, situated between the Chemin de la Maladière and the Chemin de la Zellerois;

16th The *Zellerois*, situated above and against the road;

17th The *Maison-Dieu*, situated between the road and the *Pré-Mâlin*;

18th The *Noiraude*, the *Entre-Deux-Chemins*, the *Borne-Ronde*, all together 23 ha, that were planted less than fifteen years ago and occupy the bulk of arable land below and against the road.

It is remarkable that the culture of Gamay tends to increase daily, and perhaps, not content to have invaded a part of cultivatable lands, will have replaced Pinot in all the climats other than those of the first class, the *Clos Marion, Villette, Lamblin*, the *Ormeaux* and the *Crais*. The growers, who buy almost all of the available parcels, no longer find even the vines at Mâlain productive enough; they plant now the grape called "vine of Arcenant", a fat grape with bunches whose berries are close together and that overlap to the point that those of the center never see the sun and remain green when harvested; growers are even more happy if they harvest them without rot, to which they are very prone.

The summit of the slopes of Fixey and Fixin is today completely barren. From the point where the vines stop, the scrub is completely arid. One finds only trees in the valley of Fixin, where once there existed a forest rich in vegetation that covered the whole slope exposed to the north. It does not appear to ever have been thus. In effect, in 1547, the inhabitants of Fixin demanded the permission to pull up the brush that covered the hills, saying that this would *"permit them to plant and render fruitful the brush and scrub of their village, which formerly harmed them, as it nourished wild beasts such as wolves, foxes, and others that aimed to destroy their livestock as well as fog, obscurity, and miasmas that oft-times causes frosts which destroy the vine and the grape of their vines"* (Archives of the village of Fixin).

COMMUNE DE BROCHON

Almost all of the cultivated soil in this village is consecrated to the vine. There are approximately 120 ha in Gamay and 20 ha only in Pinot Noir. The Pinot Gris is almost unknown in this vineyard; the Pinot Blanc hardly accounts for even one twentieth part. The soil and the subsoil are similar to that of Gevrey, and above all to that of Fixin. The principal climats are:

Première Cuvée

Clos de Crébillon, 68 a, belonging to M. Liégeard

Deuxième Cuvée

Croix-Violette or **Bezenne**, 4 ha, belongs to MM. Bonnet, Liégeard, and Thomas Carey.

Jeunes Royes, 7 ha, belonging to MM. Liégeard, Truchetet, etc.

Epinards, 1 ha, belonging to MM. Darcy and Raillard.

Troisième Cuvée

Mazières, 70 a, belonging to MM. Liégeard, Javelier, Denis, and Chevrey.

Vignois, 3 ha 30 a, belonging to M. Truchetet and others.

En Champs, 1 ha 30 a, belonging to MM. Tisserandot and Liégeard.

La Ruotte, 50 a, belonging to MM. Mignardot and Liégeard.

Champ-Perrier, 3 ha, belonging to M. Darcy and others.

Several vines of good Gamay belong to MM. Cazeaux, Truchetet and J. Mignardot.

I will make here an observation, applicable to the rest of all the communes of the Côte d'Or: in these fine vineyards there are many owners who I cannot cite because their holdings are too small.

The fine wines of Brochon have body and color; they keep well, and in general are good to drink only after five, six, or even eight years. They are close to many of the good wines of Fixin and Fixey. It is the climat of the *Crais-billons* that has given its name to the celebrated, tragic poet Prosper Jolyot, who was born in Dijon in 1674 and died in 1762, who took from his lands in Brochon the name of Jolyot de Crébillon.

For the modern wine lover, there are several compelling wines to explore from the Côte Dijonnaise. Few producers commercialize the wines of Dijon itself today, but there is an interesting version of Bourgogne Le Chapitre from Chenôve produced by the fashionable producer Domaine Bizot. Many producers deliver a very pleasant Marsannay rouge, and these wines are normally quite well priced. The ur-producer in Marsannay was Domaine Clair-Daü. Formed in 1950, it was one of the great domaines in Burgundy. The domaine was split up in 1985, however, due to dissent in the family, with the majority (including the fine parcels in Bonnes Mares) being sold to negociant Louis Jadot. There are two domaines in Marsannay today, however, that also share the vineyards and the legacy of Domaine Clair-Daü, Domaine Bruno Clair and Domaine Bart, both of whom produce wine worthy of exploration. Among the wines of Marsannay the whites are refreshing and the reds have an elegant expression of fruit, but the rosés are something very rare in the Côte d'Or, and are a nearly perfect summer beverage. Interesting wines are also produced in Fixin, and like Marsannay, there are several domaines worth investigating. The Joliet family still owns the Clos de la Perrière, referred to above. Domaine Pierre Gelin is based in Fixin, and produces an Hervelets as well as the Clos Napoléon, which is today their monopole.

GEVREY[41]

Today, there are nine separate grands crus in the village of Gevrey. In addition to Chambertin and Clos de Bèze, which have been renowned for more than a millennium, Chapelle, Charmes, Griotte, Latricières, Mazis, Mazoyères, and Ruchottes are all classified today as grands crus. It is interesting to see how they have progessed in esteem over time.

Chambertin proper is 12 ha 90 a 31 ca, while the Clos de Bèze is 15 ha 38 a 87 ca. Wines of the latter appellation may adopt the name of the former (although the reverse is not true), and either may declassify to Gevrey premier cru, Gevrey by itself, Bourgogne, or Côteaux Bourguignons. The wines of these two climats are distinguished because the Clos de Bèze is a warmer terroir compared to that of Chambertin. Bèze has a slightly steeper slope, which means it drains well and is better in cooler, wet years, while Chambertin tends to be better in warmer years, since it holds more water and is thus a slightly cooler terroir. Jacky Rigaux notes in his work *Grands Crus de Bourgogne*, a document in the local archives from the 15th century, refers to a Grand Chambertin of 8.5 ha and a Petit Chambertin of 4.5 ha, a distinction which has been lost. He writes that the vines at the top of the slope, planted in thinner soil, give the most elegant wines, while those planted lower on the slope give the most powerful wine and those in the middle give the wine that is the most complex.

Traveling from north to south, the first appellation classified as grand cru is Ruchottes-Chambertin, upslope from Mazis. It is composed of Ruchottes du Dessus (1 ha 99 a 23 ca), which Lavalle has in première cuvée, and Ruchottes du Bas (1 ha 31 a 14 ca), which he places with the deuxième cuvées. There is a clos at the top of Ruchottes, still surrounded by walls, which is a monopole of Domaine Armand Rousseau (purchased in 1977 from Thomas-Bassot) and is sold as the Clos des Ruchottes. Ruchottes is located at the mouth of the valley known as the Combe de Lavaux, which channels in cool air. This, combined with the fact that the vineyard is planted in very thin soils, causes the grapes to ripen very late in the season yet give nicely concentrated fruit.

Downslope from Ruchottes is Mazis-Chambertin, at the northern end of the Clos de Bèze. Today's grand cru Mazis-Chambertin is composed of the climats Mazis-Bas (4 ha 56 a 11 ca) and Mazis-Haut (4 ha 54 as 23 ca), which Lavalle classes as deuxième and première cuvées respectively. Clive Coates mentions in his book *Côte d'Or* that since the time of Lavalle a 60-are portion of the lieu-dit Les Corbeaux (lying on the northern border of Mazis-Bas) was absorbed into Mazis.

South of Mazis lies the Clos de Bèze, and south of Bèze is Chambertin itself. This is the heart of Gevrey and one of the high points of Burgundy and the wine producing areas anywhere. The vineyards are ancient, and their primacy has always been recognized. On the south side of Chambertin lies Latricières-Chambertin, grand cru today but classified as deuxième cuvée by Lavalle. The AC regulations allow 44 a 78 ca of lieu-dit Aux Combottes at the southern extremity to be included in Latricières, since it is on the same side of the road that climbs the slope to the top of the hill.

On the other side of the D122 road, known as the Route des Grands Crus, downslope from the Clos de Bèze, lies Chapelle Chambertin and just south of it Griotte-Chambertin. Chapelle Chambertin (named for the former chapel of the Abbey of Bèze) groups together En La Chapelle (3 ha 69 a 24 ca) and Les Gémeaux (1 ha 79 a 29 ca). En La Chapelle (called Chapelle Haut in Lavalle) is ranked as a première cuvée, while Les Gémeaux is classed as a deuxième cuvée. Chapelle Chambertin should not be confused with the parcel called Petite Chapelle, which is found downslope from En La Chapelle, a parcel that is deuxième cuvée in Lavalle and a premier cru today. Immediately to the south of En La Chapelle lies Griotte Chambertin. The lieux-dits to the south of the road are generally considered to produce lighter wines than those above the road.

The largest expansion of the grand crus to the south of the Route de Grands Crus, however, is the portion known today as lieux-dits Charmes or Mazoyères. Charmes (12 ha 24 a 56 ca) and Mazoyères (18 ha 58 a 68 ca) are grouped together, and either may take the name of the other, although in practice the majority are known as Charmes. These two combined equate to the second largest grand cru of Burgundy. The portion known as Charmes, downslope from Chambertin, is better regarded. Lavalle breaks Charmes into two portions, and allows the upper 3 ha of the vineyard as Première Cuvée, while the lower 9 ha are classed as deuxième cuvée. He classifies the whole of Mazoyères as deuxième cuvée. Today's Mazoyères is even larger than it was in Lavalle's day, since the portion due south from the premier cru Champs-Chenys that extends all the way to the former RN 74 was not planted in the mid-19th century. In part because of this extension, the vineyard has fairly deep soil on a bed of gravel deposited by the slope wash from the Combe Grisard.

The appreciation of the vines of Gevery is ancient indeed. Courtépée traces the origins of the vineyard to 7th century Duke Amalgaire:

> Duke Amalgaire, founder of the Abbey of Bèze, enriched [Gevrey] with several properties in Chenôve and Gevrey. This is the origin of the famous Clos de Bèze, first planted by the monks. The Abbot Hugues sold it to the cathedral chapter of Langres for 600 livres estevenants[42] in 1219; it has since been rented out to several private individuals.

He goes on to describe the other vineyards of note in Gevrey:

> One distinguishes the climats of Chambertin and of Bèze at the head of Burgundian wines. The other renowned districts are Les Saint-Jacques, Les Mazy, Les Tamisots, La Chapelle.

Dr. Morelot on Gevrey spends far less time here than Lavalle:

> Once one has passed the Clos de la Roche in Morey, one is in Gevrey, where Chambertin is found, whose European reputation has ranked it among the best wines of the world. This climat extends almost to the limit of the hill from the houses of Gevrey in a thin band, always on the lower slopes of the hill; it has a surface of approximately twenty five hectares (600 ouvrées) and has no portions as in the Clos de Vougeot that are of lower quality: here everything is of equal value, not for the quantity, which is seldom abundant, but for the excellence of the production. A bit further on, one finds again the Clos de Bèze, which approaches that of Chambertin[10,43]
>
> The other climats of Gevrey are the Clos Saint-Jacques, La Chapelle, Mazis, La Grillette, and La Fouchère. They furnish very fine wines, but they are below the level of Chambertin.
>
> All of the wines of this slope (I mean here the têtes de cuvées) can be considered as holding the first rank among those of the Côte d'Or; they are distinguished by their purity of fruit, their color, and their solid nature. The flavor that they imprint on the palate is that of the grape in perfect maturity. The wines of Morey and those of Gevrey other than Chambertin, are more rustic on the palate and do not open as quickly as those of this good climat and the superfine wines of Chambolle, at least until they are racked and fined several times. One notes again that the wines of Morey are more subject to maladies than others, and this comes from an excess of cultivation on the part of certain owners.
>
> There is one very important consideration that I must not forget to make on the particular finesse of the têtes de cuvées of Chambolle. This finesse seems to come not only from the excellence of the terrain, from the beauty of the exposition, and the nature of the red grape, but principally from a certain quantity of white grapes (Pinot Blanc). They should not be present to excess, because the wine will become thin and lose its color; but when this variety does not exceed one twelfth or even one tenth, one can say with certitude that crushed and fermented with the Pinot Noir the wine that results will always be very deeply colored, and much superior in finesse and good flavor than that which has been made only with black grapes. Several owners, concerned more with quantity than with quality, destroy the white grapes, because the yield is lower; but this is a short-sighted gambit and they lose more than they gain.
>
> The example of the good proprietors of Chambolle should be imitated by those of all the Côte d'Or. The wine could only gain in this situation, even those destined for

---

10 Duke Amalgaire gave his holdings in Gevrey in 630 AD to the Abbey of Bèze, which he had just founded. The monks began to remove the scrub from several plots and planted vines in the Clos that has long conserved the name of the Clos de Bèze.

long aging. The only deficit would be one of yield. But in the current state of the vineyards, the owners must not focus only on augmenting their production. They would still sell enough if they concentrated on making their wines as perfect as one might hope.

But this digression has removed me from my work, and there is more of this part of the Côte to describe. Up to here we have seen only the slopes, grouped more or less three by three, offering a homogeneous mass of one or two places. Here it is not the same. Each slope is more or less isolated, and each of them offers a space larger or smaller which separates it from its neighbor. At the foot of each of these is found a village, giving this part of the Côte an animated air and a more varied aspect; however, of the entire slope, this is where we find the smallest number of fine wines. We will run through these villages and be able to convince ourselves of this fact.

Dr. Lavalle's thoughts on Gevrey, including his correction of Morelot's error on the size of Chambertin:

COMMUNE DE GEVREY-CHAMBERTIN

The territory of Gevrey as revealed by the cadastral map contains 387 ha 59 ca of vines, and since the production of the real estate registry, the plantings are much more widespread on the plain at the bottom of the Route Impériale [today the D974] to the point that one can estimate the vineyard of this commune today at more than 400 ha.

Approximately half of this, situated at the foot of the slope and on the plain is exclusively planted to Gamay, and the wine that it supplies is distinguished in no way from the wine produced by the same plant in other locations – we will say nothing special in regard to it; the production is approximately 45 to 50 hl/ha.

The other half, situated on the slope and at the best exposition, is planted in Pinot Noir mixed in a few places with a bit of Pinot Blanc, without other varietal. The wines produced by these last vines form four distinct classes or qualities, as follows[44]:

1. Tête de cuvée, cru hors ligne, vin extra;
2. Première cuvée de finage, vin de dessert;
3. Deuxième cuvée, vin d'entre-mets;
4. Troisième cuvée, grand ordinaire[11]

Here are the principal climats that compose these cuvees, their substance, and the names of the proprietors who have enough to make a special cuvée.

Tête de Cuvée

Chambertin (Clos de Bèze included), 27 ha, belonging to MM. Ouvard, Serre, Marion, Thiébaut, Genret, Grachet, de Grésigny, the Belot heirs, the widow Mongin.

---

11 We will accept this classification for the following communes, which will serve henceforth as the base of all our appreciations.

Danguy et Aubertin: MM. de Blic, Bordet, the widow Dubard, MM. Gauthey cadet et fils, Fernand Grachet et fils, Guichard-Potheret et fils, Paul Guillemot, Albert et Gaston Joliet, the Marey heirs, Marion, de Morot de Grésigny, Mme. Serre, M. Thomas-Bassot et fils (Chambertin); MM. Gauthey cadet et fils, Fernand Grachet, Guichard Potheret et fils, Guillemot, Marion, de Morot de Grésigny, Mme. Serre (Clos de Bèze)

Camille Rodier has Chambertin and the Clos de Bèze alone in première cuvée, and notes the proprietors as: MM. De Blic, Bouchot-Ludot, Damoy, Duvergey-Taboureau, Ganthey, de Grésigny, Grivelet-Cusset, Guichard-Potheret, Javelier-Laurin, Albert et Gaston Joliet, Louis Latour, Liégeard, Liger-Belair, the de la Loyère heirs, Mangien-Fleurot, Marion, Poillot, Quanquin, Rebourseau-Philippon, J.-H.Remy, Armand Rousseau, Thomas-Bassot, Trapet, etc.

Première Cuvée

Saint-Jacques and **Clos Saint-Jacques**, 6 ha 52 a, belonging to MM. Duret, Marion, the widow Surget.

Fouchère [today part of Chambertin], 1 ha, belonging to M. Serrigny, the widow Mongin.

Chapelle (haute), 3 ha 89 a, belonging to MM. Grachet, Serrigny, A. Joly.

Chapelle-Chambertin provides an interesting illustration of the changing size of Burgundy vineyards over time. As noted above, Chapelle-Chambertin today includes 3 ha 69 a 24 ca of the lieux-dit En La Chapelle and 1 ha 79 a 29 ca of Les Gémeaux. Lavalle has a (slightly bigger) Gemeaux among the deuxième cuvées where Danguy et Aubertin have "Gemeaux ou Chapelle", and both authors have Petite Chapelle, which adjoins La Chapelle to the east, among the deuxième cuvées, and today it is premier cru, but Rodier has 8 ha of La Chapelle as deuxième cuvée without listing Petite Chapelle at all.

> Danguy et Aubertin: MM Bazin, Fernand Grachet, Joliet-Serrigny, Dr. Truchetet
>
> Rodier: MM Bazin, Fernand Grachet, Joliet-Serrigny, Dr. Truchetet

Mazy (haut), 4 ha, 21 a, belonging to the widow Mongin, MM. de Grésigny, Genret.

> Danguy et Aubertin: M : Bizot-Fermouche, Mme. Dubard, MM. Fremy-Tachet, Guichard-Potheret et fils, Fernand Grachet, de Morot de Grésigny, Thomas-Bassot et fils (for Mazy-Haut) ; MM: Bizot-Fermouche, Camus-Naigeon, Dr. Demorey, Devillbichot, Louis Maire-Javelier, Honoré Philippon, Rebourseau-Philippon, Thomas-Bassot et fils (for Mazy-Bas)
>
> Rodier: Bizot, Henri Gouroux, de Grésigny, Guichard-Potheret, Matrot, Louis Marillier, Rousseau-Poulot, Thomas-Bassot, Félix Tortochot, etc. (for Mazis-Haut); Bizot, J. Camus, Henri Chevillard, Fagot, Javellier-

Laurin, Félix Laroze, Marchand, Louis Marillier, Rousseau-Lebean, Thomas-Bassot, Tisserandot-Galland, etc. (for Mazis-Bas)

Ruchotte (du Dessus), 2 ha, belonging to MM. Delachère, Collot.

<u>Danguy et Aubertin</u> are the first to note the separate existence of the Clos des Ruchottes, belonging to M. Thomas-Bassot; in Ruchottes du Dessus they list only M. Tisserandot-Girod and M. Tisserandot-Grimaut; they note Ruchotte basse or Ruchotte du Bas or Mazis (which surrounds Ruchotte du Bas) as being Première Classe in the opinion of "C. Loc." although deuxième cuvée in Lavalle and deuxième classe in the Comité d'Agriculture de Beaune. They list the proprietors as MM. Boinet-Foulet, Fricot-Roblot, de Morot de Grésigny, Poillot père and Thomas-Bassot et fils

<u>Rodier</u> groups both together (as deuxième cuvées), although he notes only 3 ha 40 a, belong to MM. Grillot-Bourgeot, Magnien-Fleurot and Thomas-Bassot, etc.

Charmes (hauts), 3 ha, belonging to MM. Corbabon, Démorey.

<u>Danguy et Aubertin</u>: Dr. Demorey, MM. Gauthey cadet et fils, M. Grangier

<u>Rodier</u> has both climats grouped together as deuxièmes cuvées, with the following owners: MM. Edouard Bélorgey, Théodore Bizot, Bolnot, J. Camus, Dussauce, Léon Girard, Henri Gouroux, the widow Grey, Ch. Jantot, Albert and Gaston Joliet, Mouchet, Philippon fils, Ponsot, Rebourseau-Philippon, Salbreux, Thomas-Bassot, etc.

Grillotte (haute), 2 ha 90 a, belonging to MM. Pastol, Noël, Genret, the widow Jondot.

<u>Danguy et Aubertin</u>: M. Joliet-Serrigny, M. Rembourseau-Philippon, MM. Thomas-Bassot et fils

<u>Rodier</u>: Henri Gouroux, Rebourseau-Philippon, Thomas-Bassot, etc.

Veroilles (vieille), 4 ha, belonging to M. Joliet.

Etournelles, 1 ha 96 a, belonging to MM. Marion, Genret.

Castiers [*Cazetiers* today] (haut), 7 ha 98 a, belonging to MM. Genret, Ouvrard, Truchetet, Adenot, Noël, the widow Surget.

Deuxième Cuvée

Mazy (bas), 4 ha 38 a, belonging to MM. the Mongin heirs, the Belot heirs, Noël, Devillebichot.

Chapelle (petite), 4 ha 1 a, belonging to MM. Dubard, the widow Mongin, the Belot heirs, Serrigny, Devillbichot.

Ruchotte (basse), 1 ha 40 a, belonging to MM. de Grésigny, Delachère, Marion, the Belot heirs.

Gemeaux, 2 ha, belonging to MM. Genret, Noël, Callinet, the widow Mongin.

Charmes (bas), 9 ha, belonging to MM. Philippon, Noël, Serrigny, Chevillon.

Mazoyères, 18 ha 26 a, belonging to MM. Gournot, Molin.

Latricières, 6 ha 93 a, belonging to MM. Gournot, Ouvrard, Marion.

> Danguy et Aubertin note that although Latricières is deuxième cuvée in Lavalle, and deuxième and troisième classe by the Comité d'Agriculture de Beaune, that it sells in the region at the same price as the wines of the first class (for the property formerly owned by Gauvain), and note the proprietors as MM. Gauthey cadet et fils, Gillot, Guichard-Potheret et fils, de Morot de Grésigny, Riembaud, Savot

> Rodier: J. Camus, Gauthey, de Grésigny, Félix Laroze, J.-H. Remy, Trapet, etc.

Echézeaux, 3 ha 31 a, belonging to M. Joly.

Lavaut (haut), 9 ha 53 a, belonging to MM. Delachère, the Belot heirs, Noël, Callinet, the widow Léjéas, the widow Surget.

Troisième Cuvée

Meixvelle, 1 ha 87 a, belonging to M. Marion.

Meix-des-Ouches, 1 ha 9 a, belonging to the widow Mongin.

Craipillot, 2 ha 86 a, belonging to M. Collot.

Champonet, 3 ha 16 a, belonging to MM. Joliet, de Grésigny.

Fonteny, 3 ha 5 a, bedlonging to MM. Serre, the Belot heirs.

Corbeaux, 3 ha 60 ca, belonging to MM. de Grésigny, Noël.

Clos-Prieur (haut), 2 ha 27 a, belonging to the widow Mongin, MM. Joly, Callinet.

Cherbaude, 2 ha 20 a, belonging to the widow Jondot.

Pallut, 3 ha 37 a, belonging to M. Serrigny.

Carrougeot, 5 ha 43 a, belonging to the widow Belost, MM. Serre, Noël, Corbabon, Rousseau, Ossinot.

Combe-du-Dessus, 6 ha 43 a, belonging to MM. Corbabon, Joly, Calinet, Noël, Chevrey.

Combe-au-Moine, 2 ha 20 a, belonging to the widow Surget, MM. Noël, Chevillon-Giraud.

Danguy et Aubertin note that although Combe-du-Dessus and Combe-au-Moine are troisième cuvées in Lavalle that they are deuxième cuvées in the C. Loc.

Ensonge, 3 ha 60 a, belonging to M. Serrigny.

Vellées, 1 ha 16 a, belonging to M. Serrigny.

Motrot, 3 ha 50 ca, belonging to the widow Belost, MM. Rossigneux, J. Fricot.

Marchais, 5 ha 56 a, belonging to MM. de Grésigny, the widow Vienne.

Champs, 9 ha 67 a, belonging to MM. the Carey heirs, de Grésigny, Delachère, Bonnet, Tisserandot.

Champerrier (haut), 2 ha 36 a, belonging to MM. Grachet, Philippon, the widow Jondot.

Champeaux, 6 ha 48 a, belonging to MM. Serrigny, Tisserandot, Foulet, Jean Fricot.

Charreux, 5 ha 79 a, belonging to MM. Pastol, Genret, the widow Vienne.

Crais-du-Dessus, 5 ha, belonging to MM. The Mongin heirs, Philippon, Noël, Genret, Lenoir.

It must be observed that several of these climats, either because of the slope of the hill upon which they are found or due to other accidental causes, present greatly uneven quality in their products; thus, the Clos Saint-Jacques, Grande-Chapelle, Charmes, Grillotte and Castiers, rightly classed among the Premier Cuvées for their best products, have, however, lower slopes that would only belong in the deuxième or troisième cuvée; the Veroilles, Ruchotte-du-Bas and Mazoyères have parts that have only very recently been planted, and consequently cannot have been long classified; for one knows that the wines of young vines, wherever it grows, are very ordinary and have none of the character of great wines.

The average annual production of all of these Pinot vines is everywhere almost the same, 20 to 33 hl/ha; we speak here only of those whose husbandry is not forced, for there are owners who do not fear to alter the quality of their wine by endeavoring with fertilizers or excessive planting to produce up to double this amount from their vines.

The general and distinctive character of all wines made from Pinot in Gevrey is the firmness or the body, and it is this which has made them sought-after in the marketplace, which finds them a remedy and a sustenance for all of those who weaken; the première cuvée has the cachet of a grand vin and is little distinguished from Chambertin in the first few years; the deuxième also has the bouquet and finesse that makes of it a very agreeable wine; the troisième cuvée is the ordinaire of a prince as a vin d'entre-mets; there are below these three cuvées lowly vines that make a good ordinaire bourgeois, but of which we will not give the details because it does not distinguish itself from the same type of wine made from the other villages of the Côte.

The Original Grand Crus of Burgundy

As to the wine of Chambertin, it is almost superfluous to speak of it since it is that which the renown is the most popular and widespread throughout the world; but since the word is more practiced than the thing itself and that there are many who believe themselves to know and doubt themselves not, we will tell them that this cru possesses to the highest degree all of the qualities that constitute the perfect wine, body, color, bouquet, finesse; it is the equal of the greatest wines of the Côte d'Or; nevertheless, each of them has its particular cachet that distinguishes it to true amateurs; thus La Romanée excels by finesse; the Clos Vougeot by the bouquet; the Chambertin by body and color; but by the sum of their qualities, all three share the honor and all three would sell at the same price if the first two, which belong to the single and same proprietor (M. Ouvrard[45]) had, as this last, submitted to the effects of the competition of vendors.

The climat of Chambertin is composed of two contiguous parts which follow each other and extend to mid-slope, in the direction of north at noon, for a length of approximately 1,200 meters and a median width of 225 meters. The first of these parts, the closest to the village of Gevrey, contains 14 ha and is designated under the name of Clos de Bèze, because it was planted by the monks of the Abbey of Bèze, to which the Duke Amalgaire had given the land in the year 630. The second part, which is the extension of this, contains 13 ha, and is called Chambertin (probably from the name of some *Bertin* who had planted this *champ* [field]).

The wines produced by these two parts both call themselves Chambertin and possess, as to the elite cuvées, the same quality.[12]

The relative value of the cuvées of Gevrey that come after that of Chambertin is in the proportion of one third to one quarter, and diminishes one after another; thus when new Chambertin sell for 600 francs per cask (436 litres), the première cuvée is worth 400 francs, the deuxième 300 francs and the troisième 200 francs (all of which is, of course, only approximate, since each owner has his own manner of composing his cuvées and can give them more or less real merit). This proportion ultimately applies only to new wine, since it is quite different for old wines from good years; Chambertin, of which the perfect qualities do not appear before the age of 10 to 12 years, acquires a value double and triple these lesser cuvées, and the explanation of these phenomenon is in the nature of the subsoil and exposition; it is also in the age of the vines, which for the Clos de Bèze notably, goes back 12 or 15 centuries during which the soil, purged of all foreign plants and removed from all addition, is enriched only by the detritus of the vine, and has created an exceptional and perfectly homogeneous terrain, with which the vine, which has never changed, is in some fashion united and acquires the properties which can be given only by the conjunction of all of these conditions. Such is the privilege of the grands crus of the Côte d'Or that certain Belgian amateurs refer to them as having "race" [lineage] and certain English refer to them as "being of good family". Noble families, in effect, which inscribed in the golden book of Burgundy.

When Duke Amalgaire in 630 gave to the Abbey of Bèze his domaine in Gevrey, it was already planted at least in part to vines; however, this climat, considered as

---

12 It is here that we should rectify the error committed by Dr. Morelot of Beaune in his book entitled Statistique de la Vigne dans le Départment de la Côte d'Or, in which he says that Chambertin has a surface of 25 ha and that "a bit farther on one finds the Clos de Bèze which is similar to Chambertin."

However, if one were to separate the Clos de Bèze from Chambertin, one would say that this last offers a surface of 12 ha, and not 25, which includes the two parts (that are today 27 ha because to them has been added several areas of scrub and the upper parts of the vineyard); and that as to the quality of these two wines, the marketplace and public opinion have never distinguished between them, and, in any case, the Clos de Bèze has never been inferior.

giving good wine, was not yet counted among those whose name is widely renowned.

Until 1219 the vines of Bèze and of Chambertin (because at this time these two climats were already confused) were both the property of the Abbey of Bèze who sold them to the Chapitre of Langres. The original of this bill of sale, written in Latin on a narrow leaf of parchment, exists still in the departmental archives of the Côte d'Or. Here is the translation:

"Our Hugues, Abbot of Bèze, and all the canons of this abbey, declare to sell to the dean and to the cathedral chapter of Langres our Clos of Gevrey with all of its dependences of land, feudal obligations[46], fields, houses, vats and other adjacent properties, tithes of wine, of oats and of money, for 600 livres estevenans, and promise loyally to guarantee said sale to the cathedral chapter of Langres against all and especially against the monks of Bèze in the event that someone would be opposed to this sale. This sale has been made in the presence of Simon, archdeacon of Dijon, acting with the authorization of the episcopal seat of Langres in the year of our grace 1219."

As one can see, the monks of Bèze had, already in this period, built the Clos, and the walls, of which there are still some remains, were constructed at the beginning of the XIII century. Nevertheless, the totality of the Clos did not belong to the abbey, since in 1227, the cathedral chapter of Langres bought a plot of vines in the Clos for 24 Dijon livres 10 sols.

The cathedral chapter of Langres does not appear to have ever cultivated this domaine. They rented it out, either for wine or for money. The last tenant was a Mr. Jomard, whose nine year lease, for a rent of 100 livres yearly, expired on May 2nd, 1651. At this time the cathedral chapter of Langres consented to sell to Mr. Jomard its Clos de Bèze, containing 40 journaux, of which 36 were planted to vines and the rest in scrub and roads, "…for a yearly payment of six queues [i.e. twelve casks of 228 litres] of wine coming from these vines or of another as good, contained in new barrels, and 6 livres tournois in money, at the expense of Mr. Jomard or his heirs".

From the Jomard family, this property passed under the same conditions as above to Mr. Jobert and Mr. Grosbois de Vellemont. The former quickly became the owner of the largest part, and he thus decided to add his name to that of his domaine, which would stay in the possession of this family, known under the name of Mr. Jobert-Chambertin or Jobert de Chambertin, until the beginning of this century, when it passed directly or indirectly to the present proprietors[47].

Hardly had the cathedral chapter of Langres rented out its Clos de Bèze-Chambertin, as it was called throughout the 18th century, than the reputation of this wine grew beyond all previous levels. In 1651, the contract for sale estimated the queue of Bèze wine at 30 livres. This result was largely due to M. Claude Jobert-Chambertin, merchant of wines to the Palatine court, who popularized this wine abroad. The cathedral chapter then did all that it could to regain possession of the Clos de Bèze. A first trial to nullify the sale was carried out against Jobert in 1702 and lasted eight years. A second trial took place against him in 1761. The cathedral chapter alleged that Jobert did not deliver to them the best wine of the Clos. The tribunal decided that the renter was only obliged to give them good authentic saleable vermillion wine from the cru of Bèze, and denied the suit of the cathedral chapter. This decision was appealed and the chapter requested the restoration of their property, but without success.

We will terminate this note on this celebrated climat with the following extract from the works of [Burgundian poet, philosopher and critic] Bernard de Lamonnoye:

"There is at Gevrey, a village two leagues distant from Dijon, two celebrated vineyards, one called Bèze, the other Chambertin. One day a gallant man, who possessed a good part of the wines of Bèze, was entertaining his friends, when one of the guests sang this verse which pleased many, and above all the master of the feast:

Bèze qui produit ce bon vin	Bèze who produces this good wine
Doit passer pour très-catholique;	Must pass for a faithful catholic;
J'estime plus que Chambertin	I esteem more than Chambertin
Bèze qui produit ce bon vin.	Bèze who produces this good wine.
Si le disciple de Calvin,	If the disciple of Calvin,
Bèze, passe pour hérétique,	Bèze, passes for a heretic,
Bèze qui produit ce bon vin	Bèze who produces this good wine
Doit passer pour très-catholique.	Must pass for a faithful catholic."

There are also in existence very ancient documents concerning the climat of Varoilles. This climat was planted before the XII century. The cathedral chapter of Langres bought a first parcel in 1272, for 75 Dijon sols. In 1319, another 25 and a half *ouvrées* were acquired, and, in 1329, they purchased from Guillaume de Morey for 60 sols tournois the balance of the climat.

It seems that this climate had been pulled up in part at the start of the 18th century; for, from 1736 – 1740 the portion called the Grandes-Varoilles was replanted. M. Vienne[48] published on the Clos Saint-Jacques the following information:

"This domaine, of which the wine produced is classed among the best of the country, has passed from the hands of M. Morizot, lord of Jancigny, lawyer at Parliament, deceased in 1732, into those of M. Gonthier of Auvillars, a relative of his wife who has long survived him. The heir of this last has gone bankrupt, and, after several sales, the domaine has passed into the hands of the current proprietor."

Until the 17th century, Gevrey was long from enjoying the high reputation that honors it today, and I can never recount this fact without remarking that it has been the same for a great number of our greatest vineyards, such as, for example, Romanée-Conti. Before 1600 and until around 1680, it was considered that Dijon supplied the best wines of the region, as one will see looking over the following figures that we have extracted from the register of the deliberations of the city of Dijon and a manuscript that today is in the hands of M. Vienne, the former archivist. The *queue* of the best wines of Gevrey were taxed at the following declared values:

1613 – 36 livres	1637 – 17 livres	1661 – 22 livres
1614 – 32 livres	1638 – 28 livres	1662 – 24 livres
1615 – 24 livres	1639 – 40 livres	1663 – 45 livres
1616 – 15 livres	1640 – 35 livres	1664 – 32 livres
1617 – 27 livres	1641 – 27 livres	1665 – 39 livres
1618 – 20 livres	1642 – 45 livres	1666 – 22 livres
1619 – 24 livres	1643 – 35 livres	1667 – 24 livres
1620 – 30 livres	1644 – 66 livres	1668 – 48 livres
1621 – 20 livres	1645 – 24 livres	1669 – 24 livres
1622 – 33 livres	1646 – 17 livres	1670 – 18 livres
1623 – 27 livres	1647 – 24 livres	1671 – 28 livres
1624 – 20 livres	1648 – 30 livres	1672 – 22 livres
1625 – 25 livres	1649 – 20 livres	1673 – 32 livres
1626 – 36 livres	1650 – 57 livres	1674 – 35 livres
1627 – 23 livres	1651 – 45 livres	1675 – 44 livres
1628 – 48 livres	1652 – 38 livres	1676 – 30 livres
1629 – 18 livres	1653 – 24 livres	1677 – 21 livres
1630 – 14 livres	1654 – 64 livres	1678 – 16 livres
1631 – 17 livres	1655 – 42 livres	1679 – 25 livres
1632 – 36 livres	1656 – 32 livres	1680 – 21 livres
1633 – 22 livres	1657 – 18 livres	1681 – 21 livres
1634 – 18 livres	1658 – 26 livres	1682 - 25 livres
1635 – 24 livres	1659 – 54 livres	1683 – 22 livres
1636 – 30 livres	1660 – 30 livres	1685 – 32 livres

The prices were the same for Brochon, Fixey, and Fixin. Dijon and Chenôve were taxed at a higher rate. Thus the good wines of Dijon were valued at:

1648 – 42 livres	1660 – 45 livres	1675 – 58 livres
1651 – 60 livres	1665 – 52 livres	1680 – 25 livres
1655 – 60 livres	1670 – 27 livres	1680 – 25 livres

• *The Original Grand Crus of Burgundy* •

The climats of Bèze and of Chambertin were, in the year 1650, already carefully distinguished from the other crus of Gevrey, and they were included, all through the end of the XVII century, with the best wines of Dijon.

We have seen how since this time their reputation has increased. As soon as they were known abroad and appreciated, it only took a couple of years for them to attain the first rank.

> Camille Rodier has classified only Chambertin and Clos de Bèze as première cuvée, with the proprietors as listed above. In deuxième cuvée he lists Les Latricières, Aux Charmes, Mazoyères or Charmes, Aux Combottes, Saint-Jacques, Les Varoilles, La Chapelle, Les Mazis-Hauts, Ruchottes du Dessus and du Bas, La Grillolle and Les Cazetiers. He notes that « A part of [Cazetiers] has been classed in deuxième class, the rest in troisième. » He classified Les Mazis-Bas in troisième cuvée, along with Les Etournelles, Les Echéseaux, and Lavaux, and classifies as « Autres climats » the following : Les Gemeaux, Clos des Ruchottes, Meixvelle, Meix-des-Ouches, Craipillot, Champonet, Fonteny, Corbeaux, Les Issards, Clos Prieure, Cherbaude, Pallut, Carougeot, En Ramonée, En Labussière, Combe-du-Dessus, Combe-au-Moine, Ensonge, Vellées, Motrot, Marchais, En Champs, Champerrier, Champeaux, Charreux, Crais-du-Dessus, etc., giving this Nota Bene :
>
> « Several climats, such as Le Carougeot and the Clos des Ruchottes are worthy to be classified as deuxième cuvée. »

Domaine Armand Rousseau is at the head of a host of fine producers working in Gevrey today, including Domaine Fourrier, Domaine Denis Mortet, Domaine Dugat-Py and many other producers of quality. The wines in general are not inexpensive, but they can be among the greatest in Burgundy. This does not mean that there are not values to be found. Many observers feel that the Clos Saint-Jacques on the north side of the Combe Lavaux is grand cru quality, and Cazetiers next to it also produces some delightful, age-worthy wines. Among the best bargains, however, can be a Chambertin Clos-de-Bèze from a good grower: Domaine Robert Groffier is just one of a number of examples that are at the same time subtle, complex, elegant, powerful *and* relatively inexpensive given the pedigree of the appellation.

MOREY

There is a long and illustrious stretch of grand cru vineyards in Morey, but thoughts about the quality of these vineyards have varied over time. André Jullien places many of them in his first category, including Clos de Tart, Clos de la Roche, and Véroilles in Chambolle. Courtépée provides historical background for the Clos de Tart:

> [In Morey] The vines of the Dames des Tart in the climat of La Forge were given to them by Etienne Dojon, knight, in 1260. Duchesse Alix [de Vergy] ceded to the almshouse her clos called More and her field of Breuil in 1234...Wines justly renowned. M. Pelletier de Clery acquired Chambolle and Morey from M. de Croonembourg in 1745: MM. de Tavannes had owned this plot.

Jullien also grouped Bonnes-Mares with the vineyards noted above, even though most of this vineyard (13 ha 54 a 17 ca, out of 15 ha 05 a 72 ca) lies in Chambolle, as does Véroilles, which is an appendage at the bottom of Bonnes Mares that extends upslope towards the wood. Indeed, by the time Dr. Morelot and Dr. Lavalle were making their classifications, Veroilles was not in production. It was reclaimed only fairly recently.

Our two doctors, however, are quite a bit less generous than Jullien with their assessments of the climats of Morey. They agree on the Clos de Tart, with both of them noting it as tête de cuvée. The vineyard is located at the southern extremity of the village of Morey, and it is undeniably ancient. Jacky Rigaux speculates in his *Grands Crus de Bourgogne* that Clos de Tart dates to approximately the same period as the Clos de Bèze. Certainly, as Lavalle testifies, by the time Clos de Tart was sold in the 12th century it was already well regarded. At the time it was known as the *Climat des Forges*, and it was added to slowly over the centuries to form the present vineyard. After the Revolution, Charles Dumaine, who was a partner of Nicolas-Joseph Marey, purchased the vineyard and the ownership thus passed to the Marey-Monge family, who sold it in 1932 to the Mommessin family. The Clos has had only three owners since its formation in 1141.

The vineyard was controlled during the Marey-Monge ownership by a number of tenant farmers, including Champy and Chauvenet. It is possible to find many négociant-bottled wines from the Clos before the Mommessin era, including Vandermeulen and Nicolas. Located between Bonnes-Mares and the Clos des Lambrays, the Clos de Tart originally included a small portion of Bonnes Mares and another small portion of village-level Morey, both of which were reclassified as Clos de Tart in 1956, according to Master of Wine and Burgundy expert Remington Norman. The Clos de Tart of today has also been augmented by a small portion (27 a 80 ca) of Bonnes-Mares.

Under current regulations, all of the grands crus of Morey are equal, although some connoiseurs believe that the finest terroir in Morey is the Clos de la Roche, located at the other end of Morey, on the border with Gevrey Chambertin. Lavalle has the Clos de la Roche as première cuvée, although he has the surface area as 4 ha 57 a 40 ha. This is almost equivalent to the 4 ha 56 a 93 ca of the modern lieu-dit of the same name. The modern appellation of Clos de la Roche has been greatly expanded, with the total now 16 ha 90 a 27 ca, including parts of the Monts Luisants (a view tacitly endorsed by the Comité d'Agriculture de Beaune in 1860).

Interestingly, Monts Luisants is one of the relatively few lieux-dits (Gaudichots is another example) to be classified in three categories under the current AOC system. The top portion is village level and the next band is premier cru. In the premier cru section there are a quantity of white grapes planted, including Chardonnay, Pinot Blanc, and Aligoté. Finally, the area the furthest down the slope has been classified as grand cru Clos de la Roche, along with the lieux-dits Mochamps, Genavrières, Froichots, Chaffots, Fremières, and Chabiots.

Monts Luisants is not mentioned at all in Lavalle. Since it is located at the top of the slope, could it be that it was not planted at that time? Nor does Mont Luisants appear in Morelot, who notes "...Clos de la Roche, and on the same line the Clos Saint-Denis, where the territory of Morey finishes." Actually, there is a significant portion of Monts Luisants north of where Clos de la Roche lies, and this is the area that is grand cru today; the parcels that lie upslope from there are premier cru and village. In Danguy et Aubertin, the ownership is attributed to MM. Bordet, Claude Gremeaux, Molin, Mongeard, Ponsot, and Valby-Bornot, while by the time of Camille Rodier the owners were the Amiot Léon heirs, and MM. Domino-Motot, E. Liébaut, Claude Marchand, the widows Marchand and Mongeard, and MM. Morot, Péley, J.-B. Petit, Ponsot, J.-H. Remy, Senequier, A. Sigaut, and Emile Valby. Genavrières (located directly upslope from the lieu-dit of Clos de la Roche) is also absent from Dr. Lavalle, although it was noted by the Comité d'Agriculture de Beaune, and it appeared in Danguy et Aubertin, where the owners were listed at M. Bordet, the widow Bornot-Sigaut and MM. Louis Chevillon, Péley, Ferdinand, and François Valby. Rodier has Genavrières as troisième cuvée, and notes the owners as MM. L. Fion, Jeanniard-Martin, E. Liébaut, the widow Marchand-Truchetet, and M. Emile Valby.

Lavalle is also unimpressed with the later additions to the current Clos de la Roche: he has Mochamps, Fremières, and Chabiots as deuxièmes cuvées, and Froichots and Le Bas de Chaffots (the part that surrounds the Clos Saint-Denis) as quatrièmes cuvées. He mentions neither the rest of Chaffots (the portion south of Monts Luisants) nor Genavrières, although being located just south of Monts Luisants, perhaps they took the name of this climat at the time. AOC regulations only promoted these parcels starting in 1971, and their remainder is still classified as premier cru, although wine writer Clive Coates, endorses the homogeneity of the terroir in Clos de la Roche.

To the south of the Clos de la Roche lies the Clos Saint-Denis. This is another vineyard that has been "assembled" over time, and one that has not always enjoyed the esteem of critics. Here, too, the origins of the vineyard are monastic, having been planted by the Collégiale de Saint-Denis de Vergy prior to the 13th century, and site of the chapel of the Château de Vergy, demolished in the 17th century. Morelot comments that the Clos Saint-Denis is not as fine as the Clos de Tart and the Clos de la Roche, and Lavalle was equally unimpressed – he has the vineyard as a deuxième cuvée. At least, this is the case for the original lieu-dit of the Clos Saint-Denis, 2 ha 14 a 20 ca. It was the Beaune classification of 1861 that first promoted this site to the highest level, and included in this classification are bits of the surrounding vineyards. Today's appellation is more than triple the original amount, including another bit of Chaffots (1 ha 33 a 92 ca), along with the lieux-dits Caloluère and Maison Brûlée. Some today would have this as the least interesting of the Morey grands crus, a contentious argument.

Like Clos Saint-Denis, Clos des Lambrays has never enjoyed the same esteem as Clos de la Roche or Clos de Tart, and many modern authors and connoisseurs seem to dismiss it. Lavalle places the vineyard (which Morelot and Jullien do not mention) into première cuvée, although it was smaller in his day (6 ha 99 a 20 ca) than it is in ours (8 ha 84 a 02 ca). Today we have 5 ha 71 a 87 ca of "Les Larrets or Clos des Lambrays", 1 ha 99 a 10 ca of Les Bouchots, and 1 ha 13 a 05 ca of Meix Rentier, the whole of which was promoted to grand cru status only in 1981. Of these modern additions, Lavalle has 1 ha 17 a 05 ca of Meix Rentier as troisième cuvée. The nucleus, however, was owned in the 14th century by the monks of Cîteaux, who were considered good judges of vineyard property, and thus the higher rating is perhaps justified. Fragmented at the Revolution into the ownership of 74 different owners, Clos des Lambrays was reconstituted in 1836 (after Jullien and Morelot) by the Joly family, négociants from Nuits Saint-Georges who established their firm in the early 18th century. From the Joly family it was sold in 1865 to Albert Rodier, proprietor of the Maison Henri de Bahèzre in Nuits and grandfather of Camille Rodier, who wrote the admirable work on Burgundy, *Le Vin de Bourgogne*, classified his family's vineyard as tête de cuvée, and established Confrérie des Chevaliers du Tastevin. M. Rodier sold the estate to the Cosson family in 1938, and as the couple aged, the quality began to decline. The quality of the terroir, however, was not in question at the time – it had simply not been declared grand cru at the establishment of the AOC system because the Cosson family did not request it. Significant investments were made to the vineyard from 1979 to 1995, under the ownership by the Saier family of Algeria and other investors, and under the supervision of Thierry Brouin. Clos des Lambrays was declared grand cru in 1981. Under the present direction of Günter and Ruth Freund, the wine is enjoying a renaissance and its prices remain quite reasonable. Here is the opinion of Dr. Morelot:

> Leaving these last vineyards, one enters the territory of Morey; here there is the Clos Blanc and Bonnes-Mares, presenting together an extent of thirteen or fourteen hectares (340 ouvrées), and whose wines are the equal of those of the climats of Chambolle. A bit further is the Clos de Tart, which unites the double merit of producing a wine both very abundant and delicious, which resembles Chambertin greatly. Advancing towards the north, one meets the Clos de la Roche, and on the same line the Clos Saint-Denis, where the territory of Morey finishes. The wine of the Clos de la Roche is equal to that of the Clos de Tart; but that which comes from the Clos Saint-Denis is not as fine as that of these first two districts, although it shares in the most distinguished characteristics. The good climats of Morey present a surface of around 30 ha (720 ouvrées); they are easy to work. Their length is considerable, since they extend from the extremity of the village limits of Chambolle to those of Gevrey, and they are about 250 – 300 meters wide. Below the good districts, one finds only common wines, and above, as the slope is very steep, the vines become more and more mediocre as one climbs.

The comments of Dr. Lavalle:

COMMUNE DE MOREY

Only part of this commune is consecrated to the production of fine wine. In the climats too low, as in the points too elevated, the winegrower only cultivates Gamay, which gives him fairly agreeable common wines.

The totality of the parts consecrated to the vine can be calculated at perhaps 160 ha, among which the part with noble vines occupies only 70 ha. In these last vines, the Pinot Noir alone is cultivated, to the exclusion of all other vines. All of the Pinot Blanc and Pinot Gris that have arisen due to mutation have been pulled up. No vines are specifically consecrated to the production of white grapes. [Not true in our day]

The soil at Morey is generally formed of a strong, fat earth that compacts easily and is similar to very malleable soils. The subsoil is formed either of marl and clay as in the upper part of the Clos de Tart, or of rocks or of sand.

The average yield of the good climats is approximately 22 hl/ha.

As for the neighboring villages, one remarks the fact that all of the vines giving great wines have existed since time immemorial, and have never been pulled up or renewed except through the practice of burying a shoot from a vine so that it roots and thus renews itself. In an *ouvrée*, one generally makes 15 to 20 pits in which one buries two vines to thus produce from four to six new plants.

The number of plants that exist per *journal* can be estimated at 10,000 to 15,000.

The climats planted to Pinot Noir are:

Tête de Cuvée[13]

Clos de Tart, 6 ha 87 a 50 ca, belonging to M. Ferdinand Marey

> Danguy et Aubertin note that the vineyard belongs to M. de Blic-Marey-Monge, but that the harvests belong to Maison Champy.
>
> Camille Rodier rounds the Clos de Tart up to 7 ha, and notes that it belonged at his writing to Mlle. Marey Monge. He has the Clos de Tart and the Clos des Lambrays both capitalized.

Première Cuvée

Bonnes-Mares, 1 ha 84 a 55 ca[14], belonging to MM. Molin, Lapertot, Vaisser, Milsand, Roy, etc. In the part of this climat that is situated in the territory of Morey, between the cross of Chambolle and the Clos de Tart, the quality of wines is all exceptional and can be placed on a par with the Clos de Tart for each owner who has enough to make a dedicated cuvée.

> Danguy et Aubertin: MM. de Blic-Marey-Monge, Bordet, Guichard-Potheret et fils, A. Poupon, Molin, Pouillevet.
>
> Rodier: M. Edouard Bélorgey.

Les Lambrays, 6 ha 99 a 20 ca, belonging to M. Joly. The observations that I have made concerning the climat of Bonnes-Mares apply completely to the climat of Lambrays.

> Danguy et Aubertin: note that "C. Loc." opinion of Lambrays was "première and deuxième cuvées"; at the time of his writing it was already a monopole of M. Albert Rodier, who purchased it from M. Joly in 1868. Camille Rodier notes that "his grandsons C. and A. Rodier of the Maison Henri de Bahèzre are the proprietors", without pointing out that Albert Rodier was his grandfather, while referring to himself here in the third person. It is also clear from the map provided in Rodier that he has already absorbed the lieu-dit of Bouchots into the Clos des Lambrays as no reference is found in his work, and Danguy et Aubertin note that it was a Rodier monopole. The careful reader will note that although today the lieu-dit today is "Les Larrets ou Clos des Lambrays" that there is also 1 ha 45 a 46 ca of Les Larrets upslope from the Clos des Lambrays, as well as a Larrey-Froid. These were also owned at the time by the Rodier family, as was the lieu-dit that separated them, called La Bidaude.

Clos de Laroche [sic], 4 ha 57 a 40 ca, belonging to MM. Marey and Bizot.

> Danguy et Aubertin: MM. de Blic-Marey-Monge, Molin, Ory, Parizot, Rol-

---

13 Each time that I do not indicate that the order of the climats reflects a classification, one must consider that all of the climats grouped together are equals.

14 The balance of the climat is under the territory of Chambolle.

land, Riembault.

<u>Rodier</u>: MM. de Blic, Merme-Morizot, Mlles. Orey and J.-H. Remy.

Rodier also classes the following climats in première cuvée: Clos Saint-Denis and Les Calouères and Maison Brûlée, which make up today's Clos Saint-Denis, along with a bit of Chaffots, which is shared with the Clos de la Roche, as well as Les Mochamps, Froichot, Les Fremières, and Chabiols, which form, with Les Genavrières, the present Clos de la Roche.

For the sake of completeness, one might note that he also classifies as première cuvée Les Faconnières, Les Millandes, Clos des Ormes, Les Chenevery, and Aux Chezeaux (although here he notes that the lower part of Aux Chezeaux is classed among the troisième cuvées), and Charmes (with the note that the lower part of Clos des Ormes is classed among the deuxième cuvées). All of these last are premier cru today, as are portions of Chaffots and Monts Luisants, as noted above.

Deuxième Cuvée

Clos Saint-Denis, 2 ha 14 a 20 ca, belonging to M. Ferdinand Marey

<u>Danguy et Aubertin</u>: MM. Blic-Marey-Monge, the widow Bornot-Sigaut, and M. A. Poupon.

<u>Rodier</u> notes that this parcel belonged at his writing to MM. de Blic.

Maison-Brulée, 1 ha 84 a 25 ca, belonging to M. Marey, Mme. Milsand, Mme. Riambourg, MM. Roy and Pouillevey.

<u>Danguy et Aubertin</u>: MM. Boiget, August Maignot, Pouillevet, A. Poupon.

<u>Rodier</u>: MM. Ed. Bélorgey, Domino-Motot, the widow Victor Jonan, MM. Aug. Maignot, François Seguin.

Chabiots, 2 ha 14 a 75 ca, belonging to Mme. Rodier, MM. Roy and Armand Marey.

<u>Danguy et Aubertin</u>: MM. August Maignot, François Maignot, Marion, Milsand, Valby-Bornot, François Valby.

<u>Rodier</u>: the Amiot Léon heirs and MM. Clerget-Mignardot, Corbet, Eugène Liébaut, Alexis Maignot, Auguste Maignot, the widow Marchand-Truchetet, Emile Valby.

Fremières, 2 ha 36 a, belonging to Mme. Jondot and to M. Armand Marey.

<u>Danguy et Aubertin</u>: MM. Baud, Milsand, Parizot-Caillier, A. Poupon, Senequier, Valby-Bornot

<u>Rodier</u>: the widow Blanc-Milsaud and MM. Devante, Merme-Morizot, Alfred Parisot, Senequier

Mochants, 2 ha 51 a 20 ca, belonging to MM. Rossigneux, Lapertot, Jacotier, Ruby.

<u>Danguy et Aubertin</u>: MM. François Bordet, Alfred Paris, Parisot-Caillier, Pouillevet.

<u>Rodier</u> (who uses the modern spelling *Mochamps*): the widow Blanc-Milsand and MM. Frédéric Groffier, Guigue, Alexis Maignot, Alfred Parisot.

Faconnières, 1 ha 73 a 50 ca, belonging to MM. Armand Marey and Bizot.

Troisième Cuvée

Meix-Rentier, 1 ha 17 a 5 ca, belonging to MM. Joly, Jacotier, Molin, Milsand.

<u>Danguy et Aubertin</u>: MM. François Maignot, Molin, Joseph Morot, Milsand, Rodier

<u>Rodier</u>: the widow Blanc-Milsand and MM. Maignot, Morot, C. and A. Rodier, Senequier.

Clos Bolet, 86 a 90 ca, belonging to M. Alotte.

Godelles, 60 a 30 ca, belonging to M. Molin.

Les Crais, 3 ha 7 a 25 ca, belonging to MM. Lapertot, Vaissier, Roy, Mme. Rodin.

Millandes, 4 ha 29 a 35 ca, belonging to MM. Armand Marey, Roy Gournot.

Calouères, 1 ha 31 a 65 ca, belonging to M. Molin.

<u>Danguy et Aubertin</u>: MM. Latour-Boudrot, Molin, Mouillevet

<u>Rodier</u>: MM. E. Liébut, Merme-Morizot and Mme. Mongeard

La Bussière, 3 ha 21 a 40 ca, belonging to M. Bizot.

La Ruotte, 2 ha 47 a 70 ca, belonging to MM. Molin and de Montille.

Chenevery, 3 ha 22 a 90 ca, belonging to M. Joly.

Quatrième Cuvée

Les Larrays	Les Sorbets	Bas-Chenevary
Bouchots	Clos Sorbet	Clos Solin
Bas de Côte-Rôtie	Blanchard	Très-Girard
Le Bas de Chaffots	Charrières	Sionnières
Froichots	Clos des Ormes	Les Pourroux
Ruchots	Aux Chezeaux	

Lavalle refers only to Le Bas de Chaffots, although today the lieu-dit is simply called Chaffots, and it is divided between 2 ha 61 a 86 ca of premier cru,

7 a that are included in Clos de la Roche, and 1 ha 33 a 92 ca that are included in Clos Saint-Denis. Danguy et Aubertin allow either name, and cite as owners the widow Morizot, MM. Ponsot, Truchetet-Berthaut, and Ferdinand Valby. Rodier uses the modern spelling and has the ownership as MM. Domino Motot, Jacotier-Jacquot, Jeanniard-Martin, Lignier, the widow Marchand-Truchetet, MM. Merme-Morizot, Alphonse Noirot, Richard, Emile Sequin, Emile Valby.

Froichot is part of Clos de la Roche; Danguy et Aubertin have the owners as MM. François Bordet, Claude Gremeaux, Latour, François Marchand, Marion, Joseph Sigaut; Camille Rodier has MM. Devante, Jacquot-Bouillot, and A. Sigaut.

Lavalle continues:

> Morey has a vineyard that is very productive and excellent at the same time. Its premières cuvees are sold at the same prices as those of the best climats. Its Clos de Tart, its Bonnes-Mares, and its Lambrays approach the greatest wines and recall Chambertin.
>
> By its qualities, it is near to the wines of Gevrey. Its wines have body, color, and bouquet. One might say that they lack nothing, even though some reproach them for not having totally the same finesse and the extreme purity of the wines of Vosne.
>
> The wines of Morey in good years, cared for with intelligence in good cellars, will last easily twenty years. For several special years such as 1846, these wines can attain the age of 30 years or more.
>
> The Clos de Tart originated with a sale made in 1141 to the nuns of Notre-Dame-de-Tart by the Prior and the monks of the Maison-Dieu[49] de Brochon, who ceded all of the vines that they possessed in Morey, as well as the house and the winery used to exploit these vines. Pope Lucius III confirmed this acquisition is his bill confirming the privileges of the monastery in 1184.
>
> The property grew in 1240 through a donation made by the Gauthier family and the widow Fauconnier, as well as by acquisitions and exchanges made in the following years.
>
> Marie, Lady of Mont-Saint-Jean and Lady of Morey, freed them from the necessity of respecting the ban de vendanges[50] after the death of her husband in 1251.
>
> This property was sold during the Revolution as property of the nation, at the price of 68,200 livres, not including the expenses, to M. Charles Dumaguer of Nuits, from whom it passed to the Marey family.

Morey is a place to find interesting and profound wines. Domaine Dujac and Domaine Ponsot are the leading lights, along with the two monopole (or nearly so) producers, the Clos de Tart and the Domaine des Lambrays. Several of the members of the extended Lignier family are also making wonderful wines. Among the more intriguing values in the commune, perhaps, are the white wines whose production is authorized in all of the village and premier cru appellations. The premier cru bottlings by Ponsot (styled Clos des Monts Luisants) and Dujac are superb, and several proprietors also make a village level wine. Among the red wines, some of the best value grands crus are here. One example is the Clos de la Roche from Rousseau. A step below his top Gevrey wines, perhaps, but absolutely top notch all the same and reasonably priced. The Clos de Tart is also very good value, as is the Clos des Lambrays from the Domaine des Lambrays. Anyone who wants the best of Morey, however, must not fail to taste the Clos de la Roche vieilles vignes from Ponsot and the Clos de la Roche from Dujac.

CHAMBOLLE

In Chambolle we find that our three authorities disagree on the classification of wines from this region. Jullien includes both Musigny and Bonne Mares in a second category after the first seven of his crus, stating that they were not as well-known and did not sell for the same amount as the top group including Romanée-Conti, Chambertin, Richebourg, Clos de Vougeot, etc. Morelot includes Bonnes Mares with Morey; Lavalle does not have Bonnes Mares as a Tête de Cuvée at all. He notes that Les Musigny and Les Petits Musigny are both of this category, although he doubtless would not approve of the modern inclusion of 76 a 60 ca of Combe d'Orveau, as he notes that this vineyard is "almost a première cuvee."

It is interesting that Lavalle mentions the inclusion of a significant proportion of white grapes in Musigny, although he does not mention a cuvée of white wine being produced here. For his part, Morelot mentions a climat called *Les Nones* that he groups with Les Cras, Les Fuées, Les Véroilles, and Bonnes-Mares north of the village and upslope of the road, which neither occurs in Lavalle nor noted today. Other than these very small details, it appears that the wines of Chambolle today are little changed from their former composition. Here are the comments of Dr. Morelot:

> At the village of Chambolle the slope presents a sort of violent rupture in the bedrock, forming a fairly great interval between the two slopes. This little valley is named the Combe d'Orveau; it runs towards the west and leads to the villages of the arrière-côte. From the Combe d'Orveau, the slope forms only a single continuous mass that runs up to Gevrey where it suddenly ends. Here one finds a craggy gorge that separates the territory of this last village from that of Brochon. This narrow valley leads to the hillside villages farther to the west.
>
> The village of Chambolle is centered on this part of the slope where the exposition is superb. One sees only a portion, the balance occupying the valley of which I have just spoken; a bit further on, about a quarter league is Morey, in a charming position, and at a good half league from there, the magnificent village of Gevrey, with its beautiful homes, peopled with thirteen hundred souls. The main road from Beaune to Dijon passes at the foot of this slope.
>
> The rock that forms the slope is a limestone of great purity; it is like that of the chain of Nuits, a white marble veined with red. The exterior rock flakes away in sheets called *lavereins*, and one notes a phenomenon seen at other parts of the slope as well: it fuses together and decomposes with exposition to the air to finally form the precious soil that concerns us. One must add here another cause; the upper part of this slope encloses a large number of nonproductive marly deposits;

but when these have been long exposed to the air, they improve in quality; the rains wash them towards the lower slopes, and this alluvial matter tends to continually improve the excellent soils that lay below.

At the western edge of the Clos de Vougeot and before entering Chambolle, one finds Les Musigny, Les Amoureuses, Les Hauts-Douais, vineyards of about 13 ha (325 ouvrées), that furnish a wine that has much in common with that of the Romanées. Further down-slope are the climats of Charmes, Sordes, Babillers, that give very good wines although a bit inferior to those of Musigny.

Following the road, from the height of the village and continuing always to the north, one finds on the left Les Cras, Les Friéez [Les Fuées], Les Nones [not noted in Lavalle, or today], Les Varoilles [Véroilles], Bonnes-Mares, all distinguished climats, with an extent of about 25 ha (600 ouvrées), which produce a wine of great finesse and that differs little from the climats cited above. To the right, that is to say, moving down toward the plain, are the vineyards named Clos de l'Orme, Gruanchets [Gruenchers], Noirots, Beaux Bruns, Bandes [Baudes?], etc. The wines of these districts, although good, do not have characteristics as distinguished as those of the more elevated vineyards.

Dr. Lavalle's thoughts raise Musigny's position in the market since the time that Jullien wrote about these wines forty years earlier:

COMMUNE DE CHAMBOLLE

In the opinion of many, this village produces the most delicate wines of the Côte de Nuits. The vineyard includes approximately 155 ha, of which 75 ha are completely consecrated to the production of fine wines.

The soil of this vineyard is completely different from that of the village of Morey. The earth here is light, and will make only with great difficulty a paste when mixed with water. Clay in the subsoil is much rarer here. In the Musigny vineyard, it is found only in the corner that touches the climat of *Agillières*. In the rest of the climat, the subsoil is rock riddled with vertical crevices which the roots of the vine use to descend more than ten meters, as one can see at the base of the climat of *Amoureuses*.

As in other villages we have examined, here growers destroy as much as possible the Pinot Blanc and Gris in order to conserve only the Noir. We must make an exception for Musigny, where Pinot Blanc exists in the proportion of one twentieth and for Combe d'Orveau and Petit Musigny, where the proportion increases to one tenth.

One can consider the road from Dijon to Chalon as being the lower limit of the good crus. Nevertheless, the climats called *Aux Fosses* and *Creux-Prieur*, situated to the east of this route, are in large part planted to Pinot and give wines that are not without value.

We offer the same observations for the preceding villages as regards the age and the renewing of the grands crus.

In this village, the vine produces much less than in Morey and Vougeot. *Les Musigny* yields hardly more than five casks per hectare. The other good climats attain with difficulty seven or eight.

The principal climats in Chambolle are:

Tête de Cuvée

Les Musigny, 5 ha 89 a 50 ca, belonging to MM. de Montille, Ferdinand Marey, Piffond, Moyne, Viénot, Coste, Groffier, de Rothallier, Marguerite, de Reulle, Mallebranche, Mlle. Leguay.

> Danguy et Aubertin: MM. Jules Belin, Alberic Bichot, Léonce Bocquet, Guichard-Potheret et fils, Paul Jorrot, Alexandre Malbranche, Frédéric Mugnier, Nié frères, Noché d'Aulnay, Pierre Ponnelle, Rasse, Thomas Bassot of the house Thomas Bassot et fils in Gevrey-Chambertin, de Vogüé.
>
> Rodier: MM. Jorrot, E. Mugnier, Nicolas-Bordet, Louis Nié, Pierre Ponnelle, Comte de Vogüé.
>
> Camille Rodier has Les Musigny, Les Petits Musigny, and Les Bonnes Mares distinguished with capital letters.

Les Petits-Musigny, 4 ha 15 a 55 ca, belonging to MM. Ferdinand Marey, Coste, Groffier, Mlle. Leroy, Mme. Moyne.

> Danguy et Aubertin: MM. Alberic Bichot, Boursot-Valot, de Vogüé.
>
> Rodier: Dr. Boursot, E. Mugnier, Comte de Vogüé.

Première Cuvée

Les Bonnes-Mares, 13 ha 70 a 45 ca, belonging to MM. Ferdinand Marey, Piffond, de Montille, Roy, Groffier, Coste, Vaisser, Mercier, Marion, Mlle. Leguay, Mme. Moyne.

> Danguy et Aubertin: MM. Bichot, Joseph Jorrot, Paul Jorrot, Guichard-Potheret et fils, Frédéric Mugnier, Mignotte-Picard et Cie., Pierre Ponnelle, A. Poupon, Pujo, Rasse, de Vogüé.
>
> Rodier: MM. Edouard Bélorgey, Paul Boudrot, Boursot-Chanson, Confuron-Bornot, E. Mugnier, Outhier, H. Quanquin, J. Tabouret, R. Drouhot, J. Galland, F. Grivelet-Modot, P. Jacquot Nicolas Trapet, Valby, Comte de Vogüé.

Les Varoilles, 5 ha 29 a 5 ca, belonging to MM. de Vogüé, Marey, Piffond, de Rothallier, Joseph Jorot, Mme. Moyne.

Les Fuées, 4 ha 66 a 30 ca, belonging to MM. Groffier, de Vogüé, Marey, de Reulle, de Rothallier, de Montille.

Les Cras, 7 ha 53 a 5 ca, belonging to the same owners, to M. Piffond, and to M. Albert Demontry.

Les Amoureuses, 5 ha 25 a 50 ca, belonging to MM. Marey, Vaissier, Faivre-Guillemot.

Deuxième Cuvée

La Combe d'Orveaux, 5 ha 9 a 35 ca, belonging to Mlle. Leguay, MM. Viénot, Gournot, Coste. This is almost a première cuvée.

Les Charmes, 6 ha 64 a 10 ca, belonging to MM. Berthaut, Fourrier, Midon.

Condemènes, 5 ha 11 a 90 ca, belonging to the same proprietors.

Hauts-Douais, 1 ha 76 a 70 ca, belonging to M. Viénot.

Clos de l'Orme, 1 ha 76 a 95 ca.

Troisième Cuvée

Les Plantes	Les Sentiers	Fisselottes [sic]
Le Haut-des-Combottes	Baudes	Derrière-la-Grange
Aux Crais	Groseilles	Fouchères
Beaux-Bruns	Eschezeaux	Derrière-le-Four
Fremières	Châtelots	

All of these climats are little different from those that we have classed in deuxième cuvée and could be included in this category.

The other climats, while inferior to the preceding ones, produce nevertheless wines remarkable for their finesse and can be counted among the grands ordinaires.

The wines of Chambolle are highly esteemed by our best gourmets. Les Musigny merits to be compared with our greatest wines, and the market will pay the same price.

The Domaine Comte Georges de Vogüé, Domaine Jacques-Frédéric Mugnier and the Domaine Georges Roumier and are the undisputed leaders of Chambolle. Each of them makes a full range of wines, yet it tends to be that the best values are the Bonnes Mares and the absolute greatest bottles are from Musigny. De Vogüé has the largest holding of Musigny by far, and the wines are incredibly stylish. By contrast, Roumier produces a minute amount of Musigny that sells for an astronomical price, while Mugnier's wines strike a balance between the two. For those with less extravagant purses, the premiers crus Les Fuées from Mugnier or the Feusselottes from Mugneret-Gibourg can be particularly rewarding.

VOUGEOT

The Clos de Vougeot is a very large grand cru – 50 ha 96 a 54 ca – and any vineyard this size produces wines that vary in quality, price, and reputation, and over the course of time, the reputation of the Clos de Vougeot has varied. In the eyes of our authors it was considered among the very greatest of all the climats in Burgundy, while today it is held in much less esteem. A brief look at the vineyard and the wines will tell us why.

The comments of Courtépée are curiously brief. He comments in his note of Gilly-lès-Cîteaux that "the Clos de Vougeot [a dependency of the monastery headquartered in Gilly] is renowned for the quality of its wines. Jullien elaborated with a bit more dtail, to noting that "The products of different parts of the Clos produce wines of varying quality; the upper parts give a wine that is very fine and delicate; the lower parts, particularly the portions along the main road, give inferior wine." Morelot also commented on this division, referring to them as three separate wines and describing in detail a sort of selection process of the type now common in Bordeaux vineyards to ensure the consistency of the *grand vin*. Lavalle does not comment or offer explanations on the variables of Clos de Vougeot wines, but he notes at the beginning of his Clos de Vougeot chapter that, "Our classification, then, will be completely easy." For the modern reader, it is essential to recall that the entire Clos de Vougeot was, like Romanée-Conti, a monopole—owned by a single owner—until 1889. With the vineyard united, it was much easier to produce a sublime wine through the processes of selection and blending. No sole proprietor in the modern era has this ability, and thus for us it is essential to understand the characteristics of the different portions of the vineyard.

Lavalle classified the entire vineyard as hors ligne, intimating that its rightful place is just after that of Romanée-Conti in the Burgundy firmament. He also describes a great number of climats that were subsumed into the Clos that no longer exist, and points out that there were a few that were still recognized in his day, including "Petit and Grand-Maupertuis, Maret-Haut and Bas, Plante-l'Abbé, Garenne, Musigny-Chioures, Dix-Journaux, Quatorze-Journaux (two obviously modern names), Montiottes-Hautes and Basses, Baudes-Saint-Martin, north and south."

These lieux-dits are little-known today and do not form part of the official classification of the vineyard: the BIVB describes the appellation as having only one lieu dit called Clos de Vougeot. These older names, however, still exist with a few spelling differences that vary from producer to producer. Some producers declare them on the label; think of the Grand Maupertuis of Anne Gros or the Musigni of Gros Frère et Sœur. The map produced by the Confrerie des Chevaliers du Tastevin shows these older lieux-dits quite clearly. In the northwest corner of the Clos there is the lieu-dit Musigni, with the lieu-dit Garenne just to the south, surrounding the Château, followed by the Plant Chamel and Plant l'Abbé to the south, all still above the road that leads to the château itself. Just south of this road, there are Montiottes Hautes along the north wall, Chioures, Quartier de Marei Haut, Grand Maupertuis and Petit Maupertuis, traveling from north to south. Downslope from Montiottes Haut is the much larger Montiottes Bas, a vineyard that continues to the main route from Beaune to Dijon; downslope from Chioures lies Dix Journaux; Marei Bas is below Marei Haut, and below Marei Bas is Baudes St.-Martin, descending to the road; below the two Maupertuis are Baudes Hautes and Baudes Basses, located where their names suggest.

The documents of the INAO attached to the decree for Clos de Vougeot divide the vineyard into three sections geographically. The lowest part of the vineyard is based on Bresse marls (i.e. fairly heavy clay-based soil with good calcium content), the top of the vineyard is a slab of Jurassic limestone, and the midslope is a fractured, complex blend of the two. The top of the vineyard on Jurassic limestone is further divided, with the upper portions having thin, well-drained soils (i.e. conducive to top quality viticulture), while the lower portions are deep, lacking in calcium content, and poorly drained in the eastern part (i.e., near the road).

The lieux-dits in the top one-third of the slope are considered to produce the best wines. These include Musigni, Garenne, Plante Chamel, and Plante l'Abbé (all of which are upslope of the road leading to the château), along with the parcels just downslope, including Montiottes Hautes, Chioures, Marei Haut, Grand Maupertuis, Petit Maupertuis and Baudes Hautes. This corresponds to most of the vines upslope from the château of Château de la Tour, today known as Maison François Labet, a négociant producing very good Clos de Vougeot and bottling everything from Corsican vin de pays to Burgundian Grands Crus.

Connoisseurs include the lieu-dit Dix Journaux behind this château along with the upper parts of Baudes Basses and Baudes Saint-Martin in a second category, with the consensus being that the vines along the D974 and those in the northeast corner of the clos are the least promising, including those portions known as Marei Bas, Montiottes Basses, Quatorze Journaux, the lower part of Baudes Basses and the lower part of Baudes Saint-Martin. The three categories are sometimes referred to as the Pope's portion, the King's portion, and the monk's portion (i.e. of top quality, medium quality and lesser quality). This is an expansion of the comments of Morelot below as he describes the division of the production into three separate cuvées, although opinion among the growers today dispute the rigid division of the vineyard along these lines and suggest that a more nuanced approach is appropriate.

Dr. Morelot wrote:

> Leaving the territory of Vosne one meets with the celebrated clos known under the name of the Clos du Vougeot[15]. It contains 47 ha (1150 ouvrées). Its exposition is east-south-east, and its incline offers great differences. The upper part, which gives the best wine, has a slope of ten to twelve degrees. The extent of this clos is too large to be able to believe that the products have everywhere the same qualities and the same value. There are certainly marked differences, but they disappear through the blending of grapes which is done at the moment of the harvest, and by the care given to the production of the wine, which has, with La Romanée, Le Chambertin, and several others, the first rank among the wines of the Côte d'Or and perhaps all France.
>
> In former times, the Clos de Vougeot belonged to the monks of Cîteaux, who made three separate cuvées. That which came from the upper part was not sold; it was so exquisite that it was reserved by the Abbey to be offered to kings and queens and princes and to different ministers of Catholic nations. That of the mid part was almost equal in quality to the first, and thus it was sold for a very dear price. Finally the third cuvée was made with the grapes of the lower part; although it was not as valuable as the first two, it was however very good and sold well. The wine was made in the presses that are placed at the top of the clos and to the north. There it was racked, as it was produced, through tubes grafted together with the greatest care and fed into the cellars of the monastery about a league away. It was matured with the greatest precaution, and according to the methods that had been learned through long experience and transmitted from cellarmaster to cellarmaster. The wine of the Clos de Vougeot, according to former gourmets, was worth more than it is today, even though it is excellent, because of the minute attention paid to its fabrication."

Dr. Lavalle commented:

COMMUNE DE VOUGEOT

Outside of the famous Clos that has carried its name so far, Vougeot offers a vineyard of only extremely secondary importance. The few climats planted in Pinot that one finds have only an area of 14 or 15 ha, and among the wines harvested here, none merit, at least today, to be placed among the first rank. Our classification, then, will be completely easy; we will have;

Hors Ligne[51]

Le Clos Vougeot, 50 ha 85 a 45 ca, belonging to M. Ouvrard.

> Danguy et Aubertin: A. and L. Beaudet frères (Beaune), Léonce Bocquet (Savigny), Champy (Beaune), Dr. Boursot (Nuits), MM. Duvergey-Taboureau (Meursault), Guichard-Potheret et fils (Chalon-sur-Saône), Labouré-Gontard (Nuits), Comte Liger-Belair (Nuits), S. Lhote fils

---

15 The village of Vougeot derives its name from a very abundant fountain that takes its source in the territory of Chambolle, a bit above the Clos, and which takes the name of Vouge. This little river turns a great number of mills, passes Cîteaux, and empties into the Saône at Esbarres.

(Dijon), Moine (Beaune), Nié frères (Chassagne-Montrachet), Charles Polack (Dijon), Rebourseau-Philippon (Gevrey-Chambertin), Rouvière fils (Dijon), Jules Senard (Beaune, Aloxe-Corton).

Rodier: MM. Beaudet Frères, Dr. Boursot, E. Camuzet, Cerf, Champy Père et Cie., Confuron, Sylvain Cordier, Victor Cordier, Dufouleur Rrères, Duvergey-Taboureau, Engel, G. Faiveley, Fournier, Fribourg, Grivault-Polin, Grivelet-Cusset, F. Grivelet-Modot, J. Gros-Renaudot, Guichard Potheret, l'Héritier-Guyot, Hubert Labouré, Symphorien Lhote, Liger-Belair, Lochardet, the Martini widow, Simon Moine, Moingeon Frères, Mongeard, Mugeret, Nié-Vantey, C. Noëllat, Paufigue, H. Peloux, J. Polack, P. Quanquin, Rebourseau Frèéres, Ch. Schulz, Jules Senard

Deuxième Cuvée

La Perrière, 1 ha planted in Pinot Blanc, belonging to M. Ouvrard.

La Vigne Blanche, 1 ha 87 a 95 ca, also in Pinot Blanc, belonging to M. Ouvrard.

Les Petits-Vougeots, 7 ha 60 a 85 ca, belonging to MM. Sauvain, Porcherot, the younger Lourdereaux, etc.

Les Cras, 4 ha 60 a 95 ca, belonging to MM. Grangier, Groffier-Nortet and others.

As we see there are no première cuvée wines harvested today outside of the Clos. The perfectly exposed climat of La Perrière promises to give excellent wines, but it will only be in a few years, since this parcel has been replanted.

The white wines produced by Vigne Blanche have qualities that merit comparison with the good wines of Meursault, without placing them completely at the same level as the premières cuvées of this commune.

The red wines produced in the climats of Cras and Petits-Vougeots show purity of fruit and lack neither warmth nor bouquet, but they can only be considered as grands ordinaires.

All of our attention in this commune, then, must be concentrated on the celebrated climat known under the name of Clos de Vougeot; we will try to give, following unpublished documents, a history as complete as merited by the immense renown of this vineyard.

At the beginning of the 12th century, this precious territory called Clos de Vougeot was largely part scrub land situated at the border of the villages of Vosne, Flagey, and of Chambolle. Priests, knights attached to the house of Vergy, feudal overlords and other persons of a humbler condition possessed here and there some unplanted land and some vines planted in the shade of the forest that crowned the summit of the slope, and these vines, this scrub land, had such little value that the Grand Priory of St.-Vivant, who, according to all appearances, had received this land in its endowment and of which possession had just received a fresh confirmation from Duke Hugues II in 1131, had abandoned it and retained only the right to receive the tithe.

The renown of the holiness of the first monks of Cîteaux, the austerity of their rule, and above all their poverty, contrasted so clearly with the opulence of the other abbeys and excited in their favor the generosity that one saw demonstrated by all classes of society; and when, after long hesitations, the Cistercians wanted to indulge in the culture of the vine, the lords of the slope struggled with those of the plain for the favor of helping the new monastery grow their vineyard holdings.

Thus, as concerns Vougeot, around 1110, Hugues called the White, knight of Vergy, with the accord of his wine, of his sons and of his relatives, among which was included Hugues, the mayor of Gilly, gave a parcel of vines "near Vaonam", Liébaut, from Magny-les-Villiers, added to it the contiguous parcel; Walo Gile, knight of Vergy, ceded the terrain upon which he would later build the cellar; Eudes-le-Vert, Eudes-le-Gras and their family included also the field of Gengulphe, situated at the base of the former. These donations were ratified by the lords of Marigny and Arnout Cornut, who owned the surrounding property. Around the same time, Pierre Gros, canon of Saint-Denis de Vergy, contributed his field of Musigné, and from this moment the donations came one after another and formed the nucleus that permitted the abbey of Cîteaux to create at Vougeot, the point of the vineyard slope closest to the monastery a winemaking establishment along the lines of the barns that occupied its clearings. First the cellar was built, with the wine presses and the other buildings indispensable to the work of the domaine. The Duke of Burgundy Eudes II, on the point of dying in 1162, confirmed to Cîteaux the donations made by his predecessor and assigned to them the feudal rights for his vines in Beaune and Flagey. Two years later, Pope Alexandre III took under his protection the property of the abbey, including at least in name the cellar of Vougeot.

Assured by the Pope and the Duke of Burgundy, the monks of Cîteaux still had to fear the petty harassment that the monks of Saint-Vivant, destroyers of these villages, could inflict. In order to avoid all debate for the future, a treaty took place between the two monasteries. Here is the litreal translation:

"Let it be known to every son of the church that Etienne, prior (of Saint-Vivant) of Vergy and his chapter of monks have permitted and conceded to the monks of Cîteaux all that these monks had and were able to acquire in lands cultivated or uncultivated, from the public road from Beaune to Dijon following along the rue Morlent which continues to the summit of the Montagne de Beaumont, and from that road to the stream of the Vouge, under the condition of paying annually to the monks of Vergy for the tithe of ten journaux the sum of four sols. The vines that are situated in the above-designated limits that the monks of Cîteaux might acquire will be charged at the same rate that they had paid before. Excepted, however, is the parcel des Boetes, the tariff of which vine the monks of Cîteaux will pay one time only the sum of 17 sols. The two journaux of vines that the monks of Cîteaux possess outside of these limits will pay the same fees as those contained within the same limits. It is still stipulated that if these monks want to acquire beyond these limits from the lands of the monks of Vergy and without the consent of the Prior, there will be no resultant advantage for the monks, who will pay the same charges as the former possessors. The witnesses to this charter are: Etienne, prior; Bernard, Sichard, Bliard, Haimon, Addon; Pierre Walon, chaplain; Henri de Chenôve, Master Gauthier, Barthélemi de Noiron, Henri Maire and Bonami, his son; Nicolas Hernoux, the cook; Girard, the baker; Menu, the dean, Thierry, mayor of Vosne, and Eudes, his uncle; Pierre Milet, prevost of Vergy, and Bernard, his son; Pierre de Magny; Adhémar, Prior of Juilly, and Guillaume de Juilly, Wiric de Vergy and Hugues, his brother; Pierre, dean; Vilain, Signare; Garin, under-prior of Vergy; Richard, under-sexton; Aganon, of Beaune; Geoffroy, Pierre, Monks; Ernou, dean; Robert, monk of Cîteaux."

The Cistercians wasted no time in becoming the immutable owners of the space described above. Long years would pass before this was to be accomplished, and the abbey's cartographers testify that if in principal the liberality of pious souls laid the bases of the Clos de Vougeot, the monks would pay a high price for the right to be considered the only masters of the domaine.[16]

The limits of the enclosure were: to the south, the rue Morlent, to the east the Route de Beaune, to the west the road between Vosne and Chambolle, limits that have not varied; to the north, the monks did not surpass the road that led to the quarries where the stone for the construction of the Abbey of Cîteaux, the Château de Gilly and the buildings was found. This part of the vineyard is what one calls Vigne-Blanche, Petits Vougeots, La Perrière, with a portion of Cras or Crais, which form a subsidiary with Aux Orveaux and Aux Echeseaux on the other side of the Clos.

With the fragmented nature that one could already see long before this epoch in the vineyards of the Côte d'Or, it will be understood that many climats were subsumed into this mass, which is no less than 150 journaux (50 ha). Thus, beyond the names which we have signaled above, one finds in the 14th Century: Les Echonay, Le Quartier-d'Escoiles, Le Porchier, Pertuis-au-Cugne, Musigny-Melot, Devant-la-Maison, A la Porte Saint-Martin, Le Conroy des Echeseaux, La Combotte, Le Quartier de Maire-au-Musigny, Les Echeseaux, Le Buchilier, Aux Côtes, Le Quartier du Tites, Au Chatrel. These climats were absorbed by the following, which one still distinguishes today: Petit and Grand-Maupertuis, Maret-Haut and Bas, Plante-l'Abbé, Garenne, Musigny-Chioures, Dix-Journaux, Quatorze-Journaux (two obviously modern names), Montiottes-Hautes and Basses, Baudes Saint-Martin, north and south.

Situated too distant from Cîteaux to be able, as at the vineyard of Clairvaux, to be cultivated directly by monks who had taken vows, the Clos du Vougeot was confided to lay brothers, whose chief took the title of magister cellarii (cellarmaster), and who were joined growers from the surrounding villages.

The nearly total destruction of the ledger books of Cîteaux deprives us of precious information concerning the processes of the grape growing techniques that these monks, so advanced in this science, employed in the Clos de Vougeot. Nonetheless, if one compares the accounts of 1367, 1368, 1382, 1386 and 1387, the only years

---

16 In 1227 Geoffroy Vidard, of Chambolle, sold a parcel of vine in the Grand Clos de Cîteaux for the sum of 7 Dijon livres 3 sols. The same sold an ouvrée in the same place for 72 Dijon francs. In 1251, André Tropians, of Gilly, sold a parcel of vines in the Grand Clos de Vooget for the sum of 7 livres. The last acquisition of Cîteaux is in 1336.

that remain, with the accounts of the same epoch furnished either by the chapter of Notre-Dame de Beaune or by the viscounts of the ducal estates of Beaune and Chenôve – that is to say for the vines situated at the two extremities of the Côte d'Or, one notices techniques absolutely identical, with this difference, that these latter accomplished all of the work of the vine with the same growers, whereas in the Clos there was a division of labor that had been assigned to the lay brothers and which included all of the work, except the first two tasks, given by designated laborers known as those who burrow (fodiatores or fouisseurs) and those who hoe (picadors or piocheurs).

However, by the 14th Century the number of lay brothers had become insufficient due to the decadence of the monastic orders, and more experienced growers from Gilly and from Vougeot were substituted, and these workers were each paid, as of 1387, from four to six francs yearly.

Later when the system of sharecropping, already in place in the 14th Century, became widespread in the Côte d'Or, the abbey of Cîteaux had to conform to the general rule, with this difference: they kept the entire harvest and paid the growers their half in money calculated on the declared value of the wines of Nuits, a system that continued until the Revolution.

The abbot of Cîteaux built a fort in 1367 at Gilly to serve as a refuge in time of war, and the Clos de Vougeot, which had hitherto been independent, became a dependency of this fort and the *clestrel* or governor of the fort absorbed the post of cellarmaster. From this time and until the 17th Century, only the wine of the new harvest was kept at Vougeot, and the rest were taken and stored in the cellars of the new château, shows strong walls offered a shelter more certain than the house at the Clos, which at the time of the harvest, was guarded only by the cellarmaster and his servant, whose wages were, in 1386, one franc yearly.

The building erected on the higher part of the Clos, next to the perimeter wall that enclosed the property to the north, consisted of a modest habitation for the lay brothers, with a small chapel, the hall with the wine press, and the large cellar. As with all of the dependencies of the Cîteaux, it was a place of independence and immunity, in the seat of which all secular justice had expired. The vines inside and outside of the walls were free of feudal obligations; only, the governor of Gilly was obliged, on the Sunday after the feast of Saint Mary Magdalene, to present his vine workers to the ducal provost of Vosne, who receives their vow, judges the sins that they confess, and to never neglect, with his officers, to attend the dinner that was held on this occasion by the abbey in the cellar at Vougeot.

In 1551, Dom Jean Loisier, abbot of Cîteaux profoundly modified the former arrangement of the cellar. He demolished a part of it and subsumed the balance in the unfinished château that remains today. It is a severe edifice, composed of two main buildings at right angles, whose principal façade looks north. The entrance, facing the same way and flanked by two large square pavilions, does not lack a certain character. A delicious ornamentation in the purest Renaissance style, particularly noticeable on the doors, runs the length of the interior facades and contrasts with the antique façade of the cellar, the storage and the winery, disposed without harmony around an approximately square courtyard.

As M. Leclère said to the Congress of Winegrowers in 1844, "Only profane and vulgar tourists are able to transverse Burgundy and its beautiful capital without a pious pilgrimage to the admirable slope whose products have contributed more than one can imagine to the birth to the sympathies that France inspires in all of the peoples of the world. It is said that the Cistercians of Bernard of Clairvaux did not have the honor of creating the vineyard of Vougeot. They had only the merit of having conserved and improved it, and to have founded the traditions that have survived them. Commercial demands did not dominate these proudly independent men, and the last of them, the last of the cellarmaster fathers, could say of a young conqueror of Italy, returning from the siege of Marengo, "If he wants forty-year-old Vougeot and comes to drink here, I will not sell him any!"

A visit to the Clos is not only of interest for the intelligent winegrower; the artist can still find this place in spite of several degradations, in the state which the pious son of Saint Bernard left it. The bulk of the buildings are of a very simple construction, but its look is monumental. The vast doors are decorated with a light and tasteful decoration, in the style of the Renaissance. Enter, and you are indeed in the house of the winegrowers: here is the monastic grape press, really four antique presses, enormous, fat machines that function better, still today, than the crane-loaded press left there by M. Tourton as the sole trace of his passage[17]. Six pieces poorly linked compose the axis of these curious relics.

The vat room forms a beautiful rectangle with a central courtyard, whose galleries are thirty meters long and ten wide, each of them lit by three raised windows giving a favorable half-light. Thirty four fermentation vats of different sizes are arrayed for battle. They can ferment enough wine for 450 casks; the thickness of their walls is only three centimeters – thus one has an idea of their age. A cover descends, pierced by a single hole that covers all of them. The large aging casks [foudres] of good construction and well maintained, were fabricated with hand-split German oak by German craftsmen. Refitted casks of this type sold for 300 francs. New, with sawn staves they cost 200 francs in the country of their manufacture, and 500 francs from hand-split wood. Now, which is better, an aging vat or a smaller new casks [barriques] to receive young wine? This question has been hotly debated in this very place by knowledgeable vintners.

Partisans of the small cask assure that it leaves to each harvest its individual character and cachet, and helps the wine to finish its fermentation quickly. Others respond, however, that if it finishes the last stages of vinification quickly in the barrique it does so better in foudres, yielding a superior and more homogeneous result. The wine is less exposed to the often irritating and variable character of the wood that can be of mediocre or poor quality. It happens that at harvest time that the use of barriques exposes the proprietor to considerable losses of time and money. In this regard, foudres are more economical and give the work in the winery

---

17 This press is no longer in existence.

an advantage in security. However that may be, any of us who would climb up one of these tall foudres would declare after having plunged one's soul and experienced the blossoming of one's olfactory nerves across several of these bungs, that for Vougeot at least, a harvest can only gain by its passage in such large casks, so delicious are the perfumes of these vinous vases.

The small size of these vats is unanimously approved and sufficient for what is gathered each day, and thus the fermentation is not troubled by the addition of fresh fruit. At the Clos, the practice is to crush the fruit lightly prior to fermentation.

Two cellars, one five meters high, and the other three, can accommodate 1,600 casks. They are not vaulted, but the ceiling is laden with 66 centimeters of earth covered by tile. The light is easily regulated with the aid of shutters, and fresh air is introduced by tall narrow windows with an arch at the top. Thus thermometers vary from five degrees in the winter to twelve in the summer. It is recognized that this method of regulating the light and temperature is excellent, and it is remarked in several vineyards that where the temperature of the cellar is too uniformly maintained at ten or twelve degrees that the liquid suffers when it leaves the cellar for shipment.

Upon leaving this happy but dim place, the eye is literally struck by the vigorous greenery spread out over forty eight hectares: it is the Clos! The sacred field! A magnificent vineyard, dominated to the west by rounded and denuded crests which form the celebrated branch of the European chain known as the Côte d'Or. To the southeast, the plain inclines slightly towards the banks of the Saône. To the north and the south, the strays in the distant undulations and happy vineyards, almost all of them renowned.

The Clos is planted to Pinot Noir. The chardenet [sic], or Pinot Blanc, which twenty years ago was found in the proportion of one fifth, has been successively reduced to one fifteenth and will be further reduced to one twentieth. You know, sirs, that it is this noble plant that gives us Montrachet, considered by many oenophiles as the best white wine in the world[18]. Finally five or six hundred vines of Pinot Beurrot or Pinot Gris are disseminated in the vineyard.

The Clos gives thirteen hectolitres per hectare on average, a quantity slightly lower than one finds elsewhere in the region. In spite of what malice would say, it is evident that no fertilizer is used and one enriches the soil only with some compost and some of the remains of the skins, seeds, and stems from fermentation that have been distilled, and only for the propagation of new vines by layering. The soil is worked four times, as is the practice in Burgundy.

In 1838 there was a disastrous invasion of moths. The Clos was ravaged first, and the neighboring vineyards escaped the pest. All-out war was waged on the terrible insect, which was only vanquished after six years. During these six years, an army of children searched, plucked, and destroyed all of the leaves upon which the moth had laid its eggs. Each campaign cost 500 francs. Today the moth has not entirely disappeared, but without multiplying, it causes little harm."

---

18 The late M. de Cussy, the loveable president of the Society of Winemakers, conscientious and reflective taster, never says "Montrachet" by itself, but, eyes to the heavens, divine Montrachet.

M. Leclère finished his account with the following:

After the vine, the wine; products surrounded by all the charms of an elegant hospitality that singularly increases its merit. Our experience deepens, but within the limits of what a man of taste, a winemaker worthy of the name, think of these five types: white Chambertin, white Vougeot, and red Vougeot of 1840, 1825, and 1819. God alone knows the fine observations, the unexpected remarks, the learned discussions that have animated the room when, once and often, the reverend fathers were working! What will I tell you of it? For each type, the opinions are summed up in this single world that Voltaire, one says, attached to each verse of his illustrious master, Racine, in trying to comment upon his principal work: 'Admirable!'

At the French Revolution, the Clos de Vougeot, was confiscated and declared property of the nation, was sold on January 17, 1791 with the land of Gilly, Richebourg, and several other lands and parcels of vine to M. Focard, a landlord of Paris, for the sum of 1,140,600 francs, not including the tax. M. Focard sold it to MM. Tourton and Ravel, and from these gentlemen to the father of M. Ouvrard.

Camille Rodier added the following pertaining to the period of Ouvrard ownership:

The Clos de Vougeot passed next to his heirs, the Comte de Rochechouart, the Comtesse de Montalembert, and the Marquis de Lagarde. In 1889 this property was sold to a merchant of domaines who divided it into lots which he re-sold to about twenty owners. The château and its dependencies along with approximately ten hectares surrounding it, were purchased by M. Léonce Bocquet, who employed a large part of his fortune to restore the château and its chimneys of colossal dimension, which were truly masterpieces of the French Renaissance. It was he as well who completed the construction of the rooms on the first floor of the château which were no less than six meters in height. The Abbots of Cîteaux had judged it useless to finish them, since they had always preferred their residence in Gilly surrounded by spacious gardens.

M. E. Camuzet, Deputy from the Côte d'Or, acquired the château, its dependencies and several neighboring ouvrées. The part of the Clos de Vougeot that also belonged to M. Bocquet was sold the same day to different owners who have been discussed above.

The division of the Clos de Vougeot into so many minute constituent parts poses interesting questions to wine lovers, forcing us to select our favorite growers. Yet, is their success due to their talent or to the nobility of the terroir that they work? A talented winemaker can produce top quality with less good material, while a less endowed producer might underperform, even if they possess a very interesting parcel. In my view, there are a number of bottlings that provide extraordinary value due to the comparatively low esteem commanded by the Clos de Vougeot. This inclues the admirable bottlings produced by the various members of the Gros family: Bernard Gros at Gros Frère et Sœur produces a bottling labeled Musigni, while his brother Michel and his cousin Anne both produce one labeled Grand Maupertui. Domaine Hudelot-Noëllat also produces a very solid value wine. Château de la Tour under the direction of François Labet is producing wines of increasing interest each year, and Domaine Méo-Camuzet and Domaine Leroy both produce very highly regarded (if considerably more expensive) wines in the appellation while the Domaine d'Eugenie (the former Domaine René Engel) offers a "mid-priced" version of considerable quality.

FLAGEY-LEZ-GILLY

Unlike other villages in the Côte d'Or, Flagey does not trumpet its name loudly on wine labels. In fact, it is difficult to find it referred to at all. This is all the more surprising, since more than 60% of the total surface in Flagey is classified today as grand cru, with just over 21% classified in premier cru and 18% classified as village. The reason that Flagey is so discreet is that the wine from all of the village and all of the premier cru land is sold as Vosne-Romanée, while the grands crus (Échézeaux and Grands Échézeaux) are sold under those names alone.

The practice of referring to Flagey as a dependency of Vosne goes back at least to Jullien, who grouped Échézeaux in with the wines of Vosne. Morelot has "Les Échézeaux" in Flagey, which he esteems, but not highly enough to consider them a tête de cuvée. Lavalle has Grands Échézeaux as a tête de cuvée, although he classifies Échézeaux du Dessus as a première cuvée.

This last is an important distinction, because Grands Échézeaux is a large vineyard, 9 ha 14 a 45 ca, and it has remained constant for the past several centuries. Échézeaux, however, is another story. It began as a relatively small plot called Les Échézeaux du Dessus at 3 ha 55 a 30 ca, while the present appellation is an expansive 36 ha 25 a 83 ca. To the original Échézeaux du Dessus was added 5 ha 24 a 45 ca of Les Poulaillères (praised by Morelot and assessed as a première cuvée by Lavalle), which makes sense because Les Poulaillères is contiguous with Échézeaux du Dessus to the north and roughly at the same altitude. Also included was Les Loächausses (3 ha 12 a 20 ca, which Lavalle called Les Achausses) and Les Cruots ou Vignes Blanches (3 ha 16 a 26 ca), contiguous to Échézeaux du Dessus to the south. Also added was a fairly large bit of En Orveaux (8 ha 3 a 20 ca). Some of this lies on the border with Chambolle at the same level as Les Poulaillères, while a portion of it is located to the west at the entrance to the Combe d'Orveau. This was not the end of the expansion, however, since 2 ha 86 a 47 ca of Champs Traversins was also added, along with Les Rouges du Bas (3 ha 94 a 75 ca), both upslope; all ranked as premières cuvées by Lavalle.

Our present system, however, also includes Clos Saint-Denis (1 ha 68 a 61 ca) and Les Treux (4 ha 94 a 89 ca), both ranked as deuxième cuvées. Two portions of other climats were also added later, 96 a 82 ca of Quartiers de Nuits (which Lavalle has as a deuxième cuvée), and a very small bit of Beaux Monts Bas, (14 a 33 ca) further up the slope that he classed in première cuvée. As with Clos de Vougeot, some growers indicate the lieu-dit on the label: Jayer-Gilles produces an Échézeaux "du Dessus", and Méo-Camuzet one that is labeled as "Rouges du Bas," but this is usually not the case. Henri Jayer was very proud of his vines in Échézeaux, and claimed that Les Cruots ou Vignes Blanches was the best terroir of the appellation. The Échézeaux from Henri Jayer is always Les

Cruots, but the wine made by Henri and bottled for other members of the family came from the parcels that the family owned in Les Treux.

Here is the rather short commentary by Dr. Morelot, followed by the rankings of Dr. Lavalle:

> Hardly has one passed by the houses of Vougeot than one is in the territory of Flagey. This village, built on the plain more than a half-league from the slope, has a very extensive vineyard which comes to a point just at the slope, where the choice climats Les Échézeaux and La Poulaillère are found, furnishing delicate, deeply colored wines with a very good flavor that are the equal of those that we have just discussed.

Dr. Lavalle:

COMMUNE OF FLAGEY-LEZ-GILLY

The territory of this village, situated a distance from the plain, follows the slope in a narrow band that, separated from the vines of Vougeot and Vosne, includes a number of climats almost worthy of being noticed.

Pinot Noir only is cultivated in the vines of this slope. Gamay, as everywhere, has invaded the vineyards of the lower parts, and here again; the main road from Dijon to Châlon is the limit between the fine wines and the common wines. The total of this vineyard is around 90 ha, of which 60 are planted in Pinot and 30 in Gamay. The principal climats are:

Tête de Cuvée

Les Grands Echézeaux, 9 ha 14 a 45 ca, belong to MM. Duveaux, Chanut, Royer-Duvergey, de Bahezre, Gillotte, Marillier.

> Danguy et Aubertin: Dr. Canut, MM. Dufouleur, Duvaux, Faiveley-Fermouche, Mongeard, Rasse
>
> Rodier: MM. Choquier, Paul Faiveley, Fournier-Michel, Gaudemet, Henri Gouroux, F. Grivelet-Modot, J. Gros-Renoudot, Henri Lamarche, Lanternier, Malbranche-Morand, Modot-Fauconney, de Villaine et Chambon, A. Noirot

Rodier has Les Grands Échézeaux and Échézeaux du Dessus distinguished with capital letters.

Première Cuvée

> Camille Rodier has Échézeaux du Dessus, En Orveau, Les Poulaillères, Les Loachausses, Les Cruots, Les Champs Traversins, Les Rouges du Bas, Les Beaux Monts Bas and Le Clos Saint-Denis classified in première

cuvée. Les Quartiers de Nuits and Les Treux are both included in première cuvée as well, although it is noted that a part of each is classified in deuxième cuvée.

En Orveau, 9 ha 92 a 10 ca, blonging to MM. Audiffred-Gillotte, Chanut, Duveaux, Mollerat.

> Danguy et Aubertin: MM. Audiffred, Jules Belin, Dr. Chanut, MM. Govin, Guichard-Potheret et fils, Rasse, Viennot
>
> Rodier: MM. J. Bossu, Choquier, Paul Faiveley, J.-B. Laurier, Loison-Remy, Petit Emonin, Pierre Roger.

Les Pouaillères, 6 ha 80, belonging to MM. Duveaux, Coste.

> Danguy et Aubertin: MM. Chambon, Duvaux, Joseph Mongeard, Mugnier
>
> Rodier: MM. Bissey, de Contenson, Modot-Fanconney, A. Noirot, Thivet, de Villaine et Chambon

Les Murs-du-Clos, belonging to M. Marillier[52].

Les Eschezeaux-du-Dessus [sic], 3 ha 55 a 30 ca, belonging to MM. Royer-Duvergey, Gillotte, Duveaux.

> Danguy et Aubertin: MM. Camuzet, Clerget-Duchemin, Duvaux, Jean-Baptiste Mongeard, Jean-Baptiste Pillet, S. Lhote et fils.
>
> Rodier: MM. Henri Camuzet, Guillon, Liger-Belair, the Mongeard-Collardot heirs, J.P. Pillet, de Villaine et Chambon.

Les Achausses, 3 ha 43 a 82 ca, belonging to MM. Jacquinot, Matouillet, the elder Chanut, Gauthier, Lhot.

> Danguy et Aubertin have the proprietors of "Achausses (les) or Loachausses" as Dr. Chanut and MM. Duveaux, Gros, Jean-Baptiste Mongeard
>
> Rodier uses the modern spelling of Les Loachausses and notes the proprietors as: MM. Henri Gouroux and J. Gros-Renauidot

Les Cruots, 3 ha 28 a 95 ca, belonging to MM. Matouillet, Jacquinot.

> Danguy et Aubertin have « Cruots ou Vignes Blanches » as M : Belair, Dr. Chanut, MM. Camuzet, Faiveley
>
> Rodier: MM. Choquier, Henri Gouroux, J. Gros Renaudot, Jaillet, H. Lamarche

Les Champs-Traversins, 3 ha 58 a, belonging to MM. Marey (Félix), Royer, Duveaux.

> Danguy et Aubertin: MM. Dufouleur, Duvaux, Gros

<u>Rodier</u>: MM. F. Grivelet-Modot, Jaillet, H. Lamarche

Les Rouges-du-Bas, 3 ha, belonging to MM. Duveaux, Chanut, Groffier.

<u>Danguy et Aubertin</u>: MM. Duvaux, Faiveley-Fermouche, Trapet

<u>Rodier</u>: MM. E. Camuzet, Confuron Bornot, P. Faiveley, Galland, Liger-Belair, D. François, Thomas, Trapet

Les Beaux-Monts-Bas, 5 ha 69 a 75 ca, belonging to MM. Frantin, Matouillet, Chanut.

<u>Danguy et Aubertin</u>: MM. Duvaux, Fermouche-Lhote, Fermouche-Maignot, Grivot-Renevet and Dr. Truchetet

<u>Rodier</u>: MM. Arnoux, Gilles-Boiteux, Grivot, H. Lamarche, Mouillon

Deuxième Cuvée

Clos Saint-Denis, 1 ha 80 a 25 ca, belonging to MM. Duveaux, Collardot, Liger-Belair, Groffier.

<u>Danguy et Aubertin</u>: Note simply that Clos Saint-Denis is « very divided »

<u>Rodier</u>: MM. Henri Gouroux, Jaillet, H. Lamarche, Modot-Fauconney, Tisserandot, de Villaine et Chambon

Les Treux, 4 ha 89 a 30 ca, belonging to MM. Gauthier, Collardot, Ligger-Belair, Chanut.

<u>Danguy et Aubertin</u>: Dr. Chanut and MM. Fermouche-Maigrot, Marillier

<u>Rodier</u>: MM. Gaudemet, J. Gros-Renaudot, the Mongeard Collardot heirs, J.-B. Pillet, Thomas

Les Quartiers-de-Nuits, 2 ha 58 a 40 ca, belonging to MM. Marillier, Gournot, Chanut.

<u>Danguy et Aubertin</u>: Dr. Chanut and M. Rasse

<u>Rodier</u>: MM. Gaudemet, Loison-Remy, Mugneret

Les Violettes, 1 ha 36 a 25 ca, belonging to MM. Chanut, the elder Chanut, Lécrivain, Mongeard.

Troisième Cuvée

Les Portefeuilles, 1 ha 36 a 70 ca, belonging to MM. Salbreux, Seguin, Tanison, Chalandin.

The wines of Flagey are similar in every respect to those of Vosne, with which they are confused by the market as well as by wine lovers. I refer then to this village for the appreciation of all of the qualities of these excellent wines.

The crown of the finest wine in Échézeaux which once rested firmly on the head of Henri Jayer now is worn definitely by the Domaine de la Romanée-Conti for both their Échézeaux and Grands Échézeaux. There are several producers, however, who approach this level of quality at a much more affordable price. One must certainly mention in this regard the wines produced in both appellations by Gros Frère et Sœur and the Domaine d'Eugenie, as well as the Échézeaux produced by Louis-Michel and Thibault Liger-Belair at the separate estates. The bottlings by Domaine Méo-Camuzet, Mugneret-Gibourg, the Domaine d'Eugenie, and not least that of Henri Jayer's nephew Emmanuel Rouget all merit serious attention.

VOSNE

Every wine authority of the last several hundred years is unanimous in their opinion: Vosne-Romanée is the finest wine-producing village in the Côte d'Or. Lavalle notes, "This praise is uncontested. Our fathers and our ancestors have enviably celebrated the wines of Vosne and Flagey, and today we can only copy their formulas of homage." In this unanimous chorus of voices has been Allen Meadows, whose admirable book *The Pearl of the Côte* is an in-depth look at the wines of this village, which is home to no less than six grand cru vineyards, or eight if one lumps the vines of Flagey in with those of Vosne: Romanée-Conti, La Romanée, and Romanée-Saint-Vivant; La Tâche; Les Richebourgs and La Grande Rue.

The Abbey of Saint-Vivant de Vergy

To understand the grands crus of Vosne it helps to understand their origin, since some of the names, so familiar to us, were still in flux until well into the 19th century. The monks of the Abbey of Saint-Vivant in Vergy established these vineyards. Today, Vergy is a quiet village, but at the dawn of the 17th century, it was a center of great Burgundian power. Because of its highly defensible position at the top of the Côte, it was esteemed by Louis VII as the strongest fortress in France (and, not coincidentally, a seat of rebellion against Paris, referred to by Henri IV as a 'nest of thieves and leagues[53]').

The Abbey of Saint-Vivant was founded at the turn of the 10th century—the date is uncertain—by Manassès I "l'Ancien", lord of Vergy and Langres, Count of Beaune, Dijon, and Chalon. Convinced that he had commited sins by his brother Hervé de Chalon, bishop of Autun, Manassès I founded the Abbey to welcome the monks of Biarne (in the Jura), who carried the relics of Saint Viventius. Attached to the Benedictine Abbey of Cluny in 1087, it was richly endowed in 1131 by Hugues II, Duke of Burgundy. Hugues donated all of his uncultivated lands, woods, and fields in Flagey and Vosne to the Abbey, confirming the original gift of Manassès. The monks were responsible for clearing these lands and planting the vines. Contrary to popular belief, however, the monks of Saint-Vivant did not work the property themselves, but leased them to local growers and then collected tithes and rents.

The Abbey added to its holdings in four separate acquisitions during the 13th century. Richard Olney in his marvelous book *Romanée-Conti* notes that these purchases had already been planted to vines and suggests that they were made in order to complete Clos de Saint-Vivant. The inventory of this clos comes from a tax declaration made by the Abbey to the administration of Louis XI in

1512 after the annexation of the Duchy of Burgundy, and describes their holdings as four adjoining clos, called Clos de Neuf Journaux (referring to its size, as explained in the appendix), Clos de Moytan (five journaux in size), Clos des Quatre Journaux, and Clos des Cinq Journaux. Separated from this last clos was a plot of three ouvrées (i.e., the amount a man could work in one day) on the other side of the footpath in the vineyard belonging to the monks of Vergy.

Les Romanées

Clos des Cinq Journaux along with these three ouvrées became known in the 16th century as Cros des Cloux, and some of these vines ultimately become known as Romanée-Conti. The name "La Romanée" was not used, however, until 1651, when it is referred to in the registry of the Abbey. This designation is often thought to refer to remains of the Roman occupation although the Roman influence cannot be verified. Rather than perpetuate incorrect assumptions, the text of the AOC regulations cautiously notes that, "The Roman origin cannot be ruled out, the vine having arrived in Gaul with the invasions of armies of Julius Caesar, but 'romenie' is also an old French word, which frequently in litreature means, a mythical wine and legend." Marie-Hélène Landrieu-Lussigny suggests in the dictionary in the second half of her book *Le Vignoble Bourgignon* that "Romanée," in this instance, may refer to the footpath that leads from Vosne to Vergy, called the Sentier des Raignots. The Romanée-Conti vineyard, however, did not receive its current name until the Revolution. It was not renamed by Louis-François Bourbon, Prince de Conti, who purchased it in 1760, but rather became known as "Romanée-Conti" by association.

Much confusion stems from the similarity in names between Romanée-Conti and the parcel just upslope, known simply as "La Romanée." Yet La Romanée has little connection to its neighbor. In fact, it was formerly known as Aux Echanges, and was renamed La Romanée only in 1827 by Louis-Charles Liger-Belair, nephew of the General Louis Liger-Belair. Prior to this time, Aux Echanges had been part of Les Richebourgs, and its ownership had been divided among six different owners. After the sale of the *biens nationaux*[54], Liger-Belair was able to purchase all of these parcels, each from its separate owner. The name was only changed to La Romanée once he was in possession of all the parcels, and so it didn't exist under this name when Jullien wrote his work. Morelot speaks about both La Romanée and Romanée-Conti, although it seems he is referring to the same vineyards. Lavalle, however, gives La Romanée the same tête de cuvée status as Romanée-Conti.

Our authorities also appear to share some mixed feelings regarding the status of Romanée-Saint-Vivant. Jullien notes that its wine is inferior to Romanée-Conti, and Lavalle categorizes it as a première cuvée.

Like La Romanée, the name is also a back-formation, but an older one, first noted in 1765 to distinguish it from the parcel that had been purchased not long before by the Prince de Conti. Romanée-Saint-Vivant is [the portion of La] Romanée [belonging to the monks of the Abbey of] Saint-Vivant.

While all of the vines comprising the present extent of Romanée-Saint-Vivant were part of the original donations of Manassès and of Hugues, portions had been detached by the 16th century. The portions carved out of the whole include the northwest corner, referred to on a map of 1512 as "Vigne à Estienne Bôgnet", just north of the Clos du Moytant; and the Southeast corner, called "Vigne à Jehan Roy de Rouyres," downslope from Clos de Quatre Journaux. And yet, the Marey-Monge family between 1815 and 1823 reassembled all these detached parcels, along with the portions retained by the monks of Vergy, and this extensive vineyard (just over 9.5 ha) has seen a number of proprietors through the years.

Les Richebourgs and Les Verroilles

The northernmost of the grands crus in Vosne is Richebourg, cited by several sources as being "separated from Romanée-Conti by only a footpath." This overlooks the fact that the lieu-dit of Richebourg is considerably bigger than Romanée-Conti. In fact, it is contiguous to both Romanée-Conti and La Romanée, lying on their northern border. Lavalle lists all three vineyards as têtes de cuvées, and they are all grands crus today. He is not as sanguine, however, regarding Les Verroilles, or Les Varoilles-sous-Richebourg, as he would have it, which he has as premières cuvées. This parcel, now known as Les Verroilles ou Richebourgs ("or" Richebourgs instead of "under" Richebourgs), was joined to Les Richebourg in the twentieth century, and is another example of a grand cru expansion that was subject to a certain amount of controversy.

In 1922 de Villaine and Chambon, the owners of DRC, joined in a suit to prevent owners from Les Verroilles from selling their wine as Richebourg. This is doubly ironic. First, because they were proprietors in Les Verroilles themselves—DRC still owns nearly a hectare here. Secondly because ten years later, the plaintiffs would appear as defendants in a similar suit involving Gaudichots and La Tâche. The outcomes were the same in both lawsuits. The court of appeals in Dijon found in each instance that the less well-known site had been selling its wine for many years as that of the more well-known site without intention to defraud, and that this practice thus formed part of the "usages locaux, loyaux et constants", or "local, honest and traditional" practices of the region. This yardstick was written into a 1927 revision to the law that would eventually define the appellations d'originé controlée system.

Are the wines Les Verroilles of the same level of quality as Les Richebourgs? The question is little debated today, and most connoisseurs probably do not realize that there are in fact two separate lieux-dits. As some authors have pointed out, Les Verroilles' more northerly location means that its grapes are further exposed to the cool winds coming down from the Hautes Côtes through the combe. The exposure is less directly east than that of Les Richebourgs. Parts of Les Verroilles also lay further upslope than the balance of Les Richebourgs. As Morelot points out on the topic, "Those that cross into a greater elevation are found on a terroir subject to being washed by the rain, and do not give a liquid as perfect as those of La Romanée".

La Tâche and Les Gaudichots

The name La Tâche has always been associated with wines of the highest quality. Even today, La Tâche is ranked as second to Romanée-Conti. As noted by Lavalle, Joseph Durand (who prepared the *expertise* or valuation that accompanied the sale of this vineyard and others for the sale of the *biens nationaux* during the Revolution) wrote "...being understood that the wine of La Romanée is no longer on the market, the wine of La Tâche is accepted as the foremost wine of Burgundy." This vineyard at that time, however, was a fraction of its present size: 1 ha 40 a 5 ca, according to Lavalle (as opposed to 6 ha 6 a 20 ca today). It was sold during the Revolution and by 1815, La Tâche ended up in the hands of the Liger-Belair family, who retained ownership until 1933.

The reason for the growth in the size of La Tâche in the 1930s is that it was combined with Les Gaudichots. The text of the AOC regulation somewhat disingenuously notes, "Known since the 17th century, the place called 'La Tâche' seems to have always had one single owner. Even during the French Revolution, despite the confiscation and auction of the property of the nobility, this climat was not divided. It has had since that time only 3 owners, the last joining to the original lieu-dit, the neighboring one, known as "Les Gaudichots", whose wines are, according to customs dating back to the 18th century, similar in character and quality to those of "La Tâche"".

In fact, there are portions of Gaudichots today classed in village (5 a 26 ha), premier cru (79 a 65 ca), and grand cru, as there are 4 ha 62 a 75 a of Gaudichots included in La Tâche, and 23 a 18 ca included in La Grande Rue. Lavalle has Gaudichots as première cuvée. While much of Gaudichots has always been seen as top notch, not everyone agreed that it should have been assimilated into La Tâche. In 1932 the Liger-Belair family went to court to prevent the use of the term La Tâche for vineyards in the climat Les Gaudichots. The wine, however, had been labeled as La Tâche throughout much of the 19th century, and parcels of land in Les Gaudichots had been sold variously as Tâche, Tâche Goudichots, or Godichots et Rochottes, according to the deed of sale between M. Morellet and M. Lausseure[55].

Among the defendants in the suit were Edmond Gaudin de Villaine and Jacques Chambon, descendants and relatives of the Duvault-Blochet family, competitors to the Liger-Belair and Marey-Monge clans and proprietors, since 1869, of Romanée-Conti. They owned vineyards throughout the Côte d'Or, including holdings in Les Gaudichots. The court of appeals in Dijon found in favor of de Villaine and Chambon. This, however, was not the last reversal of fortune for the Liger-Belair family. In order to settle estate questions related to the late countess Liger-Belair, the family was forced to sell its holdings in La Tâche at auction. The parcel was purchased by de Villaine and Chambon. In 1936 the new AOC rules confirmed the court decision of four years prior and incorporated much of Les Gaudichots with La Tâche.

La Grande Rue

The final climat classed in grand cru today in Vosne is La Grande Rue, classified as "second class" by Jullien, as première cuvée by Lavalle, and mentioned by both Courtépée and Morelot. It was not promoted to grand cru in contemporary times until 1992 following a request from Henri Lamarche. Although La Grande Rue was not generally seen as tête de cuvée material, the wines did enjoy the esteem of most experts, and was classed in the first category by the Comité d'Agriculture de Beaune. It appears that its neglect during the process of establishing the current system of grands crus was due to the fact that the proprietor at the time, Edouard Lamarche, had simply not submitted it for nomination. The belief is that he wished to avoid the higher taxes that would be levied against grand cru vineyards, a distrust of the system being put in place, and a lack of confidence that grand cru status would guarantee higher prices for the wine.

The vineyard of La Grande Rue today is actually composed of 1ha 42 a 7 ca of the lieu-dit La Grande Rue, and 23 a 18 ca of Les Gaudichots. Allan Meadows relates a series of exchanges with DRC that took place in 1959 in his book *The Pearl of the Côte*: Domaine Lamarche traded 1.9 a of vines in Les Gaudichots and 2.8 a of vines in the Échézeaux climat Clos Saint-Denis for three parcels of La Grande Rue totaling 10.1 a. Until this time, the three small parcels of La Grande Rue had been used in La Tâche.

The high quality of this terroir has seldom been questioned. It is a long, narrow vineyard that begins in the village and runs up the slope to the climat Aux Champs Perdrix, bordering Les Gaudichots (La Tâche) to the south, and the Clos des Quatre Journaux part of Romanée Saint-Vivant (owned by Latour), Romanée-Conti, La Romanée, and a small bit of Aux Reignots across the road to the north. It has higher elevation and thinner soils at the top of the slope and lower elevations and richer soils at the bottom than its illustrious neighbors, yet it is certainly worthy of its current status. The Lamarche family did not apply for grand cru status for this vineyard until 1984.

A look at Vosne begins with Courtépée, who cites an endowment by Alix de Vergy in 1232 that is apocryphal according to some, even though it was widely credited in previous centuries.

> Saint-Vivant sous Vergy [is a] Priory of the Cluny order, richly endowed as an abbey c. 890, according to D. Mabillon, by Manassès de Vergy and his wife Hermengarde for 28 monks required to celebrate three grand masses daily. It was united with Cluny under St. Hugues...La Romanée de Saint-Vivant was given by Alix de Vergy in 1232. Ponce de Blaisy sold his vines in Vosne to the priory in 1246.

Courtépée goes on to note that:

> [Vosne is] The head of burgundy wine, renowned throughout Europe—the most distinguished climats (since there are no common wines in Vosne) are those of the slope above the church. La Romanée, of four journaux, belonging to the Prince de Conti; Romanée-de-Saint-Vivant, belonging to this priory and to different private owners; vast Richebourg, belonging to several proprietors; the Clos-des-Varoilles, of four journaux, belonging to M. Jacquinot of Chazan; on the other side, La Grande-Rue, of which three journaux and a bit belong to M. Lami of Samerey; La Tâche, of which four and a half journaux in a single parcel belong to M. Le Président de Bévy; Malconsort, planted in 1612; Echezeaux and Beaumonts, in the commune of Flagey. M. Jacquinot of Richemont, is the first who declared the superiority of the wines of Vosne over those of the village of Nuits in 1680.
>
> The Dukes had a hunting lodge in Vosne, which still owes a tithe of five francs to its lord. The owner was obliged to receive the master and his dogs for three days. The Ducal Prevost of Vosne named the vine-keeper of the Clos de Vougeot and was obliged to dine in the monk's cellar on the Sunday after the feast of La Madeleine in 1450. The King still had in 1537 a Prevost who named the vine-keeper and the inhabitants harvested the wine.

The parcel today called La Romanée had not yet been isolated. Courtépée does not spare his enthusiasm, which makes the (curiously brief) comments of Dr. Morelot about the wines of Vosne all the more odd:

> Upon arriving [in Vosne], one finds first Malconsorts[19], La Grand Rue, Les Varoilles, very considerable districts that necessarily offer several variations in their products in reason of their extent and exposition, but which are all precious because of their superior qualities.
>
> A bit further on one finds La Tâche: this small district of 33 ouvrées (1ha 38 a), enjoys a justly merited reputation, which it owes to the precaution of making wine only with the grapes that are harvested there. Its beautiful exposition and the excellence of the soil also contribute to give a wine of great superiority. Opposite is Romanée-St.-Vivant, whose extent is around ten hectares. This climat is circumscribed by roads and terminates at an angle to the village of Vosne.

---

19 Malconsorts was a sort of pasture covered with brush and bramble until about the year 1610. It was then cleared and covered in a vineyard of excellent quality.

Romanée-Conti is placed above; it is enclosed within a wall of one hectare seventy one ares (41 ouvrées). This climat furnishes without contradiction the best wine of the entire département. It is inclined to the southeast and forms an angle of five or six degrees[20].

Les Richebourgs are separated from Romanée-Conti only by a footpath. Their extent is around six hectares, and as they extend more over the steeper slope of the hill, their products are less exquisite than those of La Romanée; they are, however, of great value. It is even certain that if they were made only with grapes harvested at the same elevation as La Romanée, one would have an equivalent quality; but those that cross into a greater elevation are found on a terroir subject to being washed by the rain, and do not give a liquid as perfect as those of La Romanée. In spite of that one can recognize that it is the same type of wine, although with a bit less finesse and perfection, because it is the same type of terrain. The underlying bedrock is the same, and the detritus of this bedrock has the same properties.

Here are the noticeably more fulsome comments of Dr. Lavalle on Vosne:

COMMUNE DE VOSNE

This magnificent vineyard includes more than 200 ha, of which three quarters are planted to Pinot Noir. Several Pinot Blanc vines are found in the middle of these plantations of Pinot Noir, but in such small proportion that one must say that the latter plant alone produces the renowned wines of Vosne. In the middle of these excellent climats, one has difficulty establishing a classification and is obliged to set beyond its limits a significant portion of the vines.

Tête de Cuvée

Rodier has Romanée-Conti, La Romanée, Romanée-Saint-Vivant, Les Richebourg, Les Verouilles ou Richebourg, La Tâche, and Les Malconsorts distinguished by capital letters, and presented in that order.

Romanée-Conti, 1 ha 83 a 50 ca, belonging to M. Ouvrard.

    Danguy et Aubertin: the Duvault heirs

    Rodier: MM. de Villaine et Jacques Chambon

Les Richebourgs, 4 ha 93 a 45 ca, belonging to MM. Frantin, Marey, Duveaux, Liger-Belair, Lasseure, Marillier.

    Danguy et Aubertin: Dr. Chanut, the Duvault heirs, MM. Gaudemet, le Comte Liger-Belair, Marey

    Camille Rodier: MM. Julien Chambon, Gaudemet, Jules Gros Renaudot, Liger-Belair, Charles Viénot

La Tâche, 1 ha 40 a 5 ca, belonging tom. Liger-Belair, Lausseure.

    Danguy et Aubertin: the Duvault heirs, le Comte Liger-Belair

---

20 The difference in the name of this climat comes from the name of its proprietors. One part belongs to the house of the Prince of Conti, and the other part to the Abbey of Saint-Vivant. These properties have passed into other hands, and are cared for with equal dedication in order to maintain their antique reputation.

Camille Rodier: M. Liger-Belair

La Romanée, belonging to M. Liger-Belair.

Danguy et Aubertin: M. Le Comte Liger-Belair, M. Thomas Noëllat

Rodier : M. Liger-Belair

Première Cuvée

Romanée-Saint-Vivant, 9 ha 54 a 30 ca, belonging to Mmes. Jondot, Ernest Marey-Monge.

Danguy et Aubertin: The Marey heirs

Rodier: MM. Gaudemet, Louis Latour, Marey-Monge, Moillard-Grivot

Les Gaudichots, 5 ha 79 a 65 ca, belonging to MM. Lausseure, Ragonneau, Confuron, Bergeret.

Danguy et Aubertin: Dr. Chanut, Comte Liger-Belair

Rodier: MM. J. Chambon, de Champeaux

Les Malconsorts, 5 ha 94 a 65 ca, belonging to MM. Lenoir, Marey, Moissenet-Meulien.

La Grande-Rue, 1 ha 32 a 95 ca, belonging to M. Liger-Belair.

Danguy et Aubertin: the Duvault heirs, Comte Liger-Belair

Rodier: MM. J. Chambon, de Champeaux

Les Varoilles-sous-Richebourg, 3 ha 6 a, belonging to M. Frantin.

Camille Rodier: MM. Camuzet, Jacques Chambon, F. Grivelet-Modot, J. Gros-Renaudot, C. Noëllat

Les Beaux-Monts, 2 ha 42 a 30 ca, belonging to MM. Frantin, Matouillet, Liger-Belair, Sartout, Mme. Jondot.

Combe-Brulée, 1 ha 62 a 25 ca, belonging to MM. Gauthier, Matouillet, Chanut.

Aux Brulées, 3 ha, 88 a 70 ca, belonging to the same proprietors.

Les Suchots, 16 ha 12 a 10 ca, belonging to MM. Chanut, Liger-Belair, Collardot, Sartout, Royer-Duvergey.

Deuxième Cuvée

Aux Chaumes, 7 ha 32 a 25 ca, belonging to MM. Chanut, Liger-Belair, Royer-Duvergey.

Les Reignots, 1 ha 66 a 95 ca, belonging to a great number of proprietors.

Les Hautes and **Basses-Maizières**, 5 ha 55 ca, belonging to MM. Matouillet, Sermouche, and a great number of other proprietors.

Aux Réas, 9 ha 68 a 60 ca, belonging to MM. Duveaux, Gauthier, Liger-Belair, Marillier.

Troisième Cuvée

Aux Raviottes,	Aux Petit-Monts,	Champ-Goudin,
Au-dessus de la Rivière,	Bossières,	Vigneux,
Les Jacquines,	Aux Genevrières,	Aux Jachées.
Parantoux,	Aux Communes	

Quatrième Cuvée

Aux Saules,	La Folie,	Pré de la Folie,

La Croix-Blanche, etc.

« This vineyard is without contradiction, » writes one of our most competent tasters « the first of the Côte d'Or. With mellow body, extreme finesse and extraordinary bouquet, it unites all of the desirable qualities[56]. »

This praise is uncontested. Our father and our ancestors have enviably celebrated the wines of Vosne and Flagey, and today we can only copy their formulas of homage.

Of all the climats of Vosne, Romanée-Conti is the one whose reputation was the most brilliant in the previous century and at the beginning of this one. Thus I will not hesitate to publish here a curious document whose original is found in the archives of the département among the works relative to the sale of the property of the nation, and which gives us some interesting details on this celebrated cru.

Romanée-Conti is a parcel of vines celebrated for the exquisite quality of the wine that it produces. It is believed in the territory of Vosne that it has the most ideal position and thus obtains the most perfect maturity of the fruit. More elevated to the west than to the east, it presents itself to the first rays of the sun, giving it the impetus of the softest heat of the day.

The soil that nourishes these vines is sufficiently deep and of the qualities most apt for the vegetation and support of the vine. Pinot Noir is cultivated here; the vines carry their fruit well and are not subject to coulure as are the vines in many other climats.

Romanée contains forty ouvrées or five journaux. It is enclosed by walls on the east side and marked by seventeen boundary stones on the north and west.

The property of La Romanée was for a very long time the property of the Croonembourg family. We do not know when it came into their possession, only that this family possessed it in the 15th century. The precious heritage was conserved until the death of Philippe Croonembourg. André, his son, wanting to resolve the charges against the estate of his father, resolved to sell the property. The vineyard was coveted by Madame de Pompadour who was nevertheless not successful in her intrigues. Jean-François Joly, Councillor of State, made an effective proposal. Croonembourg consented to the sale of Romanée for the price of 80,000 livres and 100 Louis in gold in 1760.

This parcel of vines had been sold as if it had five *journaux*. The surveying of the vineyard had not been done before the sale took place. When it was found that the parcel was only 37 ouvrées, the seller was compelled to give three *ouvrées* that were separated from Romanée by a footpath.

The price of the property was might appear excessive at the time of the sale, especially as the parcel was subject to a tithe, payable as one-sixteenth of the fruit, and a long-term lease of thirty sols, payable to the priory of Saint-Vivant. But the renown acquired by the wines of this parcel were such and the wealth of he who would receive it were motives sufficiently powerful to incite small sacrifices. The Prince de Conti to whom Jean-François Joly had signed over his acquisition and applied for the tithe to the house of Saint-Vivant.

Before the year 1735, this parcel of vines had been cultivated by the late Nicolas Tisserandot, who had neglected them and reduced them to a poor state. They thus produced only one barrel per journaux in an average year. From 1735, it was cultivated by Denis Mongeard from Vosne until 1783. The quality vine tending and care that he gave to the vine ensured that the new proprietor employed him as well. The vine returned to a better state. What contributed even more to this improvement was the addition of one hundred and fifty truckloads of mountain turf brought by Croonembourg and spread on the parcel in 1749, in addition to the low production of this vineyard, on average one barrel per *journal*.

In 1785 and 1786, Grimelin, the estate manager for the Prince de Conti, dug a pit at the base of the parcel and removed around 800 wheelbarrows of earth and spread it in the places that had been denuded of soil and in the weak and sterile parts of the parcel. He filled in the pit with gravel and topped it with good quality new turf to renew this plot. This amelioration cost him at least 1,000 livres. A few years after this acquisition, he acquired four *ouvrées* of vines for the construction of a handsome building.

While it is true to say that La Romanée produces on average one cask per journal, one must not forget that in good years it gives much more; thus, one can make from twelve to fifteen casks. In 1772, the parcel produced eighteen casks; in 1785, twenty, in 1787, ten.

One cannot hide the fact that the wine of Romanée is the most excellent of all the Côte d'Or and even of all of the vineyards of the French republic.... Its brilliant and velvety color, its perfume, and its generosity charm all the senses. This wine, well stored and conditioned, reaches in its eighth or tenth year with augmented quality. It becomes the balm of the elderly, the weak and the ill, and brings the dying back to life.

Louis XIV, being treated for a fistula, was reduced to a deplorable and unsettling state of weakness. The doctors assembled to find the means to reanimate his forces. They were of the opinion that the most efficient remedy was to choose the most excellent old wines of the Côte de Nuits and of Beaune. The purchasing department sourced them and the invalid employed them and his health was promptly restored. Without contradiction it was that of La Romanée that performed the greatest marvels.

In 1733 and the following years, the price of the wine of Romanée, fixed by the proprietor, was 900 francs, 1,000 francs, and 1,100 francs per *queue*. Since 1750 until the time the vineyard was sold, the price of a queue was fixed, according to the quality of the year, at 1,200, 1,300 and 1,400 francs and the proprietor sold them only by the half barrel.

The Prince de Conti reserved the wine for himself during all the time when he was the proprietor.

18 Messidor year II of the French Republic[57]

Signed Renaudot, expert; Breton, mayor

        Esmonin and Mongeard, deputies »

La Romanée was sold to a Mr. Nicolas Defère, of Paris for a sum of 112,000 livres. It passed then into the hands of MM. Tourton and Ravel, who re-sold it to M. Ouvrard, the father of the current owner.

Much has been said of the origin of the name of this celebrated climat. Was it planted by the Romans? Did it belong at the time of the Roman occupation to the emperors or high officials? Had it been the site of a Roman camp? On this subject one can only make hypotheses. The only thing that is certain is that the name of La Romanée had been given in memory of some fact relative to the Roman occupation.

The climat of La Tâche produces wine not less excellent. It belonged before the Revolution to a chapter of monks from Nuits and was acquired by the younger M. Marey at a price of 900 francs per ouvrée. In the trial when the estimate of the worth of this property was calculated, the expert suggested a minimum of 650 francs per ouvrée:

> Given that, since the wine of La Romanée is not available, the wine of La Tâche passes for the first wine of Burgundy and has always been sold since the time of the sale of Romanée to the Prince de Conti at 1,200 francs per queue, with the exception of the years when the best wines are worth nothing. He estimates the average yield of each ouvrée to be 20 pintes and the expenses at half.
>
> Romanée-Saint-Vivant belonged for several centuries to the abbey of this name. The average product was evaluated from 1780 to 1790 at 18 livres

per ouvrée, all the growing expenses deducted. This domaine was sold in 1793 for 91,000 livres, including the buildings.

The other great climats of Vosne, almost all long divided into a considerable number of parcels, had belonged in large part before the Revolution to religious orders and were sold at this time as property of the nation.

What are the best wines and the best values in Vosne-Romanée today? The list is of necessity very long due to the quality of the terroir. Such a list would also have to begin with Romanée-Conti, followed by La Tâche. These are universally acclaimed as the two top appellations in Vosne and indeed among the very greatest in the world of wine and the work of the Domaine de la Romanée-Conti is here as elsewhere beyond reproach. All of their reds are the standard-bearers in their respective appellations. After these two obvious choices, the picture becomes less clear, although many wine lovers put Richebourg next. Here the Domaine de la Romanée-Conti is also at the head of the list, but there as it is not a monopole, there are other options as well. The top wine from Domaine Leroy is their Richebourg, and this is an obvious contender. Méo Camuzet is another top producer, and the wines by Thibault Liger-Belair, Gros Frère et Sœur and Anne Gros all offer great quality at a (slightly) lower price. In any discussion of the top wines of Vosne, it would be wrong to neglect La Romanée. Produced by Domaine de Comte Liger-Belair, it has been gaining each year in quality, stature and price. Some marvelous wines in Romanée Saint-Vivant also deserve mention, particularly those of the Domaine de la Romanée-Conti, Domaine Leroy and Hudelot-Noëllat.

There are also premier cru wines that bear a mention in the honor roll of Vosne-Romanée. Cros Parantoux, when produced by Henri Jayer, was easily one of the top wines in Burgundy, and today the few remaining bottles command stratospheric prices at auction. The wines today, made by Emmanuel Rouget and Domaine Méo-Camuzet, do not have quite the same allure, but the terroir, just up from Richebourg is marvelous. Another appellation on the edge of Richebourg that was made famous by Henri Jayer is the premier cru Aux Brûlées, and the versions that are produced today by Domaine Méo-Camuzet, Domaine Leroy and Domaine du Comte Liger-Belair are worthy as well. A final appellation limitrophe the top grands crus is Malconsorts, which abuts La Tâche. The wines produced here by Sylvain Cathiard, Hudelot-Noëllat and Domaine Dujac are also scintillatingly good. Not every wine here is great—it seems that La Grande Rue rarely lives up to the potential mooted by its location in the midst of the Romanées and La Tâche, but there are yet enough brillian successes to ensure that Vosne will always warrant its epithet of the Pearl of the Côte.

NUITS AND PRÉMEAUX

Nuits is one of the most compelling reasons to examine the "original grands crus of Burgundy." While the presently constituted grands crus in the rest of the Côte de Nuits have changed over time, Les Saint-Georges in Nuits is the first example of a vineyard that was unanimously seen as being at the top of the scale prior to the 20th century, but is not classified in grand cru today. As with La Grande Rue, which was promoted to grand cru in 1992, the owners of both vineyards during the formulation of the current AC regulations of the 1930s feared higher taxes and did not submit an application for this classification at the time. As with La Grande Rue, the application for Les Saint-Georges was submitted decades after the initial classification. The complicated process, which can take up to seven years to complete, is now underway. Other vineyards obtained this promotion in later years: Clos des Lambrays was promoted in 1981, and La Grande Rue in 1992.

According to Lavalle, Les Saint-Georges is an ancient vineyard, planted to vines more than 1,000 years ago. Even Lavalle, however, is puzzled by the relative lack of acclaim that it has received. One of the factors complicating Les Saint-Georges has been the fragmented nature of its ownership. While other notable climats have been concentrated in the hands of a few important growers, this has not been true of Les Saint-Georges. Nonetheless, as Thibault Liger-Belair has reminded us recently, the Côte de Nuits takes its name from Nuits. Today the wines of Nuits-Saint-Georges and Prémeaux are classified together, and there are 41 climats classed in as premier cru, with no official distinction between them.

The vines of the villages are rather spread out, and a bit of geography helps to understand them. The most northerly vines are those bordering the territory of Vosne, lying north of the little stream called the Meuzin, just downslope from the wood known at that point as the Bois de Villars-Fontaine, giving the vineyards an east-southeast exposure. Here, among others, lie the climats Aux Boudots, Aux Cras, Aux Murgers, and Aux Thorey, all singled out by Lavalle for special mention. Unlike other portions of his book, however, they are not divided neatly, but rather lumped together as "têtes de cuvées and premières cuvées", although they are described as being of "the first order" and are listed first in the text.

The second group of climats lies south of the village, with the best climats located after the valley of the Meuzin, where the hill turns to face more or less due east, downslope from the Bois de Charmois. Here Lavalle singles out Pruliers and Porrets, with this last now divided into Clos des Porrets-Saint-Georges and Porrets-Saint-Georges. Just past this point lie Les Cailles,

Les Vaucrains, and Les Saint-Georges, which are on the southern border with Prémeaux-Prissey.

The last group of climats is in Prémeaux itself. As Lavalle notes, these are the equal of any wines produced in Nuits proper. Top crus include Les Didiers, Les Forêts (also known as Clos des Forêts Saint-Georges, a monopole of the Domaine de l'Arlot), and Aux Corvées, which is now divided now into two climats: Aux Corvées itself and Clos des Corvées Pagets. In his recap at the end of his work, Lavalle has Les Saint-Georges as a "tête de cuvée N° 1," and Boudots, Cailles, Cras, Murgers, Porrets, Pruliers, Thorey, and Vaucrains (in Nuits), and Corvées, Didiers, and Forêts (in Prémeaux) as tête de cuvée N° 2.

We begin the story of Nuits with the decription of Courtépée, who refers to the climats of the village of Nuits and to the large Côte in the same breath:

> The Côte de Nuits produces the best wines of Burgundy; the most excellent without contradiction is that of Vosne, at a half league to the northwest: (see Vosne). The climat of Saint-Georges in Nuits is renowned, as is Le Boudot. We will speak later of those of Morey, Chambolle, Vougeot, Premeaux, in the articles on these villages. The first celebrity of the wines of this slope goes back only as far as Louis XIV, for whom, after a dangerous malady in 1686, Dr. Fagon ordered the most "pectoral" wine and indicated that of Nuits to be the most appropriate to reestablish his weakened forces. In 1625 two barrels of this wine sold for only 25 livres, and 50 livres in 1656.

We find much more detail in Dr. Morelot:

> A quarter of a league from Comblanchien is the village of Prémeaux[21], reputed for its beautiful water and its fountain of iron-rich water, and even more for its good wines: here begins the Côte de Nuits.
>
> The hill of Prémeaux is composed of a limestone with a very fine grain, nearly similar to that which I have spoken of earlier. The nuances of violet and the white are less noticeable than in the marble of Ladoix, but have much in common with it. This stone is excellent for construction, and as at Ladoix, one pulls out enormous blocks of stone which, when they are worked, emit a clear, metallic sound.
>
> Leaving Prémeaux, one finds Perrières, Les Corvées, Didiers; above this are Les Cailles, Les Forêts, Georges, a very distinguished district and one of the best of the slope; then Vaucrains. All of these vineyards are placed almost at the foot of the slope at a very slight incline; it is impossible to cultivate the upper parts, it is so steep that it forms an angle of nearly forty degrees. The rains and the storms have stripped away the topsoil, and thus the slope offers only a thin layer of earth mixed with large morsels of rock or stones, absolutely impossible to cultivate. The wines of this portion of the slope are very generous[22]; firm, mellow, and similar to those of Aloxe; one can only appreciate their merit after two or even three years. Les Saints-Georges is superior to all of the other wines of this slope; I will observe here that

---

21 Prémeaux offers the observer a sort of little valley that owes its birth to a fairly abundant spring, but which in former times must have yielded an immense quantity of water. These waters hollowed out the earth, bit-by-bit, and formed a deep valley, on which two slopes is built the village, crossed by the main road, whose descent was very rapid. About fifty years ago, a haute levee was constructed that rendered the crossing easier.

22 We do not know what to ascribe the disdain prior to the beginning of the 18th century for the wines of Nuits. In 1625, a barrel was worth only twenty-five livres, and until 1700, their price was always very modest. Their celebrity appears to date from an illness of Louis XIV in 1680. Fagon, his physician, prescribed them to reestablish his strength; from this time they came to favor and were justly appreciated.

they owe their quality to two causes: the first is that the wine of Saints-Georges is made only with the fruit from this climat; the second is the beautiful exposition of the vineyard; but as to the intimate qualities of the wine, they are the same. Les Saints-Georges has only more finesse, more bouquet, and much more delicacy.

At the valley of Nuits begins that portion of our slope, so renowned for the excellence of its wines, which will fail to gain precedence over those of the Côte de Beaune only because they have the reputation of being more generous, to keep better, and to deteriorate less during a voyage, which is open to dispute. This group of slopes extends to Chambolle for about one league. This part of the slope is endowed with the beautiful villages of Vosne and Vougeot; the main road passes in the midst of Vougeot, which runs right along the walls of its clos[23].

The rock that forms the base of this little chain is of a very pure limestone, with little admixture of foreign matter; it is a sort of white marble with a few thin veins of a very agreeable pink. These marbles have been seen until now only very superficially, but could become a fairly important branch of commerce if one looked deeper for blocks of a more sold and compact texture than that which one finds near the surface of the hill. The samples taken thus far are porous and filled with foreign matter.

Leaving Nuits, one climbs a bit up the slope to head to Vosne: here are found the very distinguished climats of Vignes Rondes, Bousselots, Les Cras, Chaignots, Échézeaux, Boudots. The territory of Nuits finishes in this place and it is there that Vosne begins, one of the most renowned for the excellence of its wines.

Here are the somewhat more confusing explanations of Dr. Lavalle on the same territory:

COMMUNE DE NUITS

The vines grown in the territory of the village of Nuits form two broad categories: fine vineyards planted exclusively to Pinot Noir, and common vineyards planted to Gamay.

The surface occupied by these two types of vineyard is around 240 ha in Pinot and around 350 ha in Gamay. The Pinot is rigorously limited by the nature of the soil, and is on the decline because Gamay is often substituted at high elevations and at the foot of the slope. Pinot Noir, once occupying 250 ha is now no more than 240, while the area planted to Gamay tends always to increase, and has grown in the past twenty five years from 160 ha to approximately 350 ha.

There is no parcel planted in Nuits exclusively to Pinot Gris or to Pinot Blanc called *chardenet* or *chadenet* [sic]. These two varieties are only found mixed in with Pinot Noir, and in a very small proportion, and sometimes none at all, particularly in the case of Pinot Blanc.[58]

The road from Beaune to Dijon traces fairly exactly the limit between the Pinot Noir

---

23 The summits of all these slopes were covered by great white oaks that were destroyed because it was believed that they attracted storms. Since their destruction, the storms have not been less dangerous for this part of the slope, above all for Chambolle and Morey, which are often ravaged by hail.

or *Noirien* vines and those of Gamay: east of this route, everything is Gamay, and to the west, almost everything is *Noirien*, except for several parcels situated too low or too high on the slope and several terrains at the entrance of the valley of the Musain, which are planted to Gamay.

The total extent of the vines in Pinot Noir being determined as above at 240 ha are spread over fifty climats or lieux-dits, it seems useless to give the names and the extent of each of these climats, except those that occupy the first rank and carry a name known in the market.

The climats of vines in Pinot Noir are divided into three large groups:

1st The *têtes de cuvées*, formed by grapes from a single parcel, that is to say, from vines of a single climat or two at most, neighbors and of more or less equal quality.

2nd The *premières cuvées*, formed from vines all of the first order, but that cannot take the name of any climat, since their proprietors do not possess enough of any one to make a separate cuvée; these premières cuvées have more or less a local reputation, according to the quality of the vines that compose them.

3rd The *secondes cuvées*, where inferior climats dominate; these cuvées offer multiple nuances, and it is local experience that classifies them by the names of their proprietors.

The *têtes de cuvées* and *premières cuvées* occupy approximately 110 ha, and the *secondes* about 130 ha. The 110 ha of the first order are today divided more or less as follows:

Les Saints-Georges	8 ha	Aux Boudots		7 ha
Les Vaucrains	6 ha	Aux Cras		3 ha
Les Cailles	4 ha	Aux Murger		4 ha
Porrets	7 ha	Aux Thorey		6 ha
Les Pruliers	12 ha		Total	57 ha

Danguy et Aubertin treat the climats of Nuits as the other villages instead of adopting the style of Lavalle. Their notes on the ownership of the têtes de cuvées are below. It should also be noted that Les Saint-Georges, Les Vaucrains, Les Pruliers, Les Cailles, Les Porrets ou Les Poirets, and Aux Murgers are distinguished by capital letters and presented in that order.

NOMENCLATURE
OF PRINCIPAL CLIMATS AND LIEUX-DITS

Boudots (Aux). – D.L., tête de cuvée ; C.A.B., première classe

Principal Proprietors: MM. Chalopin-Bergeret, Antonin Gandné-Baroche, Jacob Grivot, Grivot Renevey, the Hospices de Nuits

<u>Rodier</u>: MM. Gaudin de Villaine, Grandné-Clavier, F. Gremeaux, Grivot Renevey, the Hospices de Nuits, Mugneret-Clerget, Ch. Noëllat, E. Noëllat, Noirot-Marcillet, J. Reitz

Cailles (Les). – D.L., tête de cuvée ; C.A.B., première classe

Principal Proprietors: MM. André (colonel), Gautheret-Juard, de Morot de Grésigny d'Authume, Mlle. Jouard, M. Emile Jouard, the widow Marey-Monge, MM. Ragon-Morand, Roux-Jouard.

> Rodier: MM. The Louis André heirs, Cautheret-Jouard, Symphorien et Jouis Jarot, Morin Père et Fils, J. Reitz, J.-B. Rollet, Roux-Maybon

Cras (Aux). – D.L., tête de cuvée ; C.A.B., première classe

Principal Proprietors: MM. André-Argot, Chalopin-Bergeret, Claude Gaguet, Grandné-Duband, Mme. Regnault-Cogneux, the widow Marey-Monge

> Rodier: MM. Chalopin-Bergeret, Chapuzot-Camus, Confuron Himbert, Cornu-Charton, Grandné-Duban, Gremeaux-Richardot, Hudelot-Magnien, A. Japiot, Jaugey-Pelissey, Magnien-Grégoire, M. Misserey, Mongeard-Morand, G. Monin, Monin-Himbert, Mugneret-Clerget, Mugneret-Pasquier, Noëllat-Fournier, J. Reitz, Sirugue-Saconney, Mme. De Tulle

Porrets or Poirets – D.L., tête de cuvée ; C.A.B., première classe

Principal Proprietors: MM. Briet-Thomas, Faiveley-Bordeux, Claude Gaguet, l'Hospices de Nuits, M. Jouan-Boudrot, the widow Marey-Monge, MM. Morin, Ragon-Morand

> Rodier: MM. The Edme Bergeret heirs, Besaucenot-Marcillet, G. Faiveley, Garnier-Tissier, Gautherot-Jouard, Symphorien Jarot, Liger-Belair, Morin Père et Fils, Roux-Maybon, Moillard-Grivot, Trapet-Salignac

Pruliers (Les). – D.L., tête de cuvée ; C.A.B., première classe

Principal Proprietors: MM. André Argot, Berthier de Grandry, Bourgogne-Lignier, Gautheron, Morin, Ragon-Morand, Revon-Verguet, the town of Nuits

> Rodier: MM. Esprit-Dorlet, Galland-Chauvenet, the widow Gautherot, P. Gondot, A. Japiot, S. Jarot, Jeanniard Moissenet, Liger-Belair, M. Misserey, Monin-Himbert, Morin Père et Fils, Roblot-Bonnardot, Roy-Millot, Mme. De Tulle

Murgers (Aux). – D.L., tête de cuvée ; C.A.B., première classe

Principal Proprietors: MM. Jean Faucillon, the Hospices de Nuits, the widow Marey-Monge, M. Revon-Verguet, the widow Sirugue

> Rodier: MM. Bouchard-Noëllat, Manière-Virey, J.-B. Rollet, E. Sirugue

Saint-Georges (Les). – D.L., tête de cuvée ; C.A.B., première classe

Principal Proprietors: MM. André (colonel), Faiveley-Bordeux, Claude Gaguet, Gautheret-Juard, Armand Gautheron, the Hospices de Nuits, Mlle. Jouard, M. Emile Jouard, MM. Le Comte Liger-Belair, the widow Marey Monge, Mayol de Luppé, de Morot de Grésigny d'Authume, Roux-Jouard, Eugène Sirugue, Maurice Thomas

> Rodier: MM. Bourgogne, G. Faiveley, Robert Garnier, Gautheret-Jouard, the Hospices de Nuits, A. Japiot, Liger-Belair, de Lupé, J. B. Rollet, Roux-Maybon, Moillard-Grivot, Mme. De Tulle
>
> **Thorey or Torey** (Aux). – D.L., tête de cuvée ; C.A.B., deuxième and troisième classe
>
> Principal Proprietors: MM. André-Argot, Berthier de Grandry, Boulley-Clerget, Grivot-Lamy, Grivot-Murger, Guy-Neige, Trapet-Bergeret, the town of Nuits
>
>> Rodier: MM. Baillot-Pillet, Bavard-Gagnard, Bavard-Lesprit, F. Bergeret, Boulley-Clerget, Bourgogne, M. Coirier, Confuron-Himbert, Durel-Tizy, Ecard-Ocquidaut, Garnier-Grivot, the widow Grivot Lamy, A. Japiot, Jarot-Pillet, J. Jaeger, Lamy-Roy, Léger-Marchand, Moillard-Grivot, Ocquidant-Jeanniard, Tisy-Grivot.
>
> **Vaucrains** (Les). – D.L., tête de cuvée ; C.A.B., première classe
>
> Principal Proprietors: MM. Le Colonel André, Grandné-Lécrivain, Gauthron-Armamnd, Comte Liger-Belair, the widow Marey-Monge, Mayol de Luppé, de Morot de Grésigny d'Authume, Ragon-Morand
>
>> Rodier: MM. Bourgogne, Challand, Chauvenet-Pasquier, L. Estivalet, Grandné-Lecrivain, Lamblot-Gaguiard, Liger-Belair, de Lupé, M. Misserey, J. B. Rollet, Rollet-Bourret

Returning to the comments of Dr Lavalle:

> Following these but still in the first line, yet names of less importance and without preeminence are

Aux Argillas	3 ha		Les Perrières	2 ha 50 a
Aux Rousselots[59]	4 ha 50 a		Les Poulettes	2 ha
Chabiots [60]	3 ha		Les Procès	2 ha
Aux Chaignots	3 ha		La Richemone	2 ha
Chaînes-Carteaux	2 ha 50 a		Roncière	2 ha 50 a
Aux Champs Perdrix	2 ha		Aux Vignesrondes	5 ha 50 a
La Charmotte[61]	10 ha		Les Crots	8 ha 50 a
			Total	**53 ha**

General total, 110 ha

The principal proprietors in premières cuvées of the Côte de Nuits are today:

MM. Marey (Félix),			**MM. Virely,**	
Les Saints-Georges	2 ha 25 a		Aux Boudots	1 ha 55 a
Les Pruliers and others	2 ha 50 a		**Marey (widow)**	
Duret,			Les Vaucrains, Les Cailles	2 ha 20 a
Les Saints-Georges	1 ha 70 a		Moissenet-Meulien	

Les Cailles	1 ha 15 a	Les Porrets	4 ha 50 a
Aux Argillas and Aux Thorey	1 ha 60 a	**Marey-Gassendi,**	
Coirier,		Les Porrets	1 ha 25 a
Les Saint-Georges, Les Vaucrains	1 ha 20 a	**Marcand,**	
Les Pruliers	1 ha 50 a	Les Pruliers	1 ha 05 a
De Lupé (widow),		Marey-Lausseure	
Les Saints-Georges	90 a	Les Pruliers	80 a
Les Vaucrains	1 ha 20 a		
Marey-Monge (General),		**Hutteau,**	
Les Saints-Georges	65 a	Aux Boudots & Aux Murgers	1 ha 25
Les Porrets	60 a	**Gueisweiler (widow)**	
Aux Murgers	1 ha 15 a	Aux Murgers	1 ha
Faucillon,		**Janniard (widow),**	
Les Saints-Georges	50 a	Aux Murgers	85 a
Les Pruliers	75 a	Les Crots	3 ha 20
Virely,		**Royer,**	
Les Vaucrains	90 ha	Aux Thorey	1 ha 35
			37 ha
		Total	
			55 a

These 37 to 38 ha, concentrated in the hands of sixteen proprietors, furnish only the cuvées of a single climat and carrying a name; the surplus of the first-class vineyard, that is to say 72 ha, is divided into parcels more or less strong among all of the proprietors, and the union of these parcels in the fermenting tank forms the premières cuvees, more or less well known, according to the rank and the extent of the parcels that compose it.

It is essentially impossible to determine the average harvested in each climat: one can say only that the terrains the most productive are the Saint-Georges, Vaucrains, Pruliers, etc., and that those that yield the least are those of Aux Thorey, Aux Argillas, Roncière, etc. The difference in production between these is on the order of a quarter or one-fifth. The production of all of the Pinot Noir vines is around 20 hl/ha, and for Gamay from 60 to 60 hl/ha.

The relative value of the wines produced in the different crus of Nuits is more or less indicated by the classification established above. The Saint-Georges occupies the first rank for aging potential, color, bouquet, and finesse when it has attained the necessary age of ten to twenty years according to the vintage; following next for body and bouquet is Les Vaucrains, Les Pruliers, etc.; for finesse, but with less body and firmness, Les Cailles, Les Porrets, Les Perrières, Roncière, Aux Argillas, Aux Thorey, etc.

In addition, all of these distinctions are very difficult to establish, because there are very few absolutely pure cuvées, and blending in tank, far from diminishing quality, normally benefits it, giving to a cru several of the qualities that it lacks to greater or lesser degree, either the body, or the bouquet or the finesse. Thus Les Saint-Georges marries very well with its neighbor Vaucrains, Les Cailles and Les Porrets; Aux Argillas and Aux Thorey take on a bit more body with Boudots or Cras, etc., etc.

The climats that we have not yet pointed out and which can be considered as giving secondes cuvées of Pinot are: Aux Allots, Aux Athées, Aux Barrières, Au Bas-de-Combe, Belle-Croix, Les Brûlées, Chaliots-Brulés[62], Les Fleurières, Aux Herbues, Aux Lavières, Les Longecourts, Les Maladière, Les Poisets, Aux Saints-Jacques, Aux Saints-Juliens, Aux Tuyaux[63].

In Nuits there are no "third class" wines. Under this name one can only designate the wines called *passe-tout-grains*, that is to say, coming from Gamay and inferior Pinot or from pure Gamay. But almost all of these wines, produced by vines situated to the east of the Route Nationale are simply named *Passe-tout-grains* and Gamays.

The relationship between the wines of Nuits and the other wines of La Côte is not easy to establish. In general, the wines of Nuits have less firmness and strength than the wines of Gevrey and are sooner ready to drink; that have more body and color than those of Chambolle; they are similar to the wines of Vosne, and are generally of the same rank, except for La Romanée and Richebourg; Les Saint-Georges is on a par with the Corton of Aloxe and the Clos des Lambrays in Morey; finally, this slope has generally more body, vinosity, and firmness than the wines of the Côte de Beaune, which prevails over the Côte de Nuits only with a few cuvées, and only from Volnay, for finesse, bouquet and early charm, without, however, ever attaining the market value of the wines of Nuits and of Vosne[24]

In spite of our ardent desire, we have been able to find but rare references to the principal climats of Nuits, and notably of Les Saint-Georges, so famous in the past two centuries. This climat, constituted as a walled vineyard and planted with vines around the year 1000, appears to have been given in donation in the year 1023 by Humbert, the archdeacon of Autun and Elisabeth, his sister, the lady of this site to the cathedral chapter of Saint-Denis, founded by them at Vergy the same year, as the territory of Nuits was a dependency of the barony of Vergy.

In this distant epoch, and even a few centuries later, Les Saint-Georges was interchangeably designated either as an independent climat or as being part of the climat of Valerots. In 1444, the list of the territories of the Chapter of Saint-Denis mentions a rent due to this chapter for 14 ouvrées situated in Saint-Georges. This is probably the same vines that we find in 1584 when the chapter retook possession of 15 ouvrées of vines in Saint-Georges from the widow Thevenin to whom they had rented them for the period of her life.

---

24 I am obliged for the preceding information to M. Duret, the mayor of Nuits.

In 1609, the chapter had once again been displaced from its vines by a certain Mr. Haquenier. They began legal action to retake this property and were undoubtedly successful, for we find that in 1614 they sold what they owned in Saint-Georges at a price of 300 livres to J. Taveau.

The former possessions of the crown at Argilly included also vines in Saint-Georges.

COMMUNE DE PREMEAUX

The Côte de Nuits continues to the south onto the territory of Prémeaux without any modification of the surface of the soil and without any peaks or valley creating a natural separation. It is the same soil, subsoil, exposition, absolute or relative elevation, the same grapes and the same method of culture. Everything that is true of one of these vineyards is true of the other. The wines produced in the good climats of Nuits or of Prémeaux have identical qualities, and the narrow path that separates the climat of Les Saints-Georges from that of Les Didiers here is not, as it is in so many places, a limit beyond which all is quickly changed.[64]

Prémeaux produces a very important portion of excellent wines sold under the name of Nuits and its premiers crus are the equal of the most exquisite that this town can produce. Thus, for all I would say of the wines of Prémeaux, I can but reoffer the preceding description, noting only that in Prémeaux the good wines are produced in a very restricted area, and that one can consider that fine vines occupy only 61 ha. Even the culture of Gamay is not that widespread, and does not surpass 100 ha. The climats of this territory that can thus be classified:

Hors Ligne

Rodier does not distinguish any of these cuvées through the use of capital letters.

Aux Didiers, 2 ha 84 ares, of which 1 ha 33 a belongs to the Hospices de Nuits, and 1 ha to M. Moissenet-Landriot.

> Danguy et Aubertin: M. Julien Guillemot, the Hospices de Nuits, M. Promayet
>
> Rodier: The Hospices de Nuits and M. Japiot

Aux Forêts, 5 ha 2 a 95 ca, of which 1 ha belongs to the elder M. Viénot.

> Danguy et Aubertin: M. Julien Guillemot (Clos des Forêts Saint-Georges)
>
> Rodier has this as Les Forets and ascribes ownership to M. A. Guillemot.

Aux Corvées, 7 ha 83 a 40 ca, of which 2 ha belong to M. Hasenclever, 33 ha 33 a to M. Adolphe Gueisweler, and 50 a to the Hospices de Nuits.

> Danguy et Aubertin: MM. Brüninghaus, Darantiere Arsène Perrier, Rossigneux, Charles Viénot, the Galland heirs, the Hospices de Beaune

Rodier has *Les* Corvées under the ownership of MM. R. Brüninghaus and A. Rossigueux

Aux Pagets, 1 ha 33 a to M. de Curley (Alexandre); and 1 ha to Mme. Carrier.

Danguy et Aubertin: M. Cognieux-Monin, M. A. Périer, M. Viénot (Aux Corvées Pagets)

Rodier has Les Corvées-Pagets under the ownership of MM. Jean Cognieux, theHospices de Nuits and Charles Viénot

Première Cuvée

Clos-Saint-Marc, 3 ha, belonging to Mme. Carrier.

Clos-des-Argillières, 4 ha 90 a 30 ca, of which 1 ha 50 a belongs to M. Gueisweler (Adolphe).

Clos de l'Arlot, 7 ha 73 a 45 ca, of which 5 ha belongs to the elder M. Viénot.

Clos des Fourches, 15 ha 20 a 25 ca, of which 3 ha belong to M. Lemire (Etienne).

Les Perdrix, 3 ha 36 a 60 ca, of which 2 ha belong to M. Jacquinot (Edouard).

Deuxième Cuvée

Aux Leurrées, 3 ha belonging to M. Viénot and 2 ha belonging to M. Bristchgy-Viénot.

Ez Grandes-Vignes, 3 ha 90 a 75 ca, of which 2 ha belongs to the elder M. Viénot, 1 ha 50 a belongs to M. de Curley (Jules), and 70 a belongs to M. Jacquinot (Edouard).

Aux Tapones, 3 ha 47 a 70 ca, of which 2 ha 33 a belong to M. Bailly-Duret, and 1 ha to M. Haseuclever.

Aux Meix-Grands, 1 ha 50 a belonging to the elder M. Viénot.

The other parts of the territory produce only very inferior wines to the preceding, and can only be considered as ordinary wines destined to local consumption.

It seems to me that the commune of Nuits is among the most fertile hunting grounds for wines of grand cru quality at less-than-grand cru prices. Les Saint-Georges is the leading climat, but others approach it in quality. In Les Saint-Georges, Thibault Liger-Belair is the largest proprietor, followed by Henri Gouges. The most sublime Les Saint-Georges that I have ever tasted was a 1934 from Henri Gouges. It is ironic that this wine was produced just at the time that the founder of this estate was engaged in convincing his fellow growers in Nuits *not* to apply for grand cru status under the rules then being promulgated. Other leading climats in Nuits include Les Cailles just north of Les Saint-Georges and Vaucrains, just upslope (look for Robert Chevillon in these two appellations), followed by Les Porrets Saint-Georges (Faiveley) and the Gouges monopole Clos des

Porrets Saint-Georges to the north of Les Cailles as well as the Clos des Fôrets Saint-Georges (a monopole of the Domaine de l'Arlot), all superb terroirs. In addition there are a host of wonderful wines made by smaller growers and negociants in this region, and the hunt for new discoveries should prove a diverting exercise for burgundy lovers everywhere.

AROUND THE HILL OF CORTON

The vineyards of the hill of Corton are spread over three villages. It is the largest of the grands crus in Burgundy by a very large margin, at 160 ha 19 a 39 ca. As one might expect over such a large area quality can be variable, and the opinions of knowledgeable tasters have changed greatly over time. Courtépée describes the early origins of the vineyards by writing that at the dawn of the 16th century, the crown possessed a considerable vineyard of 100 ouvrées in Corton. Athough by the early 18th century, Claude Arnoux has referred to the production of Aloxe as "Vin de Primeur," and no further mention is made of the Corton climat. A hundred years later, Morelot has warmed up to Corton, and a generation further on, Dr. Lavalle opined that, "The wines of Corton are closer to the wines of Chambertin than to any other wine of the Côte d'Or." The reputation of Corton had certainly flourished during these two and one half centuries.

The true expansion of the *area* of Corton, however, occurred during the creation of the AOC rules in the 20th century. Just how much has the vineyard grown in size? Dr. Morelot writes that Corton is "ten to twelve hectares." Lavalle mentions Corton itself (11 ha 58 a 20 ca), Corton Clos-du-Roi (10 ha 82 a 90 ca), and Corton Les Renardes (15 ha 26 a 35 ca) for a total of 39 ha 67 a 45 ca. The sum of all of today's vineyards, however, that are able to market themselves as Corton total an astonishing 160 ha 19 a 39 ca. A seven-fold increase in size over roughly 180 years, due to *"usages locaux, loyaux et constants"*.

The root of these usages must due in large part to the work of Danguy et Aubertin, who expended much ink writing on the wines of Ladoix, while Lavalle scarcely mentioned the commune thirty-seven years before. Today there are 22 ha 42 a 83 ca of grand cru vineyard in Ladoix. Although Lavalle admits that *"one finds several vineyards planted in Pinot that give wines that are not without value,"* the praise seems faint indeed.

The core of what is today grand cru in Ladoix is a continuation of Renardes, Les Bressandes, and Les Maréchaudes as they wrap around the hill. It was during the last half of the 19th century that the bulk of these vineyards became known as either Le Corton, Le Roguet [sic], or Les Vergennes, as documented in Danguy et Aubertin, although there are other climats that are also included now in Corton Grand Cru, including the following:

1 ha 92 a 92 ca of Hautes Mourottes

94 a 81 ca of Basses Mourottes

8 ha 57 a 96 ca of Le Rognet et Corton

3 ha 01 a 65 ca of the Clos des Cortons Faiveley (which is also part of Le Rognet

et Corton, as above; 50 ares is for red wine only and the balance may be either)

50 a 53 ca of Les Carrières

84 a 59 ca of Les Moutottes

3 ha 45 a 17 ca of Vergennes

3 ha 04 a 40 ca of Les Grandes Lolières

10 a 80 ca of La Toppe au Vert

Parts of Hautes Mourottes, Basses Mourottes, and Le Rognet et Corton are classified mostly as Corton grand cru with some premier cru and some village parcels. Parts of Les Carrières are grand cru and some are village. Danguy et Aubertin note that these vineyards had been classified as "première, deuxième and troisième classes" by the Comité d'Agriculture de Beaune, but that local usage (indicated in their text as C. Loc.) credits them as being all of the première cuvée.

Aloxe is the heart of Corton with the most notable lieux-dits. Corton itself at the very top of the hill, a terroir, as Lavalle points out, better suited to whites than reds, and then the large swaths of vines on the east-facing slopes: particularly Renards and Clos du Roi, with Le Charlemagne at the same level of quality, and south-facing Les Chaumes right behind it. All of the other grands crus vineyards were added later, and Lavalle places them all among the première cuvées: Les Bressandes, Les Perrières, Les Fiètres, Les Grèves, Les Languettes, Les Pougets, Les Meix, Les Combes, and La Vigne au Saint. Les Maréchaudes – a large vineyard near the bottom of the slope – gives us 4 ha 45 a 97 ca in grand cru and another 1 ha 26 a 09 ca in premier cru, yet it was not mentioned in Lavalle.

Aloxe was certainly well regarded at the time of Courtépée. He documents the early history of the village, noting:

> Alosse ou Aloxe, formerly called Alousse, Alocé, Alussa, or Alussia is in the parish dedicated to Saint Médard, which is under the patronage of the College of Cannons in Saulieu to whom Charlemagne gave vines, still called the Clos de Charlemagne, which produces very good red and white wine[65]. Modoin, bishop of Autun, gave to his cathedral some vines in Aloxe, which he had been given by Jonas in 858. [There is an] Excellent climat called Corton, from the name of a neighboring wood.

> Cîteaux from the 12th century had a beautiful domaine and clos in Verconsault, with a chapel, barn, and gardens, but everything was already ruined by the wars and mortality of 1536, and was sold to Pernot Viennot and his sons in 1622. The farmhouse was a freehold with all titles and rights. M. Arbalestier found as he dug large hewn stones and a chapel pillar: it was the remains of the ancient priory.

> The barns of Sainte-Marguerite, destroyed, and currently planted to vines situated in *Neujot* or *Neuzot*. There is still a vaulted cellar, whose entrance had been blocked up by M. L'Arbalestier to whom this property belongs. He possesses also the barns

of Cîteaux and the Creux-de-la-Vallée, once wooded, where the inhabitants took refuge during the war, which is now planted to vines.

Le Charlemagne in Pernand is rather the opposite case. The village is not mentioned in Arnoux, yet the origins of the vineyards are traced back to the 8th century by Courtépée:

> The Clos du Charlemagne, given by this prince to the abbot of Saulieu in 775 is in great part within the limits [of Pernand]. The best climats are Vergelesses and Boutière on the Savigny side.

Jullien, however, ignores it two generations after Courtépée, and the reference in Morelot is brief. Dr. Lavalle, however, is enamored of the whites produced here. He points out that the south-west exposition is exceptional and still qualifies it as première cuvée, qualifying it as a sole cuvée ("cuvée unique"). Its particularity lies in its cool nature, which will give fine and racy whites with concentration and power. Danguy et Aubertin spend more time here, delving into the Celtic etymology of the name Pernand and the origins of the village in ancient Gaul. They point out, however, that while Lavalle had Le Charlemagne as première cuvée that the Comité d'Agriculture de Beaune only had it as deuxième and troisième classes, an opinion carried through to the work of Camille Rodier. Today's appellation, however, has almost all of it as grand cru (with the exception of 88 a 76 ca classed in village), and the vineyards extend almost to the bottom of the valley.

In his book *Inside Burgundy*, Jasper Morris documents the wrangling around the creation of the present extent of the Corton appellations, noting the court cases from the 1920s through the 1970s that expanded the appellations here. In addition to the relatively traditional usages of the Corton name in Pernand and Ladoix that were codified in the 1930s at the original establishment of the appellation, there have been further expansions over the years, with a significant amount of land added in Pernand in 1966 and in Ladoix in 1978.

The current reputation of the Corton appellation is low, due in part to changing fashion and perhaps in part to the expansion of the vineyard over the last century and the resulting dilution of the name. It must also be due in some measure to the somewhat lackluster nature of the wines in recent years. One imagines that this last cause is in the process of changing, with the extremely strong work done by Domaine Coche-Dury, the improvement of many traditional estates in recent years, and the appearance of the Domaine de la Romanée-Conti on the scene. Corton is, perhaps, once again on the rise.

The opinion of Dr. Morelot:

> The Côte de Beaune ends with the village of Pernand, because at a new portion of the chain of hills begins at Aloxe and extends almost without interruption to the valley of Nuits. The hill of Corton at whose foot is found this village seems to stand alone. Placed in context, it moves toward the south, with its ridge garnished with vine shoots and its summit crowned with a wood upon whose green hues the view lingers. One can hardly imagine a better exposition. The vine profits from the rays of the sun from the moment it breaks the horizon until it disappears. The products thereof also show the benefits both of this magnificent exposition and a propitious soil.
>
> The limestone that forms the mass of this portion of the slope is more pure than that of which we have just spoken. The rock is a sort of marble whose red base is nuanced with violet streaks and sprinkled with little white spots, often intermixed with calcspar and beautiful crystals. This stone is able to take a very beautiful polish; it is employed in our part of the country for fireplaces, furniture, shelves, altars, etc. It is removed from the quarries in blocks a foot thick, sometimes less, sometimes much more, and one can obtain pieces from eight to twelve feet in length; it is used above all for the jambs of doors and the crosses of buildings, and the consumption of it is considerable. One has to search far and wide for blocks for the colonnade that are easily found in the quarry of Ladoix, and the columns would be as beautiful as the polish one gives to this stone, which cedes nothing to the most beautiful marble.[25]
>
> Almost all the districts of Aloxe are of a distinguished quality. Coming out from Pernand, one finds Le Charlemagne, so named because following an antique tradition it is believed that it was first planted at the order of this prince; a bit further along, one finds les Rues-d'Aloxe, Les Dolles, Les Vergennes, Pouget, Renardes, Cervottes, Bressandes, and above all of these is placed Le Corton, which occupies the upper part of this slope; a vineyard of around ten to twelve hectares, that furnishes a wine that can pass for one of the first of the entire Côte d'Or.
>
> The wines of Aloxe, that come from the districts that I have just mentioned, have a reputation that they duly merit, and that causes all of our negociants to seek them out. They are poorly judged the first year; they have something hard or bitter that puts off he who does not know their quality. But when their second fermentation has occurred, they develop a particular warmth, a fine and agreeable bouquet, and a perfect taste. They are deeply colored, firm, fruity, mellow, and have, above all, the ability to keep, and are able to sustain a long voyage. The wines of Aloxe sent to England are always in good condition and have not suffered at all from the sea voyage.
>
> I would remark that although the wine of Corton is slightly superior to the wines that come from other climats, they differ only in that their exposition is more favorable. All the wines of Aloxe have the same qualities, which come, as I have noted, from the quality of the soil, which is composed of the same limestone. I will next

---

25 One finds around the village of Beaune, other than the stone of Ladoix, which I have just described, the Brêche of St.-Romain and of Ourche, and the beautiful marble of Bouze. The quarries are already extensive, but when the Canal de Bourgogne shall be fully operational, it is imagined that the demand will double from the requests that will be made by Paris and other cities.

demonstrate, in my analysis of the soils that this salt accounts for close to half of the composition of our slopes; it is thus not surprising that one finds a great affinity in the products of the same slope.

From Aloxe to Comblanchien, which is a good league in length, there is essentially no slope of vines, because the major part of the hill offers only patches of woods[26]. The hamlet of Buisson, which is at the southern extremity, makes a sort of a point turned to the south-east, and from this point the slope seems to heard towards the north east up to the villages of Comblanchien, where it changes direction; it takes a more variable turn and the crest of the slopes faces east-south-east and to the south-east. The territory of Buisson, Corgoloin, and Comblanchien occupy this part of the slope that provides only ordinary wines of good quality.

Between Comblanchien and Prémeaux is a clos of around 30 ha, owned by a wealthy proprietor, who, with much care and expense has created a vineyard that must be classed among the distinguished ones of our slope. This mass of vines, several years ago, was divided into an infinite number of parcels, and those that possessed them assembled the fruit with that of inferior quality, and it was impossible to appreciate their just value. Now that all of these parcels are reunited in the hands of one owner, one can better see the quality of the wine of this slope, which is well-exposed and lays on a bed of limestone which is very similar to that of Aloxe.

Dr. Lavalle:

COMMUNE DE COMBLANCHIEN

The Côte de Nuits finishes at Prémeaux. Hardly has one passed the last climats of this village and the mountain drops dramatically. The hills, with less rapid slopes, become indistinguishable from the plain. All the conditions of exposition and of height are changed, and one can divine from only the look of the place that the product of the earth must have completely different qualities than those that we have described until the present. This is, in fact, what happens. From Prémeaux up to Aloxe, that is to say in all of the places where the soil presents the conditions that we have just described, the production of great wines ceases almost completely, and there is a parenthesis that cleanly establishes the separation of the vineyard of Beaune and that of Nuits. Comblanchien produces, however, a few good wines: 16 ha are cultivated in Pinot and 45 ha in Gamay. The best cuvées of this commune are:

Aux Grandes-Vignes, 2 ha 31 a 25 ca, of which 1 ha 30 a belongs to M. Meunier, and 40 a to Mme. Maurier.

Aux Retraits, 1 ha 95 a 20 ca, of which 70 a belongs to M. Britschgy.

Aux Montagnes, 8 ha 24 a 40 ca, of which 2 ha belongs to M. Viénot-Jacquinot.

Aux Fauques, 3 ha 88 a 55 ca, of which 3 ha belongs to M. Paul Bouchard.

---

26 Several centuries ago, this whole district was a forest that extended downto Corgoloin; the villages of Serrigny and of Comblanchien were at either end. This forest was about three thousand toises [unit of meaure in pre-revolutionary France equivalent to approximately two meters] in length. We have found at Corgoloin several curious archeological objects including a beautiful bronze figurine of the emperor Hadrian, the base of a column four feet in height, and medals.

Following this:

En la Rue des Vaches, 1 ha 80 a belonging to M. Britschgy.

Aux Charmes, 3 ha belonging to M. Britschgy.

En Saint-Seine, 60 a belonging to M. Thomas, and 1 ha belonging to M. Britschgy.

The other climats produce only ordinary wine.

COMMUNE DE CORGOLOIN

One finds here the same conditions of exposition of height and of soil that one finds at Comblanchien, and consequently the same results.[66] One also can indicate here but a small number of privileged climats capable of producing fine wines. These are, in the first tier, the climats of:

En la Botte, belonging to M. Duret.

Le Clos-de-Langres, belonging to M. de Loisy.

Aux Langres, belonging to MM. Lemire and Barberet.

In second tier:

En Vierevelle, belonging to M. Edouard.

Ez Chaillots, belonging to M. Jacquinot and others.

Les Monts-de-Boncourt, belonging to M. Barberet and others.

In the climats that I have placed in the first tier, the wines have body and color. They merit an honorable place among our good wines, and when, due to age, they have acquired a bouquet, they can be compared to the premières cuvées of many more renowned villages. The yield is very slight in these climats. We estimate 15 to 16 hl/ha in Botte, and from 16 to 18 hl/ha in the Langres.

COMMUNE DE LADOUÉE[67]

It is only to satisfy geographical order that I indicate here the hamlet of Buisson and the village of Ladouée. The slope declines at the first to several wooded hillsides, and the cultivated portions of the second are arranged at the bottom of a valley that does not permit the harvest of fine wines. However, in the portions that abut the territory of Aloxe and that constitute the northern end of the magnificent climat of Corton, one finds several vineyards planted in Pinot that give wines that are not without value.

In view of the brevity of the article by Lavalle and the fact that Morelot does not even mention Ladoix, the text of Danguy et Aubertin about this village is translated here in full. This will also give the reader a sense of the style of this text and the types of information they include. Their list of principal proprietors for the climats that are today classified in grand cru is attached.

Ladoix-Serrigny

It is only in the last few years that Ladoix-Serrigny has taken on a real importance in the world of wine. Until the first half of the 19th century, the winemakers of the Côte d'Or were silent regarding this territory, or contented themselves with a simple mention in order to maintain geographic order.

At Ladoix-Serrigny, if a bit of flint has left but little trace of prehistoric man, this is not the case for the period of the Roman occupation. In the midst of antique substrata, we have found the coins of the emperors and utensils in bronze and iron. A magnificent gold hairpin was found, along with human remains, by the late M. Royer. This precious object has been part of the archeological collections of the city of Beaune since 1840.

It is certain that Ladoix-Serrigny has been devoted to the culture of the vine since the distant past.

"They are often slighted by the writers", Courtépée did not fail to mention. As for the relative importance of the location, the historian mentions, "There had been fairs and markets transferred to Beaune."

Serrigny, Sarrigne, Sariniacu, Sarriniacum, Sarrigniacum, Serrignium (1204 – 1263) is one of the most ancient villages of the Côte d'Or. The names of its rulers have appeared since the 13th century. Ladoix takes its name from the Celtic word Doix, Douix, for fountain or spring. This hamlet, attached to Serrigny, in fact possesses a fine spring that forms a little stream.

Buisson, known under this designation in 1305, is another important hamlet, originally part of the domaines of the Hôtel-Dieu de Beaune [the Hospices], and was separated from the parish of Villers-la-Faye in the 15th century to be annexed to Serrigny.

This village also counts as dependencies Neuvelle (Nova Villa in 1379) and Courcelles-sous-Serrigny (Courcellæ in 1256). Altogether, the population is approximately 1,400. The territory of the village is bordered to the east by Corgoloin and Ruffey; to the south by Vignolles and Cherey; to the west by Aloxe and Pernand; to the north by Magny-Les Villers. All of these boundaries are merely conventions, being determined only by streets and footpaths.

The latitude of the location is 47°3'39", and the longitude is 2°34'5".

A distance of 6 kilometers separates Ladoix-Serrigny from Beaune, the district and county seat.

The train station, established by the P.L.M.[68], and a public line from Beaune assure ease of travel.

Ladoix, the principal hamlet with 950 – 1,000 inhabitants, possesses its own post office and telegraph station. It is situated at the foot and along the length of the celebrated hill of Corton. The inhabitants are largely found along both sides of the Route Nationale that follows along the slope [D974, formerly the RN4].

The Original Grand Crus of Burgundy

Arriving from Beaune, to the right, at the entrance to the hamlet, one sees the former chapel of Our Lady of the Road[27], where worship has ceased since the Revolution[69].

At mid-slope of the hill at Magny-les-Villers one finds the famous stone quarries where there is red marble that takes a very fine polish that has been known since time immemorial.

Leaving the station is a road that leads to Serrigny, found on either side of a road that rejoins the main road. The total area of the village includes 2495 ha, of which about one third is planted to vines.

From the geological point of view, the bedrock of the slope (rather low elevation here) is Oxfordian limestone. On the plain one finds old alluvial soils, except around the stream of Ladoix.

Wine production is the aim and chief occupation of the majority of the inhabitants. The merchants of this commune compare their fine wines to those of Corton, whose vines occupy the same geological situation. Body, vinosity, finesse, and a delicate bouquet are their prime qualities. The growers believe that they owe these qualities to the fact that they are grown in a rocky soil with good exposition and difficult growing conditions.

With the exception of two large holdings (those of the Duke of Clermont-Tonnerre and of the Hospices de Beaune, donated in large part by M. Mallard-Gaulin), the ownership of the vineyards is very fragmented.

The lands bordering those of Aloxe and producing the premiers crus are Roguet et Corton[70], which is sometimes divided into two climats, Basses Mourolles, Carrières, Grandes Lolières, etc. The list of the others is found below. They are situated on the slope proper, and the wines produced are fairly rich in tannin, so that they can be cellared, and acquire with time a very delicate bouquet.

The Clou d'Orge, La Corvée, are situated in lighter soils. These climats give wines that are also have a fine bouquet but take less time to mature.

To the north of Ladoix on the slope opposite that of Corton, which is separated by a gorge that ends at Magny-les-Villers, is the hamlet of Buisson.

Here the wines distinguish themselves by a lower content of alcohol. According to whether their production was done in soils that are marly, gravelly, red or brown and dry, they are easy to recognize when tasting. On the other side, in the lighter soils, one produces wines that are less robust but show immediately their finesse and bouquet.

In that part of the territory that forms a little hill tying together the slope itself with the plain, one produces those table wines called passe-tout-grains, grands ordinaries, and bons ordinaires, which help to maintain the reputation of the village.

These wines, coming from a mixture of Pinot and Gamay, have a lot of body, if they come from a strong terroir, and are very forward on the nose, if they are from

---

27 V. Courtépée, t. II; - J.-P. Notice historique et archéologique sur l'ancienne chapelle de Notre-Dame du Chemin, 1861.

lighter soils. Finally, the ordinary wine is harvested further on.

After this examination of the red wines, it is just to say a few words about the white wines of the village. The upper part of the hill of Corton, above the rond-point de Buisson, produces wines that unite vinosity and finesse with a beautiful bouquet. The soils are full of pebbles, of a yellowish red hue, fairly friable, and very dry. It is common to find an agreeable taste of hazelnut upon tasting these wines.

In Buisson itself are also found renowned and appreciated white wines. Finally on the little hill of Corcelles, one can also find wine that recommends itself to wine lovers by its purity and lightness.

In conclusion, on the territory of Ladoix-Serrigny, we find everything from premiers crus and fine wines to table wines that consumers love. According to the vintage, the fine wines vary in price for the queue or two casks of 228 litres from 400 to 1,200 francs, and for ordinary wine from 160 to 330 francs.

NOMENCLATURE
OF PRINCIPAL CLIMATS AND LIEUX-DITS

[of Danguy et Aubertin]

In Camille Rodier, modern nomenclature appears in several respects. To begin with, Le Rognet et Corton (to modernize the spelling) are cited as one climat of 9 ha 19 a 50 ca, and the proprietors are given as MM. Dufouileur, Faiveley, Ligeret, etc. This is also the first time that Le Rognet et Corton and Les Vergennes have been recognized as Premières Cuvées. Rodier does not distinguish any of the climats here by listing them in capital letters.

Corton (le). – C.A.B., première, deuxième et troisième classes ; C. Loc., première cuvée

Principal proprietors : MM. Faiveley, de Loisy, Maire et fils and the Hospices de Beaune.

Roguet (le) [sp]. – C.A.B., première, deuxième et troisième classes ; C. Loc., première cuvée

Principal proprietors : MM. Bachey-Deslandes, Maire et fils.

Vergennes (les). – C.A.B., première classe ; C. Loc., première cuvée

Principal Proprietors : MM. Bachey-Deslandes, Maire et fils.

Rodier: M. Patey

Lolières (les **Grandes**). – C.A.B., deuxième classe ; C. Loc., première cuvée

Principal Proprietors: MM. Dechaux, Quentin, the widow Royer.

Rodier gives both Grandes and Petites Lolières together as Deuxièmes Cuvées, and cites the following proprietors: MM. Bussières, Capitain, the widow Fourneaux, Gros Bézulier, the Millon heirs, MM. Perronnet, the widow Begueaux, Boyer, Thomas, etc.

Tope au Vert (la). – C.A.B., deuxième classe ; C. Loc., première cuvée

Principal Proprietors : MM. Bézulier, Dorland, Lagneau, Laurent, Naudin-Mallard.

Rodier gives La Tope au Vert as a Deuxièmes Cuvée, and cites the following proprietors: MM. Gros-Bézulier, Lagneau, Laurent, Mathonillet, etc.

Basses Mourottes (les). – C.A.B., troisième classe; C. Loc., première cuvée

Principal Proprietors : MM. Louis Chapponneau, Pierre Nudant

Rodier gives Les Basses-Mourottesas a troisième cuvée, and cites the following proprietors: MM. Général Nudant, Passerotte, Pernot-Gilles, etc.

CLIMATS
PRODUCING ABOVE ALL WHITE WINE

Mourottes (les Hautes). – C. Loc., première cuvée

Principal Proprietors : MM. Bachey-Deslandes, Chapponneau, Mallard-Lucotte.

Rodier does not mention Les Hautes-Mourottes at all.

Here are the comments of Dr. Lavalle on Aloxe:

COMMUNE DE ALOXE

One counts in Aloxe approximately 140 – 150 ha of Pinot Noir. The Côte de Beaune begins with this village; the mountain juts up almost immediately, and the east-facing slopes, situated with the most magnificent exposition, serves as the base of one of the most vast and most beautiful vineyards of the Côte. The wood of Corton dominates that cultivated parts and descends to the climat of Corton itself. Several rare scraps of land have been left in scrub, several heaps of stones pulled from the vines, are, with the roads for working the slopes, the only points that designate the different climats in the magnificent carpet formed by the vines. As in all of the grands crus, no trees are cultivated in the best parts of the vineyard except the rare peach tree.

This vineyard is constituted of Pinot Noir at mid-slope and in the lower parts of the slope; Pinot Blanc and Noir at the top of the slope, and perhaps one-one hundredth of Pinot Gris planted among the white vines. We classify as follows the different parts:

Vins hors ligne

The climat of Corton, which we divide into:

Corton itself, 11 ha 58 a 20 ca, belonging to MM. Gueisweler, Marion, de Cordoue and others. This climat, planted part in Pinot Noir and part in Pinot Blanc, has an average yield of 12 – 14 hl/ha, remarkable above all for its delicious white wine and by the red wine produced on its lower slopes, but the highest zone bordering on the wood is far from similar in quality.

> Danguy et Aubertin include the mention that this climat is almost all in white wine. Their list of principal proprietors: Gauthey Cadet et fils, Louis Latour, Moreau-Voillot, Moyne-Jacqueminot.

> Rodier does not distinguish Corton with a mention in capital letters, nor does he mention the color of wine produced. He includes the following climats in Aloxe as première cuvée: Le Corton, Clos du Roi, Les Renardes, Les Bressandes, Les Pougets, Les Languettes, Les Perrières, Les Fiètres, Les Grèves, En Charlemagne, Les Chaumes and Les Chaumes de la Voierosse, La Vigne-au-Saint. Les Meix, Les Maréchaudes, and En Pauland.

> In Corton itself, he does note that the upper part of this cuvée is classified in deuxième and troisième Cuvée. He ascribes the ownership to MM. Bouchard Père et Fils, G. Faiveley, H. Gauthey, A. Girard, Louis Latour, E. Maillard, Moillard-Grivot, etc.

Corton Clos-du-Roi, 10 ha 82 a 90 ca, belonging to M. Ouvrard almost completely, with an important portion of the rest belonging to M. Maire (Simon). Completely planted in Pinot Noir, this climat gives hardly more than 13 or 14 hl/ha. It is, with the following climat, the most perfect part of the climat of Corton.

> Danguy et Aubertin: MM. Bachet-Deslandes, Charles Bernard, Robert Bruninghaus, de Clermont-Tonnerre, Gauthey Cadet et fils, Guichard-Potheret et fils, F. Hazen-Klewer, the Hospices de Beaune, Louis Latour, Maire et fils, Pernot-Gille, Royé Labaume et Cie, Jules Senard, A. de Tavernost.

> Rodier: MM. Baronne du Bay, H. Bussière, H. Gauthey, A. Girard, the Hasenklever heirs, the Hospices de Beaune, Louis Latour, Mallard-Gaulin, Comte de Mérode, Moillard-Grivot, Rameau-Lamarosse, Jules Senard, Baronne de Tavernost, etc.

Les Renardes-Corton, 15 ha 26 a 35 ca, belonging to MM. Ouvrard, Moreau, Guillemot, Volot, Desroye, Dubois, Barberet, Clermont-Montoizon, Maire (Simon), Gueisweler, Marion, and the widow Gauthet. This climat produces even lower yields than the preceding one.

> Danguy et Aubertin: MM. Arbelet, de Clermont-Tonnerre, Cunisset-Guidot, Falateuf, Gauthey Cadet et fils, Guichard-Potheret et fils, the Hospices

de Beaune, Louis Latour, Lamarosse-Barberet, Joseph Moreau, Moreau Voillot, Moyne-Jacqueminot, Royé Labaume et Cie, Jules Senard.

Rodier: MM. Gacon-Niquet, H. Gauthey, A. Girard, the Hospices de Beaune, Mallard-Gaulin, Comte de Mérode, Moreau-Voillot, etc.

We also classify as "hors ligne", although slightly inferior

Les Chaumes, 7 ha 8 a 55 ca, belonging to MM. de Grancey, and to the widow Gauthet.

We have today the grand cru climat Les Chaumes in Aloxe, which is subdivided into 2 ha 46 a 22 ca of Les Chaumes and 3 ha 87 a 80 ca of Les Chaumes et la Voierosse on the other side of the road. In Lavalle, the size given above indicates that he has combined them. They are noted separately in Danguy et Aubertin, who note the following owners: MM. Charles Bernard, Louis Latour, Alexis Maldant, Rameau-Lamarosse, Royé Labaume et Cie (Les Chaumes), and MM. Charles Bernard, Gille, Louis Latour, Alexis Maldant, Moreau-Voillot, and De Tavernost (Les Chaumes et Voierosse).

Rodier combines them again, and designates the following owners: MM. Baronne du Bay, A. Brenot, H. Bussière, Chapuis, Louis Latour, A. Maldant, Rameau-Lamarosse, Thevenot, etc.

Le Charlemagne, 16 ha 81 a 80 ca, for the white wines produced in the part of the climat situated in Aloxe and belonging to MM. Gouveau, de Grancey, Chantrier, Jules Pautet, and the Hospices de Beaune.

White wines almost exclusively are harvested in this climat.

Danguy et Aubertin: MM. Arbelet, Bonneau-Dumartray, Bussière, Louis Latour, Pavelot, Jules Senard.

Rodier refers to this climat as En Charlemagne. He does not note the predominance of white wine, and he makes the notation that « certain parts of this climat are also classified in deuxième and troisième cuvée ». He attributes ownership to MM. G. Boiveau, H. Boiveau Bonneau du Martray, A. Bussière, Chapuis, the Hospices de Beaune, Louis Latour, Pavelot-Coppenet, Thevenot, etc.

Première Cuvée

Les Bressandes, 5 ha 71 a 5 ca, belonging to MM. Sénard, Volot, Maire (Simon), Desroye, Edouard, Camus, Clermont-Montoizon, Rocaut d'Orisy, de Grancey, and Peste. These wines are perhaps more fine than those of the other climats of Aloxe, but they have much less body and they are ready to drink much more quickly.

Danguy et Aubertin: MM. Arbelet, Bachey, de Clermont-Tonnerre, Falateuf, Gauthey cadet et fils, the Hospices de Beaune, Louis Latour, Maire et fils, Alexis Maldant, the widow Mrs. Oscar Masson, MM. Naudin, L. Poisot, Royé Labaume et Cie. Jules Senard, De Tavernost.

Rodier: MM. Arbelet, Baronne du Bay, Brenot, Chapuis, H. Gauthey, Gorges, the Hospices de Beaune, Louis Latour, Loufte, the de la Loyère heirs, Comte de Mérode, V. Naudin, Jules Senard, Baronne de Tavernost, Thevenot, Yard, etc.

Les Perrières, 10 ha 73 a 70 ca, belonging to M. de Grancey.

The modern Corton Perrières includes 32 a 54 ca of the lieu-dit Le Village, not mentioned in any of the older authorities. It is surrounded by Perrières on two sides and abuts the village of Aloxe on the other. There are several more very small parcels with this name scattered around the village, but they have only communal status. To judge from the size quoted by Lavalle and Rodier, it would seem that these were simply called Perrières in former times.

Danguy et Aubertin: MM. Gauthey cadet et fils, Lamarosse-Barbaret, Moreau-Voillot, Léon Naudin, L. Poisot.

Rodier groups Perrières along with Les Fiètres (1 ha 32 a 95 ca), and attributes ownership to MM. Baronne du Bay, H. Gauthey, Louis Latour, Moreau-Voillot, V. Naudin, Poissot, Tartarin, etc.

Les Fiètres, 1 ha 30 a 95 ca, belonging to the widow Gauthet and to M. Barberet.

Danguy et Aubertin: MM. Charles Bernard, Gauthey cadet et fils, Royé Labaume et Cie.

Rodier: MM. Baronne du Bay, H. Gauthey, Louis Latour, Moreau-Voillot, V. Naudin, Poisot, Tartarin, etc., etc.

Les Grèves, 1 ha 84 a 10 ca, belonging to MM. Villiard and de Grancey.

Danguy et Aubertin: MM. Louis Latour, Alexis Maldant, Royé Labaume et Cie.

Rodier: MM. Baronne du Bay, Louis Latour, A. Maldant, etc.

Les Languettes, 7 ha 35 a 15 ca, belonging to MM. de Grancey, Rocaut, de Clermont-Montoizon, Gueisweler, and Marion.

Danguy et Aubertin: MM. Charles Bernard, de Clermont-Tonnerre, Cunisset-Guidot, Louis Latour, Léon Naudin, Regnault.

Rodier: MM. Chapuis, G. Faiveley, A. Girard, Louis Latour, V. Naudin, Regnault, etc.

Les Pougets, 9 ha 94 a 65 ca, belonging to MM. Virely, Bocquet and Marion.

Danguy et Aubertin: MM. Arbelet, Bocquet, Fernand Dumoulin, François Mathouillet, Gacon, Gauthey cadet et fils.

Rodier: MM. Chapuis, Mme. Dumoulin, H. Gauthey, Jadot, Louis Latour, Mathouillet, etc.

Les Meix, 1 ha 97 a 75 ca, belonging to MM. Sénard, Rocaut, Maire, and Villiard.

Les Meix is a climat on the southwest corner of the village of Aloxe. Lavalle and Rodier both agree on its extent, but none of the other authorities mention the climat called "Clos des Meix ou Le Meix Lallemand," a small parcel of 55 a closest to the village. Our Clos des Meix (a monopole of Comte Senard) includes both climats.

> Danguy et Aubertin: Jules Senard, sole owner.
>
> Rodier: M. Jules Senard.

La Vigne-au-Saint, 2 ha 50 a 50 ca, an extremely fragmented climat, of which a portion belongs to M. Rocaut.

> Danguy et Aubertin: MM. Gauthey cadet et fils, Louis Latour, Jules Senard.
>
> Rodier: MM. H. Gauthey and Louis Latour.

Deuxième Cuvée

Les Fournières, 6 ha 39 a 40 ca, belonging to MM. Roccion, Latour, Maldant, and the Hospices de Beaune.

Les Chaillots, 6 ha 21 a 50 ca, belonging to MM. de Grancey, Maldant, and Chantrier.

En Poland, 4 ha 65 a 70 ca, belonging to MM. Chantrier, Royer, Sénard, Vautheleret, and Bussière.

> Danguy et Aubertin has Poland ou Pauland (En): MM. Charles Bernard, Déchaux-Latour, Louis Latour, Royer, Jules Senard.
>
> Rodier has the upper third classified as a premier cru, and designates the following owners: MM. Louis Latour, Royer, Jules Senard, Baronne de Tavernost, etc.

En Boulmeau, 1 ha 52 a 35 ca, belonging to M. Camus and others.

Les Planchots, 1 ha 35 a belonging to the widow Gauthet and others.

Les Suchots, 50 ca, belonging to the same proprietors.

Les Genevrières, 1 ha 39 a 95 ca, belonging to MM. Dupont and Perronet.

Les Combes, 8 ha 67 a 45 ca, belonging to the widow Gauthet, MM. Guyot and Jules Pautet.

En Tope-Marteneau, 1 ha 69 a, belonging to M. de Grancey.

Les Guérets, 3 ha 64 a 80 ca, belonging to MM. Maire, Perronet, and the widow Gauthet.

Les Vercots, 4 ha 30 a 70 ca, belonging to M. de Grancey and the widow Gauthet.

La Saillère, 41 a 70 ca, belonging to the widow Gauthet.

Troisième Cuvée

En Caillette, belonging to M. Camus and to the widow Guidot.

Les Cras, belonging to to MM. Bussière, Dubois, Lazare Gérard, V. Latour, Volot, and to the Azincourt heirs.

La Boulotte, belonging to the widow Gauthet and to M. Peste.

Les Chapousuets, belonging to the widow Guidot, M. Latour, and others.

Les Citernes, belonging to M. Maldant and to the widow Gauthet.

Petits-Vercots, belonging to MM. Chantrier, Michelin, and Juste Desroy.

All the other climats of Aloxe give only inferior wine.

Les Maréchaudes is included here. This climat, found in Camille Rodier and in Danguy et Aubertin, straddles the border with Ladoix. While Lavalle was dismissive of the wines of this commune, he does include Les Paulands, which border Maréchaudes, as En Poland.

Les Maréchaudes, 6 ha 69 a 45 ca

> Danguy et Aubertin: MM. Bernard-Chaffotte, de Clermont-Tonnerre, Cunisset-Guidot, Duthu, Falateuf, Gauthey cadet et fils, the Hospices de Beaune, Louis Latour, the widow Mme. Oscar Masson, Léon Naudin, L. Poisot.
>
> Rodier, only the upper third is to be considered première cuvée. He notes the ownership as MM. Louis Latour, Comte de Mérode, V. Naudin, Patey, Royer, Baronne de Tavernost, etc.

Lavalle continues:

> The wines of Aloxe have a particular cachet that makes them easy to distinguish from other crus. These are the firmest and purest wines of the Côte de Beaune, and those that can age the longest time, thirty or forty years and more, in certain years. They travel well and can without danger be transported by sea if they are not too mature.
>
> The wines harvested in the climats that we have classified as hors ligne and that sell normally under the name of Corton, possess the highest degree of these qualities. A bit hard during their first years, they become pure and mellow with age and acquire bouquet and a remarkable finesse, while retaining their body and generosity. Cortons from good years are at the end of seven or eight years, perfect wines, worthy to be offered to the most delicate gourmets and to be served on the most solemn occasions.
>
> This climat is one of the most honored of Burgundy and one with which Burgundians

love to associate the glorious and cherished name with those of Chambertin, Vougeot, Romanée, Saint-Georges, Montrachet, etc., etc.

The wines of Corton are closer to the wines of Chambertin than to any other wine of the Côte d'Or. It is these that contain the most tannin.

The price that one pays in the market in the years when the quality is perfect varies from 1,000 to 1,300 francs per cask, the price at the cellar door.

We make here the same observations as those that we have already made for Gevrey and for Nuits on the nature of the cuvées of each proprietor and on the quality of each of these cuvées.

The celebrated climat of Corton, or, as it was written in ancient documents Courton, appears to have been planted, in part at least, at the same time as the climat of Charlemagne. Nothing would indicate an origin more recent, and it is more than probably that the vines given by Modoin to his cathedral were situated in this climat. In effect, in the bill of sale of goods situated in Corton, made in 1212 to the abbey of Cîteaux by Mme. Beloilet, by Guy Coque and Jean Coque, it is indicated that the Clos of the Chapter of Saint-Nazaire of Autun is associated with this property.

It would seem that formerly all the vast climat situated on the east slope of the mountain was included under the name of Courton, and we find among the former proprietors the Dukes of Burgundy, the chapter of Saint-Andoche of Saulieu, the chapter of Autun, Knights Templar, etc.

In the works relative to the parts in possession of the Dukes of Burgundy, one finds in 1335 that a cask of the wine from this climat is estimated at 30 sols; in 1337, 20 sols; in 1340, 30 sols; in 1344, 40 sols; in 1352, 5 florins. The Duke's staff worked the fields themselves, and the expense of producing this wine went as high as 74 livres 2 sols 8 derniers. [we omit here a specific account of these expenses]

In 1352, the vines of the Duke were once again leased; later, in 1400, they were cultivated again by the governor of Beaune on the Duke's behalf. At the end of the 15th century, the vines were rented, but we find however, that the vinegrower received only one quarter of the harvest.[71]

The list of royal possessions in 1507 mentions the Clos of Aloxe with the lieu-dit *en Courton* as containing approximately 100 ouvrées. In 1555 the Clos of Corton, having become property of the crown, was rented to a M. Berthelon for 15 livres yearly, which included at the time 110 ouvrées. It was reclaimed in 1618 and returned to the crown.

In 1751, the vines of the king at Corton are counted as being 80 ouvrées in vines and 20 ouvrées of scrub. In 1792, the scrub had been cultivated, the stones buried, and an exact measure gave 106 ouvrées for the portion that had belonged to the governor of Beaune.

The experts charged under the revolutionary administration with estimating the value of this property evaluated the average production of the harvest for the past ten years, less charges and expenses, at 5 livres per ouvrée, and the total that this vineyard could yield was 532 livres 10 sols. The climat was thus sold by parcel for the equivalent of 250 – 300 francs per ouvrée.

The abbey of Cîteaux possessed vines in the climat of Corton from 1180, the year in which a concession was made of a parcel by the abbey of Sainte-Marguerite. Several years later, the same abbey received vines in Corton as a gift from Henri, a priest of Châteauneuf. In 1226 it received another parcel in the same territory, in the place called Ez Echaillers-de-Corton. In the same year Pierre de Fleury, a burgher of Beaune, gave them a parcel of vines in the Clos de la Perrière belonging to the monks.

We have seen in 1212 the abbey has received from Mme. Beloilet several other parcels of vines in Corton, and notably one situated near the wood.

Urban IV confirmed in 1261 the privilege of harvesting and transporting freely their grapes to their cellar in Aloxe accorded to the abbey of Cîteaux by Alexandre, bishop of Châlon. In 1283 Etienne de Serrey of Beaune sold to Cîteaux two parcels of vines situated in Corton, amounting to an annual rent of 12 deniers.

The land registry of Cîteaux in 1483 states that the monks were proprietors of 130 ouvrées in Ronce-de-Vercovau; of the Clos de Courthon, containing 64 ouvrées; and of the Perrière de Courthon, containing 130 ouvrées. In 1620, the abbey ceded its vines in Corton to different private growers for an annual rent, and from this period these properties passed from hand to hand to the current proprietors.

In 1224 the Knights Templar of Beaune possessed in Corton a parcel of vines that had been given to them by Désiré, burgher of Chalon.

COMMUNE DE PERNANT

Situated at the bottom of a little valley whose direction can be considered to go exactly from north to south, this village has only a narrow strip of vineyards nestled between those of Savigny and those of Aloxe, and its two best climats, *Le Charlemagne* and *Les Vergelesses*, belong in part to the two preceding villages. The exposition of this vineyard is completely exceptional for the climates situated on the side of Aloxe. These vines, in effect, are more or less opposite from those of the climat of Corton, and Le Charlemagne faces almost directly south-west.

For this commune, as for those of Aloxe and Savigny, Pinot Noir has supplanted Pinot Blanc almost everywhere, and Gamay covers only the inferior climats. For these three communes, the number of vines is approximately 1,200 to 1,300 per ouvrée, sometimes more. 85 ha are consecrated to the growth of Pinot; more than 200 to that of Gamay. The climats producing the good wines are:

Première Cuvée
WHITE WINES (Cuvée Unique)

Le Charlemagne, 19 ha 70 a, belonging to MM. Bonneau-Véry.

This climat produced on average 20 hl/ha.

> Danguy et Aubertin have Charlemagne (Le or En), and list the proprietors as MM. Bonneau-Dumartray, Carret-Mareau, Denis-Soucelier, Mathouillet-Meline, Louis Latour, Louis Pavelot, and Mme. Rameau.
>
> Rodier has En Charlemagne classified as a deuxième cuvée, but notes « An important part of this climat has been classified as troisième cuvée », and ascribes ownership to MM. H. Blanchard, Bonneau-Dumartray, Louis Latour, Mathouillet-Méline, Victor Naudin, Rapet-Naudin, and Mlle. Rameau-Lamarosse.

RED WINES

Les Vergelesses, 27 ha 12 a, belonging to MM. de Chalonge, Pralon-Gillet, de Cordoue, de Joux, Sénard, Lamarosse, Peste, Desroye, the widow Gauthet, and the Hospices de Beaune. The yield can be evaluated at 15 hl/ha.

> Rodier has Les Vergelesses divided into the Ile des Vergelesses (9 ha 34 a 25 ca) and Les Basses-Vergelesses (17 ha 87 a 15 ca). He notes both in capital letters, although he states that the lower part of Basses-Vergelesses is classified in deuxième cuvée. He ascribes the ownership as follows:
>
> ILE DES VERGELESSES – MM. Henri Bussière, Mme. Dumoulin, Louis Latour, Georges Moine, Léon Pavelot, Piot-Mathouiullet, Mlle. Rameau-Lamarosse, Baronne de Tavernost.
>
> LES BASSES-VERGELESSES – MM. Chanson Père et Fils, the widow Chapeau, La Charité, Lucien Denis, Gauthey-Lamarosse, the Hospices de Beaune, Louis Latour, Mathouiullet-Métaut, Georges Moine, Vigneresse-Moine.

Deuxième Cuvée

Le Caradeaux, 20 ha 17 a 30 ca, **Les Boutières** and **Le Charlemagne**, belonging to MM. Moreau-Guillemot, Mathouillet-Chenot, de Vergnette-Lamotte, Bonneau-Véry. The yield is 20 hl/ha.

> Rodier also includes Le Caradeaux in Deuxième Cuvée, but notes that the upper part should be classified in Troisième Cuvée yet that the lower part should be Première Cuvée.

Troisième Cuvée

A troisième cuvée of red wines is harvested in the climat of Le Charlemagne by M. Bonneau-Véry.

The climat Le Charlemagne, in which was once found the Clos de Charlemagne, produces an excellent white wine, that in many particulars approaches white

Corton, and whose reputation has been hardly less in the past few centuries.

It is situated both in the villages of Pernant and Aloxe, and once produced white and red wine. Today it produces only the former.

Courtépée does not hesitate to consider that this clos had belonged to the emperor Charlemagne and as having been given to him by the monks of Saulieu. This donation took place in 775. The first document relative to this climat that we still have today dates to 1375. The chapter of Saint-Andoche de Saulieu rented its Clos Le Charlemagne. In 1385 on the 16th of October, it was given in perpetual lease to Guillaume Guinot, burgher of Beaune, for the yearly sum of two and a half casks of wine of the measure of Beaune.

In 1485, the priests of Saint-Andoche contested the legality of this rental and obtained a sentence that returned the vines to the chapter. In 1492, the chapter sold for a price of 15 livres to the lord of Briançon the right to rent a parcel of vines of 40 ouvrées situated in the same climat.

On the 23rd of August 1620, a new rental agreement ceded the Clos Le Charlemagne to M. Esmonin; but ten years later, the chapter demanded of the board of appeal of the palace the revocation of this rental agreement. It appears that it was obtained, for we see later that this chapter acquired two ouvrées to augment it and paid a sum of money to deliver earth to this site.

From this time until the Revolution, this property belonged to the chapter of Saulieu. Declared goods of the state, the Clos Le Charlemagne was sold by the district of Beaune on May 2nd 1791 for a sum of 10,800 livres, not including the tax; it contained 70 ouvrées.

In sum, Corton is not an easy appellation to understand. This being said, for the modern reader there are several interesting wines to consider. To begin with the red wine of appellation, the most important development in recent years is that the Domaine de la Romanée-Conti has leased 2.27 ha of vines in Corton from the aristocratic Belgian owners of Prince Florent de Mérode. This includes 0.57 ha of Corton Clos du Roi, 0.51 ha of Renardes, and 1.19 ha of Bressandes. Although the production of this wine is still a work in process according to the Domaine de la Romanée-Conti, the project can only bring more notice and acclaim to the better vineyards of Corton. Early vintages of the wine, tasted at the domaine, have been promising indeed. Other top red Cortons are produced by Domaine Leroy and Domaine Méo-Camuzet. The best white? Few would argue that the tiny production from the 0.34 ha parcel owned by Domaine Jean-François Coche-Dury would top the list. The Coche-Dury domaine is located in Meursault, but this wine, produced from rented vines, is one of the most sought-after white wines on the planet. The wine is unimaginably opulent and intense – more comparable to a Montrachet than to another wine from the hill of Corton. Unfortunately, the price is as well, easily outstripping even the premium that DRC is able to charge for their new Corton.

There are still a number of well-made Cortons that represent great value for money. In the value category, special mention must be made of Bonneau du

Martray. Owned by Jean-Charles le Bault de la Morinière, Bonneau du Martray is the reference standard for classic Corton Charlemagne (and the appellation's largest single landowner as well). Bonneau de Martray is also a significant (and talented) producer of red Corton. Much of the land on the Corton hill today is owned by negociants, with Faiveley and Bouchard, for example, owning large parcels and producing reliable wines and an affordable price. Other producers that deliver solid value in Corton include Domaine Rapet and Domaine Comte Senard.

SAVIGNY-LEZ-BEAUNE

Savigny, although long renowned for its wine, suffers from something of an identity crisis. Tied in name to its more famous neighbor Beaune, the village has lacked a distinctiveness of its own, although this was not always the case. In the 14th century, proud growers declined to debate the merits of their wine, according to Courtépée:

> By the act of Council in 1658, the Abbot and the Curé of the Priory of St. Maurice [in Savigny-les-Beaune] were entitled to a tithe of one basket of grapes for each sixteen harvested. In 1399, the inhabitants paid eight derniers per ouvrée rather, they said, than being constrained to swear to the quantity of their fruit, as oaths may not be sworn without peril to their souls. [...]

He was the first to relate the legend:

> The wine of Savigny is renowned. The Duke of Burgundy while passing through Dijon on the 21st of September 1703 found so good the wine presented by the President de Migieu that he said "it comes from a demi-god[72]. The best climats are Les Guettes, Les Vergelesses, Les Jarrons. There is a vineyard called La Bataillière after the Bataille family that owned it.

As Morelot points out, the village of Savigny-lès-Beaune is located in the valley of the Rhoin, a small river that flows from Bouilland to Ruffey-les-Beaune in a west-to-east direction, separating the Bois de Noël and the Bois de Chenôve from the Monts Battois and the Forêt de Savigny-les-Beaune. Vineyards on both sides of this valley are classified as Savigny-les-Beaune, although most authorities agree that the best are located on the northern (Pernand) side, since they have a south-southeast exposure. Morelot includes a portion of the climat Les Vergelesses area called Clos de la Bataillère classed as a tête de cuvée. Lavalle has Les Vergelesses as a première cuvée EXTRA (capital letters are Lavalle's emphasis), a rare designation for him. He notes that La Bataillère is the "most perfect" portion of the vineyard. It is curious then that Danguy et Aubertin do not mention Bataillère, although it reappears in Rodier. Today, although La Bataillère is visible on the map, it is not a separate lieu-dit. In fact, the total size of Vergelesses has decreased slightly, from 16 ha 97 a 85 ca in both Lavalle and Rodier to 15 ha 37 a 67 ca in today's classification.

The observations of Dr. Morelot:

> About at the entrance of the gorge where the proper Côte de Beaune finishes is found the beautiful village of Savigny with its 1,600 – 1,700 inhabitants. The little valley in which it is built, running from east to west, offers a fairly broad plain, and on

the right and on the left for a half-league are slopes covered in vines.[28] The most extensive of these slopes is called Noël; it forms a mass that extends as I have said for a half league from east to west; and then, making a turn it suddenly runs from south to north to finish in the village of Pernand.

This slope has for its base a limestone lightly white in color whose thin leafs detach easily. One finds in abundance on this slope the thin stones known under the name of *pierres tégulaires* [in the shape of roof tiles] while are used to replace the tiles covering the roofs of country houses, which are called *laves* or *laverins*. This rock is coarse and of poor quality; it is subject to shattering during a frost, and thus one seldom uses it in masonry. I don't know if one can attribute to this cause alone the difference that is noticeable in the wines, which is, however, very noticeable to gourmets.

This slope offers several esteemed districts, and furnishes good wine. Leaving Savigny, one finds Les Guettes, Les Gravins, Les Serpentières, Les Savières, and above these climats, the Clos de la Bataillère whose agreeable wines rival the best of the Côte de Beaune. It is in this place that one finds the limit of the village of Savigny and the beginning of Pernand. Here are found the climats called Les Vergelesses, Les Boutières, and a bit further, the Croix-de-Pierre and Les Carradeaux. Beyond this, as one approaches Pernand[29], the vines are still of good quality but give wines less fine.

The products of this slope all have a character more or less the same; they have fire and force, they can keep, but they have less bouquet than those of the other slopes that we have examined. One reproaches them for having a slightly herbal taste when young that will however dissipate as it ages. These diverse qualities, which are common to all of the wines of this slope, prove directly the influence of the soil on the nature of its products, and if I had need of even more conclusive proof then this slope would furnish it. As to the rest, our examination has sufficiently demonstrated this; however, those upon which we are about to embark will further prove the truth of the point that I have made.

The opinions of Dr. Lavalle:

COMMUNE DE SAVIGNY-LEZ-BEAUNE

The territory of Savigny is, as far as the surface area under vine, one of the most important of the Côte d'Or. More than 650 ha are used in the production of wine, and among these, 350 ha are planted solely to Pinot and give fine wine.

The village of Savigny, situated at the entrance of the magnificent valley of Fontaine-Froide, has its vines situated on the slopes of the two flanks at the end of the valley, one of which ends in the vineyards of Beaune and the other in those of Pernand.

It is remarkable that one finds excellent wines in these two positions so different. Nothing but Pinot Noir is grown here.

---

28 Beyond Savigny one finds the continuation of the valley as it closes and the slopes that are thus formed offer only immense masses of woods that extend for the space of two leagues. In the middle of this valley one finds a fountain deliciously called the Fontaine-Froide, whose waters are, in fact, glacial. Each year on the Monday after the fifth of August there is a tradition that attracts a crowd of curiosity seekers who come looking for pleasure. An enchanting site, waters that spring abundantly, charming shady places, games dances, picnics set up on the grass, there and there the songs of drinkers, the non-stop strolling of the visits, all make an effect of a scene which is difficult to describe.

29 This village, placed at mid-slope, has a very picturesque aspect. It is perhaps one of the most ancient of our countryside. Here were found an immense number of archeological objects that are for the most part lost now. At the base of the valley of Frétille there was an abbey that was burned at the time of the Catholic League [formed during the counter-reformation to combat Protestants]; wheat and barley were found in the rubble. This wheat had been lightly toasted during the fire and was still in good condition two centuries later and one could still use it to make bread.

We will have to note that in this commune several "extra"-quality wines in the surrounding country are considered as above the premières cuvées; a great number of vines giving wines of première cuvée level; and many climats giving good wines of the third and fourth order.

These climats are:

PREMIÈRE CUVÉE, EXTRA

Les Vergelesses, of which a portion, belonging to the widow Vauchey, is known under the name of *Bataillère* and must be considered as the most perfect part of the climat, containing 16 ha 97 a 85 ca, belonging to the widow Vauchey and to MM. Desforges-Fion, de Laloyère, Guillemot, de Joux, and to the Hospice de Beaune.

> Danguy et Aubertin do not mention Bataillère. Of Vergelesses, they note the following proprietors: Mme. Bert, MM. Chanson Père et Fils, Desforges-Truchot, Fernand Dumoulin, Célestin Gorges, de Jouix, Lavirotte, Alexis Maldant, de Maupas, Eugène Moingeon, Perdrier, L. Poisot Royé Labaume et Cie.
>
> Rodier classifies Les Vergelesses as prèmiere cuvée, and lists it at the beginning, in capital letters (Marconnets Hauts and Bas and Les Jarrons receive the same treatment). He notes, "A portion of this climat, known under the name of La Bataillère belongs to Mme. Blanlot-Morot", and notes the other owners of Les Vergelesses as the widow Dreumont, Mme. Dumoulin, MM. de Fontenay, Gorges, the Hospices de Beaune, MM. Langeron-Boursot, Charles Lavirotte, A. Maldant, Mme. Messner, Nuidan, and Louis Poisot.

Première Cuvée

Les Jarrons, 10 ha 34 a and **Les Narbantons**, 13 ha 29 a 50 ca, belonging to MM. de Lloyère, Gambeaut, de Champeau, Leblanc, to the Gauthier de Tanyotr heirs, Brberet, etc.

Les Marconnets-Hauts and **Bas**, 9 ha 45 a 70 ca, belonging to MM. Desforges-Fion, Vachey, etc.

Les Guettes, 21 ha 4 a 10 ca, belonging to MM. de Laloyère, de Vergnette-Lamotte, Gauthet, Parent, marion, Fournier, and Guillemot.

Aux Gravains, 6 ha 38 a 80 ca, belonging to the widow Vauchey and to MM. Fournier, Lamarosse, de Laloyère, and Vachey-Desforges.

Les Lavières, 18 ha 51 a 25 ca, belonging to MM. Desforges-Fion, Vachey-Desforges, and Guillemot.

Les Vergelesses-Hautes, belonging to MM. Desforges-Fion, Peste, de Laloyère, de Joux, Desforges-Bulliot.

Les Peuillets, 22 ha 93 a 75 ca, of which the western part known under the name of *Dominaudes*, merits to be classed with the premières cuvées, belonging to the same parties.

Aux Cloux, 15 ha, 61 a 75 ca, belonging to M. de Laloyère, etc.

Aux Serpentières, 4 ha 87 a 30 ca, belonging to Fournier, Lavirotte, Bourcaut, Gambeaut, Vigot, and Serrigny.

Aux Pointes, 3 hs 75 a 30 ca, belonging to MM. Larchet, Peste, Bourcaut and Vachey.

Aux Petits-Liards, 5 ha, 78 a 5 ca, belonging to MM. Lvirotte, de Laloyère, Desforges-Bulliot and Larché.

Aux Grands-Liards, 6 ha 59 a 80 ca, belonging to MM. Lamarosse, maldant, Desforges-Bulliot and Patriarche-Desforges.

Es Canardières or **Canardises**, 10 ha 77 a 55 ca, belonging to M. Marion.

Les Rouvrettes, 5 ha 74 a 50 ca, belonging to MM. Manuel, Narveault.

Les Charnières, 2 ha 6 a 75 ca, belonging to MM. Troussard de Longuy, Desforges-Fion, and de Laloyère.

Le Pimentier, belonging to MM. Peste, Parent, Serrigny, and Lavriotte.

Troisième Cuvée

Les Saucours	Les Plancots-de-la-Champane	Aux Godeaux
Le Moulin-Moyne	Les Planchots-du-Nord	Aux Champs-Chardons-Dessus
En Redrescul	Aux Liards	Les Grands et Petits Picotins
Les Bourgeots	La Champagne	

Afterwards come *Les Grenottes*, *Les Vermots*, *Les Dessus-Vermots*, *Es Fatins*, etc.

In all the other climats the growers have replaced nearly everywhere the Pinot Noir with more common vines and the wine that one harvests here can only be considered as well inferior.

The wines of Savigny, although rich in bouquet and lacking neither generosity nor force, are distinguished above all by their finesse. As they had such a grand reputation in former centuries, we search for this precious quality in our wines.

An inscription dating back two hundred years that one can still read in the village square above the cellars of M. Laloyère, characterizes thus the wines of Savigny: the wines of Savigny are nourishing, theological, and health-induing[73]

Certainly in the idea that one would engrave in stone this inscription, the praise is pompous, and although we find ourselves embarrassed to come up with a definition for the epitaph of theological, one must recognize that this praise was not above the opinion of the times of the wines of this slope.

The Duke of Burgundy, passing through Dijon on September 21, 1703, dined there, and was offered an excellent wine from Savigny-sous-Beaune. On this subject, our poet Bernard de la Monnoye composed the following couplets of a song in Burgundian patois entitled *Dialogue between Breugnette and Gros-Jean*:

He drank, not by sips,
But by hearty draughts
As much as he had, I was careful
That he didn't say a word.
The chalice was divine;
As soon as he had tasted of it
He licked his lips three times:
"It is good," he said;
"Is this manna
that has from heaven
fallen to Dijon?"
"It is Savigny-sous-Beaune,"
He was told
"from the clos of the worthy
Monsieur de Migieu!"
"I," said he "call him
Monsieur Demi-Dieu" [Mr. half-a-God]
The duke said
As he left the table
Has ever a prince of France
Spoken more justly?

The tithe in 1658 and in the years following was sixteen baskets of grapes per year. In 1399, the inhabitants preferred to pay in cash the sum of eight derniers per ouvrée rather than (as they said) be constrained to swear an oath on the quantity of their fruit, as oaths could not be made without peril to their eternal souls.

The bishop of Autun had a vineyard in Savigny in the 13th Century, in a climat called *La Serpentière*.

The climat *La Bataillère* was named after the Bataille family who owned it for many years.

The Cathedral chapter of Beaune possessed vines in *Les Vergelesses* from 1435.

Cîteaux, in 1483, had thirty ouvrées of vines in *Moulin-Moyne*, and other parcels in *Palenchot, Saulcourt, Jarron, Pimentier, Meix-de-Cîteaux*.

The Order of Malta, in 1655, had ten ouvrées in *Les Jarrons* and twenty four in *Saulcourt*.

The Carmelites of Beaune had ten ouvrées in *Lavières* and seven in *Guettes*.

Today the famous parcel of La Bataillère is a monopole of the Beaune grower Domaine Albert Morot and worth seeking out. The leading domaine in the village, however, is Simon Bize, who proposes an array of wines from the appellation that are produced in classic style at a high level of quality and a very reasonable price. It would be remiss, however, not to mention the most expensive wine of the appellation, the Savigny Les Beaune 1er Cru Les Narbantons produced by Domaine Leroy, who own 0.81 ha in the appellation. The wine is indeed a marvel, done in the rich, luxurious Leroy style. It can sell for ten times the price of many other wines from the same appellation or more.

BEAUNE

Of all the gaps in the present system, the lack of special distinction for the wines of Beaune is prominent, but perhaps understandable. Claude Arnoux, writing in 1728, begins his *Dissertation on the Situation of Burgundy*, "The town of Beaune is the center of Haute-Bourgogne; it is situated in the most fertile territory and under the most serene sky of this country…" He goes to great lengths to make Beaune the center of attention, and equates it with Bibracte, the city where the Helvetii lost to Julius Caesar in 58 BC. This description was fanciful, as was recognized even in his day, but during the *ancien régime* Beaune was certainly the most well known town of the Côte d'Or after Dijon. As such, much of the wine that was sold for use outside of the region and exported abroad went under the imprimatur of Beaune. As Jullien notes, "The territory of this town is the largest and furnishes the greatest quantities of wine, in first quality as in second," although he classified it only as being of the second class. Perhaps the lack of grands crus there dates to this early dilution of the Beaune "brand".

In 1832, Morelot includes Les Fèves and Les Grèves as têtes de cuvées. Lavalle expands this to include Aux Crais and Champs Pimonts, although he notes that Fèves is a part of Grèves (Actually, it is separated from Grèves by Bressandes.) Fixed by the two great authorities of the 19th century, one is surprised that none of the proprietors was sufficiently motivated to press the suit for promotion to grand cru when the appellation was decreed in 1936. It is often said of wines that benefited from *"usages locaux, loyaux et constants"* and yet were not decreed grands crus (such as Clos des Lambrays of La Grande Rue) that their proprietors feared increased taxes. The proprietors here, however, at least at the time of the publication of Rodier's work, were a who's who of Burgundian insiders: the Chanson and Bouchard families, M. Marey-Monge, the Duvault-Blochet heirs, as well as others. Not even the parcel that formerly belonged to the Carmelites of Beaune was created as a grand cru in spite of its special mention by Lavalle and Danguy et Aubertin.

Perhaps the lack of a grand cru in Beaune is due to the sheer quantity of wine produced in AOC Beaune. The town of Beaune is particularly well endowed with premier cru vineyards under the present system. The band of premiers crus in the hills behind the town of Beaune is wide, covering nearly the entire distance from the top of the slope to its base, and all along each of the three hillocks that provide the backdrop of the town, from Les Pierres Blanches near Savigny to Les Mondes Rondes to the south, and on to the slopes of St. Désiré. In all, 138 ha 20 a 66 ca are classified as village, 337 ha 8 a 59 ca are classified as premier cru, and only 66 ha 14 a 28 ca are classified as Côte de Beaune. There is a disproportionate amount of premier cru property, with 12.2% of the land regional appellation (i.e. Côte de Beaune), while 25.5% is village, and 62.3% is premier cru, and nearby Savigny is 62.1% village to 37.9% premier cru, and Pommard is 62.8% village and 37.2% premier cru.

Perhaps Beaune deserves a bit more grand cru property and just a bit less of premier cru, although it is ridiculous to argue from percentages. The slope undulates gracefully as it makes its way to the south, with small hills divided, some by fairly deep combes with streams flowing through them, and others just at their peaks. Following each of these faces, the vines cover them like a blanket, while underneath the limestone is fractured and differently composed in different places. Some of these climats benefit from a superb exposition and gradient of slope, and a soil and subsoil whose structure is perfectly suited to giving grand cru level wine, and yet they are only classified as premier cru. Other sites are less well endowed with natural advantages and nominally hold the same rank, a situation that can only cause the thoughtful wine drinker to wonder.

The comments of Dr. Morelot:

> The wines that come from the climats between Pommard and the valley of the Bouzaize are all of approximately the same quality, firm, deeply colored, and full of fruit; they have perhaps a bit less finesse and bouquet than those of Volnay, but if they lack these things, they have the advantage of longer ageability. They are normally worth ten francs less than those of Volnay.
>
> At the valley of the Bouzaize begins the portion of the Côte de Beaune that extends to Savigny; it forms three small hills separated only toward their peaks. The first, dominating the town of Beaune and at whose feet are the springs that nourish the Aigue and the Bouzaize, carries the name of Les Mondes Rondes; the hill that follows it is called Les Pierres Blanches, and the third, which gives shape to Savigny, is called Monts-Battois[30].
>
> The stone that forms these hills is of better quality than those of the hills between Pommard and Beaune. Although one finds a great quantity of the remains of shellfish, the stone is more compact, with a more homogeneous texture and a pink color veined with white; one sees often on the inside of blocks of this stone very beautiful crystallizations. One is generally able to polish this stone, and even before the stone of Ladoix was as often quarried as it is today, blocks were used from the quarries of Savigny for chimneys and tables.
>
> This portion of our chain, which is properly called the Côte de Beaune, offers a very considerable number of famous and renowned climats. Taking this small valley [of the Bouzaize] as a point of departure, one has the Clos de la Mousse, whose wine has a finesse and an agreeable nature all its own; next comes Teurons, and above it, Les Cras; further along are Les Grèves, whose wine is so perfect, at a small distance are Les Fèves, Les Perrières, the Sans-Vignes [Cent Vignes today], which

---

30 This hill is crossed from west to east by the ancient Roman road that leads from Autun to Besançon. This road passed before the column at Cussy [a Gallo-Roman monument dating to the 3rd century, still in existence]. The road is still well preserved in many places.

31 This village was destroyed about three centuries ago. In 1823 a winegrower, digging a trench to propagate his vine, made a hole that led to a very beautiful cave. At the foot of this hill is found the intermittent source of the Genêt. After a long rain, the water rushes out with violence from the midst of these rocks, scattering many of them; this flow ordinarily lasts just a few days, but it is generally thought that one could render it perennial.

grow today where once there was a village[31]; the Clos du Roi, Les Marconnets, all favored sites which give exquisite wine. At Marconnets the territory of Beaune ends and that of Savigny begins; there are Les Jarrons, Les Peuliers, La Dominode, etc., which give wines almost as agreeable as those of the districts that we have just cited.

The wines of this slope, when they come solely from the climats that I have just named, are the equal with the best wines of all the Côte d'Or; they are firm, fruity, deeply colored, full of fire and bouquet; they are mellow and have the precious advantage of long ageability. However, according to a former custom, when one makes the price of wines each year at the administration of the Hospices de Beaune, the wines of these slopes are esteemed to be worth ten francs less per queue, or two casks, than those of Pommard, which makes them worth twenty francs below those of Volnay.

The notes of Dr. Lavalle:

COMMUNE DE BEAUNE

Beaune merits to be classed in the first rank of wine producing towns in the Côte d'Or based on the amount of land under vines. More than 1050 ha of vines, of which 500 at least are devoted to producing Pinot, produce a quantity of wines that can reach 25,000 – 30,000 hl in an abundant year, and is not less than 12,000 in a mediocre one. Also, Beaune has long occupied without contest the first place among the territory where fine wine is produced, and common usage has given the name of Côte de Beaune to all of the slopes that extend from Aloxe to Santenay, as one designates under the name Côte de Nuits all of the celebrated climats of which Nuits is the center.

As with all of the vineyards that have passed in review until now, in Beaune it is only quality Pinot Noir that is cultivated mixed with rare Pinot Blanc in the growths of the first order, and inferior varieties of Pinot in the climats of the third and fourth order. The techniques of growing it are also the same; the number of vines per hectare does not vary greatly, etc.

The study of the principal climats of the vineyards of Beaune presents difficulties that one does not encounter to such a degree at any other point of the Côte d'Or, both as to the classification by distinct cuvées and in regards to designation of the names of the proprietors. The climats are very spread out, and consequently have different qualities in their different parts. In addition, the property is extremely fragmented and dispersed among a great number of owners, and there are very few growers who produce a cuvée from a single climat, and many obtain wines often of great quality by blending the harvest of parcels that exist in different parts of the territory or even in neighboring villages. The result of these facts is that is has often be impossible for me to point out important proprietors as measured by the sum of their harvest, for they sometimes possess no parcel of great size in any particular climat, The classification [of the wines of Beaune] by climat gives only an approximation of the relative merit of each [proprietor].

Tête de Cuvée

Rodier lists Marconnets, Fèves, Bressandes, Grèves, Cras, the Clos de la Mousse and the Clos des Mouches in capital letters. The rest appear in lower case letters, including Champs-Pimonts, which is a tête de cuvée in Lavalle.

Les Fèves (a part of the climat of Grèves), belonging to M. Jules Véry

Danguy et Aubertin: MM. Bouchard (Antonin) of the house Bouchard Père et Fils, Chanson-Pichard, Henri Darviot, Louis Lagarde, R. de Peligny, Victor Verneau, and the Hospices de Beaune.

Rodier: MM. Chanson Père et Fils, J. Lagarde, Vernaux, etc.

Les Grèves, 31 ha 75 a 95 ca, of which 100 ouvrées belong to General Marey-Monge, and important parts to MM. Masson, Leblanc-Cordier, Ligeret, the Hospice de Beaune, etc., etc. In this climat one must rank first the cuvée called l'Enfant-Jésus, belonging to M. Buretey.

Danguy et Aubertin note a great number of proprietors of Beaune Grèves. Although a list of each of them is probably superfluous, I will note that they follow Lavalle to place Les Grèves de l'Enfant Jésus above the rest of the crus here, and note that it belongs to M. Antonin Bouchard of the house Bouchard Père et Fils. It had been acquired shortly before the publication of their work: in 1889 Bouchard purchased Domaine Pommier, who had reconstituted the domaine of the Carmélites de Beaune when it had been sold during the Revolution. Elsewhere, they note that Adolphe Bouchard of the house Bouchard Aîné was also an important proprietor in Beaune Grèves.

Rodier: Mme. Adolphe Bouchard, Bouchard Père et Fils, Chanson Père et Fils, Coron Père et Fils, the Duvault-Blochet heirs, Pierre Germain, Laviolette, Charles Lavirotte, A. Ligeret, Marey-Monge, Mathouillet-Brochot, Parizot, Pierre Ponnelle, Commune d'Allerey, etc.

Aux Crais, 6 ha 99 a 55 ca, belonging to the widow Marey-Monge, to MM. Chevignard, Véry, and to the Hospice de Beaune, etc., etc.

Danguy et Aubertin have "Cras or Crais"; both refer to stone quarries. They list the proprietors as MM. A. and L. Beaudet frères, Antonin Bouchard of the house Bouchard Père et Fils, Duvault-Blochet, L. A. Montoy, Paul Patriarche, Perdrier-Arvier, Perrin de Saux, R. de Poligny, Victor Raquet, the city of Beaune.

Rodier: MM. Artault, Bouchard Père et Fils, the Duvault-Blochet heirs, Germain, Louis Latour, Montoy, Podechard, J.-B. Rivot, etc.

Champs-Pimonts, 19 ha 70 ca, of which 40 ouvrées belongs to M. Changey and the rest to many proprietors.

Danguy et Aubertin: MM. A. Beaudet, the Billardet heirs, Bouchard (Antonin) of the house Bouchard Père et Fils, Chanson-Pichard, Paul Chanson, Darviot-Ibertier, Develle-Dupont, Pierre Dubois, Duvault-Blochet, La Charité, de Juigné, Antoine Ligeret, Ernest Marey, L. A. Montoy, R. de Poligny, Jules Senard, Gustave Theuriet, the city of Beaune, the Hospices de Beaune.

Rodier: MM. Beaudet, Bouchard Père et Fils, Broichot, Chanson Père et Fils, Coron Père et Fils, the Duvault-Blochet heirs, Genin, Montoy, etc.

Première Cuvée

Les Aigrots, 14 ha 46 a 25 ca, of which 75 ouvrées belong to the widow Marey Monge, 22 ouvrées to Miss Vanderkam, and the rest to M. Naigeon and others.

Les Avots, 13 ha 37 a 90 ca, of which 60 ouvrées belong to M. de Saint-Félix, and a large portion to the widow Marey-Monge.

Clos-de-la-Mousse, 3 ha 41 a 70 ca, belonging to M. André.

La Mignotte, 2 ha 40 a 45 ca, belonging to the Hospice de Beaune.

Aux Coucherias, 22 ha 70 a 95 ca, belonging to MM. Moreau-Voillot (40 ouvrées), Rougeot, Buretey, etc.

Clos-des-Mouches, 24 ha 84 a 35 a, belonging to MM. Dubois (from Chassagne), Morelot, Loyarbe, etc.

Vignes-Franches, 9 ha 94 a 20 ca, belonging to Miss Vanderkam, M. Gravier, etc.

Clos-du-Roi, 13 ha 90 a 5 ca, belonging to M. Lavirotte, etc.

Les Blanches-Fleurs, 9 ha 26 a 95 ca, belonging to M. Masson, etc.

Es Toussaints, 6 ha 49 a 75 ca, of which 38 ouvrées belongs to M. de Champeau.

Les Boucherottes, 8 ha 65 a 65 ca, belonging to MM. Morelot, Cunier and Miss Vanderkam.

Deuxième Cuvée

Les Teurons, 13 ha 40 a 80 ca, which one should perhaps classify among the premières cuvées, belonging to MM. Moreau-Voillot, Rougeot, Lavirotte, Miss Vanderkam and the widow Bourgeois.

La Creusotte, 3 ha 50 a 20 ca, belonging to the Hospice de Beaune, etc.

Les Sanvignes-Hautes et Basses, 28 ha 1 a 75 ca, a climat of better quality in its upper portion, belonging to MM. Edouard Michaud, Rougeot, etc.

Les Reversées, 5 ha 22 a 90 ca, belonging to the widow Marey-Monge, Miss Vanderkam, MM. Rougeot, Drouhin and others.

Les Montrevenets, 9 ha 5 a 40 ca, belonging to M. Fournier and others

Les Tuvilains, 10 ha 25 a 35 ca, belonging to MM. de Charodon, Rougeot, Chevignard, Bidot, etc.

Les Pirotes, 4 ha 80 a 35 ca, belonging to M. Naigeon.

Les Chouacheux, 5 ha 14 a 35 ca, belonging to MM. Moissenet, le Marquis d'Hugon, etc.

Les Epenottes, 13 ha 63 a 55 ca ; **Les Pertuisots**, 5 ha 56 a 15 ca ; **Les Sizies**, 8 ha 26 a 65 a, belonging to MM. De Jou, de Charodon, Rogeot, etc. In all of these climats there are parts that merit to be counted among the premières cuvées.

Troisième Cuvée

Les Levées	Les Prevolles	La Maladière
Les Pirotes	Les Sceaux	Les Chelènes
Le Chardonnereaux	Le Bas des Teurons,	Les Mariages (part in Gamay)
Les Verottes	Les Bouches	Les Rôles, id.
Les Epaules	La Champagne-de-Savigny	Belissart

In the classification of the climates of Beaune that I have given above, it is not without grave reasons and without having considered the opinion of the most competent people that I believe it necessary to classify as "hors ligne" a certain number among them. One could not place at the same rank all of the climats mentioned by Dr. Morelot, and even among the proprietors with the most interest in having it thus, I found no one to support placing well above the others any one of the climats that I have mentioned as tête de cuvée.

Other than this difference, I consider the appreciation of M. Morelot as true in every point, and I think, as he does, that the grands vins of Beaune are worthy of the greatest praise. The premières cuvées cannot be distinguished from the extraordinary except by the most well practiced tasters, and are often sold at an even higher price. The wines of the second cuvée are still fit to be the daily wine of a prince, and for the tables of the bourgeoisie can even constitute the wine to accompany a roast. The troisième cuvées, finally, give delicious everyday wine possessing in their perfection all of the qualities that one must look for in these wines.

Courtépée and Béguillet, trying at the end of the last century to determine the relative merit of the wines of the Côte de Beaune, give an appreciation of white it would be very difficult, even applying it to the present day, not to recognize its very great exactitude.[74]

By reason of the considerable quantity of wines produced in the vineyards of the Côte de Beaune, each year the average price of the cuvées of each village is established, and this serves as the base for most of the commercial transactions. The documents relative to the variation of these prices have too much importance for us to neglect them. We will also do here what we have done for the Côte de Gevrey and the Côte de Nuits, giving, according to the official documents, a table of these prices. However, we cannot give a similar table for each village; we will choose those of the Côte de Beaune that have always been considered to occupy the first rank. It is thus in the chapter relative to the commune of Volnay that we will give this information. It will be easy, with the base that we have said, to derive the relative value of Beaune, Pommard, etc.

The origin of the vineyards of Beaune, as with those of the neighboring slopes, dates back to the first origins of the culture of the vine in our country, and for me there is no doubt that these are the climats that Eumenius refers to under the name of pagus Arebrignus.[75]

As far back as we can go in our archives, we find the climats that are today planted with high quality vines already clearly delimited and designated with their present names; we see that the property in vines is extremely fragmented, which is the most positive proof of its great value, and derived from its ancient cultivation; finally, in records dating to 1207 we find several climats designated as vieilles vignes (the donation of vines to the abbey of Cîteaux by Duke Eudes III in 1207 in the Departmental Archives).

The *Clos-de-la-Mousse* was given in 1220 to the chapter of Notre-Dame de Beaune by canon Edme de Saudon.

The same Chapter acquired, in 1303, 51 ouvrées of *Cras* or *Crais*, worth 62 silver francs.

Carthusian monks possessed from the 14th century vines in the best climats of Beaune. They bought vines in *Cras* in 1342 and 1377, in *Grèves* in 1345, 1389, 1489 etc. In 1381, vines in *Perrière, Blanchefleur, Crée* (Cras) and *Lavault* were given to them by the Chardenel family for the endowment of two monks.

Cîteaux received a vineyard in *Mont-Battois* from Richard Josselyn, burgher of Beaune, in 1219.

In 1483, the same abbey possessed 60 ouvrées in the *Clos-de-la-Barre* on the Chemin de Pommard, 25 ouvrées in *Sanvignes*, 6 in *Tuvilain*, 40 in *Bonfeuvres*, others in *Prenelle, Pertuisot*, etc.

The Carmelites of Beaune (the former priory of Saint-Etienne) possessed from the 13th century vines in *Grèves*, or *Territoire de Lègues* in *Tyant*.

The Order of Malta received in 1255 vines in the vicinity of *Aigue* from Hugues de Sennetier; in 1256 a vineyard in *Marconnets*; in 1263 a vineyard in *Epenots* from the Renault family of Beaune; in 1267 a vineyard in *Aigrots*; in 1288 two vineyards, one above *Aigue*, the other in *Epenots*.

In 1655, it possessed 92 ouvrées in *Marconnets*, 42 in *Aigrots*, 8 in *Lavault*, 4 in *Tuvilain*, 4 in *Belisan*, 4 in *Beaufongey*, 24 newly planted in *Aumône*, 40 in *Epenots*, 20 in *Theurons*, 10 in *Coucherias*, 8 in *Sanvignes* and 4 in *Bouche-de-Lièvre*.

The Abbey of Maizière had in the 13th century vines in the climats already indicated.

In 1507 the crown had the *Clos de Bouache* in the town of Beaune containing 200 ouvrées in a single piece.

Today the commerce in the wines of Beaune is dominated by negociants, and there are very few growers in Beaune producing wines exclusively from their own holdings. The principal negociant houses are all (comparatively) large companies with long histories, Bouchard Père et Fils, Joseph Drouhin, Louis Jadot and Louis Latour. All make well-crafted wine that represents perfectly the typicity of the Burgundy region and very good value as well. Each of these negociants has their own speciality, and some, like the Beaune Grèves Vigne de l'Enfant Jesus, a Bouchard monopole, transcend this standard to offer a superlative wine. The newest trend, however, are the so-called micro-negociants, small operations run by passionate wine lovers, such as Alex Gambal, Olivier Bernstein and Benjamin Leroux. Each of these small boutique operations brings an interesting philosophy to market, and Leroux is in addition a highly gifted oenologist whose wine should be eagerly sought out.

The other important proprietor of note in Beaune is the Hospices de Beaune. This charitable institution, founded in 1443, manages more than 80 ha of vines accumulated over the centuries through legacies from local landowners. The wines are all vinified by the winemaker on staff—the able Roland Masse is set to retire after the 2014 vintage—and are sold at an annual auction by the barrel to benefit the institution, which maintains its function as a hospital and nursing school and is also charged with maintaining the historical building and operating the vineyards and producing the wines. The purchaser of a barrel is required to assure the maturation and bottling through a contract with a third party negociant. The wines are group by cuvée, and each cuvée is given the name of an historical figure or of a significant donor. For example, the Beaune premier cru Cuvée Nicolas Rolin, named for the founder of the Hospices, is composed of 1.35 ha of Les Cent Vignes, 0.47 ha of Les Teurons, 0.36 ha of Les Grèves, 0.18 ha of En Genêt, and 0.16 ha of Les Bressandes. Cuvées originate not only in Beaune, but also in Pernand-Vergelesses, Savigny-lès-Beaune, Monthélie, Auxey-Duresses, Volnay, Pommard, Corton, Clos de la Roche and Mazis-Chambertin for reds and in Saint-Romain, Pouilly-Fuissé, Meursault, Corton-Vergennes, Corton-Charlemagne and Bâtard-Montrachet for white. One caveat - because of the way the wine is sold, it is all necessarily matured completely in new oak casks. Some of the wines blossom under such a regime, while others can be dominated by the influence of the wood.

POMMARD

Choosing the two best parcels in Beaune was not difficult for our authors: their praise of Les Fèves and Les Grèves is near unanimous. In Pommard, however, there is less agreement. Arnoux rates it as the second *Vin de Primeur*, just after Volnay, and states that "the best cuvée is that of La Commaraine." Courtépée neglects to cite a specific climat, but traces the origins of the vineyards as follows as far back as the turn of the millennium:

> [in Pommard] King Robert confirmed a gift made of a vineyard called *Polmarco* by Odo, Vicomte of Beaune, to Saint-Bénigne in 1005.
>
> Hugues III gave to the Abbey of Labussière 10 casks of wine in his Clos de la Corvée in 1187, exchanged by Duke Eudes in 1198 for 28 ouvrées that the Abbey still profited from. Jean, Count of Burgundy, sold to Duke Hugues 164 casks of wine in 1234.
>
> Our princes would give a portion of the tithe in wine to the college of cannons in Beaune, another to the Commander of Malta, and to the monks of Val-des-Choux. This college has today a third, having acquired the portion of the Knights of Saint-Jean-de-Jérusalem by transaction in 1588; 300 journals of vines and of fields are exempt from the tithe for two casks of common wine due to the village priest, by subscription made with the Dukes, who gave them to Cîteaux. The abbey sold them in 1580 to M. Brunet, who had been for a long time the advisor to the royal domaines. […]
>
> The wines of Pommard are renowned for their finesse and their purity of fruit, and follow those of Volnay for the price.

Jullien favors Rugiens and Epeneaux, while Morelot has Epeneaux and Le Clos de Cîteaux as têtes de cuvées. What of Lavalle? He elects no têtes de cuvées but comments, "No climat is placed above the others so as to merit being classed a part, but a great number of growths must be placed in the first rank and are worthy to count among the premières cuvees." He then goes on to nominate more than thirteen of them for this honor.

While Danguy et Aubertin usually agree with Lavalle and Morelot, they do not spare the "C. Loc." citations when it comes to Pommard. They begin their classification of the village by noting that C. Loc. has Argillières, Chaponnières, Croix Noires, Epenots, Fremiers, Jarolières, and Rugiens Bas (but not Rugiens Hauts) as têtes de cuvées. They also cite C. Loc. to echo or reaffirm other judgments of Dr. Lavalle, and in several instances to contradict the C.A.B., as when they note that while the C.A.B. has Clos de la Commaraine as première and deuxième classes, the C. Loc. opinion is première cuvée. The dissent of Rodier is expressed as always through the use of capital letters. He notes Les Epenots (but not Petits-Epenots), Rugiens-Bas (but not Hauts), and Le Clos-Blanc in capital letters.

The difference of opinions over the terroirs of Pommard continues to this day. Pommard wine growers are currently pressing their case for promotion of certain vineyards to grand cru status. The brief currently before the INAO includes a petition for Pommard Rugiens (both Haut and Bas), Pommard Epenots (both Grands and Petits), and Clos des Epeneaux. Jasper Morris gives us more detail about the Epenots vineyards, noting that "Grands" is smaller than "Petits" but that the vine rows are longer, while pointing out that Morelot's tête de cuvée of Clos des Epeneaux straddles both lieux-dits, while his other tête de cuvée, Clos de Cîteaux, is wholly contained within Grands Epenots. The former is today a monopole of Comte Armand, and the latter is a monopole of Domaine Jean Monnier. This last is no longer recognized as a lieu-dit in the AOC regulations. However, it is permitted for the Monnier family to refer to it on the label and they do so, also explaining on their helpful website that it is 70 ouvrées in size, planted by Eudes, the Duke of Burgundy at the beginning of the 13th century. They explain further that it was given in 1207 to Cîteaux Abbey, who sold it in March of 1557, and was purchased by Domaine Jean Monnier et Fils in 1950.

The comments of Dr. Morelot:

> As one leaves these vines, one enters the territory of Pommard that offers the excellent climats of Frémiets, Bertins, Croix-Noires, Rugiens, etc. This is the end of the Côte de Volnay.
>
> All the wines that are harvested in this part of the slope are excellent in their qualities; they have finesse, bouquet, delicacy, a suave taste which one finds in no other type of wine: also when they are neither too old nor too young, that is to say just ready to drink, one can say that they are better than all other wines.
>
> In former times, what was called vin de primeur was made in Volnay: the grapes were left in tank for only a few hours; hardly had the fermentation become established than they were pressed off; the fermentation continued in cask, covering the surface with a thick foam called *liage*. The wine, made in this fashion, was ready to drink in the second year. The inconveniences that resulted from this method encouraged the development of other procedures that seemed more sure and advantageous without diminishing the merit of the wine of Volnay.
>
> All the vines that I have just named furnish a wine of the same quality; some are better than others, but this superiority is due only to the exposition, and I do not know if the best gourmet can appreciate the difference. This identity comes, as I have said, from the nature of the soil which is everywhere the same in this part of the slope.
>
> The slope of Volnay is separated from that which is properly called the slope of Pommard by a narrow valley called La Combe. This slope extends almost to the gorge that leads from Beaune to Bouze. This part also offers three divisions, but only at the summits, the first carries the name of the Mountain of Pommard or of

Luleune; the second is named Mont Désiré, and the third, a bit separated from the others, is called Montée-Rouge. The nature of the soil is the same on these three hills; it shows itself, more visibly here than elsewhere, to be composed of the remains of sea creatures; as one browses, one sees shells, sea urchins, belemnites [squid], corals and on the summits are rocky inclusions; the stone here is of poor quality; it cracks, does not resist frosts, and by consequence is seldom employed in masonry.

This slope produces excellent wines, but ones that are different from those of Volnay. The most renowned districts as one leaves Pommard include the Clos Blanc, Clos de Cîteaux, Clos de la Commaraine[32], Les Arvelets, Epeneaux (Petits and Grands); higher up are Les Pezerolles, En Largillière, the Clos Orgelot and Les Boucherottes, Champs Pimont, Les Sizies, Les Aigrots, Clos des Mouches, etc.

Dr. Lavalle:

COMMUNE DE POMMARD

The vineyard of Pommard is, with that of Volnay and Beaune, the one that has until the present resisted the most to the invasion of Gamay. All of this territory, elevated at the zone where the best wines are found, perfected exposed, with a backdrop of bare mountains with nothing to hold the mist, is still largely planted to Pinot. In its 730 ha of vines, one finds 330 ha planted to fine vines. Pommard is thus, in terms of the production of good wine, one of the most important villages of the department.

Pinot Noir alone is cultivated. One finds scarcely one thirtieth or one fortieth part of Pinot Gris or Pinot Blanc. The method of viticulture is the same as in Beaune and the neighboring villages.

No climat is placed above the others so as to merit being classed a part, but a great number of growths must be placed in the first rank and are worthy to count among the premières cuvées; these are:

Première Cuvée

Les Arvelets, 8 ha 47 a 20 ca, belonging to MM. Alphonse Marey-Monge, Lorchardet, Ansemot, Chevignard, Parent-Ropiteaux, Buretey et Girard, mayor.

Les Rugiens, 5 ha 85 a 15 ca, belonging to MM. Febvre, de Vergnette, Edm. Marey-Monge, de Châtellenot, Chauvelot, Dumesnil, de Juigné, and the Hospice de Beaune.

> Danguy et Aubertin : MM. de Barbuat, Joseph Bouchard of the house of Bouchard Pére et Fils, MM. Chenot and Sordet, Chevignard, The Hospices de Beaune, M. Mussy-Marillier [Les Rugiens Hauts]; MM. de Blic, Joseph Bouchard of the house of Bouchard Pére et Fils, MM. Chavignard, the Hospices de Beaune, M. Rouget, de Vergnette Lamotte [Les Rugiens Bas].

---

32 The name of Commareine comes from the counts of Vienne, lords of Commarin; they possessed this excellent clos of vines even before 1100. In the titles of this period, these lords of Commarin referred to this property under the name of our property in Pommard.

Rodier : MM. de Barbuat, de Blic, Billard, Girardin, Gonnet, the Hospices de Beaune, A. Imbault, L. Jacquelin, Micault, Moine, de Montille, Le Reffait, Rieusset, Rossignol-Larochette [Rugiens-Bas].

La Refène, 2 ha 46 a 95 ca, belonging to MM. Voillot, Bourgeois, and the Hospice de Beaune.

Le Clos-de-la-Commareine, 3 ha 95 a 10 ca, belonging to M. Jobard.

Danguy et Aubertin: MM. Jobard the younger and Bernard, M. Serres.

Rodier: MM. Jaboulet et Verchère.

Les Fremiers and **Jarolières**, 8 ha 14 a 75 ca, belonging to MM. Coste, Girard, Billardet, Parent-Ropiteaux, Lejeune, Berthot, de Courtivron, de Châtellenot et Boulet.

Danguy et Aubertin: MM. de Barbuat, de Broye, Chenot and Sordet, Fellot, Mme. Jarry, M. Parent-Joannes [Les Fremiers].

Rodier: MM. Massin, Moingeon-Gueneau frères [Les Jarolières] ; MM. de Barbuat, Chenot, Mme. A. Imbault, Louis Jacquelin, Jacquelin-Terrand, Domaine Lejeune, Naudin, Parent [Les Fremiers].

Les Epenots and **Petits-Epenots**, 31 ha14 a 8 ca, belonging to MM. Manière-Clerget, Chevignard, Sirot, Parent-Ropiteaux, Morelot, Arm. Marey, Cuynet, de Vergnette, Nodot, Lejeune, Michaud-Moreil, de Charodon, General Marey-Monge, and de Drey.

Danguy et Aubertin: Danguy et Aubertin not that the Clos de Cîteaux as a monopole of M. de Blic and that the proprietors of Les Epenots are MM. de Barbuat, Comte Armand, Imbault, Jobard the younger and Bernard, Mme. Paul Marey, MM. Parent, de Vergnette Lamotte; those of Les Petits Epenots as MM. de Barbuat, Billard-Michelot, Cuinet, Louis Latour, Maire et fils, Michelot-Dubois, H. Morelot, Parent, Poillot, Tartois (François), de Vergnette Lamotte.

Rodier: MM. Comte Armand, Battault, de Barbuat, de Blic, Bourgogne, Brugnot, Changarnier, Gaunoux, Génin, Marey-Monge, Moine-Tartois, Naudin, Parent, Le Reffait, J.-B. Rivot, Vaudoisey-Caillet [Les Epenots] ; MM. Carimentran, Chenot, Génin, Gorge, the Hospices de Beaune, Latour, Michalet, Parent, Pothier-Billard, Vaudoiset [Petits-Epenots] ; Rodier does not mention the Clos de Cîteaux.

Les Charmots, 9 ha 46 a, belonging to MM. Lejeune, Jobard, Naudot, Cuynet-Gauthey, Cornet, Arm, Marey, and Rousselin.

En l'Argillère and **Pézerolle**, 10 ha 10 a 85 ca, belonging to MM. Naudot, de Charodon, Coste and Parent-Ropiteaux

Danguy et Aubertin: MM. de Barbuat, Mme. de la Breuille, MM. Fellot, Jobard the younger and Bernard, H. Morelot, Parent, Serre, de Vernette

Lamotte [Les Argillières]; Boillot-Garnier, the Hospices de Beaune, Jobard the younger and Bernard, Michelot-Dubois, Mussy-Dauphin, de Vernette Lamotte [Les Pezerolles].

Rodier: MM. de Barbuat, Brugnot, Génin, Jacquelin-Terraud, Naudin, Parent, Le Reffait, Mme. Rougé, M. Terrand [Les Argillières] ; MM. de Berle, Loluis Blondeau, Faivre, Paul Girardin, Gonuet, Michalet, Parent, de Vergnette [Les Pézerolles].

Les Boucherottes and **Clos Micot**, 2 ha 60 a 90 ca, belonging to MM. Naudot, Jobard and Tartois.

Les Poutures, **Les Croix Noires** and **Les Chaponnières**, 5 ha 65 a 35 ca, belonging to MM. de Vergnette, Jary, Billardet, Cuynet, Boulenot, Lochardet, Jobard, Lejeune et Parent-Ropiteaux.

Danguy et Aubertin: MM. de la Breuille, Mme. Jarry, M. Jobard the younger and Bernard, MM. Michelot-Dubois, Serres, Parent-Joannes [Chaponnières]

Rodier: MM. de Barbuat, Clerget-Marx, Parent, de Vergnette [Les Croix-Noires] ; MM. de Barbuat, Michalet, Michelot-Dubois [Les Chaponnières]

Les Rugiens Hauts, 7 ha 62 a 80 ca, belonging to MM. Edm. Marey, Lejeune, Coste, Bouchard, Virely and the Hospice de Beaune.

Danguy et Aubertin: MM. de Barbuat, de Blic, Joseph Bouchard, Chenot et Sordet, Chevignard, the Hospices de Beaune, Mussy-Marillier.

Rodier: MM. de Blic, Buffet, de Charodon, Clerget, Coste-Chenot et Sordet, the widow Dessus-Chevallier, the Hospices de Beaune, Parent, Jules Pothier, Ricard, J.-B. Rivot, Rouget; Rodier notes that the upper part of this climat is classed in deuxième cuvée.

Le Clos Blanc and **Clos de Cîteaux**, 4 ha 27 a 65 ca, belonging to MM. Bolanger, General Marey-Monge and Chevignard.

Danguy et Aubertin: MM. de la Breuille, M. Jobard the younger and Bernard, Mme. Paul Marey, H. Morelot, Tridon.

Rodier: MM. Boillot, Clerget, Genevois, Grivot, Jacquelin, Marey-Monge, Marx, Tridou [Le Clos Blanc].

Le Clos Marey-Monge, belonging to General Marey-Monge.

Deuxième Cuvée

Les Cras	Les Combes-Dessus	Les Tavannes
Les Platières	Les Combes-Dessous	Les Riottes
Les Trois-Folles	Es Noizons	La Croix-Blanche
Les Chanlains	Les Petits-Noizons	En Sauzille
La Combotte	Rue-ès-Porcs	

Belonging to MM. Lejeune, Lochardet, Tartois, Parent, de Vergnette, Imbaut, Coste, Chevignard, de Charodon, Morelot, de Drey, Billardet, Moreau, Cuynet-Gauthey, Voillot, Dauphin, Cornet, Orgelot, Leblanc, Arm. Marey, General Marey, Moissenet, Dumesnil, de Courtivron, Jary, Voillot, Deschamps, Boulenot, de Juigné, Chicotot, Garnier, the Hospice de Beaune, etc., etc.

Troisième Cuvée

La Lévrière and **La Perrière**, belonging to MM. Nicolle de Charodon, Ansemot, Jobard, Perreau, and Michaud-Moreil.

Le Planet and **La Croix-Planet**, belonging to MM. Lejeune, Caillet, Paret, and Tartois.

Maison-Dieu and **La Taupe**, belonging to MM. De Vergnette, Dauphin, Poulet, Buretey, Tartois, Lochardet, Voillot, Fournier, Masson, Cuynet, and the Hospice de Beaune.

All the other climats are consecrated to the production of common vines.

The slope of Pommard produces excellent wines, firm, colored, full of freshness, and possessing in high degree all of the qualities that our ancestors designated by the expressions of "honest, vermillion, and saleable".[76] Perhaps they have a bit less finesse and bouquet than those of Volnay, but they last longer and are easier to transport.

The wines of the première cuvée are sold throughout Europe under the name of our greatest wines, and in good years are worthy, in effect, to be offered as excellent wines. Those of the deuxième cuvée can constitute a superior wine to accompany a roast, or a grand ordinaire.

This vineyard is one of the most ancient of the Côte d'Or, and existed certainly at the end of the Roman occupation, along with those of Beaune and Volnay.

As in Beaune and in the rest of the region, the greatest number of vines in Pommard from the 11th or 12th century belonged to the princes or to the religious orders.

In the 13th and 14th centuries, the abbey of Maizière was the owner of vines in the climats of *Combes, l'Espinal, Epenault, Chiveau, Chaffaut, La Paule, Perrières, Ormes, Crais, Fremies de Noisey*, etc.

The Carmelites of Beaune, successors to the priory of Saint-Etienne, possessed from the 12th century vines in *La Vache, Marcau, Clos Micault, Rue-ès-Porcs, Clos-Blanc*, and *Clos-des-Ormes*.

In 1222 and 1234, Cîteaux purchased from Belin of Pommard for the amount of 30 Dijon *livres* a vineyard in the territory of *Pézerolle*, and another for 16 Dijon livres from Mr. Thiébaud-Odin.

In 1230 and 1240, Pierre de Fleury and André le Berger, bequeathed vines in the same territory to this abbey, who, in 1483 possessed in Pommard the *Clos Blanc* or *d'Espenault*, of 54 ouvrées; 16 ouvrées in *Noison*, the *Clos-de-la-Covée*, 60 ouvrées, and other parcels in *Pézerolle*, *Grèvechamps*, etc.

In 1248 the Order of Malta acquired vines in *La Faye* and in 1264 *Les Crais*; in 1655, it possessed 24 ouvrées in *Bertain* and 14 in *Rondain*.

Finally, the king possessed in 1507 the *Clos-de-Lachery* of 30 ouvrées, vines in La Pourree, later called *Petit Epenault*, 24 ouvrées in *La Boucherotte*, 24 ouvrées in *Pointe-des-Places*.

From 1400, vins de paille[77] were made in this region.

Among the most compelling addresses for top flight Pommard are the Domaine du Comte Armand for their monopole Clos des Epeneaux, vinified by Benjamin Leroux, and Domaine Michel Gaunoux for their Grands Epenots and Rugiens.

VOLNAY AND MONTHÉLIE

It seems that our earliest authors rank Volnay at the head of the second class. Arnoux has it first among his Vins de Primeur category, singling out Champans. High praise, indeed, for a blanc de noirs that was barely colored, if at all. It was the custom in the 18th century to vinify red and white grapes together and to let the juice and skins ferment together for a very short time, yielding a wine that was very light in color. In spite of the fact that the fashion of the day favored sturdy, full-bodied wines that could travel well, the wines of Volnay were still highly sought-after. Courtépée devoted considerable attention to the wines of Volnay, noting:

> Volnay had been the domaine of our ancient kings and first dukes. Hugues IV in 1250 built there or reestablished the château, which the dukes or duchesses loved to visit because of the varied view, the good air, and the excellent wines and waters of the country. […]

> This village, in the most agreeable situation and the best exposition, produces the finest wines of the Côte de Beaune; thus the proverb, "There is but one Volnay in France", and this other:

> Without Volnay there is no perfect joy

> Young wines and *vins de paille*, which once were pressed from the grapes and not aged in cask, are today red and will age for several years. The inhabitants have the privilege of choosing the harvest date, a date which the Viscount could advance or retard by a day, [this being] the day that ordinarily will determine the harvest throughout the Côte.

> It seems that nature has prodigiously gifted this region with the most precious treasures. Grains, fruits, vegetables, and dairy products surpass in taste and in goodness those of other districts; even the eggs have been so justly renowned that they have been carried to our dukes in their neighboring châteaux, as far as Argilly, and people were sent to look for them when the Duke of Bourbon was holding political assembly. The limpidity, freshness, and abundance of its fountains, so rare in the three neighboring villages, distinguish again this rich slope.

> The waters of La Cave, which spring from the mountain of Chaignot, sometimes form a considerable torrent, which is a sign that good weather is arriving after a storm, and thus the proverb: No good weather until the Cave flows.[78] Neither wine nor water has a taste of sulfur, and there is no sign that there had ever been a volcano, as some had thought. There is no sign of crevasses or of landslides.

Like Arnoux, Jullien also has Volnay near the top of his second category, noting Caillerets, Champans, and Chapelle. With this last climat, Jullien means to indicate Carrelle sous la Chapelle, a climat that borders En Champans to the north. Today there exists also Clos de la Chapelle in Volnay, but this name is of fairly recent origin. In former times, a number of the small clos surrounding the village of Volnay were known only as Le Village.

By the time of Morelot, La Chapelle has fallen from the list, and Morelot is content to echo Jullien's praise for Caillerets and Champans. While Dr. Morelot is fulsome in his praise of Volnay, Lavalle takes him to task for this and it is one of the few times that Lavalle dissents with his predecessor. Dr. Lavalle was too discreet to mention in Chapter III that Morelot was a proprietor of vines in the village and in several other climats.

Lavalle is almost ready to do what he did in Pommard and refuse to single out any crus, but in the end he, too, elevates Champans and Cailleret as têtes de cuvées. He then proceeds to classify eight other climats along with them as têtes de cuvées and to skip the category of première cuvée altogether. This may either be an oversight of the printer, or it may reflect his stated belief that all of the top climats were on a more-or-less equal footing.

All of these original têtes de cuvées were located below the road from Beaune to Autun (the present day D973). Danguy et Aubertin, however, are more than ready to cobble together all of these and more using their C. Loc. convention, which includes as tête de cuvée Les Angles, Pointes d'Angles, En Fremiers, and La Barre (now called Clos de la Barre), all of which are up the slope from this road and near the border with Pommard. The list also includes the traditional favorites of En Champans, En Cailleret, Cailleret Dessus, and Carelles-sous-Chappelle on the other side of the road as well as En Chevret (on the south side of the village), and Les Mitans and En l'Ormeau, located on the north side of the village. Rodier distinguishes with capital letters Les Fremiets, Les Champans, Les Caillerets, and Les Angles, in that order.

Today in Volnay the situation is similar to that of Beaune, where there is more premier cru property (114 ha 89 a 61 ca) than village (98 ha 37 a 15 ca). All of the climats surrounding the village (many of them with the grand-sounding "Clos" in their name) are classified as premier cru, as well as parts of the tier of vineyards even further downslope from the swath of Cailleret / Champans that Lavalle has in troisième cuvée. Wine lovers might be well served by elevating Champans and Caillerets, while being a bit more selective with the premier cru vineyards in other instances. To the south is located the ancient vineyard of Monthélie. As Courtépée notes, "[In Monthélie] Count Adalhard gave vines *in Montelio Vineolea* to Saint Nazare in the 9th century...[it has] a well-regarded vineyard".

Dr. Morelot pays scant attention to Monthélie, yet he waxes poetic about Volnay:

From the valley of Auxey there begins a third group of small hills that extend up to the gorge of Pommard. One distinguishes again three crests and as many little mountains. On the first, to the south, is built the village of Monthélie[33]. On that of the center is found the charming village of Volnay, which is located at a sort of amphitheater at mid slope[34]; finally, at the foot of the third is placed the beautiful village of Pommard, peopled with fourteen hundred inhabitants, which extends from east to west in the gorge that I have just spoken of, commonly called La Combe.

Several authors, more taken with marvels than with truth, have wanted to believe that the dip in the rock above Volnay was an extinct volcano; they have given as a reason for their opinion that this hollow, called La Cave, was shaped like a crater, and that the white wines that came from vines planted there had a taste of sulfur. They had gone to great lengths to prove something that a simple examination of the place in question would refute completely. This hollow is due to interior landslides, occasioned by rains of long duration that created a river that flowed for a day or two before drying up. The sulfurous taste is thus due to a completely different cause.

The bedrock that forms the core of this part of the slope is a limestone that fractures easily into fairly thin sheets. Below Monthélie, one finds quarries of good stone for building, but that are formed in thick layers of several inches; they are of a very fine grain, a reddish color, and often show little points with an attractive crystallization and the remains of different sea creatures.

This slope is renowned for the excellence of its wines and we can indicate the most distinguished districts within it. The first, as one leaves Meursault, is Santenots, which is still a part of this village; the wine that it furnishes, when mature, rivals all of the best wines of the Côte d'Or. After Santenots, one enters the village of Volnay, and then one finds Chevrets. Above this is Caillerets, which produces wines of the greatest finesse, and from whence the rural proverb, "He who does not have a vineyard in Caillerets does not know the value of Volnay." Following along, one finds Champans, one of the best climats of this commune, and above this is Taille Pieds. After these one finds the districts of La Chapelle, Bousse d'Or, Les Angles, etc., etc.

Dr. Lavalle:

COMMUNE DE VOLNAY

Although extensive, more than half of the vineyards of this commune are still planted to fine vines. Pinot Noir covers a surface area of approximately 220 ha divided in a great number of climats that we will indicate presently. The culture of Gamay does not attain this figure – one may estimate it at 210 to 215 ha. Admirably exposed, protected by hills with dry, bare summits, far enough removed from the plain to avoid the influence of the vapors that arise from it, Volnay can be considered as the village that, with Beaune, produces the greatest number of excellent wines. A large part of its climats are in the conditions of soil and exposition as favorable as possible; and this results in a fairly great conformity between all of the growths of

---

33 The village, or more properly the hill on which it is built, is named in the most ancient titles Mons Lyceus, a great number of antique objects have been found there through the years.

34 Volnay is a very ancient village; it was once the property of the Dukes of Burgundy. Several years ago this was the subject of a trial between the village and a private landowner who had excavated the foundations of an ancient castle that occupied almost the totality of the village on the lower side. From the type of masonry employed, it was determined that the foundations were at least eight centuries old. It is known that Hugues IV restored this château in 1250. The Duke and the Duchess often enjoyed themselves there because of the beauty of the site and the excellence of the air, the water, and the wine.

the first order so that none of them, according to many people, may be classed sufficiently above the others to occupy a place apart.

Nevertheless, it seems that in order to be just, one must distinguish several climats, notably *Caillerets* and *Champans*, and recognize that they are worthy to be distinguished under the name of tête de cuvée.[79]

Tête de Cuvée

En Cailleret, En Cailleret-Dessus, Les Caillerets, 14 ha 42 a 60 ca, belonging to MM. Masson, Dumesnil, Chauvenot, Bichot, de Châtellenot, Carnot, Serre, de Vaudremont, Morelot, Véry, Patriarche, Boulet, Bouchard, Boulet-Muzard, Duchemain, Nudan, and the Hospices de Beaune.

> Danguy et Aubertin: MM. Bonneau du Martray, Bouchard (Joseph) of Bouchard Père et Fils, Cellard-Bouchard, Massin (Armand), the du Mesnil heirs, Mme. Serre [En Cailleret] ; MM. Delagrange frères, Delaplanche-Garnier, the du Mesnil heirs, Glantenay-Bouley [Cailleret Dessus].

> Rodier: MM. Marquis d'Angerville, Boillereau, Bouchard Père et Fils, Clerget, Delaplanche-Garnier, P. Glantenay, Massin, Masson-Malivernet, de Montille, Mme. Serre, M. Zimmermann.

En Champans, 11 ha 34 a 90 ca, belonging to MM. Dumesnil, Monthélie, Chauvelot, Boche, Morelot, de Vaudremont, and the Hospices de Beaune.

> Danguy et Aubertin: MM. A. and L. Beaudot frères, the du Mesnil heirs, Hospices civils de Beaune, Imbault (Alfred), Jobard jeaune and Bernard, Malivernet, Monthélie (Armand), de Montille, Noirot.

> Rodier: MM. Marquis d'Angerville, Buffet, J. Cagear, Duchemin, Duverger, the Hospices de Beaune, Lafon-Boch, Malivernet, Monthélie, de Montille, Noirot, Pierrot.

En Chevret, 6 ha 6 a 45 ca, belonging to MM. Bouchard, Blondeau, de Vaudremont, Carnot, and Serr.

> Danguy et Aubertin: MM. Bouchard (Joseph) of Bouchard Père et Fils, Cellard-Bouchard, Mme. Serre.

> Rodier: MM. Marquis d'Angerville, Boillereau, Bouchard Père et Fils, Cellard, Massin, Baronne de Montbrun.

En Fremiers, 6 ha 50 a 45 ca, belonging to MM. Dumesnil, Chauvelot, Monthélie, and Gauvenet.

> Danguy et Aubertin: MM. Bouchard (Joseph) of Bouchard Père et Fils (Clos de la Rougeotte), Imbauld (Alfred), Joannez-Parent, the du Mesnil heirs, de Montille.

> Rodier: MM. Marquis d'Angerville, Bouchard Père et Fils, Buffet,

A. Glantenay, Mme. A. Imbault, the Hospices de Beaune, Massin, de Montille, Parent, Pillot.

En Bouze d'Or, 1 ha 96 a 85 ca, belonging to MM. Dumesnil and Patriarche.

Danguy et Aubertin: [spelled Bousse d'Or] MM. Victor Boillot, Massin (Armand).

Rodier has this as a monopole of M. Massin.

Les Angles and **Point d'Angles**, 4 ha 70 a 75 ca, belonging to MM. Dumesnil, Lavirotte, Bouchard, Chauvelot, Duchemain, Monthélie, Boillot, Loyarbe, Michaud-Moreil.

Danguy et Aubertin: MM. Cegaud, Cellard-Bouchard, Louis Latour, Masson-Boillot, Monthélie (Armand), Rouget-Perret [Les Angles] M. Imbault, the du Mesnil heirs [Pointes d'Angles].

Rodier: MM. Marquis d'Angerville, Boillereau, Cellard, Mme. A. Imbault, Latour, Monthélie, de Montille, Mme. Rougé.

La Barre, 1 ha 20 a 60 ca, belonging to M. Morel.

Danguy et Aubertin: M. Cellard-Bouchard, etc.

Rodier: M. Cellard and the Hospices de Beaune.

Carelle-sous-Chapelle and **Rougiots**, 3 ha78 a 95 ca, belonging to MM. Boillot, Duchemain, Chauvelot, Monthélie, and Gauvenet.

Danguy et Aubertin: MM. Lucien Boillot, Buffet-Machu, Gillotte-Monnot, Léon Glantenay.

Rodier: MM. Louis Boillot, the widow Bourgogne, Brugnot, Clerget, Décontlois, Dubois, Duchemin, the Hospices de Beaune, the Baron de Montbrun, de Montille, Pillot, L. Rossignol.

En L'Ormeau, 4 ha 34 a 35 ca, belonging to MM. de Vaudremont, Duchemain, Gillotte, Dumesnil, Parent-Batault, and the Hospice de Beaune.

Danguy et Aubertin: the widow Boillot-Gauvenet, MM. Camus (Auguste), Dubois-Bizot, Gillotte-Monnot, Massin (Armand), the du Mesnil heirs.

Rodier: MM. Marquis d'Angerville, Bitouzet, Boillereau, the widow Bourgogne, Brugnot, Camus, Clerget, Delagrange Frères, E., Esmonin, Glantenay-Rossignol, the Hospices de Beaune, Michelot, Verdereau, Voillot, Zimmermann.

Les Mitans, 3 ha 99 a 50 ca, belonging to MM. Gauvenet-Blondeau, Jobard, de Chatellenot, Gillotte, Chauvenet, Dumesnil, and Pétiot.

Danguy et Aubertin: MM. A. and L. Beaudet frères, the Fleurot heirs, Gauvenet, Gillotte-Moreau, Jobard jeune and Bernard, Louis Latour, the du Mesnil heirs, Rouget-Perret.

Rodier : MM. Cagear, H. Delagrange, P. Delagrange, Fr. Gillotte, Guichard-Potheret, Jobard, Latour, Parent, Pion, Mme. Rougé.

Deuxième Cuvée

Le Clos des Chênes, 16 ha 27 a 40 ca, belonging to MM. Serre, Barbet, de Vaudremont, and Blondeau.

En Taille-Pieds, 7 ha 28 a 85 ca, belonging to MM. Serre, Dumesnil, Blondeau, Bouchard, Chauvelot, Gauvenet, and the Hospice de Beaune.

En Verneuil, 79 a 45 ca, belonging to M.Gauvenet-Parent.

Les Cazelles-Dessus, 2 ha 12 a 80 ca, belonging to MM. Chauvelot and Buffet.

Les Aussy, 3 ha 32 a 75 ca, belonging to MM. Carnot, Boillot, Blondeau, and Dumesnil.

Les Roncerets, 2 ha 1 a 70 ca, belonging to M. Jeannin.

En Brouillard, 6 ha 82 a 20 ca, belonging to MM. Chauvelot, de Châtellenot, Dumesnil, Duchemain and Chauvenet.

Troisième Cuvée

Les Grands-Champs	Les Pluchots	En Vaux
La Gigotte	Les Echares	Les Chanlains
Les Combes	Les Jouères	L'Assole
Les Lurets	Les Pitures-Dessus	La Cave
Gros Martin		

Quatrième Cuvée

Sur Rocher	Les Longbois	Les Serpents
Le Pâquier	Les Petits-Gamets	Les Grands-Poisots
Les Petit-Près	Les Buttes	Les Petits-Poisots

All the other communes give only common wines consumed in the country.

The wines of Volnay are thus appreciated by one of our connoisseurs the most competent: "The wines of Volnay are exquisite by their finesse, their purity of taste and their bouquet. They are, according to us, the first wines of the Côte de Beaune, Santenots excepted".[80]

All the authors who have written on the wines of the Côte d'Or are in agreement in giving exactly the preceding appreciation. M. Morelot, in his *Statistique*, exaggerates the praise, expressing himself as follows: "All of the wines that are harvested in this part of the slope are excellent. They have a finesse, a bouquet, a delicacy, a smooth taste that are not found in any other type of wine. Thus when they are neither too new nor too old, that is to say just mature, one can say that they are preferred over all wines."

It would be at once an error and an injustice to accept in its general form the opinion emitted by M. Morelot.

Evidently, it would not be admitted by anyone that the slope of Volnay in its entirety possesses the degree of superiority that he accords it. The têtes de cuvées of several other parts of the Côte d'Or are incontestably above the best wines of Volnay, and to be correct, one can compare them only, Champans and Cailleret excepted, to wine of the premières cuvées of other climats.

Within these limits, we accept happily the appreciation of M. Morelot.

Among the climats of Volnay, Caillerets produces wines very remarkable by their exquisite finesse and merits to be carried to the rank of tête de cuvée. Thus as they say in the region "he who has no vines in Caillerets knows not what Volnay can be".

It is above all in the 13th – 16th centuries that the wines of Volnay acquired their most brilliant reputation. At this time the wines of the Côte de Nuits, still not very widespread, were enjoyed only rarely, and the wines of the Côte de Beaune were the only ones with a great renown in distant places. Among them, the wines of Volnay were held as they are today in the first rank.

Our princes gave successively to churches and to abbeys their tithes, and thus there were six who were authorized to collect tithes; only the village priest was forgotten. The tithe for wine is seven deniers for each ouvrée, according to a transaction of 17 September 1486.

I recall that from the 13th – 17th centuries the wines of Volnay and of Pommard were not meant to have a color too deep, but rather [the color of] partridge eye.[81] To this end, many vines of white grapes were grown, and producers hardly macerated their wine. M. Pézerolle de Montjeu, in a small work on grape growing published at the end of the last century and sold in Pommard by the son of M. Seguin, says that he had been the last to pull up the white grapes that were still planted around his vines according to former custom. He deplored this modification brought on by fashion, but since, as he says, "the buyer prefers color and firmness to finesse; one must content him as far as the climate will permit."

Regarding the origin of the climats of Volnay, I should repeat all that I have said of the climats of Pommard and of Beaune. As far back as we can go in the records that give a positive description, we find them with their current delimitations; since this time the soil of Volnay, fragmented into a considerable number of parcels, is in its totality planted to vines. The names under which these climats are today known almost all date to an extremely ancient time, and for the greatest number of them beyond the 8th or 9th century.

The Order of Malta became possessor in 1207 of the field of *La Caille*; in 1243 of a vineyard in *Poisot*; in 1262 of two parcels in *Aubépines*; later they had a vineyard of six ouvrées in *Cailleret*, and another in *Grande-Rue*.

The priory of Saint-Etienne of Beaune bought, in 1261, a parcel in *Essarts*; later, they possessed another in *Verseux*, in *Pointe-au-Brûlard*, in *Fremiers*, in *Angles*, in *Peluchot*, and in *Carelle*.

In vineyard lease documents prepared for six years by the priory in 1360, it is stated that the growers will receive half of the produce and shall be obliged to cultivate or to have cultivated in every detail "in good season and at the most opportune moment[35]"; that, the first year only, the priory must provide them fifty vine-stakes and a sufficient quantity of wicker [for tying the vines]; and that if it is necessary to replenish the soil that the two parties would share the expense.

The abbey of Maizière owned vines in Volnay from the 13th century in the principal climats.

In 1295, the ducal domaine had vines in La Pouture, in Fontenay, in Louvot, Sous l'Ormeau, in Creuzot, in Taille-Pieds, in Bousse-Tourte, in Chevrey, etc.

In 1340 this domaine included 360 ouvrées, of which five were in Cailleret, six in Bousse-Tourte, one hundred in Clou-Chevrier, twenty-five in Clou-Blanc, etc.

In 1507 the king owned in Volnay: the *Clos-Chevrey*, one hundred ouvrées; nine ouvrées in *Cailleret*, forty two in *Champans*, four in *Perrière*, sixteen in *Luret*, of which eight were rented for three blancs [i.e. 15 deniers] per ouvrée; six in *Raiscrit*, twenty in *Peluchot*, ten in *l'Ormeau*, three in *Chenevières*, six in *Boisse-Courte*, twenty five in *Brûlard*, twenty two in *Vaux*, five in *Taille-Pieds*, three in *Longenot*, ten in *Clos-Blanc*.

COMMUNE DE MONTHÉLIE

In spite of the small size of the territory cultivated in vines, Monthélie merits to be counted among the communes of the Côte d'Or that produce our good wines. Situated above Volnay and bordering the town of Meursault, the vineyard can be considered superior to 85 ha for the part consecrated to fine vines, gives wines that have body and good color but lack a bit of bouquet. The grape growing practices are the same as in Volnay and the vine is identical.

The price of the wines of these climats is based on that of Volnay, being reduced by this rule, that the wines of Monthélie are worth three quarters those of Volnay; thus, if those of Volnay are sold for 400 francs per barrel, those of Monthélie will be quoted at 300 francs. Three or four cuvées of the first order obtain 20 to 25 francs more. Among these one must count:

Those that come from the *Champ-Feuillot*, belonging to M. de Surget, that merits being considered at the head of the line; another cuvée from the same proprietor, coming from different vines; those of MM. Lagarde frères, of M. Bouzerand, of the widow Blondeau, coming from the climat called *Clou-des-Chênes*, etc.

---

35 In bonis et debitis saisionibus, prout saisiones exigent.

In Deuxièmes Cuvées, we note the wines of MM. Monthélie – Monthélie; Jobard the younger (*Clos-Mipont*), Virely-Thomassin, the brothers Galette, Parent Ropiteaux, the widow Blondeau and her children. These cuvées come from the climats called *Clou-des-Chênes*, *Duresse*, *Aubrain*, *Les Crais*, etc.

The wines harvested in the Combe (valley) d'Anis are highly colored without rusticity, and need four or five years in cask before bottling. They can be counted as bons ordinaires, and are designated under the name of passe-tout-grains.

Just as there are many fine terroirs in Volnay, there are a number of sources for wonderful wine as well. Any true lover of wine overlooks Volnay at their peril. Guillaume d'Angerville at Marquis d'Angerville is justly proud of his monopole Clos des Ducs—always considered his top wine, by himself and by others—but he also has an impressive holding of nearly 4 ha of Champans and more than a hectare each of Taillepieds, Frémiets and Les Angles among other holdings. These are top quality burgundy wines at very reasonable prices.

Domaine Michel Lafarge, directled today by the affable Freddy Lafarge, has a smaller holding overall, but in all the right places. In addition to his Clos du Château des Ducs monopole, there is a bit of Caillerets, nearly a hectare of Clos des Chêne and 0.4 ha of Mitans as well. As with d'Angerville, these have an extraordinary quality/price ratio.

Domaine de Montille is another good address in Volnay, with nearly a hectare of Champans, over 1.5 ha of Taillepieds and a good-sized plot in Mitans as well. Other properties to watch include the formal ducal (later royal) estate known today as the Domaine de la Pousse d'Or with their tremendous holdings that include 2.24 ha of Caillerets and the 2.39 ha monopole "Clos des 60 Ouvrées" within Caillerets; the monopole Clos de la Bousse d'Or (2.13 ha) among others. Finally, Nicolas Rossignol is undoubtedly one of the rising stars, not only in Volnay, but in all of Burgundy. Although young, he makes impressive wine from a wide array of terroirs, some that he has inherited from his family, and others leased in a sharecropping arrangement. All in all, Volnay today is teeming with excitement, quality and value.

MEURSAULT

Courtépée writes that the wines of Meursault have been appreciated for centuries:

> [Meursault has a] Good vineyard whose white wines are renowned throughout France. The best climats are Les Charmes, Les Perrières, Les Genevrières, [and] La Goutte d'Or. For red wine, Santenots, near Volnay, is where the finest Pinot Noir is produced. The passe-tout-grains are called the "doctors" of other wines, and the best ordinary wines, when aged, grace the best tables.

Buyers today often focus solely on the whites from Meursault, but the reds have also been widely appreciated, if somewhat misunderstood. As noted in the previous chapter, Morelot discusses the Santenots vineyard in the same breath as the wines of Volnay. The vineyard actually lies, however, within the limits of the village of Meursault, and this is where Dr. Lavalle and other authorities have placed it. Modern classification is not really certain where to place it, either: the red wines are labeled as AC Volnay Santenots Premier Cru, while the whites are labelled either Meursault Premier Cru (Les Santenots Blancs and Les Santenots du Milieu) or Meursault Blanc (Les Santenots-Dessous and 5 a 44 ca of Les Vignes Blanches). These last two may only be white; all of the other climats in the commune may produce red or white wine.

Since the time of Lavalle, Santenots has been seen as the finest vineyard in Meursault, although as today's appellation is much larger and thus its right to this antique esteem may be questioned. Originally, Santenots du Milieu was singled out for tête de cuvée status. Today it is divided into 6 ha 81 a 31 ca of Santenots du Milieu and 1 ha 19 a 23 ca of Clos des Santenots, while Santenots Blancs and Les Pelures (now Les Plures) were première cuvée and Santenots Dessous and Les Vignes Blanches were deuxième cuvée. All of these wines are premier cru today.

To complicate matters even further, some of the wines of Blagny are included in the modern system with those of Meursault, although this was not always the case. The village of Blagny itself lies in the hills behind Puligny, and Jullien gives them as being in the district of Puligny, placing both the whites and the reds in his third class, and noting that the whites sell for the same as the premières cuvées of Meursault. Lavalle mentions Blagny-Blanc among the premiere cuvées of Puligny, along with Bâtard-Montrachet and Les Combettes, but the list of vineyards in Blagny begins to flesh out with the addition of La Garenne in Danguy et Aubertin, and all of the modern vineyards with Rodier.

Today Blagny and Blagny Premier Cru are appellations for red wine only and whites are either Meursault (Le Bois de Blagny), Meursault Premier Cru (La Pièce sous le Bois, Les Ravelles, La Jeunellotte, Sous le Dos d'Ane, and Sous Blagny), Puligny (Le Trezin), or Puligny Premier Cru (Sous le Puits, La Garenne, Hameau de Blagny). To further confuse matters, if these wines are declassified, the reds become Blagny-Côte de Beaune but the whites become either Bourgogne or Coteaux Bourguignons. 2.8% of the vineyard surface in Meursault is planted to Pinot Noir. Complicated regulations indeed for a situation that is relatively straightforward: the wines the market endorses are overwhelmingly white and on the Puligny (southern) side of the village, not the reds produced on the northern side next to Volnay.

The comments of Dr. Morelot:

> Meursault owes its longstanding reputation to its white wines. A particular taste, resembling hazelnut, is sufficient to distinguish it. One can add a purity of aroma and an exquisite finesse. The climats of Meursault that must be set in the first line are Perrières (6 ha), Goutte d'Or (3 ha), Charmes, Genevrières, etc[36].
>
> This village, as well as that of Puligny, is very renowned for their excellent *vins ordinaires*, commonly called passe-tout-grains. These wines come from vines that are half Pinot Noir and half Gamay, and also from a specific soil. As the vines that produce them are almost on the plain, I refer to them here only as an object of note, but they are not germane to our examination.
>
> The truth of the principal that I have advanced, that the decomposition of a rock of the same nature must give identical products, seems to me evidently proved by the examination of the rock that constitutes the slope of Puligny and Meursault. It is of the same mass, of the same crystalline nature, of an aggregate of the same type of shells, taken in Meursault or in Montrachet; that is to say at the two extremities; it is the same calcium carbonate, and differs only by several exterior properties, but of the same internal composition.
>
> The wine of Montrachet, however, is superior in quality to that produced by the rest of the slope; but this is because of the exposition that inclines to the southeast; otherwise the soil of this district is cohesive but light and very permeable to the action of the air. It is composed of an admirable mixture of clay, calcium carbonate, ferric oxide, and organic matter. One must therefore attribute the superiority of the products of this climat to this happy concourse of a good exposition and an appropriate terroir. I will remark only that the other good white wines of this part of our slope approach more or less in quality the perfect one that is harvested in Montrachet.

---

36 Meursault occupies the place where there was once a forest named Muris saltus. At the summit of the hill that dominates the village, there was a castle or other construction that bore the name Montmeillan, Mons eminens. Today one can hardly find a vestige of it.

Dr. Lavalle:

COMMUNE DE MEURSAULT

The vineyard of Meursault is one of the largest and most interesting of the Côte d'Or. Until now, we have hardly noted, in all of the villages that have passed in review, several rare climats consecrated to Pinot Blanc. In many of them we have found no trace of it. In Meursault, to the contrary, more than 320 ha are consecrated to the growth of fine vines, and among these, more than half are devoted to the careful cultivation of Pinot Blanc. We must also divide the good vineyard into two parts, one is planted in Pinot Noir, the other in Chardonnay or Pinot Blanc. In the vines destined to the production of red wine, growers are careful to destroy the white vines. In those that must give white wine, the Pinot Gris is destroyed, above all in the good climats. It is also possible to say that in the renowned climats there is no more than one vine in fifty that is not Pinot Blanc or Noir.

The climat of Perrières, the first for white wine, produces hardly more than 14 or 15 hl/ha in an average year; the climats inferiors, from 20 to 30 hl/ha; Santenots-du-Milieu yields hardly more than 15 – 16 hl/ha, and the other good red vineyards from 17 – 20 hl/ha. Vine growing methods are the same as in the preceding villages.

The climats should be classified in the following order:

Tête de Cuvée

Santenots-du-Milieu, 8 ha 23 a 70 ca, a climat planted in totality to red grapes, of which the best cuvée is that of Madame de l'Ostende. A large portion belongs to M. Boch; the rest to MM. Bachet, Dumesnil, Jehannin, Delonguy, and to the Hospice de Beaune.

Danguy et Aubertin: M. C. Duverey-Taboureau, the Hospices de Beaune, the widow Jeannin, M. Maire et fils, the widow Noirot.

Rodier has Santenots du Millieu at 7 ha 99 a 60 ca, and the owners as MM. Louis Boillot-Bachelet, Lafon-Boch, the Hospices de Beaune, etc. He denotes it in capital letters.

Première Cuvée

Les Cras, 4 ha 91 a 75 ca, belonging to MM. Batault-Bretin, Serre, Bachet, and Batault-Collin. About one-fifth is planted to white grapes.

Les Santenots-Blancs, 2 ha 94 a 5 ca. This climat, formerly almost completely planted to white grapes, is now almost completely planted to Pinot Noir; the ownership is very fragmented. The principal proprietors ar MM. Jobard the younger and Bernard, Bouchard, de Monthélie, Madame de l'Ostende, Madame Blondeau, etc.

Clos-des-Mouches, 50 a 55 ca, belonging to MM. Baudot, Boch, etc.

Les Pelures, 10 ha 7 a 35 ca, belonging to MM. Bouchard, Bachet, Delonguy, Dumesnil, etc. This last proprietor has in the climat a part planted in white grapes, known under the name of Desirée, which gives white wines of the première cuvée.

Deuxième Cuvée

At the beginning we will place:

Santenots-du-Dessous, 7 ha 51 a 45 ca, belonging to MM. Bachet, Virely, Batault-Bretin, the Hospice de Beaune, etc.

Les Criots, 4 ha 54 a 80 ca, belonging to MM. Batault-Bretin, Virely, Bachet, to the Hospice de Beaune, etc.

Les Marcausses, 1 ha 96 a 40 ca, belonging to M. Batault-Bretin.

Les Peutes-Vignes, 1 ha 65 a 35 ca, belonging to MM. Boch, Monthélie-Monthélier, etc.

After this comes:

Les Terres-Blanches, 2 ha 36 a 70 ca, belonging to MM. Batault-Bretin, Gaudrelet, and Mme. Chevignard.

Les Vignes-Blanches, 2 ha 45 a 60 ca.

Les Corbins, 8 ha 77 a 50 ca, belonging to MM. Brugnot-Rolland, Brugnot-Laplanche, Dariot, Bourgogne, Garnier, Baudot, the Hospice de Beaune, etc.

En Luraule, 3 ha 32 a 30 ca, belonging to MM. Boch, Moutte, Brugnot-Batault.

Le Cromain, 9 ha 29 a 15 ca, a climat planted almost half to red wine and half to white, belonging to MM. Jobard the younger, and Bernard, etc.

Le Clos-de-Mazeret, 3 ha 16 a planted in white and red, belonging to the son of M. Jouan.

Les Meix-Chavaux, 10 ha 28 a 55 ca, belonging to MM. Dumarest, Jouan, etc.

WHITE WINES
Tête de Cuvée

Les Perrières-Dessus and **Dessous**, 17 ha 6 a, belonging to MM. Delaroche, Batault-Bretin, Macaut-Delacasne, de Berle, Madame Blondeau, etc.,

> Danguy et Aubertin: MM. Brugnot-Brazey, the Bernard heirs, MM. Jobard jeune et Bernard [sic], the widow Garnier [Perrières Dessus]; MM. C. Duvault-Blochet, Albert Grivault, Henry-Guillemard, Henry Aîné, Mme. Serre [Perrières Dessous].

> Rodier notes Les Perrièrres, Perrièrres-Dessus and Dessous in capital letters, and gives the proprietors as MM. Boillot-Buthiau, Boissard-Nicolle, Bouchard-Bouzereau, Chouet-Titard, Félix Four, the widow Mme. Albert Grivault, MM. Guillon, Lafon-Boch, the widow Lochardet, MM. Matrot-Amoignon, Gabriel Poupon, etc.

Premiere Cuvée

Les Genevrières-Dessus, 16 ha 87 a 55 ca, belonging to MM. De Berle, Bachet, de Vergnette-Lamothe, Boche, Moutte, Madame Marotte, etc.

Les Charmes-Dessus, 14 ha 89 a 25 ca, belonging to MM. Serre, Jehannin, Labaume, Jouan, Martin, de Vergnette-Lamothe, Bossu, Madame Blondeau, the Hosipce de Beaune, etc.

Les Bouchères, 4 ha 23 a 80 ca, belonging to Madame de l'Ostende, M. Dousset, etc.

Les Tessons, 5 ha 41 a 60 ca, belonging to Madame de l'Ostende, M. Dousset, etc.

La Goutte-d'Or, 5 ha 29 a 30 ca, belonging to Madame Blondeau-Cornet, MM. Titard, Boch, Bachet, Batault-Jobard, etc.

Deuxième Cuvée

Le Porusot-Dessus, 6 ha 70 a 67 ca, belonging to Madame de l'Ostende, MM. de Vergnette-Lamothe, Batault-Tavernier, etc.

Le Rougeot, 3 ha 17 a 40 ca, belonging to MM. Batault-Bretin, Macaut-Delacosne, etc. Several parts planted to red wine in this climat and the following.

Le Porusot, 3 ha 33 a 48 ca, belonging to Madame Fontaine, M. Boch, the Hospice de Beaune.

Les Grands-Charrons, 15 ha 5 a 40 ca, a very fragmented climat, of which important parcels belong to MM. Goulier, Garnier, Parent-Ropiteaux, to the Hospice de Beaune, etc.

The upper portion of this climat is of clearly higher quality than the rest, and gives wines worthy to be classed at the head of the deuxième cuvées.

The following climats, some planted to white, some to red, are most often mixed with common vines and give reds called passe-tout-grains, and second cuvées in white. These are:

Les Luchets	Les Lamerosses	Les Desbroles
Les Vireuils	Les Saussots	Les Durots
Les Porusots-Dessous	Les Longbois	Les Lurets
Les Crotots	En l'Ormeau	Les Magny
Les Pelles	En la Monatine	Les Vaux
Les Griaches	Es Cloux-Perrons	Les Belles-Côtes
Es Pellans	Es Grands-Perrons	Au Murger de Monthélie
Es Millerans	En la Barre	Sous-la-Velle
Les Forges	Les Preriots	Les Malpoiriers

The other climats are planted only to Gamay.

The first wines of Meursault, either in white or in red, can be compared only with our grand première cuvées from the best vineyards. The Santenots are firm, strong wines, with good color, rich alcohol, and have a bouquet that develops when they are eight to ten years of age. They keep well and offer a remarkably pure quality. Merchants can rarely buy them for less than 400 or 500 francs per barrel, and in the good years, these prices are greatly exceeded. In 1846, there were sold to the merchants at 750 francs straight off the press; in 1854, one had to pay 1200 francs at the same moment.

The white wines of *Perrières* sell for approximately the same price. These are wines of a perfect limpidity, of an exquisite perfume and finesse, and will hold without trouble for thirty or forty years. After Montrachet, I know of no other white wine more exquisite. The wines of Charmes and of Genevrières possess, although to a slightly lower degree, all of these qualities, and generally sell for a quarter less. This is more or less the price of the other premières cuvées in good years. The passe-tout-grain of Meursault is well esteemed and makes excellent ordinary wines.

The vineyards of Meursault are very old. Coutépée teaches us that in 1168, Sybille, the daughter of Hugues de Bourgogne, called Le Roux, gave to Cîteaux her clos of vines in *Murissalt*. The same abbey received in 1205 from Hugues, lord of Couches, the right to take from his forests all the material of which he might have need *ad opus vinearum domus* of Murissault.[82]

In 1218, the abbey of Tart left to that of Cîteaux all of its holdings in Meursault, mentioning two ouvrées of Santenots, among others.

In 1366, Jean de Mipont declared to hold as a fief of the Duke vines in *Charmes* and *Clos-Perron*.

The manor of the Lord of Meursault, belonging to the Mâlain family, included, according to the accounting given to the Dijon Chambre des Comptes, the following parcels of vines: twenty ouvrées *Derrière-le-Four*; twelve in *Treillon*; nine in *Pertuis-du-Prelet*; thirty in the *Cloux*; ten in *Charron*; sixteen in *Pechure*; fourteen in *Creben*; eight in *Visargent*; six in *Criots*.

In 1366, the manor of the Lord of Meursault, belonging to J. d'Esbarres, included a clos with a winery, with a staff of 26 and a vineyard in *Vivex*.

In 1652 the portion of the manor acquired by M. de Thésut from the Mâlain family contained sixty two ouvrées in the *Cloux*; fifteen in *Sous l'Eglise*; ten in *Charron*; four in *Creben*; fifteen in *Criot*; eight in *Petite-Vigne*; one in *Petit-Clos*; four in *Grandes-Terres*; six in *Dureau*; five in *Laussot*; five in *Cras*; twelve in *La Barre*; four in *Greissolle*; one in *Malpoirier*; six in *La Millerand*; two in *Palle*; twenty in the *Clos-de-Monthélie*. Half of this estate was willed to the Hospices de Beaune by M. de Massot in 1669.

In 1662, François de Raigecourt, from had acquired the portion belonging to M. de Montjay, declared his holdings to include twenty-four ouvrées in *Charron*; sixteen in *Moulin-Foullet*; twenty-four in *Charmes*; and ten in *Buisson-Surtaut*.

In 1666, M. Blancheton, lawyer, acquired the property of M. de Raigecourt, decared thirty-one ouvrées in *Arbues*; eighteen in *La Monatine* or *La Vigne-Blanche*; two in *Buisson-Certeau*; and thirty-nine in *Charmes*.

A small house in Volnay and twenty-five ouvrées in Santenots or Pelures, and twenty other ouvrées in *Santenots* or *Cras* coming from the Abbey of Saint-Jean-le-Grand of Autun, were sold on the 17th of March 1761 for 28,400 francs to M. Lausseure.

As one might expect, Meursault has no shortage of high-profile domaines, led by J. F. Coche-Dury as described in the chapter on Corton. Meursault makes up the majority of the production at Coche-Dury, and the Meursault wines are almost as sought-after as the Corton Charlemagne, with holdings in Perrières and Genevrières as well as Caillerets, Chevalières, and Rougeots. Domaine Guy Roulot (now run by his son Jean-Marc) is another of the giants of Meursault, although the style is different than that of Coche-Dury: concentrated, focused, and not heavy, these wines are intense but ethereal. The superb Perrières, Bouchères and Charmes are made in small amounts, but the house interpretations of various village wines such as Tillets, Luchets, Meix Chavaux and Vireuils are also worth seeking out. Domaine des Comtes Lafon is yet another international star. At Lafon there is no shortage of luxury, and the wines are powerful and full-bodied. The Charmes, from a 1.7 ha holding, is superb, and all of the top premiers crus are here: Genevrières, Perrières, Goutte d'Or. The house makes a speciality of the Clos de la Barre from their 2.1 ha holding, and there is more red wine here than at many Meursault producers, including a very large parcel in Volnay Santenots du Milieu along with a bit of Volnay Clos des Chênes, Champans, and Monthélie Les Duresses. It is also worthwhile to mention the up and coming domaine Jean-Philippe Fichet, notable for their Meursault Le Tesson and Les Chevalières. The domaine makes wines of an elegant, perfumed finesse that are delicious with food yet have the substance to age as well. Finally, Domaine Robert Ampeau (run today by his son Michel) is another interesting address in Meursault. Done is a traditional style, the Ampeau wines are not released until Michel feels they are ready, and once they are they project the essence of traditional Burgundy in their respective terroirs.

PULIGNY

The glory of Puligny is the Montrachet vineyard. This may distract the wine lover from the other marvelous wines from this commune, but Montrachet is a compelling presence – this is true now and it always has been. Little has changed with regard to Montrachet through the years. The vineyard is more or less equally divided between the villages of Puligny and Chassagne, and today we distinguish the lieu-dit of *Montrachet* in Puligny and we add the definite article for *Le Montrachet* in Chassagne. The two are nearly the same size (approximately 2 ares more on the Puligny side), and the size has not changed considerably over time.

One difference between earlier and modern systems is in the relative positions of the neighboring crus. Today Montrachet, Chevalier-Montrachet, Bâtard-Montrachet, and Bienvenues-Bâtard-Montrachet (and Criots-Bâtard-Montrachet in Chassagne) all nominally share the same status of grand cru, although historically this was not the case. Even in the 20th century a distinction was drawn between Montrachet and the surrounding vineyards: the AOC legislation cites a 1921 court case that cites the "supremacy" of the wines from the lieu-dit of Montrachet. Nevertheless the rules regarding the grands crus of Puligny and Chassagne took their present form in the late 1930s: Montrachet, Chevalier-Montrachet, and Bâtard-Montrachet were codified in 1937, and Bienvenues-Bâtard-Montrachet and Criots-Bâtard-Montrachet in 1939.

We are told in the text of the AOC regulation that the wines of Montrachet gained their renown in the 18th century. Courtépée's assertion that the wines were not known at the beginning of the 18th century is quoted, and the authors of today's regulations go on to state that it was while under the influence of the Clermont-Montoison family, lords of Chagny, that the wines came to broader notice. On close reading, Lavalle prefers the portions in Puligny ("exposed to the southeast") to the portions in Chassagne ("exposed due south"). Arnoux mentioned Montrachet in 1728, comparing it to Côte Rôtie and Muscat de Frontignan, in a historically intriguing aside.

By the time of Jullien, Chevalier and Bâtard were well defined, and he states definitively that these two were distinctly inferior to Montrachet, with Chevalier second to Montrachet and Bâtard in third place. This is the same hierarchy followed by Lavalle, although his view is much more complete and nuanced. After Montrachet, he notes Chevalier above all other wines, and then "coming next, equal in quality" the following in this order: Blagny-Blanc, Bâtard-Montrachet, Les Combettes, Les Platières, Les Refères (today spelled Referts), and Les Charmes. Many of these appellations did not make it to Grand Cru status, and there was no mention of Bienvenues (or of Criots, when we get to Chassagne).

Curiously, Lavalle does not delineate the size of each climat in Puligny as he does elsewhere. He gives Montrachet at its present size, but notes Chevalier (a première cuvée) has 27 ha 71 a 80 ca, while Rodier has it as 6 ha 24 a 30 ca, and our modern regulations have 7 ha 58 a 89 ca. Why this inconsistency?

One possibility is that Lavalle has included as part of Chevalier the portions that border it to the south as it swings around into the combe. This vineyard is today the lieux-dits En Remilly and Les Murgers des Dents de Chien, found just as the slope turns to create the valley that leads to the backcountry towards the town of Gamay. This valley, known as Les Combes au Sud, provides south-southwest expositions, most of which is today classified as AOC Saint-Aubin. Neither Lavalle nor any prior authors mention Saint-Aubin. The AOC regulations note, "In the 19th century and up to the 1930s, the fine wines of Saint-Aubin were generally sold under the flagship names of Volnay, Pommard, or even Beaune. These names, from 1936, are reserved for wines benefitting from appellations d'origine contrôlées. The appellation d'origine contrôlée Saint-Aubin, of which the reputation of the wines was established, was thus recognized in 1937."

According to the archives of the village, the village of Saint-Aubin was known as Auroux-la-Montagne under the Ancien Régime, and the name Saint-Aubin came into use only after the Revolution. Since the vineyards on the other side are for the most part accounted for, it would seem that either this is the answer, or the figure cited by Lavalle is a typographical error. This last possibility, however, begs the question of what had become of these vineyards, which predate his writing in the opinion of the authors of the AOC regulations. Our AOC of Chevalier-Montrachet today is made up of only 6 ha 30 a 91 ca of Chevalier-Montrachet, 1 ha 2 a 75 ca of Les Demoiselles, and 25 a 23 ca of Le Cailleret. Danguy et Aubertin, who do not cite the size of the climats, have included many of today's Saint-Aubin vineyards in the village of Gamay that also are not discussed in Lavalle. These include Le Charmois, Dents de Chien, Créot, and Derrière la Tour, all cited as being premières cuvées in the opinion of "C. Loc."

Interestingly, the text of the AOC Montrachet informs us that the limits of the appellation were established by a 1921 case heard by the tribunal of Beaune, brought by growers with an interest in preserving the purity of the Montrachet name. It was expressly forbidden for « anyone to use the appellation Montrachet for wines originating either from Bâtard-Montrachet, Chevalier Montrachet, [Puligny-Montrachet] Les Pucelles or other places not included in the region under the name of Grand-Montrachet, Vrai-Montrachet or Montrachet.[37] » According to Jasper Morris, however, this same decree authorized the inclusion of three small parcels from the lieu-dit Dent de Chien.

---

37 http://www.bourgogne-vins.com/le-bourgogne/le-comprendre/article/les-surprises-des-anciens-classements

Among the rest of the climats in Puligny, Lavalle groups Blagny-Blanc, Bâtard-Montrachet, and Les Combettes, vineyards that are located at diverse points within the village but united by a common level of quality. Lavalle lists them as a combined 21 ha 61 a 82 ca, fairly consistent with today's boundaries of 22 ha 90 a 45 ca. He also mentions "Les Refères [sic] and Les Charmes," cited as being 18 ha 41 a 60 ca. This evidently includes today's Les Referts that borders Meursault on downslope from Combettes, along with Les Charmes, the vineyard downslope in turn from Referts. His reference, however, must also include Perrières and Clos de la Mouchère, both part of the lieu-dit Perrières. Although he does not mention it in his tally of crus, Lavalle and Morelot both mention it in their text. The combined total of these vineyards in today's terms is 17 ha 67 ha 45 ca.

Red wine was much more common in Puligny than it is today. Courtépée's comments almost certainly refer to red wine:

> [In Puligny there is] Le Clavoillon, a good climat; J. Edouard & Marguerite Ranfer gave in 1744 three small houses and a cask of wine each year. 145 souls (80 in 1666), 511 communicants. Blagny is a dependency of Puligny with the Chapel of Saint-Denis at the Abbey of Mezières. Good wine. Exquisite game, especially the red partridge.

While he does not have any red têtes de cuvées in Puligny, Lavalle notes Les Caillerets, Le Clavoillon, and Les Pucelles as red premières cuvées. Today red wine production is forbidden in the grands crus and also in the lieux-dits of Le Trézin, Sous le Puits, La Garenne, and Hameau de Blagny (all of which surround the hamlet of Blagny), but red wine is authorized in all of the other vineyards of Puligny. Few, however, take advantage of this: Only 0.61% of the land in Puligny-Montrachet is planted to Pinot Noir.

Moving closer to our time, Blagny begins to lose its importance by commentators: Rodier cites Montrachet, Combettes, Chevalier, and Bâtard in capital letters, in that order; Blagny Blanc follows in lower case. He gives the relevant sizes of these vineyards as follows: Combettes, 6 ha 71 a 95 ca; Chevalier 6 ha 24 a 30 cal; Blagny Blanc / Hameau de Blagny (as he lists it here) 4 ha 34 a 70 ca; and Bâtard, 9 ha 73 a.

The opinion of Dr. Morelot:

> On this portion of the slope for the extent of about a league, the village of Puligny is built at the foot of the mountain, peopled with twelve hundred souls, the hamlet of Blagny and the beautiful village, or more properly the small town of Meursault, with almost two thousand inhabitants.

> The soil of this slope is best adapted to white wines; it is here between Chassagne and Puligny that the greatly renowned climat of Montrachet is found, whose delicious, perfumed wine can even rival Tokay. Above the Vrai Montrachet[83] is found a parcel called Chevalier-Montrachet, and below it is another called Le Bâtard; but

neither one nor the other provides wines that can compare to the real Montrachet, even though they are separated by only a narrow path. Puligny has other distinguished climats as well, among others La Perrière.

Blagny is surrounded by several hundred ouvrées of vines that produce only lively, light white wines agreeable to the taste, which are equal to Meursault wines of the first quality[38].

At the foot of Blagny one finds the Clos Vaillon [Clavoillon], whose red wine is highly esteemed, and which approaches in quality the best wines of our slope.

The comments of Dr. Lavalle:

COMMUNE DE PULIGNY

The largest portion of the vineyards of this village is consecrated to the culture of Gamay. Nevertheless, in the middle and upper portions of the magnificent slope where the village of Blagny is situated, one harvests white wines of an exceptional quality and red wines that are the equal of the best of the Côte de Beaune. The method of grape growing is the same as in Meursault and Chassagne; the vines are still Pinot Noir and Pinot Blanc for the climats that give fine wine. The number of hectares planted in Pinot is still more than 180 ha.

The principal climats are:

White Wines

Tête de Cuvée, EXTRA

Le Montrachet, 3 ha 95 a 30 ca, belonging to MM. le Marquis de La Guiche, Morelot, Serre, Godard-Poussignol, de Courtivron, Batault.

Danguy et Aubertin: MM. Antonin Bouchard and Julien Bouchard of the house of Bouchard Père et Fils, Ch. Drapier, de la Guiche, the widow Serre.

Rodier: Boillereau, Bouchard Père et Fils, Marquis de la Guiche, Lafon-Boch.

Première Cuvée

At the head, **Chevalier Montrachet**, 27 ha 71 a 80 ca, belonging to M. Moreau-Guillemot.

Danguy et Aubertin: MM. Antonin Bouchard and Julien Bouchard of the house of Bouchard Père et Fils, André-Brusson, Belin André, A. Billerey, Mme. Clerc-Dubois

Rodier: MM. Audiffred, Bernard, Chartron, Jouard, Leflaive, Lochardet, Martini, Poupon, etc.

---

38 The plateau of the mountain of Blagny is covered with aromatic plants, among which one finds sage (Salvia officinalis L.) that grows in abundance. This plant is often used by the inhabitants of the neighboring villages against anorexia, amenorrhea and intermittent autumn fevers.

Coming next, equal in quality:

Blagny-Blanc, **Bâtard-Montrachet**, **Les Combettes**, 21 ha 61 a 82 ca, belonging to MM. Latour, Edouard, Batault-Bretin, Villiard, Tisserand, Saugeot, Josseran, the Segault heirs, and Madame Lardillon.

> Danguy et Aubertin: MM. Josserand-Tisserand, Pamariou, the widows Tripier and Villard (Blagny Blanc); MM. André-Brugnot, A. Billerey, Brugnot-André, Brugnot-Meney, Fleurot-Labelle, Pierre-Foveau, Garnier-Meney, Lartus-Brugnot, Labouré, Moreau-Voillot, Samuel, de la Serre (Bâtard-Montrachet);

Les Platières, belonging to M. Edouard.

Les Refères and **Les Charmes**, 18 ha 41 a 60 ca, belonging to a very large number of proprietors, among whom we note: MM. Edouard, Letort, Matouillet, and the Orisy heirs.

Deuxième Cuvée

Le Champ Canet, 13 ha 57 a 45 ca, belonging to M. Serre and others.

Es Follatières, 18 ha 98 a 20 ca, belonging to diverse persons.

Many climats that could still give excellent wines and, in another epoch, had a good reputation, are today consecrated to the culture of common vines and produce only inferior wines.

Red Wines

Première Cuvée

Les Caillerets, 5 ha 41 a 50 ca, belonging to MM. Bachet and Latour

Le Clavoillon or **Clovaillon**, 5 ha 56 a 10 ca, belonging to MM. Albrier, Edouard, Drapier, de Saiseray, etc.

Les Pucelles, 6 ha 80 a 95 ca, belonging to M. Malluas and others.

No deuxième or troisième cuvées

The *Grands-Champs, Clos-du-Meix, Nosroy*, etc., produce good ordinary wine.

The climat of Montrachet, Mont-Rachet or Morachet, whose wines merit so incontestably the first rank among the white wines of the Côte d'Or, and probably among all of the white wines of the world, is situated partly in Puligny and partly in Chassagne. The middle part, known under the name of Vrai-Montrachet or simply as Montrachet, is that which gives the most exquisite wines; one also carefully distinguishes the portions upslope, designated under the name of Chevalier-Montrachet, and above all the parts downslope, which have been known for many years under the name of Bâtard-Montrachet. In the Vrai-Montrachet itself one distinguishes the part exposed almost directly to the south-east, situated in the village of Puligny, and that whose exposition is solidly to the south, which belongs to the village of Chassagne. It is in the part with the south-east exposition that Montrachet wine is produced in all of its exquisite finesse and all of its divine perfection.

In only a few hectares does one find the conditions of soil, subsoil, exposition, etc., that gives them the marvelous properties that nature refuses so often. Also, the wine of Montrachet must be considered as one of these rare marvels of which it is permitted for only a small number of the elect to appreciate the perfection. The price that one might pay is the least important thing and the easiest one to satisfy. He who may have bought a few bottles of the best years can consider himself satisfied, whatever price he has paid; he will never have paid too much. Merchants do not hesitate, in the years when the quality is perfect, to pay 2,000 francs per barrel and sometimes even more.

This climat was planted in vines many years ago. We find it already noted in 1482, and already very fragmented: since François de Perrières, Lord of Chassagne, declared at this time that he possessed five ouvrées of vines in Mont-Rachat.

In the 16th – 18th centuries, Le Montrachet belonged to diverse private individuals and for the largest portion to the family Clermont-Montoizon.

The 100 ouvrées that composed the domaine of this family, declared property of the nation during the Revolution, were sold, on 2 Germinal, year II, in two lots to M. Pourtalès, the first for 35,000 francs, the second for 37,100 francs, not including the tax. (See the commune of Chassagne that which is relative to Montrachet.)

The white wines coming from the climats that I count here among the premières cuvées can be considered worthy of being counted among the best white wines of the Côte d'Or. The red wines of the climats called Caillerets, Clavoillon and Pucelles are considered by many persons to be the equivalent of the premières cuvées of Beaune and certainly merit this reputation.

Among the documents that we have been able to gather regarding the history of the vineyard of Puligny, we find designated in 1366 the *Plante-Blanche*; in 1372, the *Vigne-Blanche*, the *Vigne-de-la-Graine*, eighteen ouvrées; in 1571, the *Clavoillon*, thirty ouvrées; the *Clos-du-Meix*, eighteen ouvrées; the *Garenne*, the *Combette*, eighteen ouvrées; *La Perrière*, seven ouvrées; the *Vigne Blanche* or les *Reuchots*, ten ouvrées, belonging to A. de Salins, husband of Catherine de Mipont; in 1628, the same climats, and in addition the *Grand Reuchot* and the *Lurot*.

The leading name in Puligny is Domaine Leflaive, whose production from the entry level through the top wines is superb. Another undisputed star is Domaine Etienne Sauzet, now run by M. Sauzet's son-in-law, Gérard Boudot. Sauzet produces wines that balance great elegance and power, developing well for years to come. The other important name to know is Carillon. Domaine Louis Carillon is a venerable estate, dating to 1632. Recently the sons of Louis Carillon have each decided to develop their own domaines. Jacques Carillon retains the name of Domaine Louis Carillon, while François Carillon has formed an eponymous domaine. Both, however, continue to work at the highest level and deserve the notice of the discerning client.

While these are some of the most important growers based in the commune, it behooves us to examine the ownership and character of the principal plots within the Puligny side of the Montrachet vineyard. The largest proprietor by far is the Marquis de Laguiche, vinified, bottled and marketed by Drouhin. This is for me the best value Montrachet on the market. Issuing from a plot that includes nearly half of the Puligny side, it is a beautiful expression of essence of white Burgundy. Another good value from the Puligny side that from the 0.89 ha owned by negociant Bouchard, who also produces an extremely well made wine that still manages to offer wonderful value for money. Domaine Ramonet has a minute plot of 0.25 ha that produces one of the most sought-after, expensive, and deliriously exciting wines produced here. The other significant owner on the Puligny side is Boillerault de Chauvigny (two plots totaling 0.8 ha), who according to Jasper Morris sell their fruit to negociant firm Louis Latour. Finally, as Saint-Aubin is not treated separately, it behooves us to note here the estate of Hubert Lamy, now run by his son Olivier, continues to produce delicious wine from a host of vineyards in Saint-Aubin and in Chassagne.

CHASSAGNE

Chassagne has long been renowned for the quality of its wine: Claude Arnoux lists it among the red wine-producing villages, remarking, "Chassagne is a vineyard that is not as considerable in extent as it is in reputation." Courtépée goes into detail about the village as well:

> [Chassagne has a] Good vineyard, of which the best climats are: the *Clos-Saint-Jean*, belonging to the Abbesse of Saint-Jean-le-Grand; *Maltroie*, belonging to M. de Beuvrand, a lawyer at Parliament; *Morgeot*, whose taxes report to Chassagne. The most famous is *Mont-Rachet, Mons Rachioensis*, of a fallow hillside, of 180 ouvrées, of which around 100 belong to the Lord of Chassagne, 36 to M. de Sassenay of St.-Aubin, 27 to M. Bonnard of Arnay-le-Duc, 24 to M. Boliveau. It was not highly regarded at the beginning of the 17th century, because the author M. Bonnard acquired in 1627, 24 ouvrées for 750 livres. The plot can yield thirty barrels at the most. It is the most excellent white wine of Europe. One distinguishes between *Vrai-Morachet*, Chevalier-Montrachet and Bâtard-Montrachet. Their prices are different. The *Vrai* is sold for 1,000 – 1,200 livres per barrel.

Today Chassagne is best known for its white wines, yet the village was originally noted for its reds. Jullien also discusses only the red wine production of Chassagne, and Morelot's chief praise is for the reds of Morgeot. After mentioning Montrachet as the single tête de cuvée in white, Lavalle has three for red wine: Le Clos-St.-Jean, Clos-Pitois (part of Brussonnes), and La Boudriotte.

While red wine production has waned in contemporary times, it is more widespread than many assume: Reds are allowed in every appellation except the grands crus of Montrachet (3 ha 98 a 73 ca), Bâtard-Montrachet (5 ha 84 a 42) and Criots-Bâtard-Montrachet (1 ha 57 a 21 ca), and 37.91% of the vineyard land is planted to Pinot Noir.

Of the climats renowned for their red wine, Clos Saint-Jean is located behind the village of Chassagne. The rest, including Clos Pitois and La Boudriotte, are located at the southern end of the village, near the hamlet of Morgeot. The original climat of this name, 31 a 15 ca, is now a general name associated with over 60 ha of vines, including Boudriotte, which itself is an "umbrella" climat with six lieux-dits totaling 15 ha 62 a 30 ca. It also includes Les Brussonnes (15 ha 75 a 89 ca), which counts Clos Pitois as a dependency.

The comments of Dr. Morelot:

> The most distinguished climats of [Chassagne] are Morgeots which surrounds the houses of the hamlet of this name, the Clos Saint-Jean, the Clos Pitois, La Maltroye, Boucherettes, Vignes-Derniers, Champs-Gains, etc. The wines that come from them are very good; perhaps less light and less agreeable than those

of Volnay; they have more body and color. One might make a slight reproach of the people of this village: they work too hard as grape growers and their vines produce too much, and, often, excessive quantity diminishes the quality.

From the valley of Gamay to that of Auxey, one encounters a mass of rocks that form the three peaks with the greatest elevation in our slope. The stone of these rocks is the most homogeneous that one will find in our region; the most compact, the hardest; it does not crumble due to frost, and is one of the best that one can employ for the construction of buildings. These rocks are shot through with crystalline limestone and quartz; one may even find entire slopes of beautiful crystalline limestone.

Dr. Lavalle:

COMMUNE DE CHASSAGNE

Chassagne is, in the Côte d'Or, the territory that produces Pinot Gris (also known as Pinot Burot or Beurot) in the greatest abundance. This fact apart, vine growing techniques are the same here as elsewhere, and all that we can say of Santenay will apply also to Chassagne. Montrachet apart, there are not more than a few ouvrées planted in Pinot Blanc, such as Ruchotte, for example, where M. de Beuvrand possesses several ares. Everywhere else, the Pinot Noir is grown in the good climats and Gamay in ordinary soil.

The number of hectares cultivated in Pinot is 175 ha. Yields can be estimated, on average, from 18 – 20 hl/ha in the best crus, and from 20 – 24 hl/ha in the good wines of the second order. The climats in which the Beurot exists in the largest quantity are Grands-Clos and Petits-Clos, where there is one vine in fifty. Elsewhere there is one vine in one hundred; everywhere the vine is being pulled up. It is regrettable that this grape is not used to make *vin de paille*.

The climats of Chassagne are:

WHITE WINE

Hors Ligne

Le Montrachet, 3 ha 53 a 89 ca (see Puligny)

> Danguy et Aubertin: MM. Carillon, Ch. Drapier, Duvergey-Taboureau, Mme. Serre, M. le baron Thénard.
>
> Rodier: MM. Duverger, Fleurot-Laroze, Girard-Gueneau, Lafon-Boch, Petitjean-Nicot, Roizot, Mme. Serre, Baron Thénard.
>
> Rodier lists in capital letters Montrachet, Bâtard-Montrachet, the Clos Saint-Jean, and La Boudriotte.

RED WINES

Hors Ligne

Le Clos-St.-Jean, 12 ha 10 a 78 ca, belonging to MM. Perret, de Beuvrand, de Courtivron, Leclerc, Lespagnol, Brunot, Petitjean de Marcilly.

> Danguy et Aubertin note that the Clos Saint-Jean is tête de cuvée in C. Loc, and specifies the owners as MM. the Brugnot heirs, Ch. Drapier, Mme. Naigeon, MM. Perret, P. de Marcilly frères, Pigneret-Pacquelin, R. de Poligny.
>
> Rodier: MM. Bazerolles, Bugnot, Gabriel Coffinet, Jacob, Mme. René Jacquet, MM. Matrot, Moine-Gérard, Marcel Paquelin, de Poligny, Polulot-Marlot, etc.

Clos-Pitois, part of the climat of *Brussanes*, belonging to MM. de Ganay, Audiffred, Maire, etc.

> Danguy et Aubertin: M. Lhomme.
>
> Rodier: M. Guyot.

La Boudriotte, belonging to M. and Mme. Audiffred.

> Danguy et Aubertin: M. Jules Audiffred, M. Massin.
>
> Rodier: Audiffred Père et Fils, Guyot, Guillon, etc.

Première Cuvée

La Maltroie, 9 ha 21 ares 60 ca, belonging to MM. de Beuvrand, Dubois, Madame Lespagnol, etc.

Les Brussanes, 15 ha 80 a 77 ca, including the *Clos-Pitois*, the *Grands-Clos*, *Petits-Clos*, *Vigne-Blanche*, belonging to MM. de Ganay, Audiffred, Maire, Delonguy, Bachelet, Gagnerot, Paquelin, Madame de la Guiche, Audiffred Faivre.

Les Caillerets, belonging to MM. Leclerc, Bachelet, Mme. Lespagnol, etc.

Les Changains, 28 ha 60 a 28 ca, belonging to MM. Dubois, Lespagnol, Perret, etc.

Deuxième Cuvée

Les Macherelles, 8 ha 2 a 42 ca, belonging to MM. de Courtivron, Paquelin-Guyot, Audiffred, etc.

Les Vergers, 9 ha 51 a 29 ca, belonging to Madame Lardillon, M. Dubois, etc.

Les Mazures, 28 ha 69 a 37 ca, belonging to MM. Dubois, Douharet-Desfontaines.

Les Chenevottes, 11 ha 36 a 97 ca, climat extremely fragmented.

La Goujonne, 26 ha 52 a 56 ca, belonging to Madame Faivre, M. Guyot, and others.

En Voillenot-Dessous, 20 ha 38 a 42 ca, climat extremely fragmented.

Coming next :

Les Chaumées, climat extremely fragmented.

Le Clos-Devant, belonging to MM. Perret and Dubois.

Les Concis-des-Champs, climat extremely fragmented.

La Grande Montagne, belonging to M. Bardot, etc.

Fontaine-Sot, climat mixed with common plants.

Les Houillères, climat both extremely fragmented and producing passe-tout-grain.

The climats called **Champ-de-Morgeot, Benoites, Platière, Carrières, Plante-Longe**, etc. give good passe-tout-grains.

The vines of other parts of the territory produce only common wines.

The good wines of Chassagne have body, color and resemble the wines of the Côte de Nuits. They have less finesse than those of Volnay, but keep better and travel more easily.

In the good years, the wines of the Clos-Pitois and of the Clos-Saint-Jean sell for 700 – 800 francs per barrel. The other wines of Chassagne, even in the premières cuvées only sometimes reach 500 or 600 francs.

In the land inventory of François de Perrières, Lord of Chassagne in 1482, he declares a clos of 40 ouvrées in front of the château. Eighty ouvrées *situated between the road that leads to Fontaine-Sot toward the north-east, bordering the vines of J. Brulez to the west, below the main road going from Gamay to Chagny, and above the public road going from Chaudenay to Chassagne;* five ouvrées in *Montrachat,* 40 ouvrées in *the Bergerie,* five ouvrées in *Chambres,* four ouvrées in *l'Orme.* [emphasis in Lavalle].

In 1366, Jean de Mipont, lord of Puligny, designated *Plante-Blanche* and *Marthe-roye* among the vineyards of his fiefdom.

In the archives relative to the manor of Chassagne, we find:

In 1477, the sale of a lease on 14 ouvrées of vines in the lieu-dit of *Sous-le-Montrachet* in the village of Chassagne.

In 1375, an exchange of vines in l'Echalier; a number of vineyard acquisitions: in 1382 a parcel in the *Meix-au-Frey*; in 1384 in *La Forge* and *Verger*; in 1391 in *Voisenot*, in 1390 in *Clos-Saint-Jean*; in 1394 in *La Maltroie* (five ouvrées for eight francs) and in *Chevenotte*; in 1402 in *Tibles*, in 1423 in *Es Ollières*, in 1438 in *Cray*; in 1452 in *Poirier-Breneau* and in *Puy-Merdereau*; in 1463 in *Concie-du-Champ*; in 1472 in *Douhe*; in 1474 in *Bauchot* or *Blanchot*; in 1484 in *l'Ouche*; in 1500 in *Coullontey*; in 1504 in *Murger*, in 1522 in *Clou-Rotam*; in 1527 an acquisition in Rebrichey, in 1528 in *Moye*, in 1566 in *Mont-Godard*; in 1593 an acquisition of six ouvrées in *Le Morgeot* for 20 écus soleil[84].

There are many wonderful growers based in Chassagne. At the head of the list one must place Domaine Ramonet, who produces powerful, concentrated wines and has ascended to superstar status. In my view the wines of Michel Niellon, produced today by his son-in-law Michel Coutoux, run a close second. For some reason they seem more popular among wine lovers in the U.S. than in other markets, but they have been consistently superb. After this, it is helpful to note the different producers belonging to several established winemaking families in Chassagne. The first is the Gagnard family. Edmond Delagrange-Bachelet was the patriarch of the clan, whose daughter married Jacques Gagnard, and his daughters in turn married Richard Fontaine and Jean-Marc Blain and formed Fontaine-Gagnard and Blain-Gagnard respectively, both known above all for their grands crus in Montrachet, Bâtard-Montrachet and Criots-Bâtard-Montrachet. Jacques' brother Jean-Noël formed his eponymous domaine, which is run today by his daughter Caroline Lestimé, a good address for elegant and perfumed whites, with an especially seductive and good value Bâtard.

Another important clan is the Morey family. Albert Morey's two sons Bernard and Jean-Marc both entered the wine business. Today Bernards sons Thomas and Vincent both have their own domaines, and Jean-Marc's daughter married Pierre-Yves Colin, who is one of the rising stars of Burgundy. Atlhough his vineyards are mostly in Saint-Aubin, they offer great value for delicious white burgundy. Pierre-Yves is the youngest son of Marc Colin, whose domaine is now run by his siblings. His uncle is Michel Colin-Deleger, whose sons Philippe and Bruno have split his property to set up their own affairs. The final producer who garners significant attention these days is Vincent Dancer whose wines are rich and structured.

The production of Montrachet on the Chassagne side is more fragmented than it is on the Puligny side. The largest by far is Baron Thénard, with 1 ha 83 a 31 ca. The next largest holding is that of Jacques Prieur at 57 a 82 ca in two plots, and then the Domaine de la Romanée Conti with three parcels totaling 32 a 14 ca and Domaine des Comtes Lafon with 31 a 82 ca. Other producers have a smaller share, including Marc Colin, with four parcels totaling 10 a 68 ca, Guy Amiot with 9 a 10 ca, Domaine Leflaive with 8 a 21 ca, Fontaine-Gagnard with 7 a 81 ca and Blain-Gagnard with 7 a 83 ca; and a Mlle. Petitjean with 5 a 42 ca. According to Jasper Morris, this is produced for her by René Lamy-Pillot, and finally the Chateau de Puligny Montrachet with 4 a 28 ca and René Fleurot with 4 a 5 ca. The best of these are spectacular, impressive wines, rather weightier than the best on the Puligny side, with a rich creamy/buttery note and often aromas of tropical fruit on the nose.

SANTENAY

Lavalle's journey ends in Santenay, as does ours. Although there are several communes producing fine wine in AC Maranges, the last of the original grands crus of the Côte d'Or are found in Santenay. Maranges is over the border, being located in the département of the Saône-et-Loire. Courtépée is the first to trace the development of the vineyards of Santenay:

> [In Santenay] Saint-Jean de Naurosse created the mill Le Bault and the farms of Morgeot where the excellent wine of this name is produced, which once belonged to the Abbey of Maizière, then to M. de la Boutière, now to MM. de Clermont & Maleteste de Villey...[Santenay has a] considerable vineyard, whose best climats are La Gravière, Le Clos Tavanes of 100 ouvrées belonging to M. Blochet and the Clos Pitois belonging to M. the Mayor of Beaune.

Lavalle, however, was the first author to cite the vineyards of Santenay as têtes de cuvées. Jullien mentions them, only to note that they are "*on a par with the second wines of Beaune, Pommard, and Volnay.*" Morelot, as noted below, also was less than enthusiastic. Lavalle, however, warmed to the region, ranking as hors ligne "Clos Tavannes, part of the climate of Brussanes", Brussanes, and Gravieres, "part of the climat of Noyer-Bart." Today, however, the lieu-dit of Noyer-Bart has disappeared from the AOC regulations, and Clos Tavannes is part of Gravières," deleting the reference to Brussanes and Noyer-Bart have disappeared from the AOC regulations, and Clos Tavannes is part of Gravières. The entire section is located on the slopes of the Bois Dessus la Montagne, essentially an extension of the Morgeot district at the southern end of Chassagne, as noted by Danguy et Aubertin.

The opinion of Dr. Morelot:

> We take our point of departure from the south to the north, leaving from one of the extremities of our chain in Santenay, the southernmost village in the département, and follow it north as far as the territory of Dijon, where our slope finishes in the valley of the Ouche.
>
> From Santenay[39] to the gorge that leads to Gamay, one finds a group of three little hills united together for the length of a league upon whose slopes are built the village of Santenay, peopled with more than fourteen hundred souls, the little hamlet of Morgeot and the village of Chassagne[40], containing approximately a thousand souls, are all situated at mid-slope, in a very agreeable position. A bit further on, following the valley, one finds the village of Saint-Aubin whose territory furnishes good wines, less fine than those of which I have just spoken, but who have many similar qualities.

---

[39] This village, located in a pleasant place, besides the advantages of its excellent terroir, possesses a mineral spring that I have analyzed with M. Paulet. A great number of ill people come each year and find that these waters will heal them. It will take only a fortuitous event to make the place a popular success.

[40] This village is very ancient, and one may still see from on the summit of the mountain one of the rocks of the Druids whose usage is disputed by anthropologists. The name of the people of this country was Tonton-Marcel.

The bedrock of these hills is a coarse limestone giving fairly good stone, and shows, above all at Santenay, a large proportion of graphite that unites them through a grey vein in the stone.

The districts of choice in Santenay are Les Gravières, Le Clos Tavannes, Noyer-Bart, etc. the wines that come from them do not have a delicate bouquet but they are firm, mellow, deeply colored, and hold well; they are not as highly regarded as those of Chassagne.

Dr Lavalle:

COMMUNE DE SANTENAY

I will finish in Santenay the slope of the good wines, although, to be truthful, our vineyards continue beyond this and end in Decize. But as the limit of the département leaves this last commune apart, I have not believed it necessary for this particular case to bend the rule that I have imposed on myself. I will say only that as much by its vineyards as by its geographic position, Decize merits to be counted in the Côte d'Or, of which it is the natural limit. Its wines are very similar to those of Santenay, and one finds in its territory a certain number of cuvées that merit being noted as première cuvée.[85]

The village of Santenay, divided in three parts, situated at mid-slope in the middle of its vines, is situated in one of the most advantageous and smile-inducing positions. At its feet flows the river of the Dheune, which the eye can follow along its undulations in the midst of the hills now bare, now wooded, which rise along its banks. From the side of the plain, the view is neither less rich nor less grandiose than at any other point in the Côte d'Or, and then has its only limits at the elevated summits of the Jura.

Completely discovered and perfectly exposed, the vines of Santenay are what is more where the grape growing is done most carefully. The production is considerable; it is not less in an average year than 18 hl/ha in the most illustrious crus, from 24 hl/ha in the deuxièmes cuvées, and more than 30 hl/ha in the vineyards that produce passe-tout-grains.

The number of vines is certainly more than 30,000 per hectare, and one must consider this excess of production that one can only partly ascribe to fertilizers of all sorts as the reason why the wines of Santenay and of Chassagne are far from having the quality that might be theirs.

Here one cultivates only Pinot Noir, and as much as possible, all white varieties are pulled up. One nevertheless sees in certain climats such as Passe-Temps and Biochots for example, much Pinot Gris, which is considered here a productive and delicate vine.

In Bieveau, one harvests excellent white wines in the parts planted to Pinot Blanc. Unfortunately, almost all of this climat is planted to poor grapes.

In Santenay, as in Chassagne, there are still a great number of vineyards planted to both Pinot and Gamay and that serve to make wines rightly called passe-tout-grains. In the other parts of the Côte d'Or we have seen that this type of practice has almost disappeared. The number of hectares planted to Pinot must be evaluated at 225 ha.

The climats planted in fine vines are:

Hors Ligne

Clos-Tavannes, part of the climat of Brussanes, belonging to M. Prudon and Madame Lacour.

> Danguy et Aubertin: MM. Bardollet-Bresset, Clair, Mme. Coqueugniot, MM. Delorme-Girardin, de Montrion, Nié-Monnot, Renaut.
>
> Rodier demotes the Clos Tavannes to deuxième cuvée, and notes the owners as MM. Demaizière-Lequin, Guillon, Roizot, etc.

Les Gravières, which is part of the climat called *Noyer-Bart*, 29 ha 37 a 70 ca, belonging to MM. Abord-Belin, Duvat-Blocher, de Drée, etc.

> Danguy et Aubertin: MM. Bachey-Deslandes, Blondeau-Lequin, Changarnier, Demaizière-Lequin, Guyot-Massin et Chambon, Hospices d'Autun, Massin-Massin, Mairet (fils), Mme. Paillard, MM. Ridard frères, Sève, de Torcy.
>
> Rodier notes Gravières in capital letters, and the proprietors as MM. Bouzerand, Forain, Jessiaume, Massin, Roizot, E. Valeau, etc.

Les Brussanes, belonging to MM. Prudon, Delonguy-Fion, etc.

Première Cuvée

En Boichot, 12 ha 82 a 82 ca, belonging to MM. Abord-Belin, Maire-Nicolle, Mme Bouchard, etc.

En Beauregard, 33 ha 99 a 74 ca, belonging to MM. de Drée, Ridard, Delonguy, etc.

En Beaurepaire, 17 ha 38 a belonging to MM. de Drée, Ridard, Duvaut-Blocher, Morelot, etc.

La Maladière, 13 ha 66 a 75 ca, belonging to M. Duvaut-Blocher, the widow Derenne, etc.

Le Grand-Clos-Rousseau, 18 ha 90 a 95 ca, belonging to M. Millard.

La Comme, 32 ha 42 a 18 ca, belonging to MM. de Drée, Ridard, the widow Derenne.

En Passe-Temps, 12 ha 49 a 87 ca, belonging to MM. Duvat-Blocher, Bouzerand, etc.

These two last climats have parts that produce very inferior quality and must figure only in deuxième cuvée.

Deuxième Cuvée

Les Prarons-Dessus, 18 ha 42 a 70 ca, belonging to MM. Duvaut-Blocher, the widow Derenne, and many others.

Les Hates, 19 ha 70 a 37 ca, a very fragmented climat, with a considerable yield, belonging to MM. Thugnot, Primard, Duvaut-Blocher, etc. Several parts of this climat merit to be counted as Premières Cuvées.

Clos-Genet, 13 ha 24 a 26 ca, belonging to MM. de Drée, Ridard, and others.

Les Cornières, 13 ha 40 a 15 ca, belonging to MM. Boursier, Abord-Belin, Duvaut-Blocher, and Madame Guillot. A small portion of this climat can be counted as giving wines of the Première Cuvée.

En Saint-Jean, 23 hja 69 a 2 ca, belonging to MM. Duvaut-Blocher, Léthorey, Millard, etc.

Next comes the *Petit-Clos-Rousseau* and the *Falconières*, that, in certain points, can be classified as deuxième cuvée, and at other points in troisième; thus the *Peurenne*, *Saint-Martin*, the *Potets*, etc., that, planted in Pinots and Gamays, give only passe-tout-grains.

The wines of Santenay are firm, mellow, with good ageability; with proper aging they easily acquire a very fine bouquet. They are nonetheless ranked after the wines of Chassagne.

Of particular note in Santenay is the Domaine Lucien Muzard, established in the 1930s. the wines, includine parcels in Gravières and Clos de Tavannes, provide exceptional value, and while they are not widely distributed outside of France, they are worthy to seek out.

A SYNTHESIS

From Dr. Lavalle:

GENERAL CONSIDERATIONS ON THE CLASSIFICATION OF WINES PRODUCED BY THE DIFFERENT VINEYARDS OF THE COTE D'OR

Until the present I have not studied the wines of each village of the Côte but as if the other villages had not existed, and the classification that I have given is only true for each of them taken in isolation. It remains, in order to be complete, to compare the villages between themselves and try to arrange them in the order assigned to them by the qualities of the wines produced in their territories.

I know that such a subject offers difficulties and how it will give rise to discussion. Thus it will be only as a draft that I submit to the interested parties and to connoisseurs the following classification, which seems to me as exact as it is possible to desire, and which I owe, except for several slight modifications, to Dr. Duret, the mayor of Nuits.[86]

Draft of a classification of the wines of the Côte d'Or

HORS LIGNE

Tête de Cuvée N° 1

Romanée-Conti, in Vosne
Clos de Vougeot
Chambertin and Clos de Bèze
Next come:

Clos-de-Tart, part of Bonnes-Mares and Lambrays, in Morey
Corton, in Aloxe (a part)
Musigny, in Chambolle
Richebourg and Tâche, in Vosne
Romanée-Saint-Vivant, in Vosne (a part)
Les Saint-Georges, in Nuits

Tête de Cuvée N° 2

Beaux-Monts, in Vosne
Boudots, Cailles, Cras, Murgers, Porrets, Pruliers, Thorey and Vaucrains, in Nuits
Caillerets and Champans, in Volnay

Clavoillon, in Puligny
Clos-Morgeot, in Chassagne
Clos-Saint-Jacques, Mazy and Varoilles, in Gevrey
Clos-Saint-Jean and Clos Pitois, in Chassagne
Clos-Tavannes and Noyer-Bart, in Santenay
Corton, in Aloxe (a part)
Corvées, Didiers and Forêts, in Prémeaux
Echézeaux, in Flagey
Les Fèves and Les Grèves, in Beaune
La Perrière, in Fixin
Romanée-Saint-Vivant, in Vosne (a part)
Santenot, in Meursault.

It is impossible to dispose the wines of these two sections in any fashion other than alphabetically without exposing oneself to numerous errors and complaints.

Première Cuvée

Aloxe, Beaune, Chambolle, Flagey, Gevrey, Morey, Nuits, Pommard, Premeaux, Volnay and Vosne.

> Under the denomination of premières cuvées I include the wines of great quality and renown, but not taking the name of a particular climat, being cuvées not from a single parcel, but composed of grapes coming from diverse climats or from parcels that do not bear a name admitted to commerce.

Deuxième Cuvée

These are the cuvées of Pinot Noir but of inferior quality. One finds a great quantity of wine of this order all along the Côte d'Or from Gevrey up to Chassagne and Santenay; within them one cannot assign them a rank; it is up to the ability of the taster to classify them, gathering information on the quality of the vines that enter into the composition of these cuvées.

WHITE WINES

Hors Ligne

Montrachet, in Puligny

WHITE WINES

Première Cuvée

Bâtard-Montrachet, in Puligny; Perrières, in Meursault; white Corton, in Aloxe. Then come :

Charmes, Combettes, Genevrières, and Goutte d'Or in Meursault; Charlemagne, in Pernant; etc.

Our Own Draft

Prior centuries lacked what today's AOC system has provided: a unified, simple system. What they have exchanged for this streamlined efficiency was a diversity of voices and a nuanced view of the wines of the Côte d'Or. A look at these varying views would be incomplete without at least an attempt to synthesize them. Let us admit at the outset that any draft of a classification of the "original grands crus" will partake of all of the faults and few of the virtues of previous classifications. I hope in advance that the reader will forgive this error. The draft classification below is not an attempt by the present author to assert his own opinion about the climats of Burgundy, an exercise that would be foolhardy and necessarily fraught with error. Rather, the list below groups them together according to the opinions of the authors we have studied, separating them into groups according to the esteem in which they were held by these authors, beginning with those climats whose esteem is universal and progressing towards that group in which he unanimity of opinion is less striking. It should be emphasized that the wine produced in all of the climats listed below was considered superb by the knowledgable authors of the past, and thus we refer to them all here as Têtes de Cuvées following the 19th century precedent.

Romanée-Conti is listed at the head of the classification, reflecting the nearly unanimous consensus that it is the finest vineyard in Burgundy. After this, the classification is organized geographically from north to south within the broad categories that we have imposed on this list of climats

Tête de Cuvée «A»

Romanée-Conti (Vosne)
Chambertin and Clos de Bèze (Gevrey)
Clos de Vougeot (Vougeot)

The climats in this top category correspond to the first three listings in the classification of Dr. Lavalle. All of our authors agree that all of these should be in the top category, and there seems no question that these were considered the very best among the original grands crus of Burgundy. As noted above, the order acknowledges the preëminence of Romanée-Conti. We imagine that few would be willing to denigrate Chambertin or Clos de Bèze, but the facts are incontestable that the market places a much higher premium on Romanée-Conti than on these other two. This must be due in part to tradition, as well as to scarcity. It is worthwhile to keep in mind, however, that a well-made wine from Chambertin or Clos de Bèze is at the very highest level of Burgundy.

It will also be noted by today's amateurs that if Clos de Vougeot does not command the same reverence today that it did in former times, then this must be due to the fragmented ownership of this vineyard. Past authors noted the uneven nature of the vineyard, and yet when the entire vineyard was under the control of the church or a single owner such as M. Ouvrard, it was possible through blending that the production achieved a very high standard. And so it should be remembered that parts of this vineyard are capable of producing wine of stupendous quality.

Tête de Cuvée «B»

Clos de Tart (Morey)
Musigny (Chambolle)
Richebourg (Vosne)
Romanée-Saint-Vivant (Vosne)
La Romanée (Vosne)
La Tâche (Vosne)
Les Saints-Georges (Nuits)

This second category includes all of the wines considered to be tête de cuvée by Dr. Morelot that were also included as "vins hors ligne / tête de cuvée n°. 1" by Dr. Lavalle in his top category, listed immediately after the top three that were also considered tête de cuvée "n°. 1" by Bertall, as well as included in the top category of André Jullien. The reader should be reminded at this juncture that while none of our authors included Gaudichots specifically in this category, the wines were often sold under the name of La Tâche. In the present day the two have been combined, and we are fortunate to be able to rely with confidence on the stewardship of the Domaine de la Romanée-Conti.

Given their pedigree, one imagines that the inclusion here of Richebourg, Clos de Tart, and Musigny is not controversial. Those who have read the works written in the 18th and 19th centuries also will not be surprised by the inclusion of Les Saint-Georges in this category, although this inclusion may surprise those having a less thorough acquaintance with the history of this vineyard. Les Saints-Georges was classed as premier cru during the formulation of the AOC rules in the 1930s, and it is often explained that a dossier was never put forward because too many growers feared higher taxes at the time. As of this writing, a dossier is now before the INAO, and in due course the issue will be decided for modern drinkers. It is incontestable, however, that this was one of the top cuvées of former times.

Romanée-Saint-Vivant has also been very highly regarded. Few would argue, however, that it has been seen consistently as a step below the portion sold to the Prince de Conti. This was certainly the case for Jullien, who stated quite explicitly that it was inferior to Romanée-Conti. Dr. Morelot finessed the issue by simply mentioned "Les Romanées" in the plural, while Lavalle was a bit more conflicted. Within the context of Vosne, he has the vineyard as a première cuvée, although at the end of his work when he compares all of the villages, a portion is counted as a tête de cuvée no. 1, and a part as tête de cuvée no. 2. By the time of the classification done by the Comité d'Agriculture de Beaune, however, the whole of the vineyard was classified as première classe, and both Danguy et Aubertin and Rodier echo this view.

The vineyard of La Romanée must surely come in here as well, although the evidence is less direct. As we have seen in Chapter XII, this portion was separated from the holdings of the church only at the sale of their land during the Revolution, and then it spent several decades as Richebourg, before being rebaptised by Louis-Charles Liger Belair in 1827, after Jullien's discourse and very close to the period when Dr. Morelot was preparing his manuscript. By the time that Lavalle was writing, however, the change had been made. Although Lavalle lists the new vineyard as being a tête de cuvée, it is not listed separately at the end. In any event, it certainly merits inclusion here: In the space of 50 years, the vineyard had been known successively as Romanée-Saint-Vivant, Richebourg, and La Romanée, all of which are included in this group.

Tête de Cuvée «C»

Clos de la Perrière (Fixin)
Bonnes-Mares (Morey and Chambolle)
Echézeaux (Flagey)
Grands Échézeaux (Flagey)
Corton (Aloxe)
Les Fèves (Beaune)
Les Grèves (Beaune)
Caillerets (Volnay)
Champans (Volnay)
Santenots (Meursault)
Clos-Morgeot (Chassagne)
Clos-Tavannes (Santenay)

In this third category, we have noticeable departures from current practice as well as some dissent among the ranks of our authorities. Traveling north to south, this is apparent at our first stop: Fixin, with Clos de la Perrière.

Today Clos de la Perrière is perhaps less well-known than it should be, yet the fact remains: it is one of the original clos established by the monks of Cîteaux whose boundaries have never changed, and it was mentioned as a tête de cuvée by Jullien, Lavalle, and Bertall. Morelot does not mention it as a tête de cuvée, but in his text on Fixin it appears as one of two vineyards that stand above the norm. He mentions that the early 19th century proprietor had been underperforming. This, however, is not germane to our subject, which is the great terroirs of Burgundy and we leave those considerations for a future work, but here must concede that this vineyard in Fixin certainly merits a place here.

Continuing to the south, we next meet Bonnes-Mares. This is a very distinguished site, and would certainly merit inclusion in the previous category were it not for the fact that Morelot does not mention it as a tête de cuvée. In his section on Morey, he mentions Bonnes-Mares by name, but only to say that it is the equivalent to the "climats of Chambolle". All of the other authors that we have cited count it as a tête de cuvee. However, Lavalle's notes are again somewhat equivocal: He places "a part" of Bonnes-Mares among the têtes de cuvées n°. 1 without explicitly disposing of the rest of it. According to his instructions, then, the rest must be counted not as tête de cuvee, but as première cuvée. Later authors do not share his hesitation.

In Flagey we find Echézeaux. This vineyard has a long history, but it is not seen as being of the first rank: Jullien has it in his second category, as does Bertall. For once the normally precise Dr. Lavalle seems a bit confused: He notes Échézeaux-du-Dessus as a Première Cuvée in his comments on Flagey, but at the end he places it as a tête de cuvée n°. 2, while in the chapter on Flagey, Grands Échézeaux is a tête de cuvee, but it is not mentioned at the end of the work. It seems fair in view of this to include both vineyards here. Morelot does not mention it either among his têtes de cuvées, but only in passing in his review of Flagey. It should be further pointed out that all of the authors above refer only to the climat of Échézeaux-du-Dessus, and not to the later accretions to this vineyard.

Corton is another vineyard that has been mentioned at the highest level but without a unanimous consensus as to the rank of the vineyard. "A part" has been put in the top rank by Lavalle, while Morelot includes it unambiguously among his têtes de cuvées. Bertall includes it among his tête de cuvées n°. 1. Jullien, however, has it as a second class vineyard (just before Échézeaux). As with Échézeaux, the modern reader would do well to recall that these comments refer only to Le Corton, and not to the other climats that have been added to it over the years.

Continuing along the Côte de Beaune we notice the following climats which appear in every classification. They are not necessarily in the top rank, but they were highly esteemed nonetheless. The first of these are Les Grèves and Les Feves in Beaune, which were classified in the second category by Jullien and among the têtes de cuvées by Morelot. Lavalle had them as têtes de cuvées no. 2 at the end of his work, as did Bertall, and Danguy et Aubertin and Rodier concur. The same is true of Volnay Caillerets and Champans as well as the vineyard of Santenots, which is located in Meursault, but is classified today as Volnay as well. The Clos Morgeot in Chassagne was also included. Finally, Clos-Tavannes in Santenay is classified at this level by Jullien, Lavalle, and Bertall, although it is not mentioned among the têtes de cuvées by Dr. Morelot. Given the scant attention paid to the reds of the Côte de Beaune today, these would seem to be vineyards that would warrant the attention of wine lovers looking for values among the red wines of Burgundy.

Tête de Cuvée «D»

Mazis (Gevrey)
Varoilles (Gevrey)
Beaux-Monts (Vosne)
Les Boudots (Nuits)
Les Cailles (Nuits)
Les Cras (Nuits)
Les Murgers (Nuits)
Les Porrets (Nuits)
Les Pruliers (Nuits)
Aux Thorey (Nuits)
Les Vaucrains (Nuits)
Les Corvées (Prémeaux)
Les Didiers (Prémeaux)
Les Forêts (Prémeaux)
Les Vergelesses (Savigny)
Epéneaux (Pommard)
Rugiens (Pommard)
Clos-Saint-Jean (Chassagne)
Clavoillon (Puligny)
Gravières (Santenay)

With the fourth category, we come to a series of climats that attracted the attention of some authors but not of others. In order from north to south, the first of these are Mazy-Chambertin and Gevrey Varoilles, both of which are ranked as a têtes de cuvées (n°. 2) by Lavalle, but were included only in the third category by Jullien, and were not mentioned by either Morelot or Bertall.

Vosne Beaux-Monts was not mentioned by Jullien or Morelot, but was classified as a tête de cuvée (n°. 2) by both Lavalle and Bertall. There are large number of climats in Nuits that also merit inclusion here. These include Les Boudots, Les Cailles, Les Cras, Les Murgers, Les Porrets, Les Pruliers, Aux Thorey, and Les Vaucrains as well as several that are located in Prémeaux but are today sold as Nuits: Les Corvées, Les Didiers, and Les Forêts. Jullien puts the commune of Nuits in his second category, along with the likes of Bonnes-Mares, Clos de la Roche, Clos de Tart, Corton, Échézeaux, and others, and says that, "all of the premières cuvées of Nuits are of approximately equal merit." They do not appear in Morelot, although they are classified as tête de cuvée (n°. 2) by both Lavalle and Bertall.

In the Côte de Beaune, Savigny-lès-Beaune Les Vergelesses is mentioned in the second class of Jullien, and as a tête de cuvée by Morelot, who singles out Clos de la Bataillère. Lavalle hedges just a bit, as he does not include it in his overall assessment at the end of his work, but he does classify it within the village of Savigny as a "première cuvée EXTRA", highlighting as Morelot has done La Bataillère. In Pommard, Epéneaux is second category in Jullien and tête de cuvée in Morelot; Rugiens is also included here by Jullien, and is a tête de cuvée in Bertall (but is not mentioned in Morelot). Too, we recall that Lavalle did not deem any of the climats of Pommard worthy to be elevated above the rest.

Further south in the Côte de Beaune, Clos Saint-Jean in Chassagne is mentioned by Jullien and Lavalle, but not by Bertall or Morelot; Puligny Clavoillon is noted for red wine by Lavalle and Bertall but not by other sources, who also praise Santenay Noyer-Bart. As to this last, Jullien has mentioned Gravières generally, while Lavalle and Bertall single out the portion of Gravières called Noyer-Bart. Oddly, this last parcel does not appear on any maps, even on the one included in Dr. Lavalle's work. As it would be odd to include a wine with such a tenuous existence, it is better to include Gravières here: It appears that it is generally considered a step down from Clos Tavannes and yet warrants inclusion. Gravières also includes Noyer-Bart, and thus including it here seems to cover any eventuality.

Other Cuvées

Clos du Roi (Chenôve)
Le Chapitre (Chenôve)
Chapelle (Gevrey)
Clos-Saint-Jacques (Gevrey)
Clos de la Roche (Morey)
Clos des Lambrays (Morey)
Les Amoureuses (Chambolle)
La Grande Rue (Vosne)

Bressandes (Aloxe)
Renardes (Aloxe)
Clos du Roi (Aloxe)
Chaumes (Aloxe)
Clos des Mouches (Beaune)
Clos du Roi (Beaune)
Les Cras (Beaune)
Dominode (Savigny)
Marconnets (Savigny)
Jarrons (Savigny)
Peuillets (Savigny)
Rugiens (Pommard)
Le Clos de Cîteaux (Pommard)
Arvelets (Pommard)
Chapelle (Volnay)
Plures (Meursault)
Les Cras (Meursault)
Maltroie (Chassagne)
Clos Pitois (Chassagne)
La Boudriotte (Chassagne)

In the fifth and final category for red wines, there are a number of wines that we mentioned by only one author and not by others. Although there may be no agreement among our authorities, one certainly finds here some interesting choices. The wines of some of these climats interest us because of their inclusion; others intrigue us in that they were not included in a higher category. In the first category are perhaps Clos du Roi and Le Chapitre in Chenôve, close to Dijon. Winemakers will sometimes make the argument that the AOC system favors crus close to cities or to transportation – perhaps this is an instance of that phenomenon? Today Clos du Roi produces Marsannay, and Le Chapitre is demoted to a regional appellation, as mentioned in our chapter on the Côte Dijonnaise.

In Gevrey we find curious omissions. We find first that Chapelle was included in the third category by Jullien (along with Clos Saint-Jacques and Véroilles). However, Lavalle does not mention it as a tête de cuvée, instead seeming to prefer Clos Saint-Jacques (and Mazy and Varoilles, all tête de cuvée n°. 2). Morelot mentions Chapelle as well (along with Clos Saint-Jacques, Mazy, La Grillette, and La Fouchère), but states distinctly that they are below the level of Chambertin. Lavalle is careful to specify that only Mazy Haut, Charmes Haut and Ruchotte du Dessus are Premières Cuvées, Mazy Bas, Charmes Bas, and Ruchotte Basse are all Deuxième Cru, as is Latricières and Mazoyères in his book.

In Morey, Clos de la Roche is mentioned by Jullien in the first class, but Morelot does not mention it. Lavalle does not mention it in his summary of têtes de cuvées at the end of his work, although, within the context of the village, the original clos is première cuvée. At the same time, some of today's constituents are deuxième cuvée or are not mentioned at all. Clos de la Roche does not appear in Bertall. And like Clos de la Roche, the Clos des Lambrays comes in only as a première cuvée in Dr. Lavalle's work, and it is not mentioned by authors elsewhere.

In Chambolle, Morelot favors Les Amoureuses, listing it as a tête de cuvée. Given the prices commanded today by wines from this climat, it seems that our modern collectors would agree. Jullien, however, had noted, a propos of Chambolle, that the "other premières cuvées differ little from the best of Beaune", and Lavalle ranked Chambolle as a première cuvée.

La Grande Rue, running along on the southern border of some of the greatest vineyards in the world, was mentioned by Jullien in his first category; in Morelot and Lavalle it is mentioned, but does not come in as a tête de cuvée.

In Aloxe, Bressandes is mentioned in the second category by Jullien and as a première cuvée by Lavalle. Morelot praises it highly in his comments on Aloxe, but he has not placed it among the têtes de cuvées, and Bertall has not mentioned it. Much of the rest of what is Corton today is also missing from this list, although Lavalle has as hors ligne Corton-Renards, Corton-Clos du Roi, and Chaumes and Charlemagne (for white) just a step below.

We note that André Jullien was much more effusive than his fellow experts regarding the wines of the Côte de Beaune, and there are a number that come in for special mention from him that are not treated with the same reverence by others. This list includes Clos des Mouches, Clos du Roi, and Les Cras in Beaune; Dominode, Marconnets, Jarrons, and Pougets in Savigny; Pommard Rugiens; La Chapelle in Volnay; Les Plures, and Les Cras in Meursault, and Maltroie in Chassagne. Other writers had their favorites here as well: Morelot praised Pommard Le Clos de Cîteaux, Bertall saw greater merit than others in Pommard Arvelets, and Lavalle favored Clos Pitois in Chassagne as a tête de cuvée n°. 2 at the end of his work, and had Chassagne La Boudriotte as hors ligne in the context of the village.

White Wines

White Tête de Cuvée «A» :

Montrachet (Puligny and Chassagne)

White Tête de Cuvée «B» :

Chevalier Montrachet (Puligny and Chassagne)
Bâtard Montrachet (Puligny and Chassagne)

White Tête de Cuvée «C» :

Corton Blanc (Aloxe)
Le Charlemagne (Aloxe and Pernand)
Perrières (Meursault)
Meursault Charmes (Meursault)
Combettes (Puligny)
Genevrières (Meursault)
Gouttes d'Or (Meursault)

As regards white wine, the situation is perhaps a bit clearer at the outset. Montrachet is universally acclaimed as the best white wine from the time of Arnoux until the present day. According to some authorities, this was not the case prior to the 18th century, but certainly from this time forward the acclaim has been universal: Montrachet is the best white Burgundy wine; French authors (and many others, of course) also would have it named the best white wine of the world. It is interesting to consider the words of Claude Arnoux, "There is no other wine of Côte Rôtie or of Muscat de Frontignan that is its equal."

Montrachet has been referred to by these authors as "True Montrachet" or "The Elder Montrachet" to distinguish it from Bâtard and Chevalier, the vineyards that surround it. These wines are also highly acclaimed, but again there is consensus that they are a step below that of Montrachet proper, and the present classification reflects this reality.

Arnoux and Courtépée also recognize the fine qualities of Meursault. Courtépée notes, « The best climats are Les Charmes, Les Perrières, Les Genevrières, [and] La Goutte d'Or ». Jullien has Meursault Perrières, Combottes, Goutte d'Or, Genevrières, and Charmes all in the second category; Morelot is initially very dismissive, but then expands the second category after Montrachet to include not only Chevalier and Bâtard-Montrachet but also Meursault and Blagny (without specifying the climats), and even adds in the white from Fixin Clos du Chapitre. There is, however, little support for this. Lavalle has Montrachet by itself, followed by Bâtard, Meursault Perrières and white Corton, in Aloxe; followed in turn by Meursault Charmes, Combettes, Genevrières, and Goutte d'Or in Meursault, and Charlemagne, in Pernant. At the end of his work, however, he leaves out Chevalier-Montrachet, although he had listed all of the whites above as premières cuvées in the context of the village, while here he places Chevalier first, although in the next breath he lists Blagny-Blanc, Bâtard-Montrachet and

Les Combettes as equal in quality. Bertall for his part has Chevalier-Montrachet, Bâtard-Montrachet following Montrachet and then Meursault Charmes, Combettes, Genevrières, and Goutte d'Or followed by Corton Charlemagne.

Given the varied opinions regarding the white wines, it would seem that our classification above reflects as accurately as possible the currents of 18th and 19th century thought, with Montrachet apart, and Chevalier-Montrachet and Bâtard-Montrachet slightly behind. It also seems, however, that a place must be given for the best crus of Meursault and the hill of Corton, both of which are reflected above.

Ultimately, the production of classifications and the minute ranking of a wine before one and after another is nothing more than a type of parlour game played by wine lovers. We should state this unequivocally: All of the wines produced in the better climats of Burgundy are delicious and so attempting to discern very fine gradations of deliciousness among them seems a presumptuous task. The best way forward is to enjoy them all, each in its place and time, with the appropriate company and complimentary food.

· APPENDIX I ·

Glossary [A. Jullien, 1836]

This is my translation of Jullien's original glossary, which he sub-titled: *Terms employed in this work to describe different qualities of wines*. Staying true to Jullien's original, the list is organized alphabetically by the French term. Any clarifications in English are set off in brackets:

Terms employed in this work to describe different qualities of wines

Acerbe: Acerbic

One qualifies thus wines made from poor grape varieties or those that have not attained maturity; they are at once hard, bitter, and sharp.

Apre: Bitter or Harsh

This word characterizes wines, which, by their roughness, leave an unpleasant sensation on the palate.

Arome: Aroma

The odor which escapes from wines; one calls this more generally the bouquet [In contemporary usage, aroma usually refers to young wines and bouquet in aged wines. I generally retain the word bouquet in the original French and translate *arome* as aroma].

Arome spiritueux: Spiritous aroma, finish

The perfume that rises from alcoholic beverages during the tasting of them. According to its strength, it continues to be sensed a greater or lesser time after the disappearance of the alcohol. In some vineyards, this is referred to as *sève* (refer to this term).

Bouquet: Bouquet

The agreeable odor that particularly distinguishes fine wines.

Bourru; Vin bourru: Rough (wine)

One calls thus that which comes from the tank or press whose transparence is troubled by the presence of a large quantity of lees.

Chais ou celliers: Barrel storage or cellars

These are the storage houses that exist on the ground floor or slightly underground where one stocks wine in cask.

Charnu: Fleshy

This term applies to wines of a certain consistency; it can appear to have this texture without having much alcoholic generosity, and thus it is distinguished from the term *corsé* [full-bodied]; see *mache* [to chew].

Collage, Coller un vin: Fine, to fine a wine

To introduce a substance to seize everything that masks the transparency of a wine and cause them to precipitate to the bottom of the vessel. The *Manuel du Sommelier* indicates the method of doing this and the substances that are employed for different wines.

Corps, Un vin qui a du corps, corsé: Body, a full-bodied wine

Expressions used to designate wines that have a certain consistency, a pronounced flavor, a vinous power, of which the substance is fleshy, it fills the mouth; the opposite of a light, dry, cold, or watery wine.

Cru, crudité: Raw

Said of a wine that is too young, which isn't ripe yet, and which still has an unpleasantly green character.

Cru: Vineyard

A *terroir* where vines are grown. One says of a wine that it is of or from a cru of a certain vineyard or a certain clos, which means only that it comes from a certain defined place; one says also that it comes from the cru of a certain slope, district, or even province, although this last usage of the term indicates an extent of terrain that can include a great number of crus whose products can differ in quality.

Cuvée: Cuvée

This word, taken in its most general sense, signifies the quantity of wine contained in a [fermentation] tank, but one employs it also to refer to the wine that comes from a distinct vineyard whose yield might fill several tanks. The term première cuvée that which is the best or first cuvée of a given region; by second cuvée that which is inferior to it, etc. This word is also sometimes synonymous with cru, and one would refer in the same way to the wine of the first, second or third cuvee, or first, second or third cru of a given vineyard. One also calls a cuvée several casks of wine of the same type that have been blended together to render them identical. *Mettre les vins en cuvée* is to blend them together in such a fashion that each cask receives an equal share of each type [of wine].

Délicat, Délicatesse: Delicate, Delicacy

A delicate wine contains little tartaric acid or color; it is neither bitter nor sharp, and may have generosity, body, and even grip, but it is necessary that these qualities are well combined and that none of them dominates.

Droit-en-gout: Purity of fruit

This is said of wine and of spirits that have no taste foreign to that which is natural to them (see *franc-de-gout*) [A clearer way of expressing this in modern English would be to say that the wines have a very pure fruit expression or great purity, i.e., that there is no discernible input of earthiness or of winemaking in the aroma].

Dur, Dureté: Hard, hardness

One qualifies new wines as hard when they have a bitter taste that disagreeably affects the palate.

Foible: Weak

Applies to wines having little body, generosity or flavor; this is a very pleasant quality, and many people prefer such wines for their daily use. These wines, if they have no other faults, can be improved by mixing them with good wines.

Ferme, Fermeté: Closed, Reticence

One uses this expression to designate those wines that combine much body, power, energy, and structure, or those which, being not fully mature, retain some green qualities. This property is a fault in wines that one would like to drink unmixed, but it is an advantage in those that will serve to refresh others.

Fin, Finesse: Fine, Finesse

A wine has finesse when it is light and delicate, qualities that can be found both in ordinary wines and fine wines, but these last must also have vigor, and above all, bouquet.

Finir (vins qui finissent bien): to age well, Wines "to make old bones of"

Said of wines that age well and gain in quality as they age and are less subject than others to be affected by complete degeneration. This quality, common to all classes of wine, is seldom found in those of low quality.[87]

Fort: Strong

A qualification given to wines that have much generosity [i.e. alcohol], body, and a pronounced taste, are appropriate to give tone to the stomach, to last a long time, and to be mixed with water and to reinforce weak or degenerate wines.

Franc[88] de Gout: Purity of fruit

One qualifies thus wines that have no other flavor than that which the grape has given them; those that has an earthy or herbal notes, albeit very natural, are not called "franc de gout"; the same is true for those to which one has made additions that can be noticed.

Franc de Qualité: Pure quality

Said of wines which have not been altered in any way.

Fumeux: Heady

An expression that indicates wines whose alcoholic and aromatic properties volatize quickly and mount promptly to the brain.

Fut, Futaille: Cask

These are two synonyms for cask; the first applies to casks either empty or full, while the second applies primarily to empty casks.

Fut, Gout de Fut: Musty [lit. « cask taste »]

A disagreeable taste given to wines by casks poorly repaired.

Généreux, Génerosité: Generous, Generosity

One calls a wine generous when the qualities that constitute it render it warming and restorative; it gives tone to the stomach, facilitates its functions and reestablishes ones forces. Horace uses this term when he says in the first book, fifteenth epistle *generosum et lene requiro*[89]" etc.

Gout du Terroir: Taste of Terroir

Flavors in wine communicated by the terrain in which it is cultivated.[90]

Gout d'Herbage: Herbal flavor

This comes, either from green plants whose roots comingle with those of the vine, transmitting their flavor to the grape, or from different vegetables employed in the compost.

Grain: Grip[91]

This term is used for a type of bitterness in young wines which, without having any disagreeable connotations, is found in the majority of dry or mellow wines when they are not very old and have not been blended with any other.

Grossier: Heavy, "four-square"

This term is used for wines that are hard and that have a pasty or thick texture, and are heavy, thick, and without finesse; wines of several good crus can appear thus when they are young, but as they age they rid themselves of the particles of lees and tartrate that mask their qualities and they become fine and agreeable. The majority of common wines, who have only the fault, are improved by mixing them with lighter wines, and above all with white wines.

Hautains: Alberate

This name is given to vines that are left to grow to a great height and whose shoots climb into the trees and interlace themselves with the branches; they produce a great abundance of grapes, but the wine is ordinarily of poor quality, because a portion of the bunches, hidden under the foliage, never mature.

Jauge: Gauge

The just measure of the capacity of a container destined to hold spirits; it is also the name of the instrument used to measure the capacity of a tank or other other vessel.

Jauger: To gauge

The action of measuring a vessel; one uses the same verb to indicate said capacity; one says, for example, "This cask gauges 200 litres."

Léger: Light

Light wines have little body, color, and grip, and can be overly generous; those that are not are weak and flat.

Liqueur, Liquoreux; Sweet, Sweetness

It is said of a wine that retains some sweetness that it has liqueur or is liquoreux, but this does not mean that it is a dessert wine, because it must remain thus after the completion of its alcoholic fermentation. White wines, which do not ferment in the cellar, are much more likely to retain some of their original sweetness, and it may happen that this characteristic is not lost for a year or longer.

Mache: Chewy

This word is used to designate a thick or pasty wine because it fills the mouth and appears to have enough consistency to be chewed.

Moelle: mellow[92]

A mellow wine is unctuous without being sweet; it has body and consistency and no bitterness.

Moelleux: Mellowness

Wines thus described have a certain consistency and are more sweet than dry and sharp. I have chosen this expression as the midpoint between dessert wines and dry wines; this seems to me the best term to apply to most of the wines of France, who, without having a sweet or bland flavor, as do many wines from Spain and Italy, are never dry or sharp as are the wines of the Rhine and the majority of the German vineyards.

Montant: Heady

A wine is said to be heady when the aromatic and spirituous parts that it exudes rise quickly to the brain; this word is also used to describe the effect of sparkling wines and other gassy beverages, when the CO_2 rises to the nose and produces a tingling in proportion to the quality of the bubble.

Mordant: Bite

This term is used for wines whose flavor dominates those with which they are mixed. Bite or a peppery character, when united with much body, generosity and good flavor, serves to improve weak wines, but it is a fault in little wines, because they are not appropriately used to ameliorate other wines.

Moustille: Prickle

This word indicates the character of a wine that not yet having completed its alcoholic fermentation conserves a sweetness and a slight prickle given it by CO_2 which continues to be released. It is not sparkling but it continues to lightly ferment; a wine that has moustille is in an intermediate state between unfermented must and finished wine.

Mout: Must

Juice recently pressed from the grape that has not yet been fermented.

Muet, Vin muet: Mute: sweet wine

Wine whose fermentation has been stopped or suspended by impregnating it with sulfur, leaving it in the state of must.

Muter: To Mute

The procedure for preparing a vin muet.

Nerf, nerveux: Nerve, Nervy

A nervy wine is one that unites sufficient body, generosity, and power to maintain for a long time a high degree of quality, and to support more easily than others transport by sea and by land, and to resist more easily the temperatures of the seasons.

Pateux: Pasty

This term designates a wine of a thick consistency that coats the mouth and whose molecules seem to attach to the palate.

Plat: Flat

Flat wines are bereft of body, flavor, and generosity; although they are often deeply colored, they are often subject to falling apart, but one can preserve them and prolong their life by blending them with full-bodied and generous wines, either red or white.

Précoce: Precocious

Said of wines that attain their maturity quickly.

Sève: Vigor

This word is often used in Bordeaux and in several other regions to indicate the vinous force and the aromatic power that develops during tasting, and, coating the palate, continues after swallowing or spitting the wine. One designates also the same quality by this term *arome-spiriteueux* (see this term). Séve differs from the bouquet in that the latter is released at the moment the wine is struck by the atmosphere, and is sensed by the nose rather than on the palate.

Soyeux: Silky

A term that refers to a wine whose contact with the palate causes an agreeable sensation undisturbed by any harshness.

Tannin: Tannin

A substance contained principally in the bark of the oak tree and is used to tan leathers; it exists in greater or lesser quantities in all wines; those that have none cannot be clarified by means of fining. The wood tannin given to white wines is considered to be one of the causes of a yellow color.

Tirage au fin: Racking

Said in Bordeaux of the operation called in other regions *soutirage*; it consists of pulling from a cask all of the clear wine, leaving in the bottom of the cask all of the lees that have precipitated.

Tonneau: Cask

A large wooden vessel used to contain liquids or other merchandise. Those used for wine vary in capacity and have different names according to the region where they are employed. As I have mentioned these in each article of this work, I believe it useless to give more details here.

One also uses the word tonneau to describe a large quantity of liquor contained in several [smaller] casks; in this usage it is not given to any particular sized vessel but to a defined quantity that is the same in every region.

Tonneau, in maritime usage, refers to a quantity of merchandise weighing 2,000 pounds, *poids de marc*[93], or a bit less than 1,000 kilograms. When used to refer to wine, it means four barrels, each containing 228 litres.

Tourner: To Turn

Said of wines that are changing or decomposing; one says that a wine turns sour or turns bitter, or turns syrupy or turns rotten when these types of decomposition become noticeable, and that it has turned sour when the decomposition is complete.

Velouté: Velvet

Said of a wine which, with beautiful color, body, and charm flatters the palate as it passes.

Velte: Velte (roughly equivalent to two gallons)

A measure formerly used for the sale of wines and spirits containing 8 Paris pints[94], equivalent to 7.617 litres in today's measure. The measure used to gauge tonneaux was also called a velte.

Velter:

To gauge a tonneau with a velte.

Vert: Green

Wines are called green when they come from unripe grapes.

Vin chaud: Hot wine

Wines are called hot when they are highly alcoholic and used to give strength to weak wines.

Vin doux: Sweet wine

Sweet wines are those that retain some natural grape sugar, not yet having completed their alcoholic fermentation. One gives this name as well to newly pressed must.

Viner: To Fortify

To give a wine more alcoholic force; this is done by mixing it with those of superior quality and power. The wines of the south of France, normally used for this purpose, have themselves been fortified before being shipped with the addition of spirit.

Vineux: Vinous

Said of a wine with much power and generosity.

Vins qui se marient bien: Wines that blend well

A term for wines appropriate to blending.

• APPENDIX II •

Table of Comparative Values [Lavalle]95

Of different measures or monies referred to in this work

The journal[96] includes 8 ouvrées, or 860 perches, or 34.284 ares.

An ouvrée[97] is worth 4.285 ares.

The petit journal is 240 perches or 22.856 ares.

The perche is a Burgundian measure of area equal to $90\frac{1}{4}$ feet or 0.095 ares.

The perche as a measure of length is $9\frac{1}{2}$ feet or 3.086 meters.

A Burgundian league is 18,000 feet or 5,847.108 meters.

The queue is worth two tonneaux, that is to say, 456 litres.[98]

The tonneaux, muid, poinçon, or pièce holds two feuillettes, that is to say, 228 litres.

The feuillette holds two *quarteaux*, that is to say, 114 litres.

The quarteau holds 57 litres.

The Dijon pint holds 1.615 litres.

Formerly, a tonneau of wine was worth 144 pints, two muids made a queue; the muid contained two feuillettes, the feuillette, nine setiers, and the setier, eight pints.

A Beaune tonneau held 2 hectolitres, 57 litres and 6 centilitres.

The émine contained 16 quarteranches, that is to say 512 litres. It was not in usage after 1683.

The quarteranche (before 1683) was the equivalent of 26 litres 76 centilitres. Since this time, it contained 32 litres and was known under the name of grande mesure.

The livre tournois[99] was worth 20 sols or 480 oboles, or 3,840 niquets.

The franc is most often the synonym of the livre. It is divided in 12 gros or 48 blancs or 144 engrognes.

The gros was worth 4 blancs; The blanc was worth 5 deniers or 3 engrognes.

The sol contained 12 deniers; The dernier 2 oboles and The obole 8 niquets.

If one would like to understand now the price of our wines, of the workday, and of the comparative value of each monetary unit in past centuries, here are several facts that could serve as a base for approximate conclusions:

During the 14th century, the price of ordinary wine from the Côte de Beaune was, on average, 1 denier per litre. However, the winegrower earned for each workday from 7 to 12 deniers. He could thus buy, with the price of a day of work from 7 to 12 litres of everyday wine.

In 1431, the pint of common wine was worth 1 engrogne, and each vineyard worker earned from 12 to 16 engrognes for salary each day. He received thus a value equal to 12 or 16 pints of wine, that is to say between 19.44 – 25.92 litres.

At the beginning of the 15th century, the good wines of Dijon were worth on average 15 francs. The winegrower received for the price of his workday from 4 to 10 sols, while the good wines of Dijon were worth 24 livres, which is to say that the price of a day's work allowed the winegrower to purchase from 2 to 5 litres of good wine.

In 1685, the different tasks of the winegrower were priced in Beaune from 4 sols 6 deniers to 8 sols 4 deniers, while the good wines of Beaune were worth, in an average year 25 francs; this made the equivalent of the price of a day's work to approximately 2 to 5 litres of good wine.

In our day, the price of everyday wine is on average 20 centimes per litre and the winegrower, who received 1 franc 75 centimes for the price of his day's work, has a salary equivalent to 8 litres of everyday wine. Good wine in general is worth 50 centimes per bottle, and the winegrower receives per day a value that represents approximately 3 litres of good wine.

Around 1450, the émine of wheat of Dijon contained 16 quarteranches, the quarteranche (26.716 litres) cost on average 20 gros. At this time, the franc was equivalent to the livre tournois, which was divided into 20 sols; in consequence, at this time a litre of wheat cost approximately 15 niquets or a bit less than a denier. The winegrower received for the price of his day 6 blancs or 30 deniers, which is to say more than 30 litres of wheat.

In our day, the double decalitre is worth on average 3 francs 50 centimes; this gives for the average price of a litre of wheat 17 centimes. From this conclusion, the winegrower who receives today 1 franc 75 centimes receives thus the equivalent of 11 litres.

The wines of the Clos de Vougeot were sold in 1380 3 livres 10 sols per muid; this gives a value of $3\frac{1}{2}$ deniers per litre. However, the everyday wines of Beaune were worth 1 denier, thus one sees at this époque this wine was worth only three and a half times the price of everyday wine. Today this wine is sold more than seven times the price of ordinary wine, showing that this wine has doubled in value since this époque. For almost all the other climats, one finds by similar calcuations that their relative value has hardly varied, and this is certainly true for everyday wine.

From these facts one sees that from the point of view of the value of wine, 1 denier, in the 14th century, was worth approximately 20 centimes of our money, which is to say that the value of silver was 48 times higher. If instead of taking the price of wine as the base and one established the calculations on the base of the price of wheat, one arrives at more or less the same conclusion.

· BIBLIOGRAPHY ·

Anonymous (Beguillet, Edme). *Dissertation sur les Vins*. Paris : Chez P. Fr. Didot Jeune, 1772. Available online : http://books.google.com/

Anselme, P. Histoire Généalogique et Chronologique de la Maison Royale de France, 1733. Paris : Compagnie des Libraires Associez. Available online : http://books.google.com/

Arnoux, Claude. *Dissertation sur la situation de la Bourgogne, sur les vins qu'elle produit*. London: Jallasson, 1728. Available online : ftp://ftp.bnf.fr/102/N1025098_PDF_1_-1DM.pdf

Barbero, Dominique; Brunet, Guy, eds. *Déclaration des biens des communautés 1665-1670* [Intendance de Dijon] ; [rédigé par l'] intendant Bouchu. Rumilly: ECU, 1978

Bazin, Jean-François. *Histoire du Vin de Bourgogne*. Editions Gisserot, 2002.

Bertall. *La Vigne. Voyage Autour de Vins de France*. Paris: E. Plon et Cie, 1878. Available online : http://gallica.bnf.fr/ark:/12148/bpt6k73212p

Coates, Clive. *Côte d'Or*. Berkeley: University of California Press, 1997.

Courtépée et Béguillet. *Description historique et topographique du Duché de Bourgogne*. Dijon: chez Causse, 1778. Available online : http://books.google.com/

Danguy, R., Aubertin, C. *Les Grands Vins de Bourgogne*. Dijon: Librarie H. Armand, 1892. Available online : http://gallica.bnf.fr/ark:/12148/bpt6k1654266

Gandelot, Abbé. *Histoire de la Ville de Beaune*. Dijon: chez Louis-Nicolas Frantin, 1728. Available online : http://books.google.com/

Guillon, Jean-Marie. *Étude Générale de la Vigne*. Paris : Masson et c^{ie}. 1905. Available online : http://books.google.com/

Guyot, Jules. *Culture de la Vigne et Vinification*. Paris : Librarie Agricole, 1961. Available online : http://books.google.com/

Hanson, Anthony. *Burgundy*. London: Faber and Faber, 1982.

Jullien, André. *The Topographie de Tous les Vignobles Connus*. Paris: L. Colas, 1832. Available online : http://books.google.com/

Jullien, André. The Wine Merchant's Companion and Butler's Manual. London: W. Anderson, 1825. Available online : http://books.google.com/

Landrieu-Lussigny, Marie-Hélène ; Pitiot, Sylvain. Climats et Lieux-dits des Grands Vignobles de Bourgogne. Paris: Editions de Monza & Editions du Meurger, 2012.

Lavalle, Jules. Histoire et Statistique et des Grands Vins de la Côte d'Or. Paris: Dusacq, 1885. Available online : https://ia600802.us.archive.org/17/items/histoireetstat00unse/histoireetstat00unse.pdf

Maupin (Agronome). La Richesse des Vignobles: Partie des Vins. Paris: Musier & Gobreau, 1784.

Meadows, Alan. The Pearl of the Côte. Winnetka: Burghound Books, 2010.

Milsand, Charles-Philibert. Bibliographie Bourguignonne. Dijon: Gustave Lamarche, 1885. Available online : http://books.google.com/

Morelot, Denis. Statistique de la Vigne dans le Département de la Côte d'Or. Dijon: Victor Lagier, 1831. Available online : http://books.google.com/

Morris, Jasper. Inside Burgundy. London: Berry Brothers & Rudd Press, 2010.

Miller, Philippe. Dictionnaire des Jardiniers. Bruxelles: Benoit le Francq, 1789. Available online: http://books.google.com/

Norman, Remington. The Great Domaines of Burgundy. New York: Henry Holt, 1996.

Olney, Richard. Romanée-Conti. New York: Rizzoli, 1995.

Rigaux, Jacky. Grands Crus de Bourgogne. Clemencey: Terre en vues, 2007.

Rodier, Camille. Le Vin de Bourgogne. Dijon: L. Damidot, 1920. Available online: https://ia601203.us.archive.org/32/items/grandsvinsdebour00unse/grandsvinsdebour00unse.pdf

Robinson, Jancis et. al. Wine Grapes. New York: Harper Collins, 2012.

Robinson, Jancis et. al. The Oxford Companion to Wine (3rd ed.). New York: Oxford University Press, 2006.

Robinson, Jancis; Johnson, Hugh. The World Atlas of Wine. London: Mitchell Beazley, 2001.

Tainturier, Abbé. Remarques sur la Culture des Vigne de Beaune et Lieux Ciconvoisins. Beaune, 1763. Reissued by Éditions de l'Armançon, 2000.

Vialay, Amédée. La Vente des Biens Nationaux Pendant la Revolution Française. Paris, Perrin et Cie, 1908. Available online : http://books.google.com/

Vienne, Henri. Gevrey-Chambertin : Notice Historique, Topographique et Statistique. Dijon, Chez Douillier, 1850. Available online : http://books.google.com/

Online sources :

http://www.bourgogne-wines.com/

http://www.domaine-jeanmonnier.com/catalogue/plus_details.php?lien=rouge8.txt

• ENDNOTES •

1. Georgics, book II, 113
2. Wines of the year
3. Wines for aging
4. See Appendix II for a discussion of the relative value of currencies and measures under the Ancien Régime.
5. Beguillet, E (1770) Œnologie ou Discours sur la meillure méthode de faire le Vin & de cultiver la Vigne. Dijon. Defay.
6. Gallia Narbonensis or Transalpine Gaul was a Roman province corresponding roughly to the modern regions of Languedoc and Provence.
7. The Pays des Éduens was that inhabited by the Celtic people found in the modern day départements of Nièvre, Saône-et-Loire, Côte d'Or, and Allier, who had Bibracte as their capital.
8. Celtic Gaul
9. Lit. "near the Saône"; the richest of the pays des Éduens
10. A Roman rhetorician born in Autun c. 235 AD
11. During the Avignon papacy (1309 – 1378)
12. Urban, a Benedictine and the sixth pope to rule from Avignon, did return to Rome in 1367, only to return to Avignon three years later under pressure from the French cardinals and from the resistance to his rule in Italy.
13. John II of Burgundy (28 May 1371 – 10 September 1419)
14. Jean Petit defended the assassination of the brother of Charles VI by assassins working for his patron, Jean sans Peur.
15. Also known as Roger Bontemps (1468-1536), secretary to François I, bishop of Auxerre
16. The different editions of Jullien's work differ in important details. For my translation I have employed the version of 1816 that is available online. Subsequently, I was able to purchase a print copy of the 1832 edition, only to notice the promotion of Corton from deuxième cuvée to Première and other substantive differences. Here I have kept to the earliest edition.
17. A French administrative division, smaller than an American state, but larger than a county
18. Semur-en-Auxois
19. A mystery. Giboudot is a synonym for Aligoté, which is common in Burgundy, but does not give red wine; the Littré dictionary defines it as a black grape grown in the Loire valley. Giboudot Noir is cited in the Vitus International Variety Catalogue (http://www.vivc.de/index.php) as a synonym of Plant d'Abraham. Could it perhaps be Tressot, formerly widely planted in Burgundy?

20	A synonym for Gamay
21	Muscadet
22	A hectare (abbreviated as "ha") is 10,000 square meters (m2) or 2.47 acres; and are (abbreviated as "a") is 100 m2, a measure not used outside of real estate, and not included in the standard definition of Bureau International des Poids et Measures that regulates the metric system; a centiares ("ca") is 1m2.
23	I translate spiritueux, lit. "spirity", as "generous". The term is not used by our authors in a perjoritive sense, and thus to translate it perhaps more litreally as "hot" or "alcoholic" would not be appropriate. When Michael Broadbent used "spirity" to refer to a wine he seems to mean that it has the sensation of alcohol without sufficient fruit flavor, and this is not the sense in which spiritueux is employed here.
24	I follow here and throughout the work the practice of standardizing and modernizing the spelling of the different crus. Where an author makes a particular point of the differences in spelling (as happens several times in Courtépée), I have left the original orthography.
25	The Clos de Prémeaux is an interesting reference. There are no less than eight today: the Clos des Forêts Saint-Georges, the Clos des Corvées, Clos des Corvées Pagets, the Clos Saint-Marc, the Clos des Grandes Vignes, the Clos des Argillières, the Clos de l'Arlot, and the Clos de la Maréchale. Morelot, however, speaks of a Clos constituted "between Prémeaux and Comblanchien" that was assembled by a wealthy landowner. He intimates that the entirety of it is worth more than the sum of its parts, and describes it as "about 20 ha". From this we can infer that this was roughly the same area that is today the Clos de l'Arlot and what is called today the Clos de la Maréchale (formerly the Clos des Fourches), since Lavalle indicated that the Clos de Fourches was 15 ha 20 a 25 ca, while the Clos de l'Arlot was equivalent to 7 ha 73 a 45 ca.
26	Today Les Plures, part of Volnay Santenots located in the commune of Meursault as are Les Santenots du Milieu, Les Santenots Blancs, and Les Santenots Dessous
27	Located between Volnay Santenots and the commune of Volnay proper
28	Clos de la Perrière
29	Here Jullien must mean the vineyard called today Combettes. It lies in the village of Puligny and borders Meursault Charmes to the south.
30	English chemist and author of Researches, Chemical and Philosophical (1778 – 1829)
31	Today we call the coloring matter in grapes anthocyanin

32	Morelot means this as a separate category; his classification is thus: Tête de cuvée Première cuvée Bonne cuvée Cuvée ronde Passe-tout-grains Gamay
33	Lit., the slope behind; now known as the Haut Côte (de Beaune or de Nuits)
34	Gypsum or calcium sulfate
35	The steep slope, located closer to home than many vineyards further down the Côte, was traditionally harvested by by women, who inadvertently displayed more than intended as they worked their way up the hill.
36	Lit: back country: those vineyards located on slopes behind the main face of the Côte d'Or
37	Legally today, Bourgogne Grand Ordinaire is may include the César and Tressot grapes as well as Pinot Noir and Gamay. It is not clear if this is the understanding of Dr. Lavalle, or if he means the term to indicate more generally everyday table wine of good quality. Further on, Lavalle speaks of ordinaire bourgeois and ordinaire de prince, and we should understand these as gradations of quality within the category of everyday wine.
38	Tête de cuvée is a term used by Lavalle which he uses to indicate the highest level of his esteem.
39	Wine made from concentrated must
40	A Cathedral Chapter (Chapitre) is a body of canons whose purpose is to assist the bishop in the governance of the diocese.
41	I adopt henceforth the nomenclature of Lavalle in the naming of the villages. While Gevrey had already appended the name of Chambertin, most of the other villages had not.
42	The livre estevenant was a silver coin struck by the archbishop of Besançon in the Middle Ages, also known under as estievenant et estevenois, it was equivalent at one time of the gold florin.
43	Morelot is of course wrong in the size of Chambertin and the location of the Clos de Bèze, as Lavalle points out twenty years later.
44	As noted above, it is best for us to adopt Lavalle's system directly without translation for the sake of simplicity. This does not, however, prevent us from understanding it. Tête de cuvée (lit. the head of the blend) is the top wine produced in a given area. Lavalle uses the word finage, and this normally corresponds to the village limits, although sometimes to the limits of the growing area commonly labeled with the name. I translate as "village" throughout. Première, deuxième, and troisième cuvée are the first, second and third rank after the tête de cuvée.

Lavalle also labels them "vin de dessert", "vin d'entre-mets" and "grand ordinaire" respectively. "Dessert" included both savory and sweet courses in the middle ages; in Lavalle's day it included the cheese course as well.

"Entre-mets" [spelled entremets today] is litreally something taken "between courses". In the 13th century, it referred to what we would call side dishes, or that which accompanies a main course; by the 17th it referred to a course after the roast and before dessert "typically composed of ragouts" according to the dictionary of the Academie Française in 1694. By Lavalle's day it could include sweet or savory courses; the Littré dictionary defines it as "pastries, eggs, fried dishes, salads, etc." Grand Ordinaire is wine for daily consumption, but of a good quality.

45	Jules Ouvrard (1798 – 1861), son of Gabriel-Julien Ouvrard, financier at the time of Napoleon. Ouvrard was one of the most important landowners in Burgundy in the 19th century, owning at one time the Clos Vougeot, Romanée-Conti, Corton Clos du Roi and large parts of Chambertin, Clos de Bèze and others.
46	Tierce: the right of a feudal lord to one-third of the produce of a piece of property
47	It is rumored in some quarters that the Ouvrard family came into possession of its vineyard property following questionable dealings during the Napoleonic wars.
48	Henri Vienne, born in 1771 in Dijon was an archivist who researched and wrote on Nuits and Gevrey as well as Toulon.
49	Almshouse
50	Proclamations regarding the harvest, including the date.
51	As noted above, this means extraordinary. As we will see, Lavalle changes his terminology slightly throughout the work. While discussing Gevrey, we see « tête de cuvée, cru hors ligne, vin extra » all on one line and one thus infers that the three terms are equal. In discussing Vougeot, however, we have « hors ligne » without any other mention. We will note in the final chapter of this section in Lavalle that he has « vins hors ligne » subdivided further, into tête de cuvée no 1 and tête de cuvée no 2, with tête de cuvée no 1 subtly subdivided again, with the following wines in this (non-alphabetic) order: Romanée-Conti, Clos de Vougeot, Chambertin and Clos de Bèze, followed by the words "coming next:" and then a further list in alphabetical order. One assumes that Lavalle means to place the Clos de Vougeot directly after Romanée-Conti in his pantheon of the great wines of Burgundy.
52	This climat appears in Lavalle and Danguy et Aubertin, but it has disappeared from Rodier and is not included in our modern list of lieux-dits. As Lavalle has not indicated the size, it is difficult to determine which climat has absorbed it. There are two small parcels between the walls of the Clos de Vougeot and the road that borders Les Grands Échézeaux, although the size of Grands Échézeaux is the same in Lavalle and Rodier, making this assumption difficult to sustain.

	53	La Ligue Catholique (the Catholic League or Holy League) was a destabilizing force in French politics in the late 16th century. Begun in Picardy in 1568, it was an alliance of forces led by the clergy in reaction to increasing tolerance of Protestants. For forty years the relative powers and importance of the Sovereign, the Pope, and the États Généraux (the assemblies of the clergy, the nobility, and the bourgeoisie created in 1302) was passionately debated. This sentiment came to a head in 1610, when Henri IV was assassinated by a fanatical catholic. During this time, Burgundy was seen as a center of anti-monarchial sentiment.
	54	Lit. "goods of the nation", Biens nationaux were properties of the church or of wealthy individuals who had fled the Revolution by emigrating that sold off during the Revolution to little profit for the fledgling state.
	55	Olney, op. cit.
	56	"Moelleux" is a word often seen in French tasting notes that can be confusing to Anglophone readers, since it can mean sweet. It is sometimes translated as "mellow", but that is not a very fashionable term today, although we retain it here. A full explanation of "moelleux" according to the Petit Robert dictionary is that it is "sweet or soft to the touch; a place where one sinks in comfortably (v. élastique); agreeable to the palate or taste; unctuous or savory…"
	57	July 6th, 1794
	58	Jancis Robinson et. al. note in their admirable 2012 work Wine Grapes that "Chardonnay was confused with Pinot Blanc until the end of the nineteenth century due to their morphological similarities".
	59	Bousselots
	60	Les Chaliots, now in village
	61	Now split into La Charmotte and La Petite Charmotte
	62	Now simply Les Chaliots, bordering Les Brulées to the south
	63	All of these are today village appellation
	64	The wines of Premeaux are today included with those of Nuits
	65	Dr. Lavalle does not quote the story of Charlemagne's gift to the church of Autun, perhaps believing it to be apocryphal.
	66	These few parcels are today classified as Côte de Nuits Villages.
	67	Ladoix
	68	Compagnie des chemins de fer de Paris à Lyon et à la Méditerranée
	69	This chapel, whose construction began in the 11th century, is one of the important landmarks in Ladoix.
	70	Much of Rognet et Corton (as we spell it today) is now classed in grand cru: 8 ha 57 a 96 ca, as opposed to 79 a 75 ca that is in premier cru Ladoix for white wine. The same parcel is classified as village for red wines
	71	Instead of half as was more common.

72	A play on words "de Migieu" [the name of a local leader] / "demi-dieu" [demi-god]
73	nourrissans, théologiques et morbifuges
74	Given in the chapter on Courtépée
75	According to Gibbon's Decline and Fall of the Roman Empire, "In the beginning of the fourth century, the orator Eumenius (Panegyr. Veter. viii edit. Delphin.) speaks of the vines of the territory of Autun, which were decayed through age, and the first plantation of which was unknown. The Pagus Aregrignus is supposed by M. de Anville to be the district of Beaune, celebrated, even at present for one of the first growths of Burgundy," cited by Lavalle as "Eumène, Discours d'actions de graces à Constantin, au nom des habitants de Flavie".
76	Loyaux, vermeil et marchands
77	Wine made by drying the bunches on straw mats to concentrate the juice
78	"Point de beau temps que La Cave ne jette"
79	In addition to Caillerets and Champans, Lavalle includes En Chevret, En Fremiers, En Bouze d'Or, Les Angles / Point d'Angles, La Barre, Carelle-sur-Chapelle / Rougiots, En L'Ormeau, and Les Mitans as têtes de cuvées.
80	Map of villages that produce the great wines of the Côte d'Or
81	œil de perdrix
82	For the work of the vines in the domaine
83	Montrachet proper; as distinct from Chevalier or Bâtard or Bienvenues-Bâtard
84	The écu soleil was minted by Louis XI, so called because of the design of a sun on the coin.
85	Lavalle here discusses the village known today as Dezize-lès-Maranges or just Maranges, and not the village known today as Decize, a Gallo-Roman city on the Loire Valley, located in the départment of the Nièvre. Dezize-lès-Maranges is located just outside of the Côte d'Or department in the department of Saône-et-Loire, but it is considered to be part of the Côte de Beaune in winemaking terms
86	Jacques Duret, doctor and botanist, was the mayor of Nuits-Saint-Georges from 1835 – 1869.
87	Note the difference here between Jullien's definition and modern English usage: it does not mean "finish" in the sense of the final sensation a wine produces after swallowing or spitting, which in French is called "arrière-gout"
88	The first sense of "Franc" in French is "honest" or "straightforward", although "honest aroma" doesn't convey the sense of "franc de gout" very well.
89	"I require [a wine] generous and soft"
90	Which we take to be separate from an "earthy" flavor, which is not necessarily unique to any one terroir; this term means the unique characteristics of each wine communicated by the place in which it is produced.

91	The term is employed in our phrase "grainy tannins", thus the adjective grip. The Dictionnaire Général de la Langue Française defines grain (among other senses) as « Aspérité grenue d'une surface » or « grainy roughness of a surface ».
92	Moelle, lit. "marrow" is a noun in French: a wine "a de la moelle" lit. "has marrow"; the best sense or at least the most common translation in English is the adjective "mellow"; it might be more accurate to say the wine is "fruity without being sweet"
93	The poids de marc is a system of weights and measure used under the ancien régime from the 14th century onward. The poids de marc are defined by a system of balance weights called la pile dite de Charlemagne, a series of baskets that fit one inside of the next, weighing a total of 12.25 K or 25 pounds.
94	From a fairly uniform system in place until the 9th century, units of measure in Europe began to change around the time of Charlemagne. The standard unit of liquid measure is the pint, which was equivalent to 1/36 of the unit known as a cubic foot known as the king's foot or the "pied-du-roi"; the English pint is equivalent to 1/50th of an English cubic foot, and an American pint is equivalent to 1/60th of an English cubic foot. The volume of a cubic foot in antiquity was known as an amphora

Name of Measure	Pints	Pouce Cubes	Modern Equivalent
Pouce	1/48	1	1.98 cl
Roquille	1/32	1.5	2.98 cl
Posson (Poisson)	1/8	6	11.90 cl
Demiard	$\frac{1}{4}$	12	23.80 cl
Chopine	$\frac{1}{2}$	24	47.61 cl
Pinte	1	48	0.96 lit
Quade	2	96	1.90 lit
Velte	8	384	7.62 lit
Pied Cube	36	1x1,728	34.28 lit
Quartaut	72	2x1,728	68.56 lit
Feuillette	144	4x1,728	137.11 lit
Muid	288	8x1,728	274.22 lit
Pipe	432	12x1,728	411.33 lit

95	These units of measure will be adopted without translation apart from this glossary
96	The definition of a journal is "the amount that can be worked in one day", which would seem variable, but is is assigned a specific value here, 34.284 ares, or roughly a third of a hectare (and an are is 100 square meters). This term is used fairly frequently in discussing wine, particularly in Burgundy.
97	The definition of an ouvrée is similar to a journal, "the amount that can be hoed by a vine grower in a day", which would seem redundant and also quite variable, but it is assigned the specific amount of 4.285 ares. The term ouvrée is used throughout the text.

98 Of all the units of measure, the most important to remember are the queue (two barrels today) and the tonneaux (one barrel), also known as a muid, poinçon or pièce, and perhaps the feuillette, a half barrel.

99 The livre tournois was both a type of currency and a monetary unit used in accounting from the middle ages nearly until modern times. It was used throughout France from the time of Philip II at the beginning of the 13th century. The livre was divided into 20 sols (or sous) as it had been since the time of Charlemagne; the sous was divided into 12 derniers. The word franc was used for a coin worth one livre tournois that was minted from the 14th through the 17th century, while in the 18th century, the word livre was reserved for the unit of account and for its representation in paper money.

At various times currencies as diverse as the écu, the Louis, the teston d'argent, the double, the Spanish doubloon, pistole, real; the Italian florin, ducat or sequin; the German and Austrian thaler and the Dutch gulden were all in use and their values were often changed by royal proclamation to serve various political or military purposes. The difficulty in fixing the value of these currencies relates to the differences in weight, purity and quality of the coins themselves, which is why the livre tournois was used as an accounting measure but not exactly equivalent to the circulating currency itself, and gradually the livre and the franc began to denote different amounts of money.

For us today, the text of the treaty for the sale of Louisiana to the United States in 1803 provides a helpful benchmark because it fixed the value as follow:

"It is agreed that the Dollar of the United States Specified in the present Convention shall be fixed at five francs 3333/100000 or five livres eight Sous tournois."

According to the consumer price index, a dollar of this period was worth slightly more than fifteen of today's dollars, and thus a French franc of the period was worth roughly three of today's U.S. dollars and a livre tournois was worth slightly less than this.

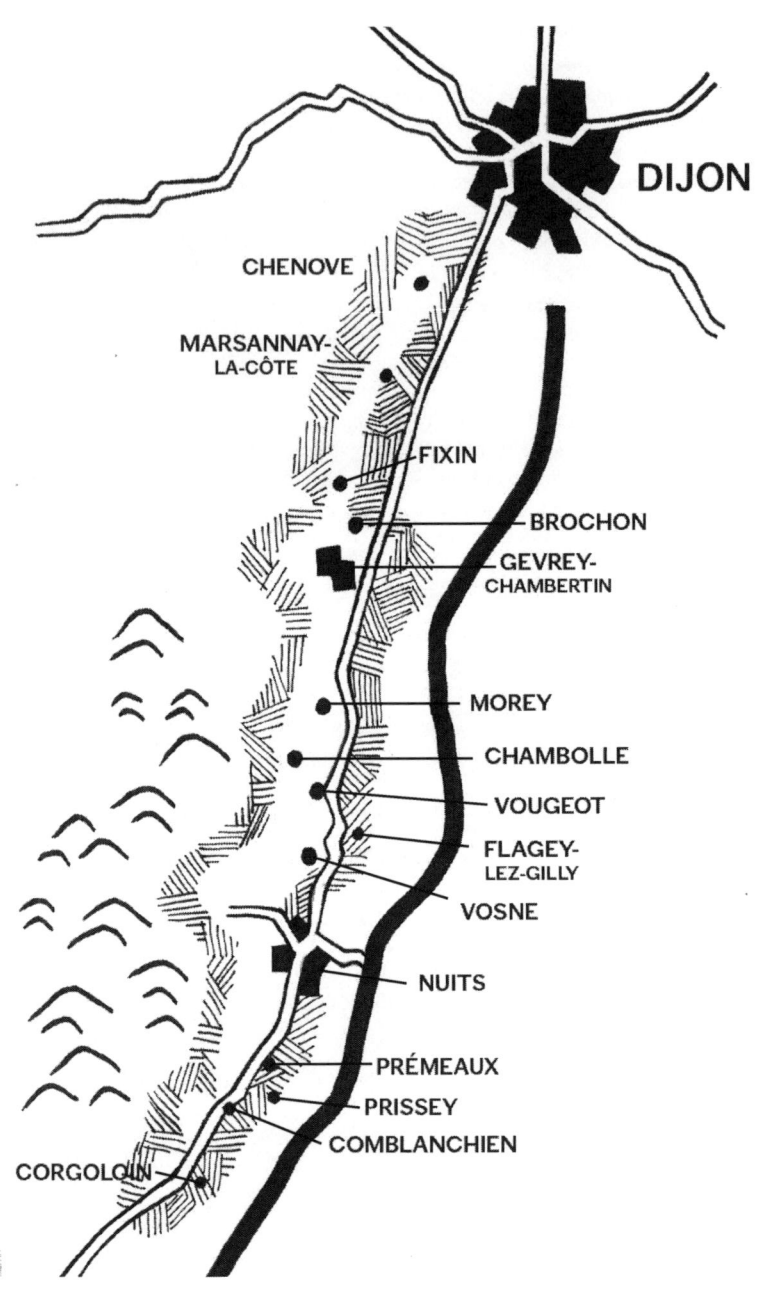

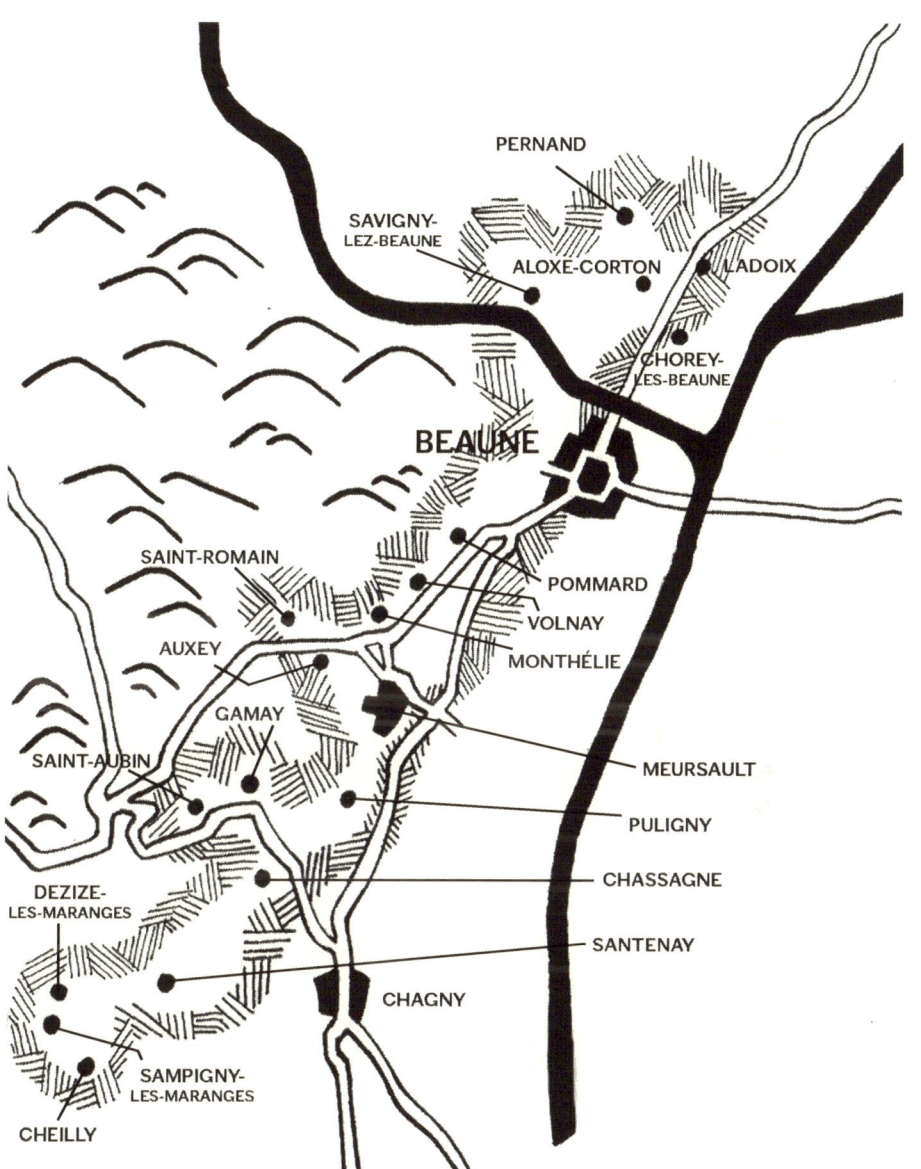

• INDEX •

A

Acerbe / Acerbic (tasting term), definition : 235
Aligoté : 52
Alix de Vergy : 66, 73, 98, 132
Aloxe : 17, 19, 31, 159, 224
Aloxe-Corton, Boulmeau : 163
Aloxe-Corton, En Toppe [Tope] Marteneau : 163
Aloxe-Corton, La Boulotte : 164
Aloxe-Corton, Les [En] Caillette : 164
Aloxe-Corton, Les Brunette et Planchots [Planchots] : 163
Aloxe-Corton, Les Chaillots : 163
Aloxe-Corton, Les Citernes : 164
Aloxe-Corton, Les Combes : 163
Aloxe-Corton, Les Crapousuets [Chapousuets] : 164
Aloxe-Corton, Les Cras : 164
Aloxe-Corton, Les Fournières : 163
Aloxe-Corton, Les Genevrières : 163
Aloxe-Corton, Les Genevrièress et le Suchots : 163
Aloxe-Corton, Les Guérets : 163
Aloxe-Corton, Les Paulands [En Poland] : 163
Aloxe-Corton, Les Petits-Vercots : 164
Aloxe-Corton, Les Vercots : 163
Ampeau, Domaine Robert : 206
Appellation, definition : xi
Apre (tasting term), definition: 235
Arbues [Meursault] : 206
Arcenant : 45
Arcenant, plant d' [Gamay] : 51
Amalgaire d'Arenberg : 66, 85
Armand, Domaine du Comte : 190
Arnoux, Claude: 16 – 19
Arome (tasting term), definition : 235
Arome spiritueux (tasting term), definition : 235
Aubrain [Monthélie] : 199
Aux Crais [Chambolle] : vin
Aux Forêts [Nuits] : 147
Aux Fosses [Chambolle] : 108

Aux Jachées [Vosne-Romanée] : 135
Aux Meix-Grands [Prémeaux] : 148
Aux Pagets [Nuits] : 148
Aux Tapones [Prémeaux] : 148
Auxey : 18, 21

B

Bahèzre, Maison Henri de : 61
Bart, Domaine : 84
Bas du Chapitre [Chenôve] : 73
Bas du Clos [Chenôve] : 67
Bas de Côte-Rôtie [Morey] : 104
Bataillière, Clos de la [Savigny Les Vergelesses] : 170
Bâtard Montrachet : 34, 46, 207, 209, 214, 224, 233
Baudes Basses [Clos de Vougeot] : 112
Baudes Hautes [Clos de Vougeot] : 112
Baudes-Saint-Martin [Clos de Vougeot] : 111-112
Beaune : 16, 20, 30, 44, 176, 224
Beaune tonneau (barrel size), definition : 243
Beaune, Aigrots [Aigue] : 180, 182, 186
Beaune, Aux Coucherias : 180, 182
Beaune, Avaux [Avots] : 180
Beaune, Belissart : 181, 182
Beaune, Blanches Fleurs : 180, 182
Beaune, Bouche-de-Lièvre : 182
Beaune, Boucherottes : 180, 186
Beaune, Champs Pimonts : 176, 179, 186
Beaune, Clos de Bouache [Clos du Roi] : 183
Beaune, Clos de la Mousse : 177, 180, 182
Beaune, Clos des Mouches : 30, 180, 186, 231
Beaune, Clos du Roi : 17, 30, 177, 180, 231
Beaune, Champagne de Savigny : 181
Beaune, La Creusotte : 180
Beaune, La Maladière : 181
Beaune, La Mignotte : 180
Beaune, La Montée Rouge : 17
Beaune, Le Bas des Teurons : 181
Beaune, Le Chardonnereaux : 181

Beaune, Les Cent Vignes [Sanvignes Hautes et Basses] : 177, 180, 182

Beaune, Les Chilènes [Chelènes] : 181

Beaune, Les Chouacheux : 181

Beaune, Les Cras [Crée, Aux Crais] : 17, 30, 176-177, 179, 182, 231

Beaune, Les Epenotes : 182

Beaune, Les Fèves : 17, 30, 44, 60, 176-177, 179, 224, 227

Beaune, Les Grèves : 17, 30, 44, 60, 176-177, 179, 182, 224, 227

Beaune, Les Grèves Vigne de l'Enfant-Jésus : 179, 183

Beaune, Les Levées et les Piroles [Les Pirotes] : 181

Beaune, Les Mariages : 181

Beaune, Les Marconnets : 17, 179, 182

Beaune, Les Montrevenots [Montrevenets] : 180

Beaune, Les Paules [Epaules] : 181

Beaune, Les Peneottes : 181

Beaune, Les Perrières: 177, 182

Beaune, Les Pertuisots : 181

Beaune, Les Prévoles [Prevolles] : 181

Beaune, Les Reversés : 180

Beaune, Les Rôles : 181

Beaune, Les Sceaux : 181

Beaune, Les Sizies : 181, 186

Beaune, Les Toussaints : 180

Beaune, Les Teurons : 180, 182

Beaune, Les Tuvilains : 181, 182

Beaune, Les Vérottes : 181

Beaune, Les Vignes Franches : 180

Beaux-Monts-Bas, Les [Flagey] : 125

Béguillet, Edme : 19

Belles-Côtes, Les [Meursault] : 204

Bernstein, Olivier : 183

Bertall, Charles-Albert Arnoux: 59

Bertall, Classification of Burgundy wines : 60-61

Bertrand du Guesclin : 55

Bévy, plant de [Gamay] : 51

Bèze, Clos de : 21, 44, 85, 88, 93, 97, 223, 225

Bienvenues-Bâtard-Montrachet : 207

Bieveaux [Bieveau] : 220

Bize, Domaine Simon : 175

Blagny, Blagny-Blanc : 31, 34, 46, 200, 207, 209, 210

Blain, Jean-Marc : 218

Blain-Gagnard, Domaine : 218

Blanc (monetary unit), definition : 243

Bligny-sous-Beaune : 46

Blochet, Jacques Marie Duvault : 219

Body (tasting term), definition : 236

Bois de Charmois : 139

Bois de Chenôve : 170

Bois de Noël : 170

Bois de Villars-Fontaine : 139

Bonneau du Martray : 169

Bonnes-Mares : 29, 30, 98, 101, 102, 107, 108, 109, 227

Bouchard Père et Fils : 169, 183, 213

Boucherettes [Chassagne-Montrachet] : 214

Bouches, Les [Beaune] : 181

Bouchots, Les [Morey] : 100, 104

Bouchu, Claude : 15

Boudot, Gérard : 212

Bouquet (tasting term), definition : 235

Bourgneuf : 31

Bourgogne Le Chapitre [Chenôve]: 31, 66, 73, 74, 230

Bourgogne Montrecul : 66

Bourru (tasting term), definition : 235

Bouzeron : 35

Brochon : 32, 67

Bruno Clair, Domaine : 84

Brussanes, Les [Santenay] : 221

Buisson : 154, 156

Bussières, Jean de : 22

Buxy : 33

Buxy, Côte de : 35

C

C. Loc, definition : 59

Calouères : 104

Carillon, Domaine Louis : 213

Carillon, Jacques : 213
Cask (winemaking term), definition : 241
Cathiard, Sylvain : 138
Cervottes : 153
Chabiots, Les [Morey] : 99, 103
Chablis : 51
Chaffots, Le Bas de [Morey] : 99, 104
Chai (winemaking term), definition : 235
Châlonnaise, Côte : 28
Chambertin : 18, 20, 28, 37, 44, 85, 88, 93, 97, 223, 225
Chambertin, Grand : 85
Chambertin, Petit : 85
Chambolle : 21, 28, 30, 224
Chambolle-Musigny, Beaux Bruns : 108, 110
Chambolle-Musigny, Clos de l'Orme : 108, 110
Chambolle-Musigny, Combe d'Orveau, La : 107, 110
Chambolle-Musigny, Derrière la Grange : 110
Chambolle-Musigny, Derrière le Four : 110
Chambolle-Musigny, Feusselottes [Fisselottes] : 110
Chambolle-Musigny, Fouchères : 110
Chambolle-Musigny, Les Amoureuses : 44, 108, 230
Chambolle-Musigny, Les Argillières : 108
Chambolle-Musigny, Les Babillères [Babillers] : 108
Chambolle-Musigny, Les Baudes : 110
Chambolle-Musigny, Les Charmes : 108, 110
Chambolle-Musigny, Les Chatelots : 110
Chambolle-Musigny, Les Condemennes [Condemènes] : 110
Chambolle-Musigny, Les Cras : 107, 110
Chambolle-Musigny, Les Echesaux [Eschezeaux] : 110
Chambolle-Musigny, Les Fremières : 110
Chambolle-Musigny, Les Fuées : 107, 108, 109
Chambolle-Musigny, Les Gruenchers [Gruanchets] : 108
Chambolle-Musigny, Les Hauts Doix [Douais] : 108, 110
Chambolle-Musigny, Les Noirots : 108
Chambolle-Musigny, Les Plantes : 110
Chambolle-Musigny, Les Sentiers : 110
Chambolle-Musigny, Les Sordes : 108
Chambolle-Musigny, Les Véroilles : 29, 98, 107, 108, 109
Chambolle-Musigny, Les Groseilles : 110

Chambon, Jacques : 129
Champ-de-Perdrix, En [Dijon] : 73
Champs Traversins [Flagey] : 122
Champs Traversins, Les [Flagey] : 124
Champy, Maison : 98
Chapelle, En La [Gevrey] : 86
Chapelle, Grande [Gevrey] : 92
Chapelle-Chambertin : 30, 85, 87, 88, 230
Charlemagne, Le : 151, 153, 161, 166-167, 225, 233
Charmes (bas) [Gevrey] : 91
Charmes-Chambertin : 85-86, 92
Charmes-hauts [Gevrey] : 90
Charnu (tasting term), definition: 235
Charron, Les [Meursault] : 205, 206
Chassagne : 17, 21, 30, 214
Chassagne-Montrachet, Blanchot [B. Dessus, Dessous; Bauchot] : 217
Chassagne-Montrachet, Champ de Morjot [Morgeot] 217
Chassagne-Montrachet, Clos Devant : 217
Chassagne-Montrachet, Clos Pitois : 60, 214, 216, 223, 231
Chassagne-Montrachet, Clos Saint Jean : 29, 60, 214, 216, 217, 223, 229
Chassagne-Montrachet, En [Les] Caillerets : 216
Chassagne-Montrachet, En Voillenot-Dessous : 217
Chassagne-Montrachet, Fontaine Sot : 217
Chassagne-Montrachet, La Boudriotte : 214, 216, 231
Chassagne-Montrachet, La Goujonne : 216
Chassagne-Montrachet, La Platière : 217
Chassagne-Montrachet, Les Benoîtes : 217
Chassagne-Montrachet, Les Brussonnes [Brussanes] : 214, 216, 219
Chassagne-Montrachet, Les Champs-Gains [Changains] : 214, 216
Chassagne-Montrachet, Les Charrières [Carrières] : 217
Chassagne-Montrachet, Les Chaumes [Chaumées] : 217
Chassagne-Montrachet, Les Chenevottes : 216
Chassagne-Montrachet, Les Concis [Concie] des Champs : 217

Chassagne-Montrachet, Les Houillères : 217
Chassagne-Montrachet, Les Macherelles : 216
Chassagne-Montrachet, Les Vergers : 216
Chassagne-Montrachet, Maltroie : 29, 214, 216, 231
Chassagne-Montrachet, Morgeot [Clos Morgeot] : 21, 29, 44, 214, 224, 227
Chassagne-Montrachet, Puits Merdreaux : 217
Châtillonnais : 51
Châtillon-sur-Seine : 33
Chausseneuz : 23
Chauvenet : 98
Chenôve : 22, 30, 33, 66, 73
Chenevary [Chenôve] : 73, 74
Chevalier Montrachet : 33-34, 46, 207, 209, 210, 214, 233
Chewy (tasting term), definition : 240
Chioures [Vougeot] : 111-112
Chorey : 45
Cinq Journaux, Clos de : 128
Cîteaux, Abbaye de : 18
Clair-Daü, Domaine : 84
Classification of vineyards, Lavalle : 88
Clermont-Montoison, baron de Chagny, Jean-François Antoine de : 219
Clos Blanc [Morey] : 101
Clos de Monthélie [Meursault] : 205
Clos des Ruchottes : see Ruchottes, Clos des
Clos du Meix [Puligny-Montrachet, Les Pucelles] : 211, 212
Clos des Lambrays : see Lambreys, Clos des
Clos Perron [Meursault] : 206
Clos de Tart : see Tart, Clos de
Clos de Vougeot : see Vougeot, Clos de
Closed (tasting term), definition : 237
Clou Rotam [Chassagne-Montrachet] : 217
Coche-Dury, Domaine : 152, 168, 206
Coffin, Charles : 23, 56
Colbert, Jean-Baptiste : 15
Colin, Domaine Bruno : 218
Colin, Domaine Marc : 218

Colin, Philippe : 218
Colin-Deléger, Michel : 218
Colin-Morey, Domaine Pierre-Yves : 218
Coller (winemaking term), definition : 236
Comblanchien : 45
Comblanchien : 154
Comité d'Agriculture de Beaune : 48
Constantine the Great, Emperor : 22
Conti, Louis-François Bourbon, Prince de : 128
Coque, Jean et Guy : 165
Corbeaux, Les [Gevrey] : 85
Corgoloin : 154
Corps (tasting term), definition : 236
Corton Basses Mourottes [Mourolles] : 150, 157, 158
Corton Clos des Cortons Faiveley : 150
Corton Clos du Roi : 151, 160, 231
Corton Hautes Mourottes : 150, 158
Corton La Toppe [Tope] au Vert : 151, 158
Corton La Vigne au Saint : 151, 163
Corton Le Meix Lallemand [Les Meix] : 151, 162
Corton Le Rognet [Roguet] et Corton : 150, 157
Corton Les Bressandes : 150-151, 153, 161, 231
Corton Les Carrières : 151, 157
Corton Les Chaumes : 161
Corton Les Combes : 151
Corton Les Fiètres : 151, 162
Corton Les Grandes Lolières : 151, 157, 158
Corton Les Grèves : 151, 162
Corton Les Languettes : 151, 162
Corton Les Maréchaudes : 150-151
Corton Les Moutottes : 151
Corton Les Paulands : 164
Corton Les Perrières : 151, 162
Corton Les Pougets : 151, 162
Corton Les Vergennes : 150, 158
Corton Renardes : 150-151, 153, 160, 231
Corton, Le Corton : 21, 29, 37, 44, 150, 158, 160, 223, 224, 227, 233
Côte de Nuits Villages, Croix-Violette [Brochon] : 83
Côte de Nuits Villages, Mazières [Brochon] : 83

Côte de Nuits Villages, Vignois [Brochon] : 83
Côteaux Bourguignons : 85, 201
Côtes de Nuits-Villages, Au Leurrey [Aux Leurrées] [Prémeaux] : 148
Côtes de Nuits-Villages, Aux Fauques : 154
Côtes de Nuits-Villages, Aux Langres : 155
Côtes de Nuits-Villages, Aux Montagnes : 154
Côtes de Nuits-Villages, En La Botte : 155
Côtes de Nuits-Villages, En Saint-Seine : 155
Côtes de Nuits-Villages, En Virevelle : 155
Côtes de Nuits-Villages, Le Clos de Langres : 155
Côtes de Nuits-Villages, Les [Aux] Grandes-Vignes 154
Côtes de Nuits-Villages, Les [Aux] Retraits : 154
Côtes de Nuits-Villages, Les Chaillots [Ez Chaillots] 155
Côtes de Nuits-Villages, Les Monts de Boncourt : 155
Couchey : 46, 67, 68, 75
Coullontey [Chassagne-Montrachet] : 217
Courcelles-les-Arts : 46
Courtépée, Claude : 19
Courton, En : 165
Coutoux, Michel : 218
Crais, Les [Monthélie] : 199
Cray [Chassagne-Montrachet] : 217
Creben [Meursault] : 205
Crébillon [Brochon] : 68, 83
Creux-Prieur [Chambolle] : 108
Criots-Bâtard-Montrachet : 207, 214
Croix-de-Pierre [Savigny] : 171
Cru (tasting term), definition : 236
Cru (vineyard term), definition : x
Cru hors ligne, definition : 70
Cruots ou Vignes Blanches, Les [Flagey] : 122
Cussy, Ferdinand de Cornot, (baron de) : 56
Cuvée, definition : xi, 236

D

Dancer, Domaine Vincent : 218
de Blaisy, Ponce : 132
de Bronzy, Cardinal : 24
de Chauvigny, Boillerault : 213
de Colleryre, Roger : 23
de Croonembourg, Philippe : 98, 135
de la Boutière, Charles : 219
de Lamonnoye, Bernard : 95
de Mérode, Prince Florent Domaine : 168
de Migieu, Abraham-Guy : 170
de Mipont, Jean : 217
de Montille, Domaine : 199
de Mont-Saint-Jean, Marie : 105
de Perrières, François : 212
de Salins, Huges : 23
de Saulx, Gaspard, sieur de Tavannes : 98
de Vellemont, Jean Claude Nicolas Perreney [Grosbois de Vellement] : 94
de Villaine, Edmond Gaudin : 129
Debroles, Les [Meursault] : 204
Defère, Nicolas : 137
Delagrange-Bachelet, Domaine Edmond : 218
Delarue : 49
Délicat (tasting term), definition : 236
Demi-queue (barrel size) : 35
Dernier (monetary unit), definition : 243
Derrière-le-Four [Meursault] : 206
d'Eugenie, Domaine : 121, 125
Deuxièmes cuvées, Rodier's definition : 63
Dezize-lès-Maranges: 220
Dijon : 18, 20, 31, 66, 72
Dijon pint (measure of volume), definition : 243
Dix-Journaux [Vougeot] : 111-112
Dojon, Etienne : 98
Dolles, Les : 153
Dom Gobelet : 56
Domaine, François : 212
Domitian : 21

Douhe [Chassagne-Montrachet] : 217
Droit en gout (tasting term), definition : 236
Drouhin, Joseph : 183
Dugat-Py, Domaine : 97
Dujac, Domaine   105 : 138
Dumaguer, Charles : 105
Dumaine, Charles : 98
Dur (tasting term), definition : 237
Durand, Joseph : 129
Duvault-Blochet : 131

E

Echaillons, Ez [Dijon] : 73
Echanges, Aux [Vosne] : 128
Echézeaux : 29, 122, 132, 224, 227
Échézeaux [Eschezeaux] du Dessus [Flagey] : 122, 124
Eduens : 21
Émine (measure of volume), definition : 243
Engel, Domaine René : 121
Engrogne (monetary unit), definition : 243
Epinards [Brochon] : 83
Erasmus : 23, 55
Es Cloux Perrons [Meursault] : 204
Es Follatières : 211
Es Grands Perrons [Meursault] : 204
Estroy : 31
Etoile, Clos de l' [Chenôve] : 67
Eudes III de Bourgogne : 73
Eudes IV de Bourgogne : 66
Eumenius : 21, 55

F

Fagon, Dr. : 23, 56
Faiveley, Domaine Joseph : 169
Ferme (tasting term), definition : 237
Feuillette : 35
Fichet, Domaine Jean-Philippe : 206
Fin (tasting term), definition: 237

Finesse (tasting term), definition : 237
Finir (tasting term), definition : 237
Finish (tasting term), definition : 235
Fixey : 32, 45, 68, 70, 75
Fixin : 32, 45, 68, 70
Fixin, Arvelets : 71, 75, 80
Fixin, Aux Cheusots : 71
Fixin, Champ-Perdrix : 76
Fixin, Champs Pennebau [Champennebau] : 76
Fixin, Clémenfert [Clémofert] : 77
Fixin, Clos de la Perrière : 68, 71, 78, 224, 226
Fixin, Clos du Chapitre : 46, 68, 70, 79
Fixin, Clos Napoléon : 71, 80
Fixin, Closmée : 81
Fixin, Crais-de-Chêne : 77
Fixin, Echéseaux : 80
Fixin, En Suchot : 71
Fixin, Hervelets : 71
Fixin, La Croix-Blanche : 81
Fixin, La Mazière : 75
Fixin, La Place : 77
Fixin, Le Champ des Arrêts : 77
Fixin, Le Clos : 76
Fixin, Le Pothey : 77
Fixin, Le Rozier : 76
Fixin, Le Tremble : 80
Fixin, Les Clos : 76
Fixin, Les Crais : 81
Fixin, Les Echalais : 76
Fixin, Les Entre-Deux-Velles : 81
Fixin, Les Foussottes : 76
Fixin, Les Herbues : 77
Fixin, Les Hervelets : 71, 84
Fixin, Les Meix Bas : 71
Fixin, Les Mogottes : 76
Fixin, Les Ormeaux : 80
Fixin, Les Petits-Crais : 77
Fixin, Meix Trouhant [Meix-Tournant] : 76
Fixin, Queue de Hareng [Brochon] : 71
Fixin, Tabeillon [Tabellion] : 77

Flagey-lez-Gilly : 122, 224
Flat (tasting term), definition : 240
Flavigny : 33
Fleshy (tasting term), definition : 235
Foible (tasting term), definition : 237
Fontaine : 45
Fontaine, Richard : 218
Fontaine d'Ouche [Dijon] : 73
Fontaine Froide : 172
Fontaine-Gagnard, Domaine : 218
Forge, La [Chassagne-Montrachet] : 217
Forges, climat des [Morey] : 98
Fortify (winemaking term), definition : 242
Fourrier, Domaine : 97
Four-square (tasting term), definition : 238
Fourches, Clos de : see Nuits-Saint-Georges Clos de la Maréchale
Franc (monetary unit), definition : 243
Franc de Gout (tasting term), definition : 237
Franc de Qualité (tasting term), definition : 237
Fremières, Les [Morey] : 99, 103
Froichots, Les [Morey] : 99, 104
Fumeux (tasting term), definition : 237
Fut (tasting term), definition : 238
Fut (winemaking term), definition : 238

G

Gagnard, Domaine Jean-Noël : 218
Gagnard, Jacques : 218
Gamay (grape) : 24, 45, 51-52
Gamay (village) : 208, 215
Gambal, Alex : 183
Gandelot, Abbé Antoine-Louis: 21
Garenne [Vougeot] : 111-112
Garnier, Joseph : 49
Gaule Narbonnoise : 21
Gaunoux, Domaine Michel : 190
Gémeaux, Les [Gevrey] : 86, 91, 97
Généreux (tasting term), definition : 238

Generous (tasting term), definition : 238
Genevrières Dessus [Meursault] : 204
Gevrey : 28, 30, 88, 224
Gevrey-Chambertin [En] Champs [Brochon] : 83, 92, 97
Gevrey-Chambertin Aux Combottes : 97
Gevrey-Chambertin Estournelles Saint-Jacques [Etournelles] : 90, 92, 97
Gevrey-Chambertin, [Les] Tamisot[s] : 87
Gevrey-Chambertin, Au Vellé [Vellées] : 92, 97
Gevrey-Chambertin, Aux Echézeaux : 91, 97
Gevrey-Chambertin, Carougeot [Carrougeot] : 91, 97
Gevrey-Chambertin, Champeaux : 92, 97
Gevrey-Chambertin, Champerrier du Dessus : 92
Gevrey-Chambertin, Champonnet [Champonet] : 91, 97
Gevrey-Chambertin, Champ-Perrier [Brochon] : 83, 97
Gevrey-Chambertin, Charreux : 92, 97
Gevrey-Chambertin, Cherbaude : 91
Gevrey-Chambertin, Clos Prieure : 97
Gevrey-Chambertin, Clos Saint-Jacques : 30, 60, 87, 89, 92, 97, 224, 230
Gevrey-Chambertin, Clos-Prieur (haut) : 91
Gevrey-Chambertin, Clos des Varoilles [Verroilles, Véroilles] : 30, 60, 90, 224, 229
Gevrey-Chambertin, Combe au Moine : 91, 97
Gevrey-Chambertin, Combe du Dessus : 91, 97
Gevrey-Chambertin, Craipillot : 91, 97
Gevrey-Chambertin, Crais [du Dessus] : 92, 97
Gevrey-Chambertin, La [En] Bossière [Bussière] : 97
Gevrey-Chambertin, En Motrot : 92, 97
Gevrey-Chambertin, En Pallud : 97
Gevrey-Chambertin, En Songe : 92, 97
Gevrey-Chambertin, Fonteny : 91, 97
Gevrey-Chambertin, Fouchère : 89
Gevrey-Chambertin, La [En] Romanée : 97
Gevrey-Chambertin, Lavaut Saint-Jacques : 91, 97
Gevrey-Chambertin, Les Cazetiers [Castiers] : 90, 92
Gevrey-Chambertin, Les Corbeaux : 91
Gevrey-Chambertin, Les Issards : 97

Gevrey-Chambertin, Les Jeunes Rois [Royes] [Brochon] : 83
Gevrey-Chambertin, Marchais : 92, 97
Gevrey-Chambertin, Meix-des-Ouches : 91, 97
Gevrey-Chambertin, Mévelle [Meixvelle] : 91, 97
Gevrey-Chambertin, Pallut : 91
Gevrey-Chambertin, Petite Chapelle : 86, 90
Gilly-lès-Cîteaux : 111
Givrey : 32, 35
Givrey, Boichevaux : 32
Givrey, Champ Poureau : 35
Givrey, Clos Salomon : 32
Givrey, La Baraude : 32
Givrey, Le Cellier : 32
Givrey, Vignes-Rouges : 32
Godelles : 104
Godichots et Rochottes [Vosne] : 130
Gout de Terroir (tasting term), definition : 238
Gout d'Herbage (tasting term), definition : 238
Grain (tasting term), definition : 238
Grand Auxerrois : 51
Grand cru, definition : x
Grands Monts de Vignes, Les [Dijon] : 73
Grande Montagne, La [Chassagne-Montrachet] : 217
Grande Rue, La : 15, 29, 127, 130, 131-132, 134, 138, 230
Grandes Terres [Meursault] : 205
Grandes-Varoilles [Gevrey] : 95
Grand-Montrachet : 208
Grands Échézeaux : 122-123, 227
Grape blend : 27, 52
Green (tasting term), definition : 241
Gregory of Tours : 22, 55
Gremeaux, Ez [Dijon] : 73
Grenan, Bénigne : 23, 56
Grillet [Chenôve] : 74
Grillolle, La [Gevrey] : 97
Grillotte-haute [Gevrey] : 90
Griotte-Chambertin : 85-86, 92

Grip (tasting term), definition : 238
Grissolle [Meursault] : 206
Groffier, Domaine Robert : 97
Gros (monetary unit), definition : 243
Gros Frère et Soeur, Domaine : 112, 125, 138
Gros, Domaine Anne : 121, 138
Gros, Domaine Michel : 121
Grossier (tasting term), definition : 238
Guillaume le Breton : 22
Guillon, G. M. : 60

H • J

Harsh (tasting term), definition : 235
Hautains (winemaking term), definition : 238
Hautes Côtes de Beaune : 51
Hautes Côtes de Nuits : 51
Heady (tasting term), definition : 237
Herbal (tasting term), definition : 238
Hospices de Beaune : 183
Hot (tasting term), definition : 241
Hudelot-Noëllat, Domaine : 138
Jadot, Maison Louis : 183
Jambles : 33
Jauge (winemaking term), definition : 238
Jauger (winemaking term), definition : 239
Jayer, Henri : 122, 138
Jayer-Gilles, Domaine : 122
Jean de Bussières : 55
Jomard, Claude : 94
Journal (measure of area), definition : 243
Jovinien (vineyards near Joigny) : 51

L

La Tâche : see Tâche, La
Labet, Maison François : 112
Ladoix [Ladouée] : 155
Ladoix , La Clou d'Orge : 157
Ladoix, La Corvée : 157

Lafarge, Domaine Michel : 199
Lafon, Domaine des Comtes : 206, 218
Laguiche, Marquis de : 213
Lamarche, Edouard :131
Lamarche, Henri : 131
Lambrays, Clos de : 100, 102, 230
Lambrays, Domaine des : 105
Lamerosses, Les [Meursault] : 204
Lamy, Domaine Hubert : 213
Lamy, Olivier : 213
Lamy-Pillot, Domaine : 218
Langres, Clos de [Comblanchien] : 155
Larrets, Les [Morey] : 100
Larrey : 66
Lassot [Meursault] : 206
Latour, Maison Louis : 183, 213
Latricières-Chambertin : 85-86, 91, 97
Lavault [Beaune] : 182
Le Haut-des Combottes [Chambolle] : 110
Le Moulin-Moyne [Savigny] : 173
League : 243
Leflaive, Domaine : 212
Léger (tasting term), definition : 239
Lepescheur : 23, 56
Leroux, Benjamin : 183
Leroy, Domaine : 138, 168, 175
Lestimé, Caroline : 218
Lieu-dit, definition : x
Liger-Belair, Domaine du Comte : 126, 138
Liger-Belair, Domaine Thibault : 126, 138
Liger-Belair, General Louis : 128
Liqueur (tasting term), definition : 239
Liquoreux (tasting term), definition : 239
Livre tournois (monetary unit), definition : 243
Loächausses [Achausses], Les [Flagey] : 122
Loisier, Dom Jean : 121
Longbois, Les [Meursault] : 204
Longbois, Les [Volnay] : 196
l'Ouche [Chassagne-Montrachet] : 217
Larmat, Louis: 48

Louix XIV : 55
Lucius III, Pope : 105
Lurets, Les [Meursault] : 204

M

Mache (tasting term), definition : 239
Mâconnais : 20
Maison-Brûlée [Morey] : 103
Maison-Dieu, [Pommard] : 189
Mâlain, plant de [Gamay] : 51
Manassès I "l'Ancien" : 127
Maray-Joly : 100
Marcs d'Or [Dijon] : 32, 70, 72
Marei [Maret]-Bas [Vougeot] : 111-112
Marei [Maret]-Haut [Vougeot] : 111-112
Marey, Nicolas-Joseph : 98
Marquis d'Angerville, Domaine : 199
Marsannay : 45, 67, 68
Marsannay, Dessus-des-Longeroies : 74
Marsannay, Diénay : 74
Marsannay, Etale : 74
Marsannay, Fer-Meulin : 74
Marsannay, Guidon : 74
Marsannay, Les Argillières : 74
Marsannay, Les Crais : 74
Marsannay, Les Favières : 74
Marsannay, Les Portes : 74
Marsannay, Les Recilles : 74
Marsannay, Rosé de : 67
Masse, Roland : 183
Maupertuis, Petit [Vougeot] : 111-112
Maupertuis, Grand [Vougeot] : 111-112
Mazis-Haut [Gevrey] : 85, 97
Mazoyères ou Charmes Chambertin : 97
Mazoyères-Chambertin : 85-86, 91, 92, 97
Mazy-bas [Gevrey] : 85, 90, 97
Mazy-Chambertin [Mazis]: 30, 60, 85, 87, 88, 224, 229
Meadows, Alan : 131
Meix au Frey [Chassagne-Montrachet] : 217

Meix-Rentie [Morey] : 104
Mellow (tasting term), definition : 240
Meloisey : 45
Méo-Camuzet, Domaine : 121, 122, 125, 138, 168
Mercury : 31
Meursault : 19, 20, 32, 34, 45, 46, 200
Meursault, Au Murger de Monthélie : 204
Meursault Blanc, Les Santenots-Dessous : 200, 203
Meursault, Clos de [En] la Barre : 34, 204
Meursault, Clos des Mouches : 202
Meursault, En la Monatine : 204
Meursault, En l'Ormeau : 204
Meursault, En Luraule [Lurale] : 203
Meursault, Gouttes d'Or : 34, 200, 201, 225, 233
Meursault, La Garenne : 200
Meursault, La Jeunellotte : 201
Meursault, La Millerand : 205
Meursault, Le Bois de Blagny : 201
Meursault, Le Buisson Certaut [Surtaut] : 206
Meursault, Le Clos de Mazaray [Mazeret] : 203
Meursault, Le Cromin [Cromain] : 203
Meursault, Les [Es] Millerans : 204
Meursault, Les [Es] Pellans : 204
Meursault, Les Bouchères : 204
Meursault, Les Charmes : 34, 200, 201, 225, 233
Meursault, Les Charmes Dessus : 204
Meursault, Les Clous [Cloux] : 205
Meursault, Les Corbins : 203
Meursault, Les Cras : 30, 202, 231
Meursault, Les Criots : 205
Meursault, Les Criots : 203
Meursault, Les Crotots : 204
Meursault, Les Durots : 204
Meursault, Les Forges : 204
Meursault, Les Genevrières : 34, 200, 225, 233
Meursault, Les Grands-Charrons : 204
Meursault, Les Luchets : 204
Meursault, Les Magny : 204
Meursault, Les Malpoiriers : 204, 205
Meursault, Les Marcausses : 203

Meursault, Les Meix Chavaux : 203
Meursault, Les Pelles [Dessus, Dessous] : 204
Meursault, Les Perrières : 34, 200, 201, 205, 224, 233
Meursault, Les Peutes-Vignes : 203
Meursault, Les Pleures [Petures] : 30, 231
Meursault, Les Ravelles : 201
Meursault, Les Rougeots : 34, 204
Meursault, Les Santenots Blanc : 200, 202
Meursault, Les Santenots du Millieu : 200
Meursault, Les Terres Blanches : 203
Meursault, Les Tessons : 204
Meursault, Les Vignes Blanches : 206
Meursault, Les Vireuils : 204
Meursault, Porusot [Dessus, Dessous], 204
Meursault, Sous Blagny : 201, 202
Meursault, Sous la Velle : 204
Meursault, Sous le Dos d'Ane : 201, 202
Miller, Philippe : 62
Mochamps [Morey] : 99, 103
Moelle (tasting term), definition : 239
Moelleux (tasting term), definition : 239
Mommessin : 98
Monbogre : 33
Monds Ronds, Les [Beaune] : 176
Monniaux, Clos [Chenôve] : 67
Monnier, Domaine Jean : 185
Montagne Saint-Désiré : 17
Montagny : 33
Montant (tasting term), definition : 239
Mont-Godard [Chassagne-Montrachet] : 217
Monthélie : 32, 198
Monthélie, Le Clou des Chênes : 198
Monthélie, Le Meix de Mypont [Clos-Mipont] : 199
Monthélie, Les Champs Fulliot [Feuillot] : 198
Monthélie, Les Duresses : 199
Montiottes-Basses [Vougeot] : 111-112
Montiottes-Hautes [Vougeot] : 111-112
Montrachet : 19, 20, 21, 33, 37, 46, 201, 207, 209, 210, 214, 215, 224, 232
Montrachet Ainé : 33

Montrecul, En [Dijon] : 72
Monts Luisants, Clos des : 105
Monts-Battois : 177
Mordant (tasting term), definition : 239
Morey [Saint-Denis] : 30, 98, 224
Morey, Albert : 218
Morey, Domaine Bernard : 218
Morey, Domaine Jean-Marc : 218
Morey, Domaine Thomas : 218
Morey, Domaine Vincent et Sophie : 218
Morey-Saint-Denis, Aux Chezeaux : 104
Morey-Saint-Denis, Bas-Chenevery [Chenevary] : 104
Morey-Saint-Denis, Clos Baulet [Bolet] : 104
Morey-Saint-Denis, Clos des Ormes : 104
Morey-Saint-Denis, Clos Solon [Solin] : 104
Morey-Saint-Denis, Clos Sorbé [Sorbet] : 104
Morey-Saint-Denis, La Bussière : 104
Morey-Saint-Denis, La Riotte [Ruotte] : 104
Morey-Saint-Denis, Les Blanchards : 104
Morey-Saint-Denis, Les Chaffots : 99
Morey-Saint-Denis, Les Crais: 104
Morey-Saint-Denis, Les Faconnières : 104
Morey-Saint-Denis, Les Genavrières : 99, 103
Morey-Saint-Denis, Les Larrets : 104
Morey-Saint-Denis, Les Pourroux : 104
Morey-Saint-Denis, Les Ruchots : 104
Morey-Saint-Denis, Les Sionnières : 104
Morey-Saint-Denis, Les Sorbès [Sorbets] : 104
Morey-Saint-Denis, Millandes : 104
Morey-Saint-Denis, Monts Luisants : 99, 100
Morey-Saint-Denis, Très-Girard : 104
Morisot, Antoine : 95
Morot, Domaine Albert : 175
Morris, Jasper : 152, 185
Mortet, Domaine Denis : 97
Moulin-Foullet [Meursault] : 206
Moustille (tasting term), definition : 240
Mout (winemaking term), definition : 240
Moye [Chassagne-Montrachet] : 217
Moytan, Clos de : 128

Muet (winemaking term), definition : 240
Mugneret-Gibourg, Domaine : 110
Mugnier, Domaine Jacques-Frédéric : 110
Muid (barrel size), definition : 243
Murger [Chassagne-Montrachet] : 217
Murs-du-Clos, Les [Flagey] : 124
Musigni [Vougeot] : 111-112
Musigny : 29, 30, 37, 44, 223, 226
Musigny, Les [Chambolle] : 107, 109
Must (winemaking term), definition : 240
Mute (winemaking term), definition : 240
Muter (winemaking term), definition : 240
Muzard, Domaine Lucien : 222

N

Nantoux : 45
Naurosse, Saint-Jean de : 219
Nerf (tasting term), definition : 240
Nervy (tasting term), definition : 240
Neuf Journaux, Clos de : 128
Niellon, Domaine Michel : 218
Niquet (monetary unit), definition : 243
Noirien, definition : 51
Nones, Les [Chambolle] : 108
Norman, Remington : 98-99
Noyer-Bart [Santenay] : 219, 220, 224
Nuits : 18, 28, 139, 224
Nuits-Saint-Georges, Au Bas-de-Combe : 146
Nuits-Saint-Georges, Aux [Les] Cras : 139-140, 142-143
Nuits-Saint-Georges, Aux [Les] Perdrix : 148
Nuits-Saint-Georges, Aux Allots : 146
Nuits-Saint-Georges, Aux Argillas : 144
Nuits-Saint-Georges, Aux Athées : 146
Nuits-Saint-Georges, Aux Barrières : 146
Nuits-Saint-Georges, Aux Boudots : 139-140, 142, 223, 229
Nuits-Saint-Georges, Aux Bousselots : 141
Nuits-Saint-Georges, Aux Corvées [Prémeaux] : 140,

147, 224, 229

Nuits-Saint-Georges, Aux Herbues : 146
Nuits-Saint-Georges, Aux Murgers : 139-140, 142-143, 223, 229
Nuits-Saint-Georges, Aux Rousselots : 144
Nuits-Saint-Georges, Aux Saints-Jacques : 146
Nuits-Saint-Georges, Aux Saints-Juliens : 146
Nuits-Saint-Georges, Aux Thorey : 139-140, 142, 144, 223, 229
Nuits-Saint-Georges, Belle-Croix : 146
Nuits-Saint-Georges, Chabiots : 144
Nuits-Saint-Georges, Chaignots : 141, 144
Nuits-Saint-Georges, Chaînes-Carteaux : 144
Nuits-Saint-Georges, Les Chaliots [Chaliots-Brûlées] 146
Nuits-Saint-Georges, Clos de la Maréchale [FKA Clos des Fourches] [Prémeaux] : 148
Nuits-Saint-Georges, Clos de l'Arlot [Prémeaux] : 148
Nuits-Saint-Georges, Clos des [Ez] Grandes-Vignes [Prémeaux] : 148
Nuits-Saint-Georges, Clos des Argillières [Prémeaux] 148
Nuits-Saint-Georges, Clos des Corvées : 60
Nuits-Saint-Georges, Clos des Corvées Pagets : 140
Nuits-Saint-Georges, Clos des Forêts Saint-Georges [Prémeaux] : 60, 140, 224, 229
Nuits-Saint-Georges, Clos des Porrets-Saint-Georges 139
Nuits-Saint-Georges, Clos Saint Marc [Prémeaux] : 148
Nuits-Saint-Georges, Échézeaux : 141
Nuits-Saint-Georges, Lavières : 146
Nuits-Saint-Georges, Les [Aux] Didiers [Prémeaux] 140, 147
Nuits-Saint-Georges, Les Cailles : 139-140, 142-143, 223, 229
Nuits-Saint-Georges, Les Cras : 141, 223, 229
Nuits-Saint-Georges, Les Crots : 144
Nuits-Saint-Georges, Les Didiers [Prémeaux] : 60, 224, 229
Nuits-Saint-Georges, Les Fleurières : 146

Nuits-Saint-Georges, Les Longecourts : 146
Nuits-Saint-Georges, Les Perrières : 144
Nuits-Saint-Georges, Les Poisets : 146
Nuits-Saint-Georges, Les Porrets-Saint-Georges : 139, 223, 229
Nuits-Saint-Georges, Les Procès : 144
Nuits-Saint-Georges, Les Pruliers : 139-140, 142-143, 223, 229
Nuits-Saint-Georges, Les Saints-Georges : 20, 21, 29, 37, 44, 139, 142-143, 223, 226
Nuits-Saint-Georges, Les Vaucrains : 139-140, 142, 144, 223, 229
Nuits-Saint-Georges, Roncière : 144
Nuits-Saint-Georges, Vignesrondes [Vignes Rondes] 141, 144

O · P

Obole (monetary unit), definition : 243
Ormeau, En l' [Volnay, Mitans] : 192, 195, 198
Ouvrée (measure of area), definition : 243
Pagus Arebrignus : 182
Palle [Meursault] : 205
Passe-tout-grains : 69
Pasty (tasting term), definition : 240
Pateux (tasting term), definition : 240
Pavet, En [Dijon] : 73
Pechurs [Meursault] : 206
Pelletier de Clery, François : 98
Perche (measure of area), definition : 243
Pernand [Pernant] : 17, 21, 152
Pernand, Vergelesses : 21
Pernand-Vergelesses, En [Le] Caradeaux : 167, 171
Pernand-Vergelesses, Ile des Vergelesses : 167
Pernand-Vergelesses, Les Basses-Vergelesses : 167
Pernand-Vergelesses, Les Boutières : 167, 171
Perrière, Clos de la : 29
Perrières Dessous, Les [Meursault] : 203
Perrières Dessus, Les [Meursault] : 203
Perrigny-les-Dijon : 46

Pertuis du Prelet [Meursault] : 206
Petit Clos [Meursault] : 205
Petit journal (measure of area), definition : 243
Petit-Près, Les [Volnay] : 196
Petite-Vigne [Meursault] : 205
Petits Musigny, Les [Chambolle] : 107, 109
Petits Vougeots Les [Vougeot] : 114
Petrarch : 22, 55
Pézerolle de Montjeu, Étienne : 197
Philippe II (the Bold) Duke of Burgundy : 22-23, 24, 52
Philippe III (the Good), Duke of Burgundy : 24
Philippe V, King of Spain : 24
Pièce (barrel size), definition : 243
Pierre Gelin, Domaine : 84
Pierres Blanches, Les : 176
Piquon, Au [Chenôve] : 74
Pisse-Vin, En [Dijon] : 73
Plafond limite de classement : 52
Plante Chamel [Vougeot] : 112
Plante l'Abbé [Vougeot] : 111-112
Plante-Longe [Chassagne-Montrachet] : 217
Plat (tasting term), definition : 240
Plombières : 45
Poinçon (barrel size), definition : 243
Pointes d'Angles [Volnay] : 192, 195
Poirier-Breneau [Chassagne-Montrachet] : 217
Polmarco : 184
Pommard : 16, 20, 22, 29, 44, 185, 224
Pommard, Clos Blanc [d'Espenault] : 185, 189
Pommard, Clos de Cîteaux : 44, 185-186, 231
Pommard, Clos des Epeneaux : 185, 229
Pommard, Clos Micot: 188, 189
Pommard, Clos Orgelot [Pezerolles] : 186
Pommard, Croix-Noires : 185
Pommard, En Sauzille : 188
Pommard, Frémiets : 185, 189
Pommard, Grands-Epenots : 186, 187
Pommard, Jarolières : 187
Pommard, La Combotte : 188
Pommard, La Commaraine [Clos de la Commaraine] : 17, 184, 185-186
Pommard, La Croix Planet : 189
Pommard, La Croix-Blanche : 188
Pommard, La Lévrière : 189
Pommard, La Perrière : 189
Pommard, La Refène : 187
Pommard, Largillières [Argillières, En l'Argillières] 184, 186
Pommard, Le Planet : 189
Pommard, Les Arvelets : 59, 186, 231
Pommard, Les Bertins : 185
Pommard, Les Boucherottes : 188, 190
Pommard, Les Chanlains : 188
Pommard, Les Chaponnières : 184
Pommard, Les Chaponnières : 188
Pommard, Les Charmots : 187
Pommard, Les Combes-Dessous : 188
Pommard, Les Combes-Dessus : 188, 189
Pommard, Les Cras : 188
Pommard, Les Epenots [Épeneaux] : 44, 184, 186
Pommard, Les [Es] Noizons : 188, 190
Pommard, Les Petits-Noizons : 188
Pommard, Les Petits-Epenots : 186, 187
Pommard, Les Pézerolles : 186, 189
Pommard, Les Platières : 188
Pommard, Les Poutures : 188
Pommard, Les Riottes : 188
Pommard, Les Rugiens : 59, 186, 231
Pommard, Les Rugiens-Hauts : 185
Pommard, Les Tavannes : 188
Pommard, Rue au Port [Rue-ès-Porcs] : 188-189
Pommard, Trois Follots [Les Trois-Folles] : 188
Pommard, Village [Clos Marey-Monge] : 189
Pommard, vin de paille : 190
Ponneaux [Dijon] : 32
Ponsot, Domaine : 105
Pope Benoit XIII : 22
Porrets, Les [Nuits-Saint-Georges] : 139, 142-143
Poulaillères, Les [Flagey] : 122, 124
Pousse d'Or, Domaine : 199

Précoce (tasting term), definition : 240
Precocious (tasting term), definition : 240
Prémeaux : 139
Prémeaux, Clos de : 29, 154
Premières cuvée, definition : 44, 70
Premières cuvées, Rodier's definition : 63
Preriots, Les [Meursault] : 204
Probus : 21
Provinage : 52
Puligny : 19, 33, 45
Puligny-Montrachet Champ Canet : 211
Puligny-Montrachet, Clavoillon [Clovaillon] : 21, 209, 211, 212, 224, 229
Puligny-Montrachet, Clos de la Mouchère : 209
Puligny-Montrachet, Combettes [Combottes]34, 211, 225
Puligny-Montrachet, Hameau de Blagny : 201, 202, 209
Puligny-Montrachet, La Garenne : 201, 202, 209, 212
Puligny-Montrachet, Le Cailleret : 208, 209
Puligny-Montrachet, Le Trézin : 201, 202, 209
Puligny-Montrachet, Les Charmes : 207, 209, 210
Puligny-Montrachet, Les Grands-Champs : 211
Puligny-Montrachet, Les Nosroyes : 211
Puligny-Montrachet, Les Perrières : 209, 212
Puligny-Montrachet, Les Platières : 207, 210
Puligny-Montrachet, Les Pucelles : 208, 209, 211
Puligny-Montrachet, Les Referts [Refères] 207, 209, 210
Puligny-Montrachet, Les Reuchaux [Les Reuchots, Grand Reuchot] : 212
Puligny-Montrachet, Sous le Puits : 211
Purity of fruit (tasting term), definition : 236

Queue (barrel size), definition : 243
Racking (winemaking term), definition: 241
Ramonet, Domaine : 213, 218
Rapet, Domaine : 169
Rendement butoir : 52
Richebourg [Les] : 20, 28, 44, 59, 128, 132, 133, 223, 226
Rigaux, Jacky : 85, 98
Roche, Clos de la : 29, 30, 99, 101, 102, 230
Roguet, Le : 157
Roi, Clos du [Chenôve] : 31 , 70, 73, 74, 230
Rolin, Cuvée Nicolas : 183
Romanée, La : 20, 21, 37, 44, 134, 226
Romanée-Conti : 28, 60, 127, 128, 133, 135, 138, 223, 225
Romanée-Conti, Domaine de la : 126, 138, 152, 168, 218
Romanée-Saint-Vivant : 28, 129, 132, 134, 223, 224, 226
Rossignol, Domaine Nicolas : 199
Rouges du Bas, Les [Flagey] : 122, 125
Rouget, Emmanuel: 126
Rough (tasting term), definition: 235
Roumier, Domaine Georges : 110
Rousseau, Domaine Armand : 97
Roussotes, Ez [Dijon] : 73
Ruchotte du Dessus : 231
Ruchottes-Chambertin : 90
Clos des Ruchottes [Gevrey] : 97
Ruchottes-du-Bas [Gevrey] : 91, 92
Rues-d'Aloxe : 153
Rugiens-Bas [Pommard] : 185
Rully : 32
Ruotte, La [Brochon] : 83

Q · R

Quarteaux (barrel size), definition : 243
Quarteranche (measure of volume), definition : 243
Quartier de Marei Haut [Vougeot] : 112
Quatorze-Journaux [Vougeot] : 111
Quatre Journaux, Clos de : 128

S

Saillère, La [Aloxe-Corton] : 164
Saint-Aubin : 208
Saint-Aubin, Derrière la Tour : 208
Saint-Aubin, En Créot : 208
Saint-Aubin, En Remilly : 208

Saint-Aubin, Les Murgers des Dents de Chien : 208
Saint-Denis, Clos [Flagey] : 122, 124
Saint-Denis, Clos [Morey] : 99, 101, 103
Saint-Jacques, En [Dijon] : 73
Saint-Jean-de-Vaux : 33
Saint-Marc (Côte Chalonnaise) : 33
Saint-Martin : 32
Saint-Romain : 18, 45
Saint-Vallerin : 33
Saint-Vivant de [sous] Vergy, Abbaye de : 127
Santenay : 21, 30, 219
Santenay, Beauregard : 221
Santenay, Beaurepaire : 221
Santenay, Clos de Tavannes [Tavanes] : 21, 30, 219, 220, 221, 224, 227
Santenay, Clos Genet : 222
Santenay, En Boichot : 221
Santenay, En Passe Temps [Passetemps] : 221
Santenay, Grand Clos Rousseau : 221
Santenay, La Comme : 221
Santenay, La Maladière : 221
Santenay, Les Cornières : 222
Santenay, Les Gravières : 21, 30, 219, 220, 221, 229
Santenay, Les Hâtes : 222
Santenay, Les Prarons-Dessus : 222
Santenay, Saint Jean : 222
Santenots [Meursault] See Volnay Santenots
Santenots-du-Milieu [Meursault, AC Volnay-Santenots] : 202, 202
Saules : 33
Sausses, Ez [Dijon]: 73
Saussots, Les [Meursault] : 204
Sauvignon : 52
Sauzet, Domaine Etienne : 212
Savigny, Au Pointes : 173
Savigny, Aux Champs Chardons : 173
Savigny, Aux Clous [Cloux] : 173
Savigny, Aux Godeaux : 173
Savigny, Aux Grands-Liards : 173
Savigny, Aux Gravains : 172

Savigny, Aux Petits-Liards : 173
Savigny, Aux Serpentières : 173
Savigny, Connardises [Canardières or Canardais] : 173
Savigny, La Bataillère : 44
Savigny, La Dominode : 30, 231
Savigny, Les Bourgeots : 173
Savigny, Les Charnières : 173
Savigny, Les Dessus-Vermots : 173
Savigny, Les Grenottes : 173
Savigny, Les Guettes : 170, 172
Savigny, Les Hautes Vergelesses : 172
Savigny, Les Hauts Marconnets : 172
Savigny, Les Jarrons : 30, 170, 172, 231
Savigny, Les Lavières : 172
Savigny, Les Marconnets : 30, 172, 231
Savigny, Les Narbantons : 172, 175
Savigny, Les Peuillets : 173, 231
Savigny, Les Planchots de la Champagne : 173
Savigny, Les Planchots du Nord : 173
Savigny, Les Saucours : 173
Savigny, Les Serpentières : 171
Savigny, Les Vergelesses : 30, 170, 172, 229
Savigny, Les Vermots : 173
Savigny, Pimentier : 173
Savigny, Redrescul : 173
Savigny, Rouvrettes : 173
Savigny-lès [lez]-Beaune : 17, 21, 31, 170
Seloncourt [Chenôve] : 73
Senard, Domaine Comte : 169
Serrigny : 156
Setier (barrel size), definition : 243
Sève (tasting term), definition : 240
Sol (monetary unit), definition: 243
Sous l'Eglise [Meursault] : 205
Soyeux (tasting term), definition : 240
St. Désiré, Montagne : 176

T

Tâche Goudichots : 129

Tâche, La : 28, 37, 44, 59, 130, 132, 133, 223, 226
Talant : 45
Tannin (tasting term), definition : 240
Tart, Clos de : 29, 30, 44, 98, 101, 102, 223, 226
Tastevin, Confrerie des Chevaliers du : 61
Taupe, La [Pommard] : 189
Terroir (tasting term), definition : 238
Terroir, definition : x
Tête de cuvée, definition : xi, 44, 70
Thénard, Domaine Baron : 218
Tibles [Chassagne-Montrachet] : 217
Tirage au fin (winemaking term), definition : 241
Tonneau (winemaking term), definition : 241
Touches : 31
Tour, Château de la : 112
Tourner (winemaking term), definition : 241
Treillon [Meursault] : 206
Treux, Les [Flagey] : 122, 124
Tyant, Territoire de Lègues [Beaune] : 182

V • W

Vaches, En la Rue des [Comblanchien] : 154
Valadons [Chenôve] : 73
Valadons, Ez [Dijon] : 73
Varoilles, Clos de [Vosne] : 132
Vaux, Les [Meursault] : 204
Velouté (tasting term), definition : 241
Velte (winemaking term), definition : 241
Velter (winemaking term), definition : 241
Velvet (tasting term), definition : 241
Verroilles ou Les Richebourgs [Varoilles-sous-
    Richebourgs] : 129-130, 132, 134
Vert (tasting term), definition : 242
Vézelien (vineyards near Vézelay) : 51
Vienne, Henri : 95-96
Vigne à Estienne Bôgnet : 129
Vigne à Jehan Roy de Rouyres : 129
Vigne Blanche, La [Vougeot] : 114
Vignes Blanches, Les [Meursault] : 200

Vignes Derniers [Chassagne-Montrachet] : 214
Vigor, vigorous (tasting term), definition : 240
Vin chaud (tasting term), definition : 242
Vin doux (winemaking term), definition : 242
Vin extra (definition) : 70
Vin muet : 47
Viner (winemaking term), definition : 242
Vineux (tasting term), definition : 242
Vinous (tasting term), definition : 242
Violettes, Les [Dijon] : 66, 72
Violettes, Les [Flagey] : 125
Visargent [Meursault] : 206
Vivex [Meursault] : 205
Vogüé, Domaine Comte Georges de : 110
Voisenot [Chassagne-Montrachet] : 217
Volnay : 16, 20, 28, 44, 224
Volnay, Caillerets : 29, 44, 191, 194, 197, 223, 227
Volnay, Caillerets-Clos des 60 Ouvrées : 199
Volnay, Carrelle sous la Chapelle : 29, 191, 193, 195, 231
Volnay, Champans [En Champans] : 16, 29, 37, 44, 191,
    194, 198, 223, 227
Volnay, Clos de Chênes : 196
Volnay, Clos de la Barre : 192, 195
Volnay, Clos de la Bousse d'Or [En Bouze d'Or] : 193
Volnay, Clos de la Rougeotte [Rougiots] : 195
Volnay, Clos des Ducs : 199
Volnay, Clos du Verseuil [En Verneuil] : 196
Volnay, Cros Martin : 196
Volnay, En Cailleret : 194
Volnay, En Cailleret-Dessus : 194
Volnay, En Chevret : 192, 194, 198
Volnay, En Vaut [Vaux] : 196
Volnay, Ez Echards [Les Echares] : 196
Volnay, Frémiets [En Fremiers] : 192, 194, 198
Volnay, La Cave : 196
Volnay, La Gigotte : 196
Volnay, Lassolle [l'Assole] : 196
Volnay, Le Pasquiers [Pâquier] : 196
Volnay, Le Ronceret [Les Roncerets] : 196
Volnay, Le Village : 192

Volnay, Les Angles : 192, 193, 195, 198
Volnay, Les Aussy : 196
Volnay, Les Brouillards [En Brouillard] : 196
Volnay, Les Buttes : 196
Volnay, Les Carelles [Cazelles]-Dessus : 196, 198
Volnay, Les Chanlains : 196
Volnay, Les Grands-Champs : 196
Volnay, Les Grands-Poisots : 196
Volnay, Les Jouères : 196
Volnay, Les Lurets : 196, 198
Volnay, Les Mitans : 192, 195
Volnay, Les Petits-Gamets : 196
Volnay, Les Petits-Poisots : 196
Volnay, Les Pluchots : 196
Volnay, Les Serpens [Serpents] : 196
Volnay, œil de perdrix wine style : 197
Volnay, Pitures-Dessus : 196
Volnay, Santenots [Meursault] : 21, 30, 37, 44, 200, 205, 224, 227
Volnay, Sur Roches [Rocher] : 196
Volnay, Taille Pieds [Taillepieds, En Taille-Pieds] 193, 198
Volnay, vin de paille : 191
Vosne : 21, 22, 29, 127, 224
Vosne-Romanée En Orveau [Flagey] : 124
Vosne-Romanée, Au-Dessus de la Rivière : 135
Vosne-Romanée, Aux Brûlées : 134
Vosne-Romanée, Aux Champs Perdrix : 131
Vosne-Romanée, Aux Communes : 135
Vosne-Romanée, Aux Malconsorts : 132, 134
Vosne-Romanée, Aux Ravioles [Raviottes] : 135
Vosne-Romanée, Aux Réas : 135
Vosne-Romanée, Aux Reignots : 131, 134
Vosne-Romanée, Bossières : 135
Vosne-Romanée, Champ Goudins : 135
Vosne-Romanée, Cros Parantoux [Parentoux] : 135
Vosne-Romanée, La Combe Brûlée : 134
Vosne-Romanée, Les [Aux] Chaumes : 134
Vosne-Romanée, Les [Aux] Petit-Monts : 135
Vosne-Romanée, Les Beaux Monts : 132, 134, 223, 229

Vosne-Romanée, Les Gaudichots : 99, 129-131, 134
Vosne-Romanée, Les Jacquines : 135
Vosne-Romanée, Les Suchots : 134
Vosne-Romanée, Maizières Basses : 134
Vosne-Romanée, Maizières Hautes : 134
Vosne-Romanée, Porte Feuilles [Flagey] : 125
Vosne-Romanée, Pré de la Folie : 135
Vosne-Romanée, Quartiers-de-Nuits, Les [Flagey] : 125
Vosne-Romanée, Vigneux : 135
Vougeot, Clos de : 20, 21, 28, 37, 44, 110, 223, 225
Vougeot, Clos de la Perrière : 114
Vougeot, Les Crâs : 114
Vrai-Montrachet: 208, 209, 211, 214
Wine tasting, preferred technique [Lavalle]: 54

Printed in Great Britain
by Amazon.co.uk, Ltd.,
Marston Gate.